South African Writing in Transition

Also published by Bloomsbury:

The Slow Philosophy of J. M. Coetzee, Jan Wilm
South African Literature's Russian Soul, Jeanne-Marie Jackson

South African Writing in Transition

Edited by
Rita Barnard and Andrew van der Vlies

BLOOMSBURY ACADEMIC
LONDON • NEW YORK • OXFORD • NEW DELHI • SYDNEY

BLOOMSBURY ACADEMIC
Bloomsbury Publishing Plc
50 Bedford Square, London, WC1B 3DP, UK
1385 Broadway, New York, NY 10018, USA

BLOOMSBURY, BLOOMSBURY ACADEMIC and the
Diana logo are trademarks of Bloomsbury Publishing Plc

First published in Great Britain 2019

Cover design: Eleanor Rose
Cover image © Getty Images

A catalogue record for this book is available from the British Library.

A catalogue record for this book is available from the Library of Congress.

ISBN:	HB:	978-1-3500-8688-3
	ePDF:	978-1-3500-8689-0
	eBook:	978-1-3500-8690-6

Typeset by Integra Software Services Pvt. Ltd.

To find out more about our authors and books visit www.bloomsbury.com and
sign up for our newsletters.

Contents

Acknowledgments

This collection had its origins in a very productive seminar at the annual meeting of the American Comparative Literature Association (ACLA) at Brown University in 2012. Since then history and politics—and our scholarly reflections on them—have shifted dramatically, both in South Africa and in the United States and the United Kingdom, where many of us are based. But this remains a good occasion to thank the ACLA for providing such a stimulating platform for intellectual exchange on South African writing over the years. We are grateful to all seminar participants, both those who contributed to this book and all those who generously shared their thoughts with us in Providence, including Mark Sanders and Stephen Clingman.

Other gatherings and communities that have also enlightened us include the 2017 colloquium on South African Temporalities at the Johannesburg Institute for Advanced Studies, the Institute for Humanities in Africa at the University of Cape Town, the Theory Workshop at Stellenbosch University, the Latitudes Research Forum at the University of Pennsylvania, the English Department at Ithaca College, the Postcolonial Seminar at the University of Cambridge, the "Writing South Africa Now" conferences, and the Postgraduate Research Seminars at the Departments of English at Queen Mary University of London and King's College London. These opportunities for exchange shaped the editors' conception of the terrain we collectively traverse in this volume.

Special thanks by name to Patrick Flanery, Ronit Frenkel, Neville Hoad, Chris Holmes, Shamil Jeppie, Simon Lewis, Sophie Oldham, Deborah Posel, Daniel Roux, Paul K. Saint-Amour, Jennifer Spitzer, Hedley Twidle, and Chris Warnes. Timothy Wright and Steven Robins will see how they left their mark on the introduction to this volume.

In addition to our colleagues at the University of Pennsylvania, Queen Mary, and the University of the Western Cape, we would like to thank Derek Attridge and David Attwell for their support and their seminal work in South African literature. Sarah Nuttall also deserves our warm recognition as the scholar, intellectual instigator, and voice of conscience she is. Her generosity and that of WISER, which she heads so ably, has been a deep resource to everyone in the field for many years.

A good portion of the editorial work for this collection was done in the beautiful Women's Studies Cottage at the University of Colorado. Thanks to the staff there, to our dear colleague Laura Winkiel, and the university's First Scholars Program, which enabled both editors to spend some glorious summer days in Boulder.

We could not have had a more gracious, efficient, and encouraging editor than David Avital. Thanks to him and his colleagues at Bloomsbury Academic, and also to the two anonymous readers, whose appreciative understanding and critical insights alike have enhanced this collection considerably.

Contributors

Rita Barnard is Professor of English and Comparative Literature at the University of Pennsylvania, where she directs the undergraduate program in Comparative Literature. She holds a secondary position as Professor Extraordinaire at the University of the Western Cape. Her books include *The Great Depression and the Culture of Abundance, Apartheid and Beyond: South African Writers and the Politics of Place*, and the edited collection, *The Cambridge Companion to Nelson Mandela*. She was for many years coeditor of *Safundi: The Journal of South African and American Studies* and has published numerous essays on South African and modernist literature and culture.

Katherine Hallemeier is Associate Professor of English at Oklahoma State University. Her monograph, *J. M. Coetzee and the Limits of Cosmopolitanism*, draws on affect theory and gender studies to explore how Coetzee's later fiction tests conceptions of cosmopolitan community. Her writing on cosmopolitanism, Afropolitanism, and human rights discourse in Anglophone African fiction has been published in journals such as *ARIEL: A Review of International English Literature, Studies in the Novel*, and *English Studies in Africa*. She is currently working on a book on American dreams in contemporary African fiction.

Christopher Holmes is Associate Professor of English at Ithaca College. His work has appeared in *Contemporary Literature, Novel, Diaspora*, and *Literature Compass*. He is completing a book manuscript titled "At the Limit: The Contemporary Novel at the Ends of Form." He teaches Anglophone world literatures and is the founder and codirector of Ithaca College's New Voices Literary Festival.

Tsitsi Jaji is Associate Professor of English and African and African American Studies at Duke University. Her book, *Africa in Stereo: Modernism, Music and Pan-African Solidarity*, earned the First Book Award from the African Literature Association. She is also the author of two works of poetry, *Beating the Graves* and *Carnaval*. Jaji has held fellowships from the Radcliffe Institute for Advanced Study, Mellon Foundation, Center for Black Music Research, the NEH/Schomburg Center, and National Humanities Center, among others.

Sarah Lincoln is Associate Professor of English at Portland State University, where she teaches postcolonial and other global literatures, ecocriticism, and critical theory. Her essays on consumerism, waste, and ecology have appeared in *Social Dynamics*, *small axe*, *The Journal of Commonwealth Literature*, and in several edited collections. Her current book project, *The Idea of Gardening: Postcolonial Literature and the Ethics of Cultivation*, studies the political, cultural, and environmental stakes of contemporary gardening.

Erica Lombard is a Postdoctoral Research Fellow at the University of Cape Town, South Africa, where she is working on a book-historical account of the development of South African literature after apartheid. Her work has appeared in the *Journal of Commonwealth and Postcolonial Studies, English in Africa* and the *Journal of Literary Studies*, and she is coeditor of *Fighting Words: Fifteen Books that Shaped the Postcolonial World* (2017). Her chapter in this collection was written during a postdoctoral fellowship at the University of Johannesburg.

Brenna M. Munro is Associate Professor at the University of Miami. Her book South *Africa and The Dream of Love to Come: Queer Sexualities and the Struggle for Freedom*, published by the University of Minnesota Press in 2012, was nominated for a Lambda Award. She has written on Caster Semenya, Winnie Mandela, and the queer figure of the child soldier. Her current project examines sexual politics in literature from Nigeria and its diaspora.

Annel Helena Pieterse is an ACLS African Humanities Program Postdoctoral Fellow at the University of the Western Cape, South Africa. Her current project, "Texts Bewitched: Reading the supernatural in South Africa," examines the distortion and opacity of the sign around issues of the occult in textual representations in South Africa. She has published in *Current Writing: Text and Reception in Southern Africa, English in Africa*, and *South African Theatre Journal.*

Monica Popescu is William Dawson Scholar in African Literatures and Associate Professor in the Department of English at McGill University. She has published two books, *South African Literature Beyond the Cold War* (which won the 2012 Arlt Award in the Humanities) and *The Politics of Violence in Post-Communist Films*, and is the coeditor (with Cedric Tolliver and Julie Tolliver) of a special issue of the *Journal of Postcolonial Writing* on *Alternative Solidarities: Black Diasporas and Cultural Alliances* during the Cold War. She has published articles on the Cold War in Southern Africa, postapartheid literature, and Eastern European culture. Currently, she is working on a book on African Literature and the Cold War.

Lily Saint is Assistant Professor of English at Wesleyan University, where her research explores the nexus between ethics and cultural practice in the global South. Her book, *Black Cultural Life in South Africa: Reception, Apartheid and Ethics*, is forthcoming from the University of Michigan Press in Fall 2018. Recent writing appears in *NOVEL: A Forum on Fiction*, *The Cambridge Journal of Postcolonial Literary Inquiry*, and in the *Los Angeles Review of Books*.

Erica Still is Associate Professor in the English Department at Wake Forest University, where her teaching and research interests focus on African-American and South African fiction, considering questions of racial subjectivity, trauma, and memory, and the intersections between constructions of masculinity and moral agency. Her comparative study of representations of racialized trauma, *Prophetic Remembrance: Black Subjectivity in African American and South African Trauma Narratives*, was published in 2013 by the University of Virginia Press.

Andrew van der Vlies is Professor of Contemporary Literature and Postcolonial Studies at Queen Mary University of London, and Extraordinary Associate Professor at the University of the Western Cape in South Africa. He has published widely on South African literatures, print cultures, art, and sexuality, including in *The Cambridge History of South African Literature* and *Oxford History of the Novel in English*. Books include *Present Imperfect: Contemporary South African Writing*, *South African Textual Cultures*, and, as editor, *Print, Text & Book Cultures in South Africa* and Zoë Wicomb's *Race, Nation, Translation: South African Essays, 1990–2013*. He is lead editor of *Safundi: The Journal of South African and American Studies*.

1

Introduction

Rita Barnard

In April 2016, Sisonke Msimang wrote a passionate blog for the *Daily Maverick* in which she tried to capture her response to the news (backed up by official statistics) that young South Africans were less educated than their parents were twenty years ago—and increasingly less employable. The predominant feeling she registers is one of betrayal. "Our betrayal," she says, "has a particular smell":

> It is the stench of pit latrines and bodies baking in the sun in Marikana, shot down by police rifles. It smells like another murder in Bredasdorp....betrayal smells like the cabin of a private jet bound for Dubai. And yes, betrayal also emanates just as powerfully from the sight of a blind woman begging unsuccessfully in traffic. Betrayal smells like trash....We pick our way across the detritus and hold our breath to avoid the reality of how much South Africa stinks.[1]

This repellent sensorium also has a temporal dimension—of disappointment, suspension, and radical uncertainty: "All I know," Msimang declares, "is that we are living in the almost-times." These are times, she elaborates, when it is hard to know if "we are ascending or descending," if people will take action in ways that end up making themselves proud, or if South Africans will remain ashamed— ashamed especially of a president so outrageously unashamed of his reversal of the promises of a hard-won democracy.

Temporality in the aftermath

This was the distressing situation—the final years of Jacob Zuma's regime of ineptitude and corruption—in which the chapters in this volume were originally conceived. Since then the country has acquired a new president in Cyril Ramaphosa: a change that has brought justifiable relief, if not quite the new dawn some have wanted to claim. Msimang's overall assessment of South Africa's stark inequalities and her emphasis on its uncertain trajectory still remain relevant. Indeed, current speculations about how long "Ramaphoria" can endure only serve to underscore the fact that intellectual space has opened up for a new critical consideration of South African temporalities. It is striking how frequently political commentators in recent years tried to capture something of the pace and affective characteristics of lived time. In April 2017, Eusebius McKaiser evoked the protracted frustration engendered by the treacle-slow pace of Zuma's demise: "We are…experiencing a painfully inelegant final movie scene that the directors should have cut thirty minutes ago," he lamented.[2] But others, attentive to the rumblings of change spelled by the student protests in 2015 and 2016, noted the growing momentum of a new politics of impatience.[3] By early 2018, as Zuma's recall became likely, history itself seemed to accelerate. The columnist Stephen Grootes pronounced this a time "when political events don't splutter and ebb, but shake and gust"; "meanders" suddenly turned into "rapids"—and then into a veritable "waterfall."[4] Once Zuma finally resigned, a new structure of feeling was clearly in place. The gonzo commentator, Richard Poplak, declared that it was time to bring out the bubbly: "It's JC Le Roux o'clock. The hangover looms like Day Zero, but that's tomorrow's problem."[5]

But despite this renewed sense that "the future is going to be different from the past" and hopes that something of the glow of the old rainbow can be reignited, we are still living in "almost-times"—and we should still be responsive to Msimang's urgent call for action and engagement.[6] Indeed, this is a moment in which the meaning of "transition," a key term in this volume, is once again open for consideration.

In the course of investigating its meanings here, we enter into an implicit dialogue with the work of other scholars, especially in African studies, who have asked whether the received conceptual frameworks and narratives of the postcolonial period, including the teleology of democratic transition, still retain any interpretive power—especially in the face of historical phenomena like the Zuma kleptocracy with its mindboggling rapacity and twisted transnational dimensions. The effort to emerge from this interpretive impasse will certainly require the "inventive fabrication of novel concepts and stories through which past, present, and future can be productively reinhabited" that Goldstone and Obarrio have called for in their meditations of African futures.[7] The project of our collective work in this volume, accordingly, is to trace precisely such inventions in literary texts, clarify them, and propose an array of terms—hope, betrayal, precariousness, nostalgia, waiting, longing, mutation—that might help illuminate not only South African culture and its trajectories, but potentially also the uncertain and uneven temporalities of the world at large.

For a while, back in the 1990s, it was possible to see South Africa in the mode of progress or even, more transcendently, of the political sublime.[8] The transition to democracy and the inauguration of Nelson Mandela presented itself as the happy culmination of revolutionary anticipation. The nation, once stuck in the retrograde racist agendas of apartheid, seemed finally to be moving along with the rapid pace of global modernity. The trauma of the past, such was the message of the Truth and Reconciliation Commission, would be overcome and the bad old days would cease to haunt the present. But, as all the chapters in this volume assert, the nation's trajectory has not proven this simple, and it is now time to consider the many loops and twists, the stasis and acceleration, the paralysis and hope of postapartheid experience.

The project of attending to the temporalities of South African life and letters (and we may briskly define "temporality" as the way in which we live and imagine the relation between past, present, and future) implies a shift in scholarly focus.[9] From about 1995 until 2010—the periodization is rough—it seemed as though space and place were the major critical concerns in South African literary and cultural studies.[10] There are excellent reasons for this. The impact of what was then the new critical human geography and the work of theorists like Henri Lefèbvre, David Harvey, Michel de Certeau, and Edward Soja was felt in many disciplines; it furnished South African scholars with themes and methodologies that felt relevant and applicable. And beyond the spatial turn in the academy, there was the unavoidable fact that apartheid was a spatial mode of exercising power, of segregating, dividing, confining, policing, and impoverishing the majority of the population with brutal deliberation. To explore the transition— to write the "now," as Sarah Nuttall urged in those years—was to trace out the new demographics of cities and new ways of living in them: a task undertaken not only in scholarship, but in many of the great novels of the 1990s, including Nadine Gordimer's *None to Accompany Me* (1994), Marlene van Niekerk's *Triomf* (1994), and Ivan Vladislavić's *The Restless Supermarket* (2001).[11]

While we must not forget the insight embedded in Bakhtin's term "chronotope," namely that time and place tend to be dialectically entangled, it nevertheless seems as though an interest in temporality is beginning to supersede the earlier geographic preoccupation. The derailing of the dream of liberation, starkly manifest in the material legacies of apartheid's spatial engineering, has brought us to a point where speculation about the pace, direction, and meaning of our times is pervasive. In addition to the rhetorical flourishes of the bloggers and opinion columnists already discussed, we should note the interventions of major scholarly works like Jennifer Wenzel's pioneering *Bulletproof: Afterlives of Anticolonial Prophecy in South Africa and Beyond* (2009) and Andrew van der Vlies's *Present Imperfect: Contemporary South African Writing* (2017), which have offered imaginative theorizations of the archives of prophetic memory and disappointment, respectively. Inspired by Bloch and Benjamin, both of these studies assert the need to read against the grain of linear histories of progress with their seemingly irreversible outcomes. Contrary to the positive structures of feeling imposed by expectations of inevitable liberation, Wenzel and Van der Vlies invite us to find creative and critical potential precisely in failures and bad feelings: such negations, they argue, work to preserve imaginings of radical change in dark and discouraging times.

We should note here that it is not only the contemporary pathology of our "almost-times" that makes South Africa's time sense intriguing. The country has always seemed curiously out of synchrony with the rest of the world. As both Wenzel and James Ferguson have reminded us, South Africa was colonized in the seventeenth century, 200 years before the rest of Africa; it ratified a racist regime and political agenda right at the time when the rest of the world began to work against such overt discrimination; and while other African nations were decolonized in the 1960s, the promise of freedom for South Africa's majority arrived only in the 1990s.[12] Furthermore, the country had to forge a sense of national identity at the very moment when economic globalization made the sovereignty of all nation states seem like yesterday's dream.[13] South Africa, one is tempted to say, is temporally exceptional and its history disables easy periodization. And yet, as several chapters in this volume show, there are also congruities between South African and global structures of feeling, including the paranoia characteristic of the Cold War era and, in recent years, a pervasive feeling of disappointment and diminished expectations, a sense of entrapment in the distracted present of social media and consumption, and an intensification of rage and impatience: all of which, however various, are identifiably transnational predicaments. Indeed, recent anthropological work on the affective registers of anxiety, anticipation, hope, and revelation in Africa at large show many connections with contemporary South Africa. This is especially evident in what Achille Mbembe has decried as the most brutal effects of neoliberalism on the continent: "The generalization and radicalization of a condition of temporariness," impermanence, and insecurity.[14] It is therefore a tricky matter to figure out the relationship between national specificities and global conditions, not least because what might seem local, anomalous, and retrograde may actually turn out to be predictive for the world at large. For, as Jean and John Comaroff have pointed out, the global South in fact may be ahead of the global North in many respects, not lagging behind.

South Africa, in sum, is not only fascinating as an extreme case for the territorialization of power (thence the lasting explanatory force of the term "global apartheid"), it is also, as Ferguson judges, a very interesting place for thinking experimentally about time.[15] The point is readily proven by the Comaroffs' radical questioning of the usual trajectories of development, but I would suggest additionally that even the temporalities of apartheid are worth reexamining, especially in light of the efflorescence of scholarly work on global modernities. Afrikaner nationalism has perhaps too readily been thought of as turning back of the clock. After all, in the self-understanding of its movers and shakers, apartheid was resolutely forward-looking and it was clearly modern in terms of its architectural design, its bureaucratization of the state apparatus, and the sheer scale of the social engineering it wished to undertake.[16] Such intriguing contradictions and anomalies remain material for ongoing scholarly investigation.

Let me revert, however, to an earlier moment in my argument. If critical interest in South African space was energized and shaped in the 1990s by an apt theoretical framework, the same is true today for the study of South African temporalities.[17] The term "postcolonial" (as well as postapartheid) has always stimulated discussions about time and periodization in literary studies.[18] But a growing body of scholarly work—new reflections on African futurities, new scholarship on the time sense of global neoliberalism, and fresh debates on the concept of world literature—has offered additional perspectives that resonate with the work brought together in this collection. Since a comprehensive overview of this terrain is impossible (for what study of narrative is not in some measure a reflection on temporal imaginings?), I will discuss three inventive—and very different—contemporary studies that seem to me particularly pertinent to the nexus of themes unfolded in our collection.

Let us start with an intervention in the world literature debates, since South African literature is increasingly discussed under this rubric and many of the chapters in this volume provide transnational perspectives on the issues they engage. I am thinking here of Pheng Cheah's *What Is a World?* (2016), which sets out a compelling argument for emphasizing temporality in any discussion of world literature; indeed, temporality is, in his view, indispensable for a viable conception of the "world." Cheah judges that in the much-discussed oeuvre of David Damrosch, Pascale Casanova, and Franco Moretti, the term "world" means, essentially, the globe: it is a spatio-geographical projection.[19] The world is imagined, in other words, as the product—indeed, the reflection—of the unified market created by global capitalism. In much of this literature, he argues, the terminology of World Systems theory is deployed with hardly any modification: the emphasis is on centers versus peripheries, and on circulation. (The latter notion is key, to the point that if a work of literature is read globally, as some have argued, it thereby becomes *world* literature.) To counter this flat-world materialism, Cheah reminds us that in Goethe's foundational essay on the subject, world literature has not only a spatial but also a temporal dimension. It *creates* the world by providing a narrative, implicit or explicit, of an unfolding of human achievement: a vision of humankind, in all its difference, achieving self-expression.[20] The "world" in world literature is therefore an ethico-political concept; it is the constitutive modality of cosmopolitanism.

At stake in Cheah's argument is also a reminder that for Marx the vision of a global market is an alienated optic, in which social relations are invisible. But Cheah is not concerned so much with making social relations freshly visible. What is important to him is rather the idea of "worlding" as a temporal project, even perhaps a teleological one (though teleology, in his understanding, need not be linear: it involves a manifestation of promise that could expressed as circularity).[21] By reintroducing this normative conception of world literature, Cheah feels that literature may have some claim to a causal impact: the "worlding" it accomplishes may bring about "the being with of all peoples."[22]

The way in which Cheah's polemic pertains to our collective subject matter here (he is both fellow traveler and counter-voice) will reveal itself slowly over the course of the book as a whole. Suffice it to say for now that while his insistence on development and teleology seems highly problematic in relation to our suspended antipodal "almost-times," there is nevertheless a line of inquiry in our collection—simultaneously skeptical and utopian—that probes the conditions for that "being with of all peoples," one that asks on what grounds we could become "temporary together," or how South African literature might, in Edouard Glissant's beautiful phrase, become a "writing in the presence of all the languages of the world."[23]

This is to say that there is something appealing and apt about Cheah's proposed shift in emphasis from the spatio-geographical to the temporal, and his rearticulation of the normative qualities and agency of literature. But what he offers is a curiously ahistorical approach to temporality; in a society as riven by race and class as South Africa, the universalizing aspects of this argument cannot escape a stern critical gaze. The work of the anthropologist David Scott in his

Omens of Adversity (2014), by contrast, is deeply interested in the period-specific character of any given time sense. His work, moreover, is particularly applicable to postapartheid South Africa (several of our contributors find it indispensable), since he so vividly addresses the predicament of living in the aftermath of former futures.[24] Scott's specific subject matter is the overthrow of the Marxist revolution in Grenada in 1983: a marginal event, one might be tempted to say, but one that Scott endows with world historic significance and the dignity of tragedy. In his view, Reagan's military intervention (and the lack of much global response to it) marked the termination of the period of decolonization and revolution initiated at the Bandung Conference in 1955. This is a development with profound implications for our temporal experience, for, as Scott reminds us, the idea of revolution is quintessential to the modern organization of time. The emergence of nations, classes, subjects, and populations was always organized around a notion of change and, indeed, progress: a linear succession of presents to be transcended in a better future. But the hegemony of neoliberalism profoundly altered this time-honored way of imagining the relation between past, present, and future—to the point where one might say that temporality and history (which before had marched in step) came to feel out of joint. The result is a pervasive sense of a stalled present, of living in the aftermath of anticipated futures: a predicament that has somehow made time more conspicuous—and therefore more available for theorization.

This, as I have already suggested, is also South Africa's predicament. Scott's vision resonates with that of many of the contributors to this book: it explains a great deal about the conditions of waiting, stuckness, disappointment, and nostalgia they variously diagnose in postapartheid literature. For we cannot forget that the dramatic political changes in the country were precipitated by the fall of the Soviet Union and that South Africa's *de jure* liberation from apartheid, though belated, still overlapped with the rise of neoliberalism. Thus, we may well detect in the disappointments of our "almost-times" a staggered congruity with the global structures of feeling Scott diagnoses so poignantly.

But it seems to me that we cannot end there, especially since there are signs in the volatile terrain of contemporary South Africa of accelerated and varied forms of activism and protest. These do not necessarily restore the revolutionary modality for which Scott retains a certain nostalgia; but they hint at imagined futures in the very ruin of Mandela and Tutu's rainbow nation dreams. It seems important here to use the plural, "futures," especially given what Leon de Kock has aptly defined as the generalized sense of "plot loss" of recent years: a singular national story has become difficult to conceive.[25] The final theoretical framework

I would propose, then, is one provided by anthropologist Anna Tsing, in her recent study *The Mushroom at the End of the World: On the Possibility of Life in Capitalist Ruins* (2015). Tsing writes passionately about the multiple futures that "pop in and out of possibility" when one relinquishes the assumption that the future is "a singular direction ahead."[26] Even though her immediate subject matter is remote from ours (the book is by no means a monograph on decolonization, postcolonialism, or even narrative), Tsing's work begins to sketch out a time sense beyond neoliberal suspension, one that adds global resonance to certain imaginings that have already emerged in South African culture and ways of life.

The premise of Tsing's study of the global practices around the collecting of matsutake mushrooms, a fungus that sprouts in industrially devastated landscapes, is that we live not only in the ruins of revolutionary dreams, but in the even vaster ruins of an extractive modernity and destructive ideologies of development. This is to say that Tsing adds an ecological and viscerally material dimension to Scott's vision of living in the aftermath of catastrophe. In a memorable formulation, reminiscent of De Kock's diagnosis of South Africa's "plot loss," Tsing declares that we have lost "the handrails of stories that tell where everyone is going and, also, why."[27] The result, she argues, is that the condition of precariousness, once the fate of poor, has become a common predicament: "All our lives are precarious, even, when, for the moment, our pockets are lined."[28] To accede to this view does not mean that we should discard Njabulo Ndebele's critique (cited by several contributors) of the global privilege of white folk, which in South Africa stands in the way of their national belonging and "being at home" with all their contemporaries.[29] We can retain his stern admonition, while also recognizing that none of us will in the end be immune to environmental and climatic catastrophe, which in South Africa is bound to take the form of drought and fire (as the Western Cape disasters of 2017 suggest). Unlike Ndebele, however, Tsing imagines something far beyond the national home: she speaks of a "temporal polyphony" involving numerous improvised global networks, which she describes as "open-ended assemblages of entangled ways of life."[30] Such informal networks already operate in South Africa, especially for African immigrants, as revealed by research by of AbdouMaliq Simone and others into the new life forms of informal settlements and city centers.[31]

The new time sense or structure of feeling that Tsing outlines, moreover, is distinctly autumnal (the mushrooms that arrest her attention grow in the fall). Such a sensibility, which is already palpable in South Africa, implies an abandonment of the vernal metaphors the "new South Africa" elicited during the early transition years (we might recall here, for example, the 1990 collection

Spring is Rebellious: Arguments about Cultural Freedom). But the autumnal affect feels somehow appropriate, not only in the ravaged forests where Tsing's beloved mushroom might arise, but also in the blighted urban areas, the dusty townships, and the drought-stricken rural areas of South Africa where lives continue to be creatively patched together on the improvisatory edges of global modernity.

At stake in this vision of survival in unpropitious and risky places and times is a recognition that the world will not be made new: we will not be saved by global revolution. But Tsing's wager is that this sober recognition, to which we have been blinded by notions of progress, will stimulate a capacity to live fully in the present, which, elusive though it may be, is really the only time we have ever had.[32] Only such an attitude, she argues, will spark the modes of attention and curiosity necessary to our adaptation to and understanding of the contemporary conditions of our existence, where we are all touched by the global political economy of late capitalism, but bereft of the benefits it once promised—of stable incomes and regular jobs.

The relevance of Tsing's reflections to contemporary South Africa is striking (let us not forget that this discussion began with Sisonke Msimang's dismay about the dire job prospects facing her young compatriots). They allow us, most specifically, to imagine in richer detail the time sense that might emerge from what Sarah Lincoln, in her provocative contribution to this volume, has termed "precarious time." We might also gauge their resonance by considering briefly Timothy Wright's fascinating work on the figure of the mutant and the trope of mutation in recent fictions about Johannesburg.[33] To be sure, the mutant is not a mushroom; but mushrooms and mutants things do have something in common: they signal modes of transformation in situations where, as Imraan Coovadia argues, the conditions for transcending the present are hardly to be conceived.[34] The trope of mutation, in other words, invites us to imagine change in circumstances where one cannot presume a preset future or any sort of linear teleology of progress. The logic of mutation, after all, is discontinuous: mutations are sudden and experimental; they might succeed or fail within the material circumstances that produce them.

It is interesting and apt, then, that two of the texts Wright discusses, Neill Blomkamp's film *District 9* (2009) and Lauren Beukes's *Zoo City* (2010), discussed in this collection by Brenna Munro, are speculative narratives (perhaps even science fictions), but they are oriented to the present. Indeed, we might think of the bizarre mutations they stage as bodily analogues to the defamiliarizing curiosity Tsing celebrates, in that they transform the stalled contemporary world rather than imagining an escape from it into past and future. Moreover, the Joburg mutants—the "animalled" subjects of *Zoo City* or the Afrikaner bureaucrat-turned alien of *District 9*—do not operate in any sort of national allegory: their radically transformed existences have nothing to do with historical progress or the oppositional resistance tied to a story of liberation. Like Tsing's mushrooms (which she describes in all their spongey, odiferous materiality), they figure resistance simply by staying alive: the mutant's creatureliness (though still presented in rather phobic ways in these texts) forces us to imagine the new in a much more material, nonhuman, and environmental manner than is the case in nationalistic, revolutionary, and modernist master narratives. Finally, both Tsing's and Wright's experimental reflections return us to the point I made earlier, but then bracketed, regarding Bakhtin's brilliant notion of the "chronotope." It is impossible to completely disconnect discussions of time and temporality from place and space. Wright's meditations on mutation and its temporalities ultimately yield a completely new (and I think accurate) vision of Johannesburg, the ruined modern city, as a purely physical rather than a cultural, pedagogical, or ideological environment. Much like the plundered and damaged forests of Tsing's fieldwork, the scavenged and "shattered landscape" of the city has become a new kind of nature, where, as Wright puts it, "forms of dynamism might lurk unseen behind its facade of stagnation."[35]

On transition

Wright's work moves us, then, to consider the biological and material—or radical and desperate—modes of transformation at stake in the notion of mutation. Nevertheless, it is not "transformation" but "transition" that remains the keyword in this volume, and it does commit us, to a considerable degree, to a contemplation of South Africa's fate as a nation, or at least a polity.[36] "Transition" is a shifty and problematic term, not least because, as Monica Popescu once noted, it marks a lack, gesturing as it does toward an arrival that has not yet occurred.[37] And it inevitably raises a number of unsettling questions. Which years, after all, are we referring to when we use the term? For how long can a nation that has gone through a major change be said to be in transition? Does "transition" inevitably impose a teleology, or could it (like the word "crisis" as habitually applied elsewhere in Africa) suggest an array of temporal experiences and affective registers? It is no wonder that some South African scholars have taken issue with the term, proposing that we have entered a "post-transition" phrase, while others have turned to a backward-looking term "remains," in order to de-emphasize the assumption of a destination or deferred arrival in favor of a sober recognition of the residue of past in the present.[38]

Yet, unsatisfactory and slippery though the term "transition" may be, and ambiguous in terms of its periodization, it remains unavoidable. Indeed, it seems to me that Leon de Kock is entirely right when he asserts that the entire field of South African writing since 1990 pivots around the idea of transition.[39] Though he provides us with a dutiful tracking of the various refinements of periodization and terminological shifts, De Kock ultimately—and judiciously— dismisses their usefulness. After all, the very disillusionment with the rainbow narrative of secular redemption is an index of the extent to which the social imaginary "continues to hold dear the founding tenets of the new democracy."[40] And to say that "transition" is pivotal is to say that postapartheid literature is fundamentally animated by temporal concerns and questions. There are perhaps only two very basic questions: What has been the fate of a promised new beginning inaugurated so stirringly in 1994? How do we imagine and represent "the social relation … between past (the time of memory), present (the time of conscious awareness), and the future (the time of anticipation)"?[41] The fact that this relation is unclear and contested—occulted, even, as De Kock puts it, by "contending regimes of information and legitimation"—in no way diminishes its centrality to the literary and political imagination.[42]

As editors, Andrew van der Vlies and I have therefore made no attempt to rein in or homogenize the various uses of the term offered in this volume, nor to follow the lead of those scholars who suggest that we are already somehow in transition's aftermath.[43] The desire to retain this openness is also premised on an understanding that literature does not abide by any accepted historical demarcations and that it inspires us to make meaning precisely out of the fluidity of time, out of the complexity—or perplexity—of lived history, especially of the ever-porous "almost-times" of the present. And while this collection does, cumulatively, offer a wide-ranging exploration of postapartheid writing, the volume's purpose is not so much to collect writings about literary works representing a transition period, bracketed by certain dates, than to offer a meditation on how "transition" may be reconceived, not as a settled temporal marker, but as a practice crucial to democracy (as Chris Holmes proposes in his chapter) and crucial to the narrative imagination.

Since this book is concerned with temporal complexities, with the way the present is shot through with the past and shaped by dreams for the future, it has not been possible to organize the chapters in any strict chronological fashion. Rather, in order to make the logic and coherence of the contributions stand out, the volume is conceptualized as a sequence of thematically paired chapters. It moves, broadly speaking, from reflections on different historical conjunctures and representational modalities to theoretical meditations on what it might mean to *read* in transition: how we might devise modes of encountering the literary text that eschew the usual boundaries of nationality, territory, context, and periodization. This said, the volume is undeniably shaped by its own context and origins. The idea arose from the ALCA conference at Brown University in 2012 (thence the preponderance of essays by young and mid-career US-based scholars) and it is determined throughout by the frustrations and intellectual provocations of the Zuma years, during which history has moved along (even as we wrote, in the days before Zuma's fall, we felt obscure rumblings of change under our feet), but refused to flow according to preconceived expectations. It was a situation that demanded—and continues to demand—interpretive ingenuity. We can only hope that we have shown some and warmly invite other writers, wherever they be, to extend our inquiry and redirect it as seems necessary.

On hope and betrayal

The collective work of this book is initiated by Monica Popescu's reflections on "revolutionary time." Her chapter presents Mongane Wally Serote's novel *To Every Birth Its Blood* (1981) as a key text of the late apartheid years and, in its crucial transnational aspects, of the late Cold War era. This double interpretive gesture reveals some of the difficulties at stake in periodizing the Cold War and provides further evidence of South Africa's anomalous temporalities. Scholars agree that the Cold War was hardly a homogeneous and unchanging period: the optimistic sentiments of the late 1940s and the 1950s eventually yielded to a darker mood, as hopes for radically reshaping the future started to wane. But they suggest different dates for this turn: Ann Douglas, for example, locates the shift in the 1960s, while David Scott, as we have seen, locates it in 1983, with the overthrow of the Marxist government in Granada—a moment that for him signals the global advent of neoliberalism and the end of revolutionary dreaming. When one brings South African history into play, periodizing gestures become even more problematic. For in South Africa the year 1983 marked the formation of the United Democratic Front and initiated a period of renewed activism, along with precisely the future-oriented, militant optimism that Scott thought to be in retreat worldwide.

The anticipatory temporality of the liberation struggle is suggested by the very title of novel Popescu analyses, but it is most evident, she insists, in the performative dimension of the work: Serote's aim in *To Every Birth Its Blood* is to write revolution into being. In its representational dimension, however, the novel is less unidirectional. To be sure, its two parts trace a development: a shift in the focal character's experience from his initial inward-looking, melancholic drifting to a more resolute goal-oriented commitment. Yet, as Popescu points out, Serote registers both vanishing and emergent modes of thinking and feeling, along with those that come to assume dominance in the narrative present. The novel stages the attitudes of three generations of activists: the cautious long-term strategizing of the characters shaped by the repressive 1960s, the disillusionment of those shaped by Black Consciousness in the 1970s, and the volatile, eager daring of the young, shaped by the renewed militancy of their day. The narrative, in other words, brings multiple, layered, and contradictory temporalities into play. And the complexities only deepen, Popescu argues, when we take our present preoccupations into account: it is impossible to reread Serote's work without a sense that it is concerned with a future that has already passed. In Zuma's stalled South Africa, the novel's anticipatory and pedagogical qualities, its expectation of a new revolutionary birth, could not be shared, except perhaps in the modality of nostalgia.

Far from desiring to transcend or reduce these complexities, Popescu provides a term that assists us in thinking about them more productively. She proposes, as a methodological imperative, that we strive to discern a work's "affective-temporal structure": that we read with an alertness, not only to the overall thrust of the narrative, but also to the disjoint temporal experiences and sentiments that shape the memories and possibilities, the paralyses and aspirations at stake in a given text or historical conjuncture. This approach, of course, harkens back to Raymond Williams's "structures of feeling," a concept intended to foster a mode of periodization—and interpretation, for the activities are inseparable—that does not rely on preset macroscopic ideas about classes or modes of production, but rather on microscopic changes. These are often *felt*, rather than *thought* changes and they are discoverable in literary texts, par excellence. In Popescu's work and that of others in this volume, the possibilities of Williams's provocatively vague term are inflected and enriched by the affective turn in contemporary criticism. Desire, regret, disillusionment, shame—such inclinations, she insists, determine the forms by which we give narrative shape to events, as well as our ways of reading about them.

Popescu's meditations on revolutionary time are extended and reversed in the following chapter, Annel Pieterse's "After Marikana: The Temporalities of Betrayal." Though she does not deploy the term "affective-temporal structure," such is precisely Pieterse's concern. She seeks to describe the angry disillusionment of present-day South Africa: sentiments that are most potently marshaled around the Marikana Massacre of September 2012, when forty-one striking workers at the Lonmin Platinum mines were shot down by police. This event, Pieterse argues, ruptured the sanctioned national myth that casts the present as the culmination of a linear narrative of redemption and transcendence: the mythic story of how the liberation movement courageously defeated apartheid and brought freedom and equality to all. Against this simple teleology, with its good-guys-bad-guys cast and its happy outcome, Pieterse bring into play a narrative of betrayal. It is a twisted sort of narrative, for betrayal is disturbing, unsettling—it demands a reordering of our understanding of the past.

Such a reordering, Pieterse contends, is accomplished by two recent works: Jacob Dlamini's *Askari: A Story of Collaboration and Betrayal in the Apartheid Era* (2015) and Niq Mhlongo's novel *Way Back Home* (2013). These works are set in the past (in the late 1980s and early 1990s—the precise moment that interests Popescu), but the chapter treats them in a rather Benjaminian way, showing how the present—the time of the now—is shot through by the fragments and recurrences of the past: the scattered clues, in this case, of the violence perpetrated by the ANC and by blacks on other blacks, violence that those in power today would rather suppress. The close readings of Dlamini and Mhlongo reveal the sinister particularities of South Africa's border wars and the Vlakplaas death farm in all their local specificity. Yet the history in question in this chapter is not solely that of South Africa; for behind the linear nationalist narrative of the South African liberation struggle lies the equally simplistic global narrative of the victory of liberal democracy over capitalism. The (re)vision brought to us by betrayal narratives serves to subvert both of these myths by means of their dark reminders of repressed complexities and complicities. They enable us, above all, to see the extent to which the official history of the struggle has been appropriated for financial gain, thereby falling in line with the market logic of neoliberalism. "The rhetoric of revolution," Pieterse declares, has become "a political lubricant legitimizing rent seekers squatting atop every conceivable source of wealth."

Even so, the chapter considers the Marikana moment in dialectical ways. During the period of protracted disappointment, when frontal criticism of the ANC government was destined not to stick, the revelation of past secrets—a kind of deferred exposé or "stutter," in Pieterse's metaphor—seemed to retain some hope for change. This is why she ultimately eschews the temptation to cast Marikana simply as repetition, a reenactment with different agents, of the Sharpeville massacre. For betrayal narratives, she asserts, do not proclaim stuckness: they offer an implicit critique of the present and brush against the grain of the ANC's legitimating master history. Indeed, their reordering of the past prompts Pieterse to ask whether the Marikana protests and the recent student uprisings should not be seen as part and parcel of what Alain Badiou has described (in terms curiously reminiscent the title of Serote's revolutionary novel) as the first new stirrings of a global popular uprising: "a powerful contraction in the rebirth of history."[44]

On mellowness and vulnerability

The next pair of chapters engages with a different set of temporal modalities: waiting and precarity.[45] The former has long been grasped as a particularly South African structure of feeling. During the apartheid era (once described by J. M. Coetzee as "a viscous, sluggish chronicity, charged with eruptive potential"), waiting seemed to be a condition of whites, living in the expectation of a cataclysmic, violent overthrow.[46] But since the end of apartheid, waiting (as distinguished from revolutionary hope) has also become part of black experience. Researchers have recounted the ways in which millions of poor people find themselves in a state of suspension or, more vividly, "sitting around" [*sihlezi*], in unsatisfactory living circumstances, yearning for the stability of permanent housing that would enable them to be able to plan their futures, to have privacy and independence—to cease to be immature dependents and claim full adult subjectivity and citizenship.[47]

In her chapter, "Still Waiting? Writing Futurity after Apartheid," Katherine Hallemeier recognizes this predicament, but puts forward the provocative premise that the anticipation of either collective disaster or collective transformation presupposes a particular notion of eventfulness and agency that is far from universally available. Drawing inspiration from Nadine Gordimer, Ivan Vladislavić, and especially Njabulo Ndebele, Hallemeier raises the question of whether a pressing sense of futurity, anxious or eager, does not serve to narrow present experiences and demean the lives of those, notably poor women, who are not included in the triumphal national story. Must the end of waiting—the "waiting to come back home" referred to at the end of Gordimer's story "Amnesty"—necessarily depend on an idea of national belonging and, more specifically, on property ownership?

To answer this question, Hallemeier turns first to Vincent Crapanzano's *Waiting: The Whites of South Africa* (1985), an anthropological study of a small-town

Afrikaans community during the late apartheid years. This influential text of its day has recently come in for trenchant criticism by Derek Hook, who has faulted Crapanzano for not grasping that white South Africans' anxious waiting was symptomatic of an unarticulated sense of guilt and an apprehension of justified revenge.[48] While acknowledging the force of this critical reinterpretation, Hallemeier homes in on a positive moment in Crapanzano, namely his feeling that the narrow and banal experiential world of white South Africans could have been quite different had they not focused on a singular dreadful telos, but rather on transforming and enriching their quotidian interactions with their countrymen in a myriad small ways. In so doing, they might cumulatively have transcended the impoverished lager mentality of apartheid and hastened its end. This idea is counterfactual and utopian, to be sure, but it resonates with Ndebele's call during the same period for a "rediscovery of the ordinary."[49] For Hallemeier, the intuition of an alternative affective-temporal structure in Crapanzano's work is enabling: Why not imagine a more present-oriented structure of feeling, an alternative to the contemporary frustrations of waiting? Her attention is therefore drawn to those moments in *The Cry of Winnie Mandela* (2003), Ndebele's curious fictional-philosophical symposium on women's waiting, where he does precisely this. The closing moments of the work are particularly telling. Ndebele allows his female narrators, who have spent years in suspension on the margins, to embark on a fun road trip complete with *padkos* and sing-alongs, in the company of both the nation's and the world's most famous waiting women: Winnie Madikizela-Mandela, sporting a fabulous pair of sunglasses, and (unlikely as it may seem) Penelope of ancient times, now reimagined as a footloose hitchhiker and feminist oracle. If Serote, as Popescu would have it, writes a revolutionary time into being, Ndebele, or so Hallemeier argues, celebrates and sings an alternative (and antithetical) affective-temporal structure, one he terms—quite beautifully— "mellowness." From his comic and very mellow final scene, she draws some bold conclusions. She challenges Homi Bhabha's oft-cited claim in *The Location of Culture* that postcolonial writing reveals the unhomed condition of postcolonial society and stages a vision of "the world-in-the-home," by insisting instead that feminist literature from the global South can reveal "a home-despite-the-world." This condition will be mobile and rootless, but rich in present engagement and distinct, therefore, from the dominant temporalities of national liberation and global capitalism alike.

The next chapter, Sarah Lincoln's meditation on what she calls "precarious time," is also engaged with Ndebele's thought, although the primary fictional texts explored are Zakes Mda's *Ways of Dying* (1995) and Nadine Gordimer's

July's People (1981). Her starting point is Ndebele's 2000 Steve Biko Memorial Lecture, "Iph'Indlela? Finding Our Way into the Future," with its searching comments on the idea of home. Ndebele's argument here is that national belonging for all cannot be predicated on heredity or identity, or even, as Hallemeier also suggests, on expectations for the future. "Home" must rather be found in the now, in modes of relation in the present, and it comes with a rather strenuous ethical requirement, especially for white South Africans. They need to understand that their security and comfort, maintained at the expense of others, must be relinquished and that this involves a sharing of the vulnerability and exposure that is the day-to-day experience of so many of their fellow citizens. One might see this mode of living together as the unlearning of privilege that Gayatri Spivak has always urged; but Lincoln's chapter renders the process in concrete, abjectly material ways. It is defined, in the works she analyzes, by three characteristics: a narrative temporality of instability and indeterminacy; a metaphorics of waste and superfluity; and, finally, a certain linguistic impenetrability, encountered in disconcerting personal experiences that prove untranslatable and irreducible. It is only through this loss of a privileged state of immunity—a trope Lincoln theorizes via Derrida, Butler, and Ed Cohen—that the privileged subject may become a true contemporary in the sense of "being temporary together." If Hallemeier's chapter affirms the mellowness of an enriched present, not dependent on the eventfulness of national historical time, Lincoln affirms, through her readings of Mda and Gordimer, a state of being that is risky, perhaps exhilarating, perhaps sad: one that is not only present and material, but impermanent and discomfiting, open to a common predicament of perpetual loss, change, and vulnerability. It is also a state of being which tends to erase South African's vaunted exceptionality; for, as Goldstone and Obarrio insist, temporariness may well be the most important concept for understanding the conditions of existence on the African continent today.[50]

On trauma and nostalgia

The next pair of chapters explores modes of memory in South African literature and probes two further affective-temporal structures: trauma and nostalgia. Erica Still's chapter, which takes Yvette Christiansë's powerful slave narrative, *Unconfessed* (2007) as its primary text, sets out with a discussion of two antithetical approaches to the past and specifically to the racial trauma of slavery and apartheid.

The first approach has already been touched on—almost taken as read—in other chapters, namely the state-sponsored reclamation of the past through the institution of the TRC. Clinically speaking, trauma is a temporal disruption, a repetition of a violent or painful experience in the present, which prevents the sufferer from moving on with his or her life. It is, as Still reminds us, a modality that arises from the past, but profoundly affects present and future experience. The vast narrative event that was the TRC offered a framework through which "proper" temporal relations could be restored: a laudable goal, but one that ultimately subordinated the past to the demands of the future, insisting on reconciliation in the interest of a narrative of overcoming.

The second approach to trauma, that of David Scott, offers critique of this mode of transitional justice. He argues that the stalled present of neoliberalism with its scant commitment to a transformed future has meant that the unjust past is no longer something to be transcended, but to be accommodated. Thus, the contemporary fixation on trauma and trauma studies is for him symptomatic of an attenuated sense of the political as an ongoing demand for emancipation. The task Still sets herself, then, is to find a way to consider trauma—to confront the past and renegotiate its relationship to the present and the future—without seeing it as a mere resource for memorializing and nation building on the one hand and an apolitical escape on the other.

Her response, like that of other authors in this volume, is profoundly literary. Christiansë's novel, Still argues, deals with trauma in a way that is, not unlike trauma itself, reiterative, revealing its secrets only by accretion—and then incompletely. *Unconfessed* is radically heterotemporal, as emphasized by the shifting point of view of the novels' three sections (which goes from third-, to first-, to second-person narration). The language of the law in the first section, which casts the slave woman's experience as a sequence of causes and effects, is in tension with the elusive, incomplete, fragmentary self-discovery of the first-person narrative in the second section. Both these modes are eschewed in the novel's coda. Addressing the reader as "you," it refuses to provide a singular assertive climax to the text: it offers instead a multiplicity of possible endings, with the iteration of the phrase "some say … some say …." Free speculation and invention, in other words, come to replace the linear, authoritative "whereas" of law. Such an ending is not amenable to a reading that is "political" in any simple and utilitarian way. For unlike the state *in* transition, which would, in Still's graceful formulation, "turn the past into a known but distant place," literature offers "a state *of* transition in its very uncertainly and open possibilities regarding past, present, and future." In this, paradoxically, she discovers political energies:

it is in the very multiplicity of the potential outcomes to the slave woman's story, that the text mimics the multiplicity and open-endedness of democracy itself.

An important point made in Still's chapter is that the proliferation of temporal descriptors that have been applied to contemporary South Africa—postapartheid, post-antiapartheid, transitional, and post-transition—is an indication that the task of negotiating the relationship among past, present, and future is ongoing. The following chapter by Erica Lombard, by contrast, specifically designates its interests as post-transitional. The chapter concerns a recent subgenre: the return of the exile to the deathbed of a parent. Such novels, Lombard suggests, are made possible by the unraveling of the once-persuasive teleological story of national liberation to the point where it has become possible to think of the past not only in terms of trauma or trauma transcended, but also in other registers—most notably nostalgia.

Yet Lombard's interests, like Still's, lie in the mediation of past, present, and future. Drawing on the now-classic work of Svetlana Boym, she suggests that nostalgia can perform such a task. This claim is not uncontroversial, for earlier commentaries on nostalgia in postapartheid South Africa have tended to view it as conservative and politically suspect—and suitable for whites only. But, as Lombard points out in her commentary on Jacob Dlamini's wry memoir about growing up in Kathlehong township, *Native Nostalgia* (2009), nostalgia can also function as a counternarrative to the simplistic and spectacular narrative of suffering and heroism. In it the demonstration of the ordinariness of the apartheid past Dlamini's text affirms the full humanity of those who lived it. The readings of Mark Behr's *Kings of the Water* (2009) and Anne Landsman's *The Rowing Lesson* (2007) that follow explore two further versions of nostalgia, defined respectively by Boym's "restorative nostalgia," with its spatialization of time, and "reflective nostalgia," with its temporalization of space.[51] Behr's novel, accordingly, stages a return to a place (a family farm edenically named "Paradys") and to the tropes of the familiar Afrikaans genre of the *plaasroman*. The latter novel is less place-bound and offers instead, as its central metaphor, the coelacanth, a fish once presumed to be extinct, but then discovered alive in the waters off the Eastern Cape. It is a figure in Lombard's reading for a complex temporality, signaling not linear process and transcendence, but rather the coexistence of heterogeneous times—times in which the residual lives on, along with the dominant, and in which "home" is discovered not in rootedness but in flux. The rowing lesson teaches that one may "reach forward, into the past." The chapter's analysis of these recent novels, in sum, permits a rethinking of nostalgia as an embrace of the past that is not necessarily closed off from imaginings of the future. However, as Lombard reminds us in conclusion, such an embrace must acknowledge the fact that South African subjects have very unequal access to consoling memories. The indulgent, fun, and merely stylish nostalgia of, say, the TV show *Mad Men* is probably still not available, she observes, in a country where history has been so divisive and violent.

On criminals and queers

If Lombard's chapter features a recent and specifically South African genre and Still's a genre with both national and diasporic relevance, the following two chapters engage with two well-established forms, both inseparable from global modernism: the crime novel and the short-story cycle. Both forms have flourished in South Africa and crime has proven particularly marketable, with the international success of writers like Deon Meyer, films like the Oscar-winning *Tsotsi* (2005) and, in the academic sphere, the far-reaching work on law and order by scholars like Jean and John Comaroff. One might presume, then, that recent crime fiction, the subject of Brenna Munro's chapter, would adapt to the conditions of circulation laid out by Franco Moretti in his "Conjectures on World Literature": global form, local contents, and local voicings.[52] But Munro implies that there may be other parameters as well. She suggests that crime and the crime novel in South Africa have become difficult to separate from the story of HIV/AIDS, thus producing a surprising generic variant she calls, after Lauren Beukes, "muti noir." In her reading, HIV/AIDS is not merely a matter of additional content: it may in fact be one reason for the insistent way in which time is made visible and problematic in these texts. After all, HIV/AIDS and crime are the two phenomena that, more than any other, have derailed the normal unfolding of individual lives since 1994 and troubled any hopeful sense of South Africa's teleological trajectory toward the promises of liberation.

The novels Munro investigates, Deon Meyer's *Blood Safari* (2010), Diale Tlholwe's *Ancient Rites* (2008), Sifiso Mzobe's *Young Blood* (2011), Lauren Beukes's *Zoo City* (2010), and Kgebetli Moele's *The Book of the Dead* (2010), emplot past, present, and future in remarkably varied ways. These include (in Munro's deft summary) the following: an eruption of the trauma of the apartheid past into the present; a negotiation between traditions presumed to be archaic and the routines of contemporary life; an immersion in a narcotic present tense of crime and rapidly sated consumerist desire; and a relentless fixation on the futureless repetition of destructive serial actions. Munro's engaging reading of these diverse crime novels reveals a great deal about the unfolding shape of the present in South Africa. They present a range of generational and gendered concerns, from the wounds of white men struggling with new institutional orders to the malaise of black youths, bored with the paltry rewards of working-class chrononormativity. But these novels reveal something about global affective-temporal structures as well. If their content extends to crime syndicates that reach across national borders (as is often the case with Meyer), the affective-temporal structures they evoke are also shaped transnationally—by the consumerist and apolitical orientation of neoliberal economies in which not only the characters, but also the books themselves, as circulating commodities, must function.

One global feeling expressed here is paranoia. To be sure, it may have specifically South African inflections (Munro reminds us of the "black-intruder" alibi in the Oscar Pistorius murder case), but paranoia is also, as Sianne Ngai has observed, a sentiment of discontent with the "obstructed agency" so many feel today: with "one's perceived status as small subject in a global system."[53] South Africa's crime wave (as well as its obsession with the counter-discourse of law) is then one of the many signs of the end of its putative exceptionalism: evidence, as Munro puts it, that "the country is becoming more like everywhere else." "Neoliberal time is global," she declares, "and so is crime"—especially when one grasps crime, as several of these novelist do, as merely an alternative mode of production and profiteering, unofficial but parallel to the official capitalist marketplace and the kleptocratic state.

Andrew van der Vlies's chapter investigates another genre, the short-story cycle, in light of S. J. Naudé's innovative *The Alphabet of Birds* (2014), first published in Afrikaans as *Alfabet van die voëls* (2011). The inherently ambivalent nature of the short-story cycle, hovering between the coherence of novels and the disconnection of mere stories, made it an important form in apartheid-era South Africa: it hinted at the persistence of collectivities at a time when such collectivities and communities were rent asunder by the systemic and direct violence of the state. In Naudé's hands, the form, hovering between relation and looseness, also becomes expressive of the fate of the work's contemporary characters—typically expatriates, typically Afrikaners, typically homosexual. Its formal ambivalence, moreover, perfectly captures what Van der Vlies would propose as yet another affective-temporal structure of contemporary South African literature, namely queer longing. This is, he explains, a contradictory structure, involving a yearning for some kind of future redemption and satisfaction, but simultaneously also a resistance to it: a perverse clinging to the painful pleasures of disavowal and postponement.

Naudé's collection contains several stories that feature the trope of the exiled child returning to the parent's deathbed, foregrounded also in Lombard's chapter, and it is clear that generational and familial relationships are crucial but always problematic in the work's social imaginary. But the presiding modality here is not nostalgic. One of the most striking images (arising in the story "The Noise Machine") is that of a child, drowned, but visible beneath the surface of an icy lake. The image evokes a condition of failed development or frozen potential, which resonates with the state of suspension and disappointment that seems to define contemporary South Africa. But it can also be read in light of Euro-American queer theory, especially Lee Edelman's polemic against a sentimental fixation on the figure of the child as a guarantor of futurity. This is to say that the affective-temporal structures in Naudé—of failure, stasis, and longing—are far from local or national. Indeed, Van der Vlies is able to draw extensively on the examination of "bad feelings" in the work of scholars like Sara Ahmed, Lauren Berlant, and Heather Love, who have argued that queer unhappiness is not necessarily equated with despair, or to a failure to imagine that things can be different. At stake, in this body of work—and in Naudé's stories—is a validation of that which counters, negates, or simply refuses to go along with prescribed trajectories, whether of heteronormal bourgeois lives, or of the nation—so often figured as a heterosexual reproductive family. In Van der Vlies's reading, the melancholy fragments of these strange stories, with their failed relationships, illness, mistranslations, and ambivalence about place and nationality, are not without redemptive potential. On the contrary, the very disappointment they register, their holding back and holding open, affirms Ernst Bloch's understanding of the methodology of hope as residing in the *not yet*. This is why so many of Naudé's stories retain what we might call (after the title of one of them) a kind of looseness—as does the collection too: loose ends are necessary to that deferral or postponement, which, as Van der Vlies's argues, stands as the promissory note for nonnormative forms of fulfillment and liberation.

On heterogeneity and incompletion

The final pair of chapters in this collection deals with two of the most important writers to have come to prominence since 1990: Ivan Vladislavić and Marlene van Niekerk. These chapters, however, take a contemplative step back from the task of applying a periodizing hypothesis or fixed formal template to the literary work, offering instead a critique of the very terms of such approaches, notably "genre" and "context," and suggesting new modes of reading.

In her chapter, "History and the Genres of Modernity: Marlene van Niekerk's *Agaat*," Lily Saint provides a useful list of the predominant concept-metaphors that have been deployed to describe present-day South Africa. First, there is the idea of lateness (as in "post-apartheid"), second is the idea of rebirth and renovation (as in "the new South Africa," or Thabo Mbeki's short-lived "African Renaissance"), and, third, our old friend "transition"—that in-between temporality, presided over by Walter Benjamin's Janus-faced angel of history, "gazing back at the traumas and nostalgias of colonialism and apartheid, while simultaneously careening forward into the anxieties and desires of future teloi." But Saint opts for none of these, reflecting instead that period demarcations, like those of literary genres, tend to settle into ready-made definitions. Thus, we have been taught to think of South African history as constituted by the sequential moments of, say, the colonial period, the Mfecane, the apartheid era, the interregnum, and the postapartheid years, or, more conceptually, by rupture and continuum, event and duration, and kairos and chronos. These designations have the effect, Saint declares, of fixing, naming, and setting apart—thereby eliding evidence of continuity, indeterminacy, and contingency.

In her reading of *Agaat* (2004), she therefore refuses to test the novel out in relation to the genre of the *plaasroman* (as others have done), to claim it (as one could) as the quintessential postapartheid novel, or to contextualize it in terms of the historical period it spans (1948–1996). Her chapter, in other words, does not deploy the strategies of political formalism that would articulate the logic of a period subgenre, nor does it, like other chapters in this book, attempt to define the contours of a particular affective-temporal structure. Saint's strategy is, instead, to turn to Derrida's observation that while "the law of genre," literary or historical, is to categorize, decree separation, and banish contamination, it always fails. Thus, "the law of the law of genre" yields heterogeneity: the very principle that *Agaat*'s dizzying, proliferating genres and representational modes—stream of consciousness, diary entries, hymns, poems, telegraphese, shopping lists, folksongs, European classical music, maps, embroidery— relentlessly and exuberantly perform. The same argument, Saint points out, goes for the laws of political segregation, whose failure is evident in the colored servant Agaat's (arguably pyrrhic) victory over her white mistress and, more generally, in the persistence of hybridity in South African culture and its lived realities. This paradoxical situation is beautifully summed up in the line from Breyten Breytenbach that Saint quotes for us: "*Apartheid is the law of the bastard.*"

This observation entirely destabilizes any pure Afrikaner identity, the historical excuse for apartheid, which, as Van Niekerk shows, is actually the result of, not the cause for, segregation.

With its four discrete narrative modes, *Agaat* is a highly structured novel: so much so that one might want to call it a belatedly high-modernist text in its rage for order, its allusiveness, and poetic tautology. But even though its form strives for experimental elegance (just as its main character strives for racial and class segregation), the novel constantly reveals its inadequacy and the failure of its attempts to provide closure. If this is modernism, Saint argues, it could perhaps be seen as akin to the versions of black modernity—traumatized, polyglossic, fugitive, syncretic, and hybrid—foregrounded by Paul Gilroy and David Attwell. *Agaat*, in other words, requires a redefinition of modernity and equally, Saint suggests, of our understanding of the present. It is a novel that exposes all our strategies for dealing with temporality, in order to make time newly and acutely visible.

If Saint's chapter provocatively aligns her reading of *Agaat* with Breytenbach's judgment that apartheid was "the law of the bastard," then Chris Holmes's reading of Ivan Vladislavić in the next chapter of this volume is aligned to Breytenbach's description of the transformation and democratization of South Africa as "*die groot Andersmaak*" [the great Othermaking]. In his chapter, "Transition as Democratic Form: The Unfinishable Work of Ivan Vladislavić," Holmes does entertain the thought that there might be a period genre of "transition writing," but he suggests that "transition" needs to be subjected to very careful reconsideration. Acknowledging that the term has frequently been used as a period designation (gesturing to the years of the emergency, the release of Mandela, the turbulent period of negotiations, the 1994 election, and its immediate aftermath), "transition," in his view, is best seen as a radically uncertain temporality. If, for Zoë Wicomb, "transition" signals a failure of democratization, Holmes suggests that democracy itself is always transitional: it will never be fully achieved. Citing Thomas Docherty, he proposes that democracy is in a sense continuous with culture itself. It entails the discovery of a selfhood that is always becoming, always marked by alterity, "a condition of being-with-otherness."[54]

This conception has literary implications, which open up Vladislavić's oeuvre in new ways and permit a rethinking of the relationship of literature to history. To articulate this relationship, Holmes turns to Rita Felski's critique of the use of "context" as a kind of box to constrain and delimit interpretation. His main theorist, however, is Vladislavić himself. Holmes is particularly intrigued by one of Vladislavić's recent works: *The Loss Library and Other Unfinished*

Stories (2012), a collection of fragments, notebook, excerpts, and still-born stories written during the period 1990–1994, the most turbulent years of South Africa's transformation. The questions this work raises are twofold: Why did Vladislavić find these pieces impossible to complete at the time, and why should they be republished, with the demand, as it were, that the contemporary reader thaw the "frostbitten pages" with his or her breath? (The metaphor, we should note, is particularly apt, since one of the fragments concerns an artist's monumental "frieze" of incidents in South African history: an artifact that deploys precisely the periodizing or "freezing" of set historical eras rejected by Saint.) The answer Holmes offers is that Vladislavić (even in *The Restless Supermarket*, with its fascinating record of Hillbrow's racial transformation as mediated by a very crusty observer) works against any promise of capturing history in amber, and against understanding literature's meanings in relation to historical context. The unfinishable stories in *The Loss Library*, even though they come with devices that signify their historical moment—dates, footnotes, and introductions—ultimately do not represent the transition to democracy so much, as capture its form (and we might bring to mind here Still's earlier comments on *Unconfessed* as mimicking democracy's multiplicity). In Holmes' reading, Vladislavić's oeuvre is therefore not "transitional" in the sense that it depicts the period or even its structures of feeling. Rather, it suggests that we might think of transition—on its very incompletion—as a figuration of thought itself. Novels, as Felski asserts, are not things to be known, but things to know with; reading them will yield not "a solution to the problem of nations," a phrase cited in the chapter's epigraph, but a restless negotiation with change essential to the practice of democracy and freedom.

In search of scholarly futures

In the manifesto-like coda to this volume, Tsitsi Jaji joins Holmes in proposing an extended notion of transition, one that might spill over temporal boundaries (like those staked out by founding of South African democracy in 1994), as well as territorial frontiers (like those of the increasingly xenophobic South African state). This vision would require a mode of imaginative border crossing: a rearrangement of past, present, and future that would transcend South Africa's exceptionalism and encourage a new transnational imaginary, mindful of what the poet Keorapetse Kgositsile, one of the many inspirational voices Jaji evokes for us, has called "love armed with future memory."[55] Deliberately turning to history as a resource for navigating the present, Jaji offers a rereading of Sol Plaatje's *Mhudi* (1930) as work of transition. The novel, she makes clear, will not permit us to forget the grinding quotidian inequalities of "racial time."[56] But it nevertheless enables us, in her reading, to return to a long-standing, but deflected anti-racist and transnational project. Along with many of the postapartheid works considered in this conclusion and in this volume as a whole, *Mhudi* suggests an alternative vision of cross-border solidarity and of the future: a vision of a continual commitment to human rights, dignity, and openness.

It seems right, then, to think about ongoing lines of inquiry rather than offer a definitive *finis* to our collective meditations. What kind of scholarly or literary work is merely trendy and symptomatic of the temporal pathologies of our day and what might have the potential to initiate new storylines, new modes of thought? Should we be suspicious of conventionally developmental forms or fixations on past trauma? If so, would a different set of theorists emerge as useful? As we have seen, the chapters in this volume tend to replace the usual postcolonial interlocutors with queer theorists, anthropologists attentive to heterotemporalities, and philosophers like Benjamin and Bloch, but are there other thinkers we could draw on? Furthermore, which new archives might we tap in order to identify different modalities of time? Would such archives (I think, for instance, of the astoundingly rich archive of South African apocalyptic imaginings across the decades that Michael Titlestad has brought together) amplify or displace the established archive of the TRC, which has to date been counted as the great collective narrative of the transition?[57]

And as to literature and literary form: Does the attention to heterotemporalities often called for in this volume imply that we are no longer looking for a major work, for a "great South African novel"? Is the task, rather, to seek out minor, nonfictional, or even failed works: fractured forms, registering the opacity of the present moment in various innovative ways? And what should future scholars make of the idea of slowness? Have the rapid changes and profound pressures of political history in South Africa prevented us from responding fully to the necessary deceleration and recalibration demanded by climate change and the Anthropocene? If we did respond, would a different set of literary texts from those we have discussed here accrue interest and urgency (one thinks, for example, of Ingrid Winterbach's *Book of Happenstance* and *To Hell with Cronje*, with their meditations on the slow evolution of life on the planet, or, say, James Whyle's *The Excavations*, with its wildly imaginative postapocalyptic futurism)? And what, we might ask with equal urgency, do we make of the new accelerated pace of experience brought to us by contemporary social media and what Achille

Mbembe has called the new politics of impatience?[58] Does it mean that literary study will remain important, or is the time the public invests in consuming news and opinion online, whether distractedly or passionately, rendering literature an outmoded cultural practice with a time signature too rarified for the present? Readers—and we hope they are out there (for if there is a hope shared by contributors to this volume, it is that literature can train our attentiveness to polyphonic beat of contemporary experience)—will find answers to some of these questions in this volume. Where they do not, we hope the very gaps we have left will help set an agenda for future investigations.

Notes

1   Msimang, "Zuma's South Africa." On the phenomenology of disappointment as a matter of both time and affect, see the introduction to Van der Vlies, *Present Imperfect*, viii.
2   McKaiser, "It's Radical Economic Gibberish."
3   Mbembe, "The State of South African Political Life."
4   Grootes, "A Whiplash Kinda Day," and "Cometh Zuma's Day of Reckoning?"
5   Poplak, "Hasta la Vista, JZ."
6   Grootes, "Ramaphosa's Final Victory."
7   Goldstone and Obarrio, "Introduction: Untimely Africa," 17.
8   On the political sublime, see Barnard, "Introduction," 2–3.
9   As early as 2006, David Attwell called for a shift in South African literary historiography "from an emphasis on how to write about sameness and difference, to writing about *temporality*" (*Rewriting Modernity*, 8). The matter of sameness and difference, however, has not disappeared at all (how could it?); indeed it has become all the more fraught and complicated. See, for example, Leon de Kock's comments on "good difference" and "bad difference" in the contemporary public and literary sphere (*Losing the Plot*, 40–42).
10 The wonderful foundational text is by Judin and Vladislavić, *Blank ____: Apartheid, Architecture and Beyond*; see also Beavon, *Johannesburg*; Barnard, *Apartheid and Beyond*; Bremner, *Writing the City into Being*; Graham, *South African Literature after the Truth Commission*; and Nuttall and Mbembe, *Johannesburg: The Elusive Metropolis*.
11 Nuttall, "City Forms and Writing the 'Now.'"
12 See Wenzel, *Bulletproof*, 16–17; Ferguson, "Theory from the Comaroffs."
13 See for instance Comaroff and Comaroff, "Naturing the Nation."
14 Mbembe, "Africa in Theory," 222.
15 Ferguson, "Theory from the Comaroffs." And so, in somewhat different ways, is the African continent at large. Though historically a "formidable laboratory of

modernity," Africa has consistently been portrayed as "not being in sync with the pace and direction of planetary history," its extremely varied and vibrant localities cast as "remote spaces frozen in time, precariously governed by custom and calamity." See Goldstone and Obarrio, "Introduction: Untimely Africa," 17.

16 See Posel, "The Apartheid Project, 1948–1970," 343–45.

17 In addition to the works specifically described in this brief introduction, readers might consult Osborne, *The Politics of Time*; Boym, *The Future of Nostalgia*; Agacinski, *Time Passing*; Hoy, *The Time of Our Lives*; and West-Pavlov, *Temporalities*.

18 See, for example, West-Pavlov's chapter on "Postcolonial Temporalities," *Temporalities*, 158–74, and Ganguly, "Temporality and Postcolonial Critique." Particularly relevant to this collection is Neil Lazarus's re-invigoration of Raymond Williams's term "structure of feeling" in his *The Postcolonial Unconscious*, 79ff.

19 Cheah, *What Is a World?*; see also his "World against Globe," 309.

20 Cheah, "World against Globe," 318–20.

21 Ibid., 320.

22 Ibid., 326.

23 Levin, *Memories of the Moderns*, 7. This is cited in Lincoln's chapter in this collection. Glissant, "J'écris en présence de toutes les langues du monde," is cited in Tsitsi Jaji's conclusion.

24 Scott, *Omens of Adversity*, 2. See also De Kock on the "future-anterior," an idea he adopts and applies to contemporary South Africa from Hal Foster and Ashraf Jamal, in *Losing the Plot*, 14, 58–59.

25 De Kock, *Losing the Plot*, 2 and ff.

26 Tsing, *The Mushroom at the End of the World*, viii.

27 Ibid., 2.

28 Ibid.

29 Ndebele, "Iph'Indlela?" 53.

30 Tsing, *The Mushroom at the End of the World*, 8, 4.

31 See, for example, Simone, "Globalization," 173–187.

32 Tsing, *The Mushroom at the End of the World*, 2.

33 Wright, "Mutant City," 417–34.

34 Coovadia, *Transformations*, 56–57.

35 Wright, "Mutant City," 418.

36 I am tempted, nevertheless, to propose that the term "transition" functions in the South African context in a similar fashion to the equally pervasive term "crisis" in the context of Africa at large. Both terms, after all, designate a turning point, a decisive moment, but one that gets extended to the point where it seems like an ongoing state of affairs: a condition. Like "crisis," "transition" thus functions as a discursive figure, a deictic. It names not so much an object of study, entity, or a period, but a shifting "place from which one claims access to and knowledge of history." Goldstone and

Obarrio, "Introduction: Untimely Africa," 5–8; Roitman, "Africa Otherwise," 31. To posit a connection between (African) "crisis" and (South African) "transition," then, is to register something of the fictionality of South African exceptionalism, while also recognizing our national and historical specificities.

37 Popescu, "South Africa in Transition," 29.

38 I am thinking here of Minkley et al.'s collection, *Remains of the Social*. We might note, however, that while "remains" in the title is focused on the traces of the past, the subtitle's "desiring" retains the future orientation embedded in the idea of transition. This dual impulse would seem to support Grant Farred's diagnosis of a "double vision" characteristic of postapartheid writing, in "The Not-Yet Counterpartisan," 589–605.

39 De Kock, *Losing the Plot*, 2.

40 Ibid., 3–4.

41 Scott, *Omens of Adversity*, 1.

42 De Kock, *Losing the Plot*, 4.

43 Frenkel and MacKenzie, eds., "Conceptualizing 'Post-Transitional,'" 1–121.

44 Badiou, *The Rebirth of History*, 5.

45 Jedediah Purdy has described that the graceless neologism "precarity" is "a theory-head word for 'precariousness,'" and I share his distaste for the term (though it has come to seem unavoidable). See "The Mushroom that Explains the World."

46 Coetzee, *Doubling the Point*, 209.

47 Motsemme, "'Loving in a Time of Hopelessness,'" 70–72.

48 Hook, "Petrified Life," 13.

49 Ndebele's famous essay of that title first appeared in 1986.

50 Goldstone and Obarrio, "Introduction: Untimely Africa."

51 Boym, *Future of Nostalgia*, xviii.

52 Moretti, "Conjectures on World Literature," 65.

53 Ngai, *Ugly Feelings*, 298–331.

54 Docherty, *Aesthetic Democracy*, xii.

55 Kgositsile, "Ivory Masks in Orbit," in *This Way I Salute You*, 13.

56 Hanchard, "Afro-Modernity," 266.

57 Titlestad, "South African End Times," 52–70.

58 Mbembe, "The State of South African Political Life," 14.

Works Cited

Agacinski, Syliane. *Time Passing: Modernity and Nostalgia*. New York: Columbia University Press, 2003.

Attwell, David. *Rewriting Modernity: Studies in Black South African Literary History*. Athens: Ohio University Press, 2006.

Badiou, Alain. *The Rebirth of History: Times of Riots and Uprisings*. Trans. Gregory Elliott. London: Verso, 2012.

Barnard, Rita. *Apartheid and Beyond: South African Writers and the Politics of Place*. New York: Oxford University Press, 2005.

Barnard, Rita. "Introduction." In *The Cambridge Companion to Nelson Mandela*. Ed. Rita Barnard. New York: Cambridge University Press, 2014. 1–25.

Beavon, Keith. *Johannesburg: The Making and Shaping of the City*. Pretoria: University of South Africa Press, 2004.

Boym, Svetlana. *The Future of Nostalgia*. New York: Basic Books, 2002.

Bremner, Lindsay. *Writing the City into Being: Essays on Johannesburg, 1998–2008*. Johannesburg: Fourthwall Books, 2010.

Cheah, Pheng. *What Is a World?: On Postcolonial Literature as World Literature*. Durham, NC: Duke University Press, 2016.

Cheah, Pheng. "World against Globe: Towards at Normative Conception of World Literature." *New Literary History* 45.3 (Summer 2014): 303–29.

Coetzee, J. M. *Doubling the Point: Essays and Interviews*. Ed. David Attwell. Cambridge, MA: Harvard University Press, 1992.

Comaroff, Jean, and John L. Comaroff "Naturing the Nation: Aliens, Apocalypse, and the Postcolonial State." *Journal of Southern African Studies*. 27.3 (2001): 627–51.

Comaroff, Jean, and John L. Comaroff, *Theory from the South, Or, How Euro-America is Evolving toward Africa*. New York: Paradigm, 2012.

Coovadia, Imraan. *Transformations*. Cape Town: Umuzi, 2012.

De Kock, Leon. *Losing the Plot: Crime, Reality, and Fiction in Postapartheid Writing*. Johannesburg: Wits University Press, 2017.

Docherty, Thomas. *Aesthetic Democracy*. Stanford, CA: Stanford University Press, 2006.

Ferguson, James. "Theory from the Comaroffs, or How to Know the World Up, Down, Backwards, and Forwards." *Johannesburg Book Salon* 5 (2012). http:jwct.org.za/salon_volume_5.htm.

Frenkel, Ronit, and Craig MacKenzie, eds. "Conceptualizing 'Post-Transitional' South African Literature in English." Special Issue of *English Studies in Africa* 53.1 (2010): 1–121.

Ganguly, Keya. "Temporality and Postcolonial Critique." In *The Cambridge Companion to Postcolonial Literary Studies*. Ed. Neil Lazarus. Cambridge: Cambridge University Press, 2004, 162–80.

Glissant, Edouard. "J'écris en présence de toutes les langues du monde." *Congrès Eurozine 2008: Crosswords X/Mots croisés*.

Goldstone, Brian and Juan Obarrio, eds. *African Futures: Essays on Crisis, Emergence, and Possibility*. Chicago: University of Chicago Press, 2016.

Goldstone, Brian and Juan Obarrio. "Introduction: Untimely Africa." *African Futures*. 1–22.

Graham, Shane. *South African Literature after the Truth Commission: Mapping Loss*. New York: Palgrave Macmillan, 2009.

Grootes, Stephen. "A Whiplash Kinda Day and Other Zuma-related Injuries."
  Daily Maverick, February 7, 2018. https://www.dailymaverick.co.za/
  article/2018-02-07-reporters-notebook-a-whiplash-kinda-day-and-other-zuma-
  related-injuries/.

Grootes, Stephen. "Cometh Zuma's Day of Reckoning?" *Daily Maverick*, February 12,
  2018. https://www.dailymaverick.co.za/article/2018-02-12-analysis-cometh-zumas-
  day-of-reckoning/.

Grootes, Stephen. "Ramaphosa's Final Victory over his Predecessor." *Daily Maverick*,
  February 17, 2016. https://www.dailymaverick.co.za/article/2018-02-17-sona2018-
  ramaphosas-final-victory-over-his-predecessor/.

Hanchard, Michael. "Afro-Modernity: Temporality, Politics, and the African Diaspora."
  Public Culture 11.1 (1999): 245–68.

Hook, Derek. "Petrified Life." *Social Dynamics* 41.3 (2015): 438–60.

Hoy, David Couzens. *The Time of Our Lives: A Critical History of Temporality.*
  Cambridge, MA: MIT Press, 2009.

Judin, Hilton and Ivan Vladislavić. *Blank ____: Apartheid, Architecture and Beyond.*
  Cape Town: David Philip, 1998.

Kgositsile, Keorapetse. *This Way I Salute You: Selected Poems.* Cape Town: Kwela, 2007.

Lazarus, Neil, ed. *The Cambridge Companion to Postcolonial Literary Studies.*
  Cambridge: Cambridge University Press, 2004.

Lazarus, Neil. *The Postcolonial Unconscious.* Cambridge: Cambridge University
  Press, 2012.

Levin, Harry. *Memories of the Moderns.* New York: W.W. Norton, 1980.

Mbembe, Achille. "Africa in Theory." Goldstone and Obarrio. 211–30.

Mbembe, Achille. "The State of South African Political Life." *Africa is a Country,*
  9 September 2015. http://africasacountry.com/2015/09/achille-mbembe-on-the-
  state-of-south-african-politics/.

McKaiser, Eusebius. "It's Radical Economic Gibberish." *Mail and Guardian*, April 21,
  2017. https://mg.co.za/article/2017-04-21-00-its-radical-economic-gibberish.

Minkley, Gary, Maurits Van Bever Donker, Premesh Lalu, and Ross Truscott, eds.,
  Remains of the Social: Desiring the Postapartheid. Johannesburg: Wits University
  Press, 2017.

Moretti, Franco. "Conjectures on World Literature." *New Left Review* 1 (2000): 54–68.

Motsemme, Ntabiseng. "'Loving in a Time of Hopelessness': On Township Women's
  Subjectivities in a Time of HIV/AIDS." *African Identities* 5.1 (2007): 70–72.

Msimang, Sisonke. "Zuma's South Africa: When Shame Means Nothing at All." *Daily
  Maverick*, April 25, 2016. https://www.dailymaverick.co.za/opinionista/2016-04-25-
  zumas-south-africa-when-shame-means-nothing-at-all/#.

Ndebele, Njabulo. "Iph'Indlela? Finding Our Way into the Future." *Social Dynamics* 26.1
  (2000): 43–55.

Ndebele, Njabulo. "The Rediscovery of the Ordinary." *The Journal of Southern African
  Studies* 12.2 (April 1986): 143 57.

Ngai, Sianne. *Ugly Feelings*. Cambridge: Harvard University Press, 2005.

Nuttall, Sarah. "City Forms and Writing the 'Now' in South Africa. *Journal of Southern African Studies* 30.4 (2004): 731–48.

Nuttall, Sarah, and Achille Mbembe, eds. *Johannesburg: The Elusive Metropolis*. Durham, NC: Duke University Press, 2008.

Osborne, Peter. *The Politics of Time: Modernity and the Avant-Garde*. London: Verso, 1995.

Popescu, Monica. "South Africa in Transition: Theorizing Post-Colonial, Post-Apartheid, and Post-Communist Cultural Formations." PhD dissertation, University of Pennsylvania, 2005.

Poplak, Richard. "Trainspotter: Hasta la Vista, JZ." *Daily Maverick*, February 14, 2018 https://www.dailymaverick.co.za/article/2018-02-14-trainspotter-hasta-la-vista-jz/.

Posel, Deborah. "The Apartheid Project, 1948–1970." Ross, Mager, and Nasson. 343–45.

Purdy, Jedidiah. "The Mushroom that Explains the World." *New Republic*, October 8, 2015. https://newrepublic.c0m.article/123059/foraging-meaning.

Roitman, Janet. "Africa Otherwise." Goldstone and Obarrio. 28–38.

Ross, Robert, Anne Kelk Mager, and Bill Nasson, eds. *The Cambridge History of South Africa*. Cambridge: Cambridge University Press, 2011.

Scott, David. *Omens of Adversity: Tragedy, Time, Memory, Justice*. Durham, NC: Duke University Press, 2014.

Simone, AbdouMaliq. "Globalization and the Identity of African Urban Practices." Judin and Vladislavić. 173–87.

Titlestad, Michael. "South African End Times: Conceiving an Apocalyptic Imaginary." *Journal of Literary Studies* 51.2 (2014): 52–70.

Tsing, Anna Lowenhaupt. *The Mushroom at the End of the World: On the Possibility of Life in Capitalist Ruins*. Princeton, NJ: Princeton University Press, 2015.

Van der Vlies, Andrew. *Present Imperfect: Contemporary South African Writing*. Oxford: Oxford University Press, 2017.

Wenzel, Jennifer. *Bulletproof: Afterlives of Anticolonial Prophecy in South Africa and Beyond*. Chicago: University of Chicago Press, 2009.

West-Pavlov, Russel. *Temporalities*. London: Routledge, 2013.

Whyle, James. *The Excavations: A History of the End of the World*. De la Rey and Reitz: Kindle, 2017.

Winterbach, Ingrid. *Book of Happenstance*. Trans. Ingrid and Dirk Winterbach. Rochester, NY: Open Letter, 2011.

Winterbach, Ingrid. *To Hell with Cronje*. Trans. Elsa Silke. Cape Town: Human & Rousseau, 2014.

Wright, Timothy Sean. "Mutant City: On Partial Transformation in Three Johannesburg Narratives." *NOVEL: A Forum on Fiction* 51.3 (2018): 417–437.

2

Revolutionary Times:
Mongane Wally Serote and Cold War Fiction

Monica Popescu

In a 2012 speech commemorating the death of the activist Ruth First, Albie Sachs bemoaned the "death of revolution" and the disappearance of the "tunnel vision" that had characterized the last decade of the antiapartheid struggle. He mourned not only First, but a sense of political purpose and clarity, which had dissipated by the end of the 1980s: a moment that corresponds significantly with the end of the Cold War.[1] The opinion expressed by the ex-freedom fighter and Constitutional Court judge also resonates across several recent literary texts that articulate a nostalgia for the Cold War era as a temporal dimension structured by clearer moral and ideological principles than the disorienting present. In Zoë Wicomb's *David's Story* (2000), for example, the eponymous protagonist—an Umkhonto we Sizwe cell leader—contrasts the transparency of the rules of engagement, the moral and political code during the struggle, to the confusion brought about by the early 1990s: "Those were the days, David sighs, when things were clear and we knew what had to be fought, what had to come down" (133). In Mandla Langa's *The Memory of Stones* (2000), the narrative counterintuitively renders the recollected antiapartheid struggle as more present and alive than the decade succeeding the first democratic elections: a perception that translates into a narrative reversal. The narrator's use of the present tense enlivens past moments; his use of the past tense to recount recent events, by contrast, suggests the relative emotional remoteness of the present.[2] The energy of the antiapartheid struggle and the freedom fighters' commitment to bring about a new form of social organization elevated those years and set them apart in a temporal category of their own: revolutionary time. It is with this temporal dimension of revolution and violent social transformation that my chapter is concerned.

How is revolution perceived as it is unfolding and how does literature enable us to grasp this specific temporality? Does the topic lend itself to specific literary forms—a category of texts that could be labeled "novels of revolution"? If so, to what extent do local and global events combine to shape the form and themes of such texts? African novels depicting revolutionary situations record rapidly shifting perceptions of temporality, as those engaged in the struggle renew their commitment to the future, make sense of the present, and reckon with the past. I am interested in examining the way in which literary texts, like Mongane Wally Serote's *To Every Birth Its Blood* (to which I will return later in the chapter), record this experience of temporality—the characters' perception of the present moment and the intuition of the advent of a larger structure that is becoming historical. To do so, I introduce the concept of affective temporal structures.

Literary narratives are privileged sites where cultural critics can identify emergent ideas. Fascinated with the processual aspect of concept formation— the minute changes in dominant and submerged ideas that emerge only diachronically—Raymond Williams describes barely perceptible conceptual nuclei as "structures of feeling." He starts from the observation that individuals do not experience the world in terms of fully articulated formulations of currents or ideologies, but instead are caught in the ever-shifting and incompletely articulated experience of the present. Unlike other Marxist theorists concerned with a macroscopic view of society, Williams finessed the relation between art and society by attending to microscopic changes: "[t]he idea of a structure of feeling can be specifically related to the evidence of forms and conventions— semantic figures—which, in art and literature, are often among the very first indications that such a new structure is forming" (133).

Instead of taking up Williams's term, I borrow some conceptual tools from the current "affective turn" in the humanities and the social sciences.[3] Recent developments in the theory of affects have highlighted their relevance for thinking not only about individuals but also social bodies, by illuminating causal interrelations at work.[4] For instance, Lauren Berlant is interested in how aesthetically mediated affective responses exemplify a shared historical sense.[5] My argument develops from this social dimension of affect, yet it preserves the small-scale scope of analysis, attending to groups of people united in their perception of temporality by their geographical, sociopolitical or cultural situatedness.

Affective temporal structures are ways of perceiving the present moment and establishing relations (whether of continuity or rupture) between the present, on the one hand, and the past and the future, on the other. Affective temporal structures are social, allowing individuals to see themselves as part of a community, to be affected by and to affect others. While informed by geopolitical location, as well as access to financial and cultural capital, they circumvent the need to make generalizations about the sense of historicity shared by a social class, nation, gender group, or generation. As affects are not yet articulated, they offer a way of addressing the transient moment and ways of thinking about the world that are not yet conceptually fixed.[6] They allow us to conceive of emergent (or waning) ways of apprehending temporality without having to subsume artists to established ideological positions, accepting that even when politically involved, artists do not reflect the textbook version of ideas espoused by larger political or cultural entities.

Affective temporal structures generate narratives that we overlay on the concatenation of events; they make us see history as directional, or cyclical, or hopelessly fragmented. These structures refer to the desires, aspirations, or disillusionment that we invest in projections of the future. To simplify: we may imagine a positive unfolding of the future, a good conclusion to our collective or personal life narratives, or we may see the future frustrating our aspirations to meaningfulness, truthfulness to ourselves and to our ideals, or as a collapse of avenues of progress into a nightmarish repetitive cycle.

For instance, David Scott identifies the success of the Grenada revolution of 1979 and its subsequent defeat in 1983 as watershed moments: moments that shifted perceptions of temporality for his generation of Caribbean intellectuals. It was not only that the perception of possible political futures had changed for one small Caribbean nation. While the revolution itself had been "a vindication and culmination of a certain organization of temporal expectation and political longing" (20), its defeat led to a "palpable sense of dissolution of the political temporality of former futures" (9).[7] In other words, the sense of defeat that accompanied the US intervention in Grenada marked the way in which at least an entire generation of Caribbean leftist intellectuals came to see the future as depleted of any emancipatory hopefulness. Scott emphasizes the generational import of this event, in the same way in which intellectuals in Africa who witnessed the beginning of decolonization with Ghana's independence in 1957, or those who turned and returned compulsively to the pages of Frantz Fanon's *The Wretched of the Earth* in search of a blueprint to produce revolutionary futures, had a shared sense of what the temporal arc of past-present-future might produce. Reading the same texts and sharing similar sociopolitical circumstances is bound to engender similar, although not identical, affective temporal structures. As both archive and germinating fund for such perceptions of temporality, fiction presents us with a range of affective temporal structures that reflect the imaginative possibilities of this time frame.

The affective temporal structures of revolution

In this chapter, I turn to Mongane Wally Serote's 1981 novel *To Every Birth Its Blood*, a text that crystallizes a shift in perceptions of temporality, as it attempts to make sense of then-contemporary events in South Africa and the rest of the world. Begun at a moment when the South African society was on the verge of going up in flames during the 1976 Soweto Uprising, the novel attests to a change in perceptions of temporality that Serote likely underwent at that time.[8] In dialogue with—yet not beholden to—mainstream ideas about social change, this novel reflects on the liberation struggle in Southern Africa in the late 1970s and imagines its future trajectory into the 1980s. It prefigures the arduous road ahead in the struggle against apartheid. Serote's focus on process identifies his fiction as a privileged site for observing the emergence of new conceptual paradigms that envision social transformation.

Serote's novel, with its emphasis on revolution, charts a genealogy of the ideas of liberation in Southern Africa—a lineage that intersects with various Cold War-era conceptions of social transformation. The novel ends with the blood-suffused image of a birthing mother to whom revolutionary Jully serves as midwife. It is a metaphor for the arduous process of decolonization that, despite its painful beginnings, announces the hopefulness of a new life. Serote's understanding of the temporality of revolution, viewed against the background of Cold War, enables us to reassess the impact of this conflict on the cultural landscape in Southern Africa. At first glance, the novel might display only superficial connections with the Cold War; however, its affective temporal structures, which I will discuss in more detail, connect it to this global conflict.

To Every Birth Its Blood has stimulated an energetic debate regarding its unusual form, more so, perhaps, than other literary texts from the same period. The novel has a bipartite structure that was either deemed disjointed and therefore stylistically lacking, or singularly apposite to depict the mass struggle in the wake of the 1976 Soweto Uprising.[9] The first part of the novel presents daily oppression under apartheid through the lens of journalist Tsi Molope's first-person narrative of personal dilemmas; the latter half abandons the focus on the protagonist and democratically distributes the third-person narrative perspective among a multitude of focalizers. Onalena, John, Dikeledi, Tuki, Oupa, Themba, and, eventually, Tsi, the only character who continues to narrate in the first person, convey the accelerating energies of revolution. Moving beyond rage and a feeling of helplessness after the 1976 Soweto Uprising was crushed, characters discuss the violent character of the apartheid state, witness political trials, and hear about torture in detention; they are recruited to the antiapartheid movement and engage in sabotage actions, or they are driven to exile in neighboring countries from where they mount the final attack against the racist state. Initially, at various stages of political consciousness and engagement with the struggle, this constellation of characters gradually comes to embrace a sense of imminent change and revolution.[10]

Although narrated in the past tense, Serote's novel conveys an acute sense of immediacy. The combination of formal elements (clipped dialogue, increasingly shorter narrative vignettes, the frequency of the present tense adverb "now," belying the past tense narration) and thematic aspects (the characters' increasingly clearer political consciousness, the heightened tempo of strikes against the apartheid regime that the movement mounts) gives the impression of unfolding events that might take unpredictable directions. At the same time, the antiapartheid struggle is presented as having continuity with the anticolonial battles of the past, in an ever-unfolding present of resistance:

> The Movement is old. It is as old as the grave of the first San or Khoikhoi who was killed by a bullet that came from a ship which had anchored at Cape Town to establish a stop station. The Movement is as young as the idea of throwing stones, of hurling one's life at the armed men who believe in God and shoot with guns. (179)

The shift between overall past tense narration and a present tense that paradoxically reflects a sense of historicity is only one of the startling ways in which Serote handles perceptions of temporality. Written during and in the aftermath of the Soweto Uprising, the novel moved with the events and ended up trying to anticipate the course of the struggle in the 1980s.[11] As Michael Green has pointed out, along with Nadine Gordimer's *July's People* (1981) and Christopher Hope's *Kruger's Alp* (1984), the novel is an example of the "future histories" penned in the 1980s. They are "works that seek to comment upon the past and present by projecting the implications of the past and the present forward in time."[12] Serote's novel charts the present moment as it accrues significance while the protagonists consider possible future outcomes.

There is an abrupt change in the affective temporal structures displayed by *To Every Birth Its Blood*, a shift that coincides with the transition from the first to the second part of the novel. More minute changes are also discernible in the second part. As Tsi Molope struggles to figure out the meaning of his life and his limited ability to connect to other people hampered by apartheid-era racism, a spiraling, inward-looking, and pessimistic temporal structure is set in place. It is displaced in the second part, where the affective temporal structure becomes teleological and future oriented, making the text a novel of revolution, committed to the world that is to be born. The ending of the novel takes place in an imaginary future in the 1980s, when a second student uprising propels the country into revolution. The Border War has spread from Angola to Botswana, where South African exiles and the local population alike are bombed by SADF planes and attacked by commando troops; yet Tsi, the narrator from Part I, is confident that this Southern African expression of the Cold War will end with the victory of the antiapartheid movement. This shift in affective temporal structures from a pessimistic to an optimistic outlook appears to contradict established views about the periodization of contemporary African history. While macro-level approaches cannot explain this transformation, a focus on understanding the present as process, as revealed through the concept of affective temporal structures, can give us an insight into these differences.

Large-scale attempts at periodization fail to explain the upsurge in optimistic perceptions of temporality that took place in South Africa in the 1980s. Cultural critics have made pronouncements about changes in the perception of temporality during the latter half of the twentieth century, changes driven by global events such as the tide of decolonization of the 1950s and early 1960s, or the hardening of Cold War ideological lines behind a rhetoric of militarization and nuclear arms race, or the rise of an increasingly triumphalist neoliberal capitalist discourse in the 1980s. In her landmark article "Periodizing the American Century: Modernism, Postmodernism and Postcolonialism in the Cold War Context," Ann Douglas divides the Cold War into two periods—an optimistic stage that lasted until the beginning of the 1960s and the collapse of optimism from the mid-1960s onward, when innocence and authenticity were no longer possible after neocolonial politics and interventionism had ruined the hopefulness of newly independent nations (84). If we follow Douglas's argument, we expect that the affective temporal structures of the second half of the Cold War would correspond to the skepticism and pessimism that characterize numerous African novels from the late 1960s onward, such as Ayi Kwei Armah's *The Beautyful Ones Are Not Yet Born* (1968) and Ousmane Sembene's *Xala* (1973), or South African texts like Christopher Hope's *Kruger's Alp* (1984) and J. M. Coetzee's *Waiting for the Barbarians* (1980).

However, as mentioned earlier, David Scott places the tidal change at the beginning of the 1980s, when the revolution in Grenada was defeated and intellectuals on the left had to reassess their perception of past, present, and future: the years ahead no longer holding the possibility of socialist victory, the postcolonial dreams smashed under new forms of imperialism. While both Douglas and Scott agree that at some point during the second half of the twentieth century the effervescence of the post–Second World War independence movements and people's former belief in the possibility of attaining social justice died out, they do not necessarily agree when this turn took place. If we add to the mix—as I did in the beginning of this chapter—the South African intellectuals' nostalgia for the 1980s as a period of hopefulness, political clarity, and purposefulness, the picture becomes even more confusing. Instead of relying on generalizing chronologies of African or postcolonial literature, here I focus on smaller-scale perceptions of temporality that necessarily account for a writer's response to global blocs and fault lines, while also attesting to the artist's embeddedness in local microstructures (like class and generational position).

The decolonization struggles in Southern Africa were still in full swing during the second half of the Cold War, as Angola and Mozambique gained their independence in 1975 yet continued to battle internal and external enemies; Zimbabwe shrugged off white rule in 1980, Namibia in 1990, and South Africa only in 1994. Thus, a number of Southern African novels bring an important contribution to the postcolonial literary archive by displaying cautiously optimistic affective temporal structures, such as those underlying Serote's novel *To Every Birth Its Blood*. This optimistic affective temporal structure, which we see in other works of fiction (for instance, the promise of change at the end of Alex La Guma's *In the Fog of the Season's End* and *Time of the Butcherbird* or Nadine Gordimer's *A Sport of Nature*), is primarily due to the fact that South Africa, unlike other former colonies, had not experienced either the elation of independence or the disappointment of the "morning after" that we see in numerous postcolonial novels, such as Armah's *The Beautyful Ones Are Not Yet Born*. Therefore, numerous 1970s and 1980s South African texts penned by writers associated with the antiapartheid struggle upheld the optimistic affective temporal structures that had characterized 1950s and 1960s decolonization literature elsewhere on the continent.[13]

The concept of affective temporal structures allows us to record the minute changes in the perception of the present as experienced by characters, reflecting shifts in levels of political consciousness and commitment, and to relate them to literary strategies. This focus on emerging structures illustrates Serote's own changing position, as he gradually abandoned the Black Consciousness (BC) perspective and embraced a view of revolution in consonance with that of the African National Congress (ANC)-South African Communist Party (SACP) alliance. The novel fictionalizes some of Serote's formative experiences. For instance, Tuki and Dikeledi are part of a township theater group that stages plays reflective of the lived experience in Alexandra. Similarly, Serote and artist Thami Mnyele cofounded the Mihloti Black Theatre in Alexandra in 1971.[14] Together the artists read and discussed works by Frantz Fanon, Amilcar Cabral, Agostinho Neto, Malcolm X, and Marcus Garvey (29). Later, Serote expressed his belief in the value of togetherness and community action, an idea that finds an echo in the shift from individualistic self-absorption in the first part of the novel to the multiple, yet conjoined, action of characters in the second part of the novel: "Changes take place when people are informed, when people are conscious, when people identify common goals and common objectives, and in certain circumstances are prepared to make sacrifices for that."[15] This belief in collective action is informed by and has ramifications for the affective temporal structures displayed; it also highlights the genealogy of political concepts that informed Serote's vision of revolution, to which I turn in the next part of the chapter.

Writing revolution

Mongane Wally Serote has been described as a revolutionary writer who, during the apartheid era, was ready to use both words and weapons to overturn the regime.[16] But what does revolution mean in his literary works? Who is to participate and how does it unfold? Does political action suffice or is blood to be shed? How long is revolution supposed to last? His novel offers a snapshot of the mélange of emergent, crystallized, and vanishing political ideas, with their attendant affective temporal structures, during the late 1970s and early 1980s. I explore the genealogy of Serote's idea of social transformation in South Africa to tease out the cultural texts and programs reflected in his writing and, simultaneously, his contribution to shaping the conceptual components and aesthetics of revolution in South Africa. The intellectual history of the idea of revolution as reflected in South African fiction not only displays its conceptual makeup, but also highlights the cultural forces and the global political landscapes that have modified or supplanted this idea. To revisit the concept of revolution is to find new ways of thinking about the period and of historicizing the scholarship that engaged with or circumvented it.

Consistent with Serote's idea of literature as a form of social commitment—he encouraged readers to think of authors as "cultural workers"—writing about revolution also entailed writing the revolution into being in South Africa.[17] In a roundtable with Ngũgĩ wa Thiong'o in 1988, Serote was asked whether his political involvement in the liberation struggle or his interest in writing came first. His response followed a line oftentimes expressed by ANC-SACP activists in the 1980s, which gave culture an instrumental role, turning it into a "weapon of the struggle": "Participation in the struggle became an inspiration. Because one wanted to express the condition of one's people, one also had to further understand what it is that made us an oppressed and exploited people, what it was that was going to liberate us" (35). This view of the function of the writer is the distillation of his political journey, from an adept of BC philosophy to an ANC cadre, as he became a "poet of revolution."[18] This progression, which unfolds against the background of the Cold War, is also inscribed in the novel's focus on the present and the text's shifting affective temporal structures. The novel is able to record these minute changes otherwise difficult to chart in history studies because, as Raymond Williams pointed out, the "practical consciousness" recorded in literature and the arts "is almost always different from official consciousness" (130).[19]

Writing about the meaning of revolution and social transformation in Africa in the late 1970s and early the 1980s happened in a variety of venues, from strategy and policy-making documents issued by the political entities involved in liberation struggles to essays and analyses penned by those close to decision-making structures, and from journalism and academic writing to fiction. When Tuki, one of the main characters in Serote's *To Every Birth Its Blood*, proclaims that "South Africa is going to be a socialist country, this is going to come about through the will, knowledge and determination of the people" (185), his statement obliquely speaks to a history of conceptual roadmaps for surpassing apartheid that had variously clashed or coexisted. During the first wave of decolonization in the late 1950s, it was not a foregone conclusion what specific forms of social organization would eventually prevail in Africa; it wasn't clear either—to political observers and participants alike—whether these forms of statehood would be established peacefully or by means of revolution.[20] As the euphoria of new beginnings started to dissipate and the reality of neocolonialism and a sharply polarized Cold War climate set in, fewer real options remained for Southern African countries seeking independence in the 1970s and the 1980s. Until the Pretoria government became interested in negotiating with the ANC in the late 1980s, thereby creating a glimmer of hope for a peaceful transition to a democratic form of organization, the ANC-SACP alliance envisioned revolution and armed struggle as the only available roads for social transformation in South Africa.[21] This process of conceiving trajectories for social transformation came to a head with the Soweto Uprising of 1976.

Serote is one of the few South African novelists who rendered "the Power days," the moment of the antiapartheid struggle spearheaded by the BC Movement that culminated in the Soweto Uprising.[22] His novel records the shift in public consciousness from a focus on BC philosophy to a growing awareness of "the Movement" (Serote's fictional representation of the ANC-SACP alliance) as leader of the struggle. The militancy and the immediacy of response (black pride, the resumption of African names, street battles, and the refusal to surrender the townships to state control) change into a longer-term perspective (initiation into the movement, study groups to conscientize freedom fighters, underground operations, and the continuation of the struggle in exile). As an ANC member who came to political consciousness under the influence of BC, yet who received military training in Botswana, Angola, and the USSR as an Umkhonto we Sizwe (MK) member, Serote is exceptionally positioned to understand the elements of ideological continuity and disjuncture within the antiapartheid struggle during the late 1970s and the early 1980s.[23]

Revolutionary method and the time frame within which apartheid could be abolished had preoccupied the ANC leadership from the early 1960s, when Nelson Mandela rejected the efficacy of nonviolent protest and spearheaded the formation of the armed branch of the party, MK. In the aftermath of the 1963–1964 Rivonia trial, the ANC-SACP alliance was seriously debilitated in its power to strike back against the apartheid state, as a result of the imprisonment or the escape into exile of the MK High Command. The model of revolution or political change that had worked in other African colonies was impracticable in South Africa, where the white minority was entrenched in its controlling position over the political, economic, and legal apparatuses. After the ANC and the SACP regrouped in exile, in the wake of the 1969 Morogoro conference, they set in place a new strategy for conducting the armed struggle. However, the resilience of the Portuguese empire and the obstructing presence of white minority rule in Rhodesia and South West Africa prevented guerillas from infiltrating and launching operations within South Africa.[24] The early 1970s were marked by the clash between the leaders' long-term approach and the rank and file members' impatience, as the latter desired to be sent home immediately after receiving military training abroad in order to start a revolutionary war.[25] It is only after 1975 and, respectively, 1980, when Angola, Mozambique, and Zimbabwe became independent, that the idea of revolutionary warfare could actually be concretized.

This politically favorable situation was ideologically strengthened by the impact of BC, in turn boosted by dialogue with the Fanonist school of thought as well as the Black Power and the Civil Rights movements in the United States.

Serote's oeuvre reflects the growth of his revolutionary consciousness under the influence of Steve Biko and the BC Movement especially in his first two volumes of poetry, *Yakhal'inkomo* (1972) and *Tsetlo* (1974).[26] Frantz Fanon's idea of violence as a cathartic reappropriation of the activist's abused self and as a means of recapturing the pride of being black entered the South African discursive field with the BC Movement.

Fanon had influenced Serote's thinking as a young writer, as evidenced by his invocation of the Martinican activist and philosopher as part of a line of secular, revolutionary saints:

> I've been a looked after
> black seed; by black saints and prophets
> by Sobukwe Mandela Sisulu
> Fanon Malcolm X George Jackson.[27]

In *To Every Birth Its Blood*, Dikeledi draws on the famous Fanonian argument to summarize the idea that freedom can only be brought about through struggle: "She felt sad because she knew, she understood so well that South Africa had shut out all other choices. [...] She understood that there was no such thing as freedom being asked for, that freedom must be fetched, must be won, must be fought for" (132). Fanon had pointed out that the psychological damage inflicted by colonialism—the fear and self-hatred experienced by the colonized—could only be undone through cathartic violence, participation in revolution, and a "change [of] the order of the world" (2). The idea of revolutionary transformation through insurrection and armed struggle, through a necessary period of violence that would make space for a new world, is epitomized in the title of Serote's novel. *To Every Birth Its Blood* establishes a correlation between the birth of the postapartheid society and revolutionary violence.

However, Serote's relationship with revolutionary violence has been far from straightforward. While he saw the resort to arms as a normal expression of the anger felt by his generation, which marked a new form of "consciousness and responsibility" that enabled their rise as political interlocutors to be reckoned with, "[t]he gun was never an end in itself for me, although the struggle to use it responsibly was never easy. It was part of a bigger quest for a goal that reached beyond killing."[28] *To Every Birth Its Blood* reflects this uneasy relation with violence: characters are recruited to be part of the movement (John and Dikeledi are inducted by Oupa) and members plant bombs to destroy governmental targets (Onalena detonates a bomb in a parking lot outside a state institution); they kill black collaborators (Mandla executes a policeman who had terrorized

Alexandra during the Power days), retaliate to state violence by attacking its representatives (Tuki, Mandla, John, and Onalena participate in a dangerous mission to kill officers responsible for numerous township deaths), and finally extend the armed struggle into the countryside by "dealing with" farmers. Described euphemistically or in a matter-of-fact style, the escalating violence imagined by Serote in the novel as a necessary component of the revolutionary struggle in the 1980s was at odds with the changing ANC-SACP policies, which varied between acknowledging their limited resources and hopes of starting an urban-based "people's war."[29] "[M]y writing enabled me to understand what I was doing and why I was doing it."[30] Serote observed, as he had to reconcile a superseded Fanonist emphasis on the psychological benefits of violence, the humanist abhorrence of bloodshed inherited from his grandmother, and changing ANC-SACP strategies in the late 1970s and early 1980s.

However, as the characters progress through various stages of political involvement, the novel makes clear that Fanonism and BC are insufficient intellectual and tactical weapons and the truly revolutionary program is the one proposed by the movement:

> While he [Dikeledi's father] encouraged her, he also made it clear, somehow, that he regarded what was going on as something which still had to be cooked, looked into. Whenever they talked, he was careful. He questioned her. Made it known when he thought something was wrong, or when he disagreed. "I want you to understand that colour here must not be the issue. Once we get to understand that, then we can talk on, but I am afraid that you have put too much emphasis on the colour question," Ramono used to say to her. (142)

Serote implies that a race-based alliance as advocated by Pan-Africanism and BC is not tenable. As further proof, Yaone—the artist in exile in the United States—professes that African-Americans are not able to fully grasp the situation in South Africa. As Americans and citizens of a neocolonial power, they are indirectly complicit in apartheid.[31]

In a move that places the novel squarely within the international Cold War context and draws attention to the role of superpowers in creating or enabling crisis situations in the rest of the world, Yaone voices his concern with American complicity: "They call it Soweto here. Sometimes, when I am sitting around and talking about the Soweto issue, with both the black and the white Yankees, I feel like saying okay now, you bloody shits, did you know that as I am sitting here and talking, I think that you are directly responsible for the deaths in this, *your* Soweto?" (emphasis Serote's,106). This view of the responsibility of old and new imperial powers in creating and maintaining iniquitous regimes is in keeping with both the ideas put forth by Kwame Nkrumah in his path-breaking analysis of neocolonialism and the astute social and political analysis produced by members of the ANC-SACP coalition such as Ruth First.[32]

The novel traces the process of acquiring social and political literacy, starting from John's observation of seemingly disparate realities that he intuits to be nonetheless interlinked by means of opaque economic mechanisms to his realization that change must be brought on by the people through a necessarily violent overthrow of the regime:

> The people of this country are locked in a tight embrace which is going to destroy them. The white people. The black people. The gold. The diamonds. The guns. The bombs. South Africa, such a beautiful country. The bright sun, the warm days and nights, the rainy days, the mountains, trees, rivers, such a unique country. John felt *illiterate*, naïve and stupid, thinking all these things. What had all these to do with a reality which was death? [my emphasis]. (107)

The questions John tries to answer connect apparently disparate entities. Rendered in short sentences, consisting mostly of noun phrases, the seeming disjuncture between these proximate yet conflicting elements highlights the contradiction between the bountiful landscape of South Africa and the poverty and violence to which the majority of its inhabitants are subjected. A few pages later, Oupa points out that the police defends the property of the big owners (110), indicating that the deployment of state violence served financial and industrial interests. As writer and ANC member, Serote takes part in the ANC-SACP coalition's efforts in the 1970s to present apartheid as a systematic and far-reaching denial of human rights. These extended over the political, economic, legal, social, and cultural realms and had beneficiaries across the globe. As Ruth First, one of the strongest intellectual voices against apartheid, pointed out in the coauthored *The South African Connection: Western Investment in Apartheid* (1972), the vested interest in preserving the political status quo was made evident from a study of international business interests and investments in material and human resources in South Africa. To preserve control over gold, diamonds, and fertile land, the white minority in power deployed violence and technologies of subjugation, such as guns and bombs. Without spelling it out, the earlier paragraph hints that death was dispensed not only by the state but was inextricably connected to international powers that tacitly accepted the situation or permitted South Africa to acquire or manufacture military equipment.[33] Posed as a puzzle that cannot be articulated in complete sentences yet, this enumeration of disparate yet invisibly interconnected elements enables John, intradiegetically, and readers, extradiegetically, to begin to become politically literate. Apartheid is therefore presented as having far-reaching ramifications and as entangled in the Cold War global setup.

In keeping with ANC-SACP strategy, the novel suggests that this entanglement of interests could only be counteracted through a well-planned revolutionary solution. The "Strategies and Tactics" document, adopted at the 1969 Morogoro conference in Tanzania, proposed a long-term plan for seizing power in South Africa. In the aftermath of the Soweto Uprising, with numerous young people secretly leaving the country to join the MK training camps, the militarization of the movement increased and, consequently, the idea of revolution carried more weight.

Revolution is envisioned differently by various characters: the younger generation, like Oupa, are impatient for action; those who came of age during the BC Movement and the Soweto Uprising wonder if the people will have sufficient strength to fight apartheid successfully; at the same time Michael Ramono, Dikeledi's father, a spokesperson for the older generation in the ANC, advocates long-term strategy and careful planning for decisive action: "This is a long, long struggle; it has long been here, we used to talk about the same things which you are talking about" (133). One of the leitmotifs of the second half of the novel is the statement "they have heard that before," which reflects a repeating stalemate with apartheid forces that this time, despite initial doubts, propels the characters into action. For instance, both John and Dikeledi had participated in protests during the Power days and had lost loved ones or were marked by violence; they had been mobilized by revolutionary thoughts, yet later they lapsed into an uneasy adjustment to the tense life in the townships. However, when the still-teenaged Oupa displays his faith in the movement and its transformative powers, they agree to be recruited. Their views of temporality, vacillating between hopefulness, despondency, and confidence again, trace some of the affective temporal structures crystallized in this novel.

As the antiapartheid struggle was a protracted process spanning four decades, therefore taking much longer than decolonization struggles in other parts of the African continent, the characters have to negotiate between an ominous sense of repetition and a distant horizon of hopefulness, on the one hand, and the realization that a different strategy and the clear leadership of the movement will lead to liberation, on the other. "When the Power days were over there was silence" (108), John observes, while also keeping an ear attuned to what new local and international events indicated. Serote is interested in rendering the formation of revolutionary energies as well as the characters' increased confidence in the success of the struggle. *To Every Birth Its Blood* makes room for the processual dimension—the formation of mass consciousness, people's new or renewed commitment to the future, as they become convinced of the necessity to join the struggle and follow the program laid out by the movement.

Both the ANC's 1969 "Strategy and Tactics" document and the SACP's 1962 program "The Road to South African Freedom" envisioned the struggle as a two-stage transformation—a national revolution that would eliminate racial discrimination followed by a socialist revolution that would transform the economy of the country by empowering the working class and abolishing private property.[34] Oupa's statement that the movement stands for "the destruction of oppression and exploitation" (143) alludes, through its precise choice of nouns, to the two stages of revolution endorsed by the ANC-SACP coalition. At the same time, read retrospectively, the novel serves as a reminder that the available options and models during the late Cold War era necessarily informed the ANC-SACP strategy. At the beginning of the 1980s, neither the antiapartheid movement nor writers could envision the collapse of the Eastern Bloc, the invalidation of socialism, or the possibility of peaceful transition to a democratic society as it actually came to happen.[35] Therefore, the imagined futures were shaped by Cold War geopolitical landscapes.

Nonetheless, as Serote's novel is not the ideological mouthpiece of the ANC-SACP alliance, characters debate the meaning and substance of revolutionary action and the time necessary to carry it out. For instance, Oupa reads V.I. Lenin's *What Is to Be Done?*, a political pamphlet that criticizes the reliance on the spontaneous revolt of the masses and emphasizes the party's leadership role. Despite his engagement with this pamphlet, Oupa favors spontaneity, arguing that "this is the moment to hit," contrary to what "The Center of Directives" advises (163). Characters debate and contest the possibility of relying on models. While Oupa foreshortens the affective temporal structures by focusing on immediate action, his elder peers take a longer-term approach:

[Oupa:] The boers are fighting us, as simple as that. We have to pitch up a battle, fight back, that is all. All this that is happening now, happened to many other people. It happened in Guinea Bissau, Algeria, Angola, Mozambique, Vietnam, Cuba, you know: the people there pitted their strength against the mighty, the strong. [...] We too have to fight and win our country back.

Both John and Dikeledi looked anxiously at Oupa but said nothing. They were alarmed by the enthusiasm that suddenly lit up his face as he said this. They wondered whether he knew what he was saying. They had heard this so many times. (140)

Beyond their concern for a generation that seems too young to be thrown into battle, John and Dikeledi are also alert to the simplifying comparisons that propose Mozambique or Algeria (with their extremely violent conflicts drawn out by Western interventionism), not to mention Angola or Vietnam (true Cold War battlefields), as examples to be followed by the antiapartheid movement. Also, as part of a slightly older generation that came to political consciousness with the BC Movement, Dikeledi and John are initially uncertain whether the end of the antiapartheid struggle could be foreseen. The corresponding affective temporal structures are similarly without a clear future horizon. "Now, there was a sense of loss, a sense of defeat; there were no more fists and shouts of Power. It seemed quiet" (133), Dikeledi observes, meditating on the difference between the years when the BC Movement was spearheading the struggle and the early 1980s. Having been faced with the violent response of the state, Dikeledi and John lack the strategy and the vision that the movement brings. Elsewhere Serote discussed his sense that BC had exhausted its energy by 1974, when he left South Africa to pursue an MFA in the United States.[36] It was the encounter with a determined group of ANC activists in Botswana in the late 1970s that persuaded him that the party's vision for the future, with its attention to political, military, ideological, and cultural aspects of the struggle, was worth following (42).

Serote suggests that with its echelons bridging generations—from the older Michael Ramono, to the middle-aged Mandla, and to young comrades like Oupa—the movement provides the strategy, the teleological outlook, and the belief in victory. The affective temporal structure emerging at the end of the novel looks confidently toward the future. "Push, push, push" (206) are the final words of the novel, referring both to Jully's injunction for the mother-to-be and the collective effort of pushing through the final arduous stretch of the battle against the state.

There are two revolutions taking place in Serote's novel: while it is evident that the novel envisions the struggle and radical social transformation in South Africa, the text also participates in a writing revolution that discards a high modernist style of writing (seemingly embraced in the first half of the novel) for a more apposite realist prose style, a literature that participates in the struggle. As Michael Titlestad has persuasively explained, the novel "sounds a cautionary note in its exploration of the limits of modernist improvisation in the face of violent oppression" (108). He argues that by relinquishing the narrative mode of organization based on jazz and improvisation, as well as the modernist rendering of individual breakdown, *To Every Birth Its Blood* makes a statement about the forms of literature appropriate for a society in crisis. A narrative that renders the growth of the political consciousness of a multitude of characters and their unity of purpose is preferable to the solipsism of one consciousness, even if the latter is presented in a formally innovative way. Serote implies that a revolutionary writer disdains the claims to the autonomy of fiction, which was a distinctive mark of modernist authors. Instead, he sees the writer as just another type of worker, a cultural worker, who contributes to the creation of a new society. This movement away from the belief in the autonomy of art to a collective effort of creation it is a journey undertaken by other African writers.[37] Not only thematically, but also by means of its form, the novel allows Serote to enter a dialogue with his contemporaries regarding the role of art in times of social turmoil and transformation. The emphasis on the social function of the writer and the thematic focus on revolution signal that the Cold War was the background against which these cultural battles unfolded.[38]

In the later decades of the twentieth century, critics paid attention to the politically committed fiction of Serote and his contemporaries. However, the increasing distance from the years of the struggle and the emergence of documents that were kept secret or difficult to access at that time give us the possibility to revisit them in a new light now, set them in dialogue, and see how themes articulated in political documents find echoes in cultural texts and vice versa. As a result, a submerged Cold War landscape, sometimes tacitly grasped yet other times completely invisible, can now be traced in all its manifestations.

Notes

1   Albie Sachs made these remarks at the thirty-year commemoration of Ruth First's assassination. See Sachs, Introductory Comments.

2   Popescu, *South African Literature Beyond the Cold War*, 50.

3   See Hardt and the collection of essays *The Affective Turn*.

4   Michael Hardt argues that affects signal "both our power to affect the world around us and our power to be affected by it, along with the relationship between these two powers" ("Foreword," ix).

5   Berlant, *Cruel Optimism*, 3.

6   Like Williams, Berlant perceives the idiom of feelings and affects as appropriate for developing "an architecture for apprehending the perturbed world with all the

kinds of knowing to which one has access, from the neuro-affective to the rationally processed" ("Thinking," 6).

7   The defeat of the Grenada Revolution, Scott argues, contributes to "a wider critical discussion of the ethical-political experience of the temporal 'afterness' of our postcolonial, postsocialist time" (20).

8   Biographical evidence supports this sense of trepidation: Serote seems to have started writing the novel in exile in the United States, a few months before the Soweto Uprising, and the dramatic events forced him to change narrative gears (Visser, "Fictional Projects and the Irruptions of History," 69). Relocating to Botswana in 1977, where he became involved with the MEDU Ensemble, he moved geographically closer to the struggle and received military training as an MK member (Ngũgĩ and Serote, "The Role of Culture in the African Revolution," 42).

9   For debates on the significance of the two-part form, see essays by Titlestad, Bethlehem, Visser, and Sole ("'This Time Set Again'").

10 Serote emphasizes the importance of representing a collective character in his works and is critical of Hollywood movies that focus on individual achievement (Interview with Solberg, 82).

11 Titlestad, "Mongane Serote's *To Every Birth Its Blood*," 110–11.

12 Green, "Nadine Gordimer's 'Future Histories'," 15.

13 Yet not all novels conform to this pattern (as Hope's and Coetzee's works suggest), and even within the same literary work not all narrative strands convey the same affect.

14 Miles, "Word and Image," 29.

15 Serote, Interview with Solberg, 182.

16 See Barboure; Villa-Vicencio and Soko.

17 See 1988 discussion with Kenyan writer Ngũgĩ wa Thiong'o (33, 40–41). Also, in his interview with Solberg, Serote emphasized the interconnection between his political and writing activities (180).

18 Patel, "Literary Profile," 183.

19 In *Marxism and Literature*, Williams discusses the experience of a mode of perception that seems private yet later becomes codified into "institutions and formations" (132).

20 Aside from the statehood models offered by the Western world and the Eastern Bloc, newly independent nations could also contemplate regional unions or forms of social organization tailored to local history, as proposed by the supporters of African socialism. See Byrne, "Africa's Cold War," 104.

21 Ellis, *External Mission*, 281–93.

22 Sole, "The Days of Power," 65.

23 Villa-Vicencio and Soko, "Mongane Wally Serote," 244.

24 Ellis, *External Mission*, 60–64.

25 See ibid., 62–63, on the ill-fated Wankie campaign, when insufficiently equipped MK cadres were sent to infiltrate Rhodesia, with the hope that they would

eventually reach South Africa. On the clash between the ANC-SACP leadership's long-term planning and the impatience of guerillas, see also Serote's rendering of this conflict in his novel *Scatter the Ashes and Go*.

26 For instance, the poem "What's in This Black Shit" weaponizes language, as the expletive "shit" changes from reflection on township life, to insult, and to a form of linguistic resistance.

27 Serote, *Tsetlo*, 34.

28 Villa-Vicencio and Soko, "Mongane Wally Serote," 244.

29 Ellis, *External Mission,* 281–83.

30 Villa-Vicencio and Soko, "Mongane Wally Serote," 244.

31 Yaone's estrangement and personal crisis in the United States are reflections of Serote's own views on the isolation of exile. In 1974, Serote received a Fulbright Scholarship that enabled him to complete an MFA degree at Columbia University (Villa-Vincentio and Soko, "Mongane Wally Serote," 242).

32 See Nkrumah, *Neo-colonialism*, and First et al. *The South African Connection*.

33 For such indirect relations, see also Borstelmann.

34 The ideological unity and similarities between these two guiding policy documents arise not only from the increasingly tighter links between the ANC and the SACP, but also derive from Joe Slovo's significant role in the formulation of both documents (Ellis, *External Mission*, 77).

35 A compelling example is Nadine Gordimer's *A Sport of Nature* (1987): the author is able to envisage the inauguration of a black president in South Africa who closely resembles Nelson Mandela, yet she is unable to envision the collapse of the Soviet Union and the end of the Cold War.

36 Serote and Ngũgĩ, "The Role of Culture in the African Revolution," 40.

37 Popescu, "Aesthetic," 8.

38 See also Stonor Saunders and Caute.

Works Cited

Barboure, Dorian. "Mongane Serote: Humanist and Revolutionary." In *Momentum: On Recent South African Writing*. Eds. M. J. Daymond, J. U. Jacobs, and Margaret Lenta. Pietermaritzburg: University of Natal Press, 1984.

Berlant, Lauren. *Cruel Optimism*. Durham, NC: Duke University Press, 2011.

Berlant, Lauren. "Intuitionists: History and the Affective Event." *American Literary History* 20.4 (2008): 845–60.

Berlant, Lauren. "Thinking about Feeling Historical." *Emotion, Space and Society* 1 (2008): 4–9.

Bethlehem, Louise. "'A Primary Need as Strong as Hunger': The Rhetoric of Urgency in South African Literary Culture under Apartheid." *Poetics Today* 22.2 (Summer 2001): 365–89.

Borstelmann, Thomas. *Apartheid's Reluctant Uncle: The United States and South Africa in the Early Cold War*. Oxford: Oxford University Press, 1993.

Byrne, Jeffrey James. "Africa's Cold War." *The Cold War in the Third World*. Ed. Robert J. McMahon. New York: Oxford University Press, 2013. 101–23.

Caute, David. *The Dancer Defects: The Struggle for Cultural Supremacy during the Cold War*. Oxford: Oxford University Press, 2003.

Ellis, Stephen. *External Mission: The ANC in Exile 1960–1990*. New York: Oxford University Press, 2013.

Fanon, Frantz. *The Wretched of the World*. Trans. Richard Philcox. New York: Grove, 2004.

Field, Roger. *Alex La Guma: A Literary and Political Biography*. Woodbridge: James Currey, 2010.

First, Ruth, Jonathan Steele, Christabel Gurney. *The South African Connection: Western Investment in Apartheid*. New York: Harper & Row, 1973.

Green, Michael. "Nadine Gordimer's 'Future Histories': Two Senses of an Ending." *Wasafiri* 19 (Summer 1994): 14–18.

Halim, Hala. "Lotus, the Afro-Asian Nexus and Global South Comparatism." *Comparative Studies of South Asia, Africa, and the Middle East* 32.3 (2012): 563–83.

Hardt, Michael. "Foreword: What Affects Are Good For." In *The Affective Turn: Theorizing the Social*. Eds. Patricia Ticineto Clough and Jean Halley. Durham, NC: Duke University Press, 2007. ix–xiii.

Langa, Mandla. *The Memory of Stones*. Boulder, CO: Rienner, 2000.

Miles, Elza. "Word and Image: A Dialogue—The Art of Thami Mnyele." In *Thami Mnyele and the MEDU Art Ensemble*. Eds. Clive Kellner and Sergio-Albio Gonzales. Jakana: Auckland Park, 2009. 29–35.

Moore, Gerald. "The Transcription Centre in the Sixties: Navigating in Narrow Seas." *Research in African Literatures* 33.3 (Fall 2002): 167–81.

Ngũgĩ wa Thiong'o, and Mongane Wally Serote. "The Role of Culture in the African Revolution: Ngũgĩ wa Thiong'o and Mongane Wally Serote in a Round-Table Discussion." *The African Communist* 113 (Second Quarter 1988): 31–48.

Nkrumah, Kwame. *Neo-colonialism: The Last Stage of Imperialism*. London: Panaf, 2004.

Patel, Essop. "Literary Profile. Mongane Wally Serote: Poet of Revolution." *Third World Quarterly* 12.1 (January 1990): 187–93.

Popescu, Monica. "Aesthetic Solidarities: Ngũgĩ wa Thiong'o and the Cold War." *Journal of Postcolonial Writing* Special Issue on *Alternative Solidarities: Black Diasporas and Cultural Alliances during the Cold War*. Eds. Monica Popescu, Cedric Tolliver and Julie Tolliver 50.4 (2014): 384–97.

Popescu, Monica. *South African Literature Beyond the Cold War*. New York: Palgrave, 2010.

Sachs, Albie. Introductory Comments, "Ruth First: A Revolutionary Life 1925–1982." Symposium, The Institute of Commonwealth Studies, University of London, June 5, 2012. https://www.sas.ac.uk/videos-and-podcasts/politics-development-and-human-rights/ruth-first-revolutionary-life-1925-1982-0.

Saunders, Francis Stonor. *The Cultural Cold War: The CIA and the World of Arts and Letters*. New York: The New Press, 2003.

Scott, David. *Omens of Adversity: Tragedy, Time, Memory, Justice*. Durham, NC: Duke University Press, 2014.

Serote, Mongane Wally. Interview. With Rolf Solberg. *Writing South Africa: Literature, Apartheid, and Democracy, 1970–1995*. Eds. Derek Attridge and Rosemary Jolly. Cambridge: Cambridge University Press, 1998. 180–86.

Serote, Mongane Wally. *Scatter the Ashes and Go*. Serote, Mongane Wally. *Tsetlo*. Johannesburg: Ad Donker, 1974.

Serote, Mongane Wally. *To Every Birth Its Blood*. London: Heinemann, 1981.

Serote, Mongane Wally. *Yakhal'inkomo*. Johannesburg: Renoster, 1972.

Sole, Kelwyn. "The Days of Power: Depictions of Politics and Community in Four Recent South African Novels." *Research in African Literatures* 19.1 (Spring 1988): 65–88.

Sole, Kelwyn. "'This Time Set Again': The Temporal and Political Conceptions of Serote's *To Every Birth Its Blood*." *English in Africa* 18.1 (May 1991): 51–80.

Titlestad, Michael. "Mongane Serote's *To Every Birth Its Blood*: History and the Limits of Improvisation." *Journal of Literary Studies* 19.2 (2003): 108–24.

Villa-Vicencio, Charles, and Mills Soko. "Mongane Wally Serote: Poet, Soldier and Healer." *Conversations in Transition: Leading South African Voices*. Cape Town: David Phillip, 2012. 242–51.

Visser, Nick. "Fictional Projects and the Irruptions of History: Mongane Serote's *To Every Birth Its Blood*." *English Academy Review* 4.1 (1987): 67–76.

Wicomb, Zoë. *David's Story*. New York: Feminist Press, 2001.

Williams, Raymond. *Marxism and Literature*. Oxford: Oxford University Press, 1977.

3

After Marikana:
The Temporalities of Betrayal

Annel Helena Pieterse

This chapter explores the struggle for meaning that has been taking place in South Africa in the wake of the Marikana massacre of August 16, 2012, when members of the South African Police Service (SAPS) shot and killed thirty-four mineworkers taking part in a wildcat strike at the Lonmin platinum mine near Rustenburg, in South Africa's North West province. The violent confrontation between striking miners, policemen, security officers, and National Union of Mineworkers (NUM) members had begun on August 11, 2012; five days later, members of the SAPS corralled a group of miners and shot them in cold blood. Evidence after the fact indicates that many of the miners were shot in the back while running away, and were pursued by the police and shot when they sought refuge among the rocks on a nearby hill.

The shocking images of the event that circulated in public in the weeks and months following the massacre drew comparisons with those that circulated in the wake of the Sharpeville shootings of March 1960. However, the irruption of violence at Marikana cannot be understood only in terms of repetition. What are the temporal implications of the massacre? How have South Africans narrativized violence in the wake of this spectacle of police brutality, the likes of which they had not seen in the twenty years since the end of apartheid? I contend that the pervasive disappointment of the working classes in a state governed by the party of liberation is reflected, in displaced fashion, in a series of stories of betrayal on the part of the liberation movement during the late struggle period of the 1980s and early 1990s. Betrayal, it seems, is not only an important emerging theme, it is one that requires new forms of periodization and that expresses a new sense of lived temporality.

Then and now: Making sense of violence

In October 1998, the new ruling party in South Africa, the African National Congress (ANC), tried to obtain a last-minute interdict to prevent the release of the final report of the Truth and Reconciliation Commission (TRC). The TRC's "Findings on the ANC" held the ANC accountable for "gross human rights violations," including the practice of "necklacing,"[1] the protection of the identity of mutineers who had killed unarmed soldiers accused of being spies, and the decision not to disclose the identity of many who were known to be enemy agents.[2] Ostensibly, the ANC was concerned that the report would treat the liberation movements in the same way as it did the apartheid government. In their official online response the ANC is very clear: they were waging a just war and to equate their struggle with the apartheid state's abuse of power would be "immoral and unacceptable."[3] The ANC thus flatly refused to entertain any ambiguity that may attend on their own role, or to acknowledge the violence perpetrated from within the ANC on its members: "It was through the courageous actions of our cadres that this evil system was defeated. To accuse these heroic fighters of 'gross human rights violations' in a lawful and just war is a slap in the face."[4] In this way, the South African transition narrative locates South African history between the binarist oppositions of good and evil, heroes and perpetrators. This transition narrative formulates the history of South Africa as a linear progress from a past of injustice and oppression under Afrikaner rule, to a present of freedom and equality brought about by the actions of the liberation movement.

In *Country of My Skull*, one of the cornerstone accounts of the role of the TRC in constructing the prevailing South African national narrative of the transition, Antjie Krog recalls the ceremony at which Archbishop Desmond Tutu handed over the five volumes of the TRC's final report to then president Nelson Mandela, on October 29, 1998:

> Mandela speaks: "I therefore take this opportunity to say that I accept the report as it is, with a-a-all its imperfections, as an aid that the TRC has given us to help reconcile and build our nation." Mandela is such a solid party man. For him to take a stance different from his party must have been exceptionally difficult.[5]

Closely attuned to the breakdown of language throughout her account of the TRC process, Krog picks up on Mandela's stammer at this crucial instant in the nation's emerging identity. In this moment, Mandela is speaking as a statesman: he is producing the national narrative about the TRC. But his stammer on the word "all" is an indicator of the contestation at the heart of this national narrative. It draws our attention to the processes and contradictions by which struggles for meaning were taking place at the time. At this particular historical moment, the official national (and public) discourse cannot accommodate all the implications signified by that "a-a-all." By accepting the report with "all" its imperfections, as Krog notes, Mandela adopts a stance at odds with that of the party, placing him in a position where his implicit acknowledgment of the findings on the ANC might very well have been read as a betrayal of the party itself. But the "all" marks a place—it keeps open a path to a parallel narrative that cannot be countenanced at that nation building moment. This parallel narrative is one that emerged through perpetrator hearings at the TRC, which revealed the politics of violence in the liberation movement itself. The figure of the traitor hovers like a shadow in this parallel narrative.[6] In addition to the incidents of necklacing and the protection of the identity of mutineers and enemy agents mentioned earlier, one of the most high-profile examples of this parallel narrative emerged during the hearing of Winnie Madikizela-Mandela, who appeared in front of the commission because of her suspected involvement in the kidnapping, torture, and death of fourteen-year-old child activist, Stompie Seipei, believed to be an informer. This parallel counternarrative comprises "all" the "imperfections" in the TRC's final report: the troubling, hidden issues that remain unresolved, all these years later. These "imperfections" can be read as pointing to a future moment where the discursive space marked by Mandela's hesitating stammer could be revisited and expanded. That moment, it seems, is upon us.

Nearly twenty years after the handover of the TRC's final report, we encounter another ANC president, Jacob Zuma, speaking at the Tshwane University of Technology on June 23, 2015. Two days before unexpectedly releasing the long-awaited report of the Farlam Commission of Inquiry into the massacre of the thirty-four striking mineworkers at Marikana, Zuma hinted at the potential need to reinstate apartheid tactics to police potentially violent protests: "Otherwise the culture of Apartheid that used violence to suppress people will have to be looked at again, and I don't want it. We don't want the police to use violence because they are stopping violence."[7] A heckler from the Economic Freedom Fighters, an opposition party led by former ANC Youth League leader, Julius Malema, then called out: "They killed people in Marikana!" Zuma replied: "And those people in Marikana had killed people and the police were stopping them from killing people."[8] One cannot help but read Zuma's comments as condoning the force employed by police, as well as the police view of the miners as "muti-crazed and hell-bent on violence."[9] More significant for my argument, however, is Zuma's comment on the need for a return to apartheid-era policing to subdue social dissatisfaction, and the threat that it implies: of the deployment of violence as a political instrument. This kind of statement would have been unimaginable in 1998, during the golden years of Mandela's conciliatory nation building, but its possibility—as I have been suggesting—is already indicated in Mandela's stammer. Zuma's comment is an indicator of the ANC-led government's likely ongoing reliance on the coercive, internal violence revealed during the TRC processes.

In the wake of the Marikana massacre, the very comparisons with the apartheid state that the ANC had sought to avoid in 1998 were evoked in the repetition of the familiar image of black men running from police with assault rifles, crouched behind armored vehicles. Achille Mbembe[10] has made the point that these killings were extrajudicial executions, suggesting continuity with the security practices of the apartheid state, where, as Jacob Dlamini concludes, extrajudicial execution of political activists was "all of a piece with the bureaucratic and political workings of apartheid."[11] Repetition, as Hedley Twidle has suggested, is an inadequate trope for understanding the temporal implications of this event. To be sure, commentators were prompted to return to the apartheid past, drawing comparisons between the events at Marikana and the Sharpeville shootings of 1960.[12] However, as Twidle contends, this return flattens out history in "a series of all-too-usable episodes" that reveals "the limited repertoire of conceptual shapes available in the public culture as South Africa tries to imagine the relation between past and present."[13] The Marikana massacre clearly destabilizes the transition narrative of a progressive historical trajectory from oppression and inequality to freedom. But if this event cannot be understood in terms of repetition, how might we instead think of its temporal implications?

One of the most formative critiques of the Marikana massacre is the 2014 documentary film *Miners Shot Down*, directed by Rehad Desai. The opening sequences of the film juxtapose images of the miners being fired upon with archival footage of the 1960 Sharpeville shootings, drawing a direct analogy between the events. As background to the wildcat strike, the film proceeds to emphasize the dire economic conditions of the miners, presented as illiterate citizens trapped in a cycle of poverty that denies them the possibility of full personhood. The film thus indicts the failure of the ANC-led government to deliver on its transition-era promises of free, quality education and economic parity and the viewer is left with the overwhelming impression that the dream of the revolution has been betrayed.

Indeed, betrayal of black solidarity emerges as a powerful theme in this film: in an arresting scene from police footage taken on August 13, 2012, the striking miners are returning to "the mountain" (a nearby hill that they had appropriated as their strike headquarters) when they encounter a police cordon. In the exchanges that follow—in Fanagalo, the Zulu-based pidgin language of the South African mining industry, with English subtitles supplied—one of the strike leaders, Andries Ntsenyeho, addresses the police, saying: "The pain that I am feeling when I look at you, I only see faces similar to mine. That makes me very sad. When I'm killed by another black brother like me. Someone of my kind." This speech is particularly poignant, given that Ntsenyeho was one of those shot dead three days later. The violence perpetrated on the exclusively black strikers is executed by predominantly black subjects, at a mine whose "public face" in the documentary is that of a black man, Barnard Mokwena, senior vice president at Lonmin.[14] Moreover, the film overtly constructs the figure of the traitor in the image of Cyril Ramaphosa, then the incumbent deputy president of the ANC and, since mid-February 2018, South Africa's fifth post-transition president.[15] In voiceover, Desai explains that Ramaphosa, erstwhile founder and leader of NUM, now a nonexecutive director of and shareholder in Lonmin Mining Company, was a man "who once saw South Africa's working class as a force to bring about change, [but who] now found himself on the other side of the table. At the time of the massacre, he was a board member of Lonmin."[16] Desai's framing of Ramaphosa suggests that Ramaphosa has betrayed the workers whom he once represented by protecting the interests of white capital.

Miners Shot Down has been accused of sensationalism and criticized for its failure to address the role of white "corporate Lonmin" in the lead-up to the massacre.[17] Problematically, as reviewer Gillian Schutte notes, the film represents these events as "a purely black affair, a reworking of the black-on-black violence discourse from the 1980s into the contemporary common sense 'capitalist-black' black-on-black violence discourse as if white economic imperialism had nothing to do with this heinous event."[18] Schutte's critique of Desai's film is compelling, but if one cannot accept the film's representation of events at face value, how does its representation of the violence perpetrated on black bodies at Marikana, as well as the casting of villains, fit into an emerging discourse about the role of apartheid-era black collaborators in the oppression of black subjects in a postapartheid democracy?

Betrayal features at every level of the Marikana narrative: betrayal of the workers by the unions as well as the government that appears to have sided with white capital, and, by extension, betrayal of the revolutionary ideals of the liberation struggle. Betrayal provides us with an understanding of the temporal implications of the Marikana massacre that complicates and questions both the trope of repetition and the optimistic, progressive, and linear national narrative.

Mapping temporal coordinates

The linear narrative of the South African transition is set against the backdrop of another global linear narrative, namely the victory of liberal democracy over communism. The photojournalist Greg Marinovich notes in his extensive account of the genesis of the Marikana tragedy that the end of the Cold War ushered in a commodities boom and a new age of consumerism in South Africa.[19] Access to extractive industries such as mining attracted high-risk investors who tend to have a "frontier approach to business, labor relations and the law."[20] Despite the economic boom, the gap in income inequality has widened and the Gini coefficient measures South Africa as the worst in the world.[21] Most blue-collar workers earn below subsistence wages. As Marinovich describes it, in the new political and economic climate, the revolution itself was appropriated for capital gain, with "politically connected labour union elite" fast becoming "an integral part of the commercial environment": "top union officials and office bearers earned corporate-level salaries" and the "rhetoric of revolution" was reduced to "a political lubricant, legitimizing rent seekers squatting atop every conceivable source of wealth."[22] The betrayal of the dream of economic freedom by the representatives of the workers' revolution had a key influence on the way in which events at Lonmin played out. In the months leading up to the wildcat strike, miners across the platinum belt had lost faith in their NUM representatives, who were seen to be in the pockets of management.

In terms of local coordinates, the temporal implications of the Marikana massacre thus need to be understood in relation to the promise of freedom and economic equality on which the ANC came to power. At the very moment when a socialist revolution seemed imminent in South Africa, the collapse of the socialist states ushered in a new era of liberal democracy and human rights, and South Africa became a leading example of this victory, with Mandela co-opted as a global icon of its success. Recent global events demand that we revisit this teleological narrative of the success of neoliberal capitalism, however. Alain Badiou reads the 2011 uprisings in the Arab world as the "first stirrings of a global popular uprising" against gains made by neoliberal capitalism since the 1980s.[23] The invocation of the Marikana massacre during the ongoing South African student protests that erupted in late 2015 suggests that the strike and the subsequent massacre of the miners, when read in a global context, fits into this pattern of growing resistance to globalized capital, and might be understood, following Badiou's argument, as a powerful contraction in the rebirth of History.

But let's return first to that pervasive sense of the ANC's historical betrayal. In recent South African narratives of the antiapartheid struggle, we find a preoccupation with the figure of the traitor and the afterlife of the secret. These accounts are retrospective, returning readers to the historical moment of the late state of emergency and the early transition. In other words, these narratives take us back to the moment of the collapse of not only apartheid, but of revolutionary socialist possibility. The protagonists are poised on the brink of revolution—and then history ends. The temporal terms in which David Scott has described the fate of the leaders of the Grenada Revolution are applicable here:

> Their era had vanished, and now they were like leftovers from a former future stranded in the present [...] [T]hese former revolutionaries would be obliged to save themselves [...] in a political world *redefined* in a new jargon of authenticity that no longer admitted the legibility, much less recognized the legitimacy, of their former political ambitions, their former political languages, their former political lives.[24]

The return to this moment at the "end of history" in recent South African narratives appears to be part of an attempt to understand the particular local fate of the socialist revolutionary in this New South Africa, this New World, redefined by the jargon of neoliberalism. In his "Theses on the Philosophy of History," Walter Benjamin argues for a reading of history in which the historian "grasps the constellation which his own era has formed with a definite earlier one."[25] These retrospective narratives about the transition seem to adopt a similar approach to historical time: they return to an earlier era in order to understand how the "time of the now" is shot through with the fragments of this earlier time.

The act of betrayal affects our lived experience of time: our sense of temporality. While not all acts of betrayal are necessarily violent, the temporal consequences of the act of betrayal appear similar to those of the act of violence. Betrayal and violence both cause a rupture or interruption in our lived experience of time, terminating previous social relations. The anthropologist Robert Thornton has argued that violence is a process that relies on multiple, ongoing evolutions of meaning, and that it is therefore inappropriate to reduce violence to sequences of causes. "The crucial result of violence," he argues, "is that it must be inserted into the narratives and subsequent frameworks of meaning that we cast for it."[26] Similarly, we might argue that the act of betrayal results in an irrevocable shift in the way in which we attribute meaning to particular actions or events. Ato Quayson has suggested that when victims of violence interrogate the past, they do so because the interrogation might help them to exist in the present.[27] However, the meaning revealed through this historical recall is part of a contradictory process, "some of whose implications reside in the unfolding present, articulated from within the discursive framework of the new South Africa and from which the events can be publicly recalled and acknowledged in the first place."[28] Once the act of betrayal becomes the lens through which previous actions or events are read, they take on new meaning. The act of betrayal exposes the ambiguity of power relations, demanding a reappraisal of the past, and by extension of the present. This reappraisal inevitably calls for a reconfiguration of the processes by which we understand the significance of an historical event. Betrayal thus introduces uncertainty in our experience of the past. The retrospective view that betrayal initiates is not a question of excavating or surfacing repressed memories, but rather a question of reassigning meaning to memories that may very well have been on the surface all along. The incidents of internal violence that the ANC sought to suppress with their interdict of the TRC report are in the public record, but the import of these events has been historically displaced by the celebratory transition narrative. Recent betrayal narratives bring these violent events to the fore, re-reading the national narrative through the lens of these painful and intimate betrayals. The result is something like a feedback loop, allowing information to stream from past to present, running interference with the established narrative. I propose, then, to put a selection of betrayal narratives, fictional as well as historical accounts, into play with one another, in an attempt to identify the way in which these works retrospectively illustrate the struggle for meaning at the moment of the South African transition.

Beyond "Victim" and "Perpetrator"

Contestations in the construction of meaning were present at the very inception of the postapartheid national narrative, signaled, as I've somewhat fancifully suggested, by Mandela's stammer. The TRC hearings were central to establishing the powerful victim/perpetrator binary that has tended to dominate the South African imaginary in the past two decades, because the TRC's Human Rights Violations hearings were split between the testimonies of victims and the confessions of perpetrators. However, as Antjie Krog observes in *Country of My Skull*, two contending positions on reconciliation and change were vying for supremacy at the time of the perpetrators' amnesty hearings (58).[29] There were those who, like Kader Asmal, held that it was "not a question of bad apples on both sides" but rather of "a bad tree, a weed, on the one hand, and an apple tree on the other" (58). This metaphor invokes the biblical trope of the Garden of Eden and the tree of the knowledge of good and evil (Genesis 2:9). On the one hand, there is the garden gone to seed in the image of the bad tree or weed, suggesting the neglect of a God-given task. On the other hand is the image of the apple tree, often associated with the tree of knowledge of good and evil. The metaphor implies that the distinction between right and wrong is obvious, and excesses that occurred within the framework of resistance to apartheid were justified. This approach to reconciliation, adopted by many of the new leaders, including then deputy president Thabo Mbeki, held that reconciliation might only be possible if whites acknowledged that they were culpable for the evils of apartheid. Krog notes that this political line "freezes the debate in tones of black and white and gives no guidance on how the individual can move forward" (58). Another antithetical approach was the position the TRC itself had to adopt following the hearings on human rights violations. These revealed that human rights violations suffered by black people had been perpetrated not only by whites, "but also by blacks at the instigation of whites" (58). The TRC therefore had of necessity to formulate a position on reconciliation that made it available to all South Africans.

The narratives that have been constructed in the wake of the Marikana massacre have similarly challenged the once clear distinction between victim and perpetrator. The commission of inquiry led by a retired judge, Ian Farlam, heard testimony from the bereaved relatives of the NUM members and policemen ostensibly killed by striking miners in the days before the massacre. These testimonies illustrate the complicated position of the policemen and present them as victims of violent circumstances. Similarly, the relatives of the dead miners had to work consciously against perceptions that had been established of the mineworkers as a criminal, faceless mob.[30] If the final report of the TRC already contained indications of the instability of the victim/perpetrator binary, then betrayal stories emerging now seek to fill in the silences and gaps that cannot be explained by the white/black binary. One reason for the emergence of these narratives certainly has to do with the natural passage of time. As Rebecca Davis, reviewing Jacob Dlamini's *Askari* (2014), suggests: "Perhaps it is a sign of our growing historical distance from Apartheid's formal structures—though not from its legacies—that our democracy can begin to countenance narratives that destabilize the certainty about the identity of victims and perpetrators."[31] Another reason may be the growing sense that the revolution has been betrayed, that the "utopian future in which the alienated, reified time of capitalism is overcome and socialist humanity coincides with its destiny,"[32] is no longer a possibility. Nothing signals this betrayal more clearly in South Africa than the Marikana massacre, where the protection of multinational capitalist interests trumped the value of workers' lives. Indeed, an overwhelming feature of these narratives that destabilize the victim/perpetrator distinction is the preoccupation with the seeming failure of the socialist project just at the moment when the South African revolution seemed imminent. The temporal effect, as Scott argues, is "the experience of temporal *afterness* that prevails" in which the trace of futures past hangs over what feels "like an endlessly extending present."[33]

If the moment of transition signals a shift in the way that meaning is constructed, then betrayal narratives return to that moment as the surface against which the event of betrayal might be read. Discussing the unstable referential locus of trauma and the challenges that attend on determining historical "truth," Ato Quayson argues:

> The "kernel" of history is not a secret but the contradictory processes by which the event becomes historical and gains magnitude. It is the configuration of these processes, conceived of not as stable but as always in motion that provides the "surface" against which the significance of the historical event is then read. Thus, there is no easy distinction to be drawn between kernel and surface; both are in a restless interplay.[34]

Quayson goes further to argue that the same principle applies in the literary-aesthetic domain, "where it is the configuration of all the levels in the text interrelated as a literary process that allows a surface to be grasped."[35] He therefore urges scholars to bring "the literary configuration-as-surface" into dialogue with the "historical configuration-of-process-as-surface," to "'hold it up to nature' in such a way as to mirror nature as a process of discovery."[36] The question, for Quayson, "is not just how true or false a literary or historical account is to discrete events," but whether it "encapsulates the process and contradictions by which struggles for meaning take place in the world."[37] The betrayal narratives to which I now turn offer configurations of the past and present that illustrate the complex position of the figure of the traitor and the processes by which this figure is constructed, as well as the repercussions of living on in the wake of the betrayal of the dream of a socialist revolution.

Both Niq Mhlongo's *Way Back Home* (2013), a novel, and Jacob Dlamini's *Askari*, a work of nonfiction, are preoccupied with the experiences of individuals who went into exile during the apartheid era to join uMkhonto weSizwe (MK), the military wing of the ANC. These narratives trouble the easy distinction between victim and perpetrator that has prevailed in standard assessments of the South African past. Instead, these works seek to highlight the complexities of the relationship between past and present.

"A Knife which Severs the Flow of Time"

Askari tells the story of Glory Sedibe, a member of the ANC and MK. In 1986, betrayed by the Royal Swazi Police and possibly by his own comrades in the ANC, he was abducted by an apartheid death squad from his hiding place in Swaziland, taken back to South Africa, interrogated, and tortured. The book explores the choices Sedibe made in his turn "from resister to collaborator, insurgent to counterinsurgent, and, to his former comrades, from hero to traitor."[38] Dlamini offers a composite picture, the various fragments of which challenge established narratives about the operation of ANC cadres during the late 1980s and early 1990s, the final years of the antiapartheid struggle. The narrative loops back and forth in time and creates a strong sense of the continental and transnational spatial connections forged during the late struggle period. The narrative is offered from multiple points of view and using hybrid genres. Additionally, Dlamini's account of Sedibe's life is reconstructed from several divergent sources, characteristic of the "archival turn" in recent South African literature.[39] The stories brought to light explore what the silences in official narratives mean—that to live with the effect of a secret is to live in a temporal state that has stagnated. "A secret," Dlamini quotes David Xiao as saying, "is like a knife which severs the flow of time, leaving a scar which will sometimes masquerade as the secret itself" (250).

Dlamini is preoccupied throughout with the question of betrayal and its temporal implications. Citing Gabriella Turnaturi, he notes: "betrayal affects not only relations between individuals but also the individuals' sense of a shared space and time" (97). *Askari* begins with a map of South Africa and its immediate neighbors to the east demarcating the arena of the struggle insofar as it relates to Sedibe's individual story of exile and return. The only indication that this is not a recent map of the region is the fact that the city of Polokwane and the town of Makhado still appear under their apartheid-era names, Pietersburg and Louis Trichardt: the reader is compelled to make a small perspectival shift in order to read the otherwise contemporary landscape through the lens of the late struggle period. This accommodation attends upon a temporal shift that results in a kind of defamiliarization; the reader must reorient herself in time and, consequently also, in space. Notably, this compelling spatial reorientation is offset by a focus on the temporal in the final chapter of the book, entitled "The past, the present and the future." The account thus opens with a focus on space and ends with a focus on time.

Structurally, the narrative in *Askari* is organized in a nonlinear series of vignettes. Each chapter foregrounds a different aspect of Sedibe's life, that helps readers to understand his choices. So, for example, in the seventh (and central) chapter, "The Village," Dlamini explores Sedibe's social background, but sets his personal story against the story of the asbestos mining town of Penge, the village of the chapter's title. Dlamini traces its origins to the nineteenth-century European and North American demand for asbestos, and the rise of British-owned multinational mining companies in South Africa, sketching a cross-section of the (international) history of the exploitation of resources and labour in South Africa, that demonstrates how the events of Sedibe's life and the consequences of his actions in the late 1980s are entangled with South Africa's deeper past.

As Dlamini points out, the story recounted does not have a reliable narrator: Sedibe is a liar whose word cannot be trusted. The opinions of the individuals who knew Sedibe and were interviewed by Dlamini are questionable. By enumerating in such detail the unreliability of the text before us, Dlamini foregrounds its ontological instability, but he also links it to a temporal state of belatedness: "The historian is always late and cannot for that reason record 'what in fact happened exactly in the way that it happened'" (5). Dlamini's reconstruction of the conditions that led to Sedibe's decision to turn is notable for its generic hybridity. Interspersed between the biographical accounts of Sedibe's life, constructed from various sources, we find autobiographical accounts of Dlamini's own life, as well as accounts that the reader is advised to treat as fiction. These often-surprising autobiographical and fictional digressions serve to create a sense of the texture of everyday black life under apartheid. Additionally, they illustrate certain concepts in Dlamini's analysis of the psychology of black collaboration under apartheid. So, for example, in the final chapter, Dlamini states:

> There is nothing neat about the history presented here. Sedibe's story is not the whole story. The experience of one man can only be understood in a wider context. Many of these stories exist in a world of shadows that has yet to be explored. There are stories that continue to refuse to be told. How might we go beyond that refusal? One way, it seems to me, is to engage honestly with the "fatal intimacy" at the heart of human relations in South Africa. It is in our persons that the secrets of the past have found a home. We must open up these archives and tell these stories. (255–6)

Dlamini anticipates mixed reception of his advice to open up these archives and reveal these secrets, and, in order to illustrate the implications of this "fatal intimacy" (255),[40] recounts a story that the reader is "advised to treat as fictional" (256). Tellingly, it deals with the ambiguous status of a suspected traitor within the intimate social unit of the extended family. A young, unnamed man, who may or may not be Dlamini himself, has a "dodgy" uncle, who has been known to tell people he's a cop, "yet no one can claim to have seen him in a police uniform" (256). The young man confronts the uncle with the question: "Have you ever spied for the police?" The uncle avoids answering him, and later that day the young man tells his closest cousin about the exchange. Although the cousin also has doubts about the uncle, he is horrified that the young man has voiced these doubts to the uncle: "Why? How could you? Why do you want to know?" (257). The young man "takes these questions in his head in turn" and finds himself "face to face with the notion of a legitimate secret" (257). This process raises all sorts of uncomfortable questions:

> Does the young man, and by extension his family, really want to know if there is a collaborator in their midst? Does the family want to know if one of their own was an informer for the apartheid police? Would knowledge of the uncle's past, if he had been an informer or agent of some sort, change the uncle's standing in the family? The young man decides, after a struggle with himself, that he does not want to know. He decides that maybe some things are not worth knowing. There ends our fiction. (257–8)

The story highlights the pervasiveness of betrayal and the extent to which it is tied up with intimacy. It also shows how difficult it is to "out" a suspected collaborator, thus "allow[ing] the secrets of the past to gain an afterlife" (250). Through a self-reflexive gesture, Dlamini emphasizes his authorial distance from the event he is about to recount, while at the same time alerting the reader to his or her own predispositions. The configurations presented in his reconstruction of Sedibe's life complicate the way in which we think about apartheid and its legacies, because it shows how narrow a category race is for understanding individual loyalties and allegiances.

Dlamini ends his account by advising that, as a nation, South Africans need to examine the "taboos, the secrets and the disavowals at the core of our collective memories" (260). The effects of these secrets afflict victims and perpetrators alike, as they remain mired in a temporal state of stagnation. It is only by confronting these secrets that we might reenter, or perhaps reroute, the flow of time.

The returning ghost

The "afterlife" of the secret is a central theme in Niq Mhlongo's *Way Back Home*, in which the effect of the secret is tellingly linked to the return of a ghost. In a public conversation with his publisher, James Woodhouse of Kwela, during the 2014 Stellenbosch Woordfees, Mhlongo noted that the novel is preoccupied with the fact that the ANC's own apartheid-era transgressions were never fully disclosed.[41] Because the fate of the victims has not been disclosed, their families have not been able to perform the necessary rites that will release the spirits of the dead and allow them entry into the ancestral realm. The current dispensation's continued refusal of full disclosure, and insistence on their own status as victims, means that the nation is haunted by the spirits of those exiles in a perpetual state of "returning." A joke made by Woodhouse during the conversation offers a clue to the novel's temporality: looking for "new" South African literature that dealt with postapartheid issues, the publishers had been adamant to steer away from novels about apartheid when Mhlongo presented a manuscript for a novel that is essentially *about* apartheid. The anecdote illustrates the way in which postapartheid issues are shot through with "fragments" of the apartheid past—a key concept in the novel itself.

The protagonist in *Way Back Home*, Kimathi Tito, is "a real son of exile" (19). Born in Tanzania to a Xhosa father and a Tanzanian mother, Kimathi is named for his father's struggle hero, Kenyan Mau-Mau leader Dedan Kimathi Waciuri. Kimathi's pedigree illustrates the kind of continental connections forged during the liberation struggle. A "soldier of the South African revolution," Kimathi has accumulated wealth and gained influence in the new South African democracy. Repressed memories of his actions in an ANC training camp in Angola are beginning to surface, however. Along with this psychological haunting, he is also afflicted by a spiritual haunting as the ghost of a young woman begins to appear regularly to him. The temporality of the novel shifts constantly between a present that is emptied out of all historical meaning, and a past characterized by violence and betrayal, in which change is anticipated, and is imagined as revolutionary. The setting underscores a sense of porousness and movement, of action beyond and across the boundaries of the late apartheid state, mapping the intercontinental pathways of the returning exile, who is a global subject with pan-African and transnational, socialist connections. However, despite this movement across time and space, the novel's overwhelming atmosphere is one of claustrophobia. It presents a futureless world—a sense of stasis is achieved by Kimathi's obsession with signifiers of status that are repeated like a mind-numbing litany. In this world, "The Movement" itself is little more than a convenient pickup line, and Mhlongo's depiction of the manner in which the rhetoric of revolution is glibly employed as Kimathi seals self-enriching deals is a powerful illustration of the manner in which the language of socialist revolution has been co-opted for capitalist gain. There is no sense of a future, except in Kimathi's anticipation of immediate rewards. Kimathi is concerned only with the accumulation of wealth and status, and his point of view is replete with references to designer labels, extravagant cars and expensive whiskey. His venality is signaled by the ease with which he hands out vast amounts of cash to "make sure everything is in order" with his business transactions, but claims to be too broke to pay child support (43).

Kimathi's preoccupation with "present opportunities" rather than "emergent order" denotes him as belonging to "the entrepreneurial present," a concept introduced by Dawid de Villiers in his analysis of Ralph Ziman's 2008 film, *Jerusalema*. De Villiers argues that revolutionary time is characterized by the "enabling function of the past, of the historical perspective, in the present," while in the world where the revolution has already happened (like the world presented in *Jerusalema* and in *Way Back Home*), "the present is merely the *result* of the past; it is no longer sustained or impelled by it."[42] De Villiers' description chimes with David Scott's notion of an "endlessly extending present," a "stalled present [...] that stands out in its arrested movement."[43] In this stalled present, revolutionary rhetoric is employed cynically in the pursuit of capital gain and sexual conquest. As Brenna Munro argues in her chapter in this book, the "failures of futurity" enacted in recent South African narratives reveal the difficulties of imagining political alternatives in South Africa at the moment.

Kimathi thrives in this stagnant, posthistorical present until it is severely disrupted by a ghost from the past. This moment marks a change in the narrative of the present, which takes on a surreal and symbolic quality. The temporal shift is heralded by an ominous portent: driving along the freeway on a dark and stormy night, Kimathi pulls over after hitting an owl—a harbinger of death—with his car. A blurry figure in white approaches through the rain and gets into the car with him, causing Kimathi to faint from fear. When he regains consciousness, a beautiful young woman is sitting next to him. She tells him that her name is Senami, and that she's on her way back home. As Senami's story unfolds, we learn from her parents that Senami went into exile in 1986 and never returned. The woman Kimathi encounters is the ghost of the exile, trying to "make [her] way back home," in a perpetual state of returning. The appearance of Senami introduces another temporal plane in the novel: that of the supernatural. Senami tells Kimathi that she lives "in another world," a comment that is intended literally, not metaphorically. The spirit realm is thus established as part of the reality of secrets and betrayal that marks the chronotope of this novel: by establishing the dead as actors with vested interests in the events of the present, Mhlongo extends the effects of secrets and betrayals beyond the natural world. Senami's ghost is an important signifier; her appearance indicates a temporal rupture—time is out of joint, if you will.

Kimathi's use of psychoactive medication, as well as his unstable psychological state, might lead the reader to assume that the ghost is simply a hallucination, a symptom of his psychopathy. But we soon learn that the same ghost also haunts Senami's parents, and that it is only by discovering her fate in exile and performing the proper burial rites for her remains that her spirit might be laid to rest. Kimathi harbors the secret answer to Senami's fate. Thus, the novel suggests that victims like Senami and her parents, and perpetrators like Kimathi, are all suffering the effect of the secret. This depiction of the relationship between victims and perpetrators finds its echo in what Jacob Dlamini, citing Njabulo Ndebele, calls the "fatal intimacy" at the heart of apartheid, which has allowed the secret to gain an afterlife in South Africa.[44] The victims of violence must live with the perpetrators, often in the same communities, with the unresolved question of betrayal between them.

The investigation into Senami's disappearance leads Kimathi and her parents to Angola and the now abandoned Amilcar Cabral camp, where "nothing's changed": time has looped back on itself. We have returned to the moment when the secret severed the flow of time. In the preceding flashbacks, the reader has gradually witnessed the atrocities committed by two characters, who go by the *noms de guerre* Comrade Idi and Comrade Pilate respectively, and who persecute "traitors" at the camp. These characters are representations of those "mutineers" responsible for the deaths of innocent comrades accused of being spies, who were protected by the ANC during the transition. Senami, known in the camp as Lady Comrade Mkabayi, is detained because she refuses to have sex with them. She succumbs to her wounds after being beaten, raped, and stabbed by the pair, and four fellow prisoners lay her to rest in a shallow grave. It is this grave that Kimathi points out to the *sangoma* Makhanda, a traditional healer who has accompanied them on the journey. The *sangoma* acts as the mediator between the world of the living and the spirit world. The relationship with the spiritual presented in this novel is firmly rooted in an African cosmology, which brings into sharp relief discourses of forgiveness and reconciliation based on a primarily Christian worldview such as those that emerged at the TRC.

Way Back Home offers an ambivalent view of reconciliation. While Senami's bones are exhumed, Kimathi wanders away from the group. Alone in the old "Doomed Spies" block, he is again visited by the ghost of Lady Comrade Mkabayi/Senami, who demands that he tell the truth of what happened to her. The only way he can save himself is to confess all his crimes. The ghost, then, does not necessarily seek revenge—she offers him an opportunity at a kind of reconciliation. Kimathi, however, cannot admit that he has done wrong, he can only see himself as a victim of circumstances: he "had no choice," he was following the instructions of the commanders, the "orders of The Movement" (204–5). His insistence on his innocence precludes the possibility of reconciliation, and thus he becomes the subject of revenge: a life for a life. Outside, Mongezi, a comrade who has helped Kimathi arrange the journey to the camp, breaks down and tells the group that Kimathi was responsible for Senami's death, as well as the deaths of several other comrades. Mongezi admits that, as Comrade Bambata, he was the one who falsely gave Senami up for a spy after being tortured. A dust cloud that rises from the site of the grave then leads them to the Doomed Spies block, where they find Kimathi hanging dead from his belt. Some reviewers have found this ending abrupt and troubling, since it offers no answer to the question of how South Africans can reconcile the past with the present.[45] However, this conclusion misses the point of the final words in the novel. Senami's father, Napo, states: "At least we have found closure and we'll be able to carry our daughter's spirit home with us" (208).

The novel leaves the reader with a clear conclusion, that in order to reconcile the past with the present in South Africa, a full disclosure is called for. Only once the correct rituals to release the spirits of the dead and allow them to "return home" have been enacted can South Africa really begin to move past the time of the returning exile, the moment of constant transition in which we appear to have been caught for the past twenty years.

Conclusion: *A luta continua*

Both *Askari* and *Way Back Home* feature present time characterized by stasis and suspension. In this sense, these narratives share with apartheid-era literature a failure to imagine the future. However, whereas apartheid-era literature "often found itself stuck with the urgencies of the present," as Meg Samuelson argues,[46] both Mhlongo and Dlamini emphasize the enduring effect of the shared secret between collaborators and victims, and the need for a proper excavation of the past.

This chapter began by identifying the recent emergence of a body of work on South Africa that is characterized by a preoccupation with the question of betrayal, particularly within the structures of the liberation movement during the late struggle period. The Marikana massacre and its aftermaths—poignant reminders of the betrayal of the revolutionary ideals of the antiapartheid struggle—can be understood within this series of emergent betrayal narratives. During South Africa's transitional phase, accounts that undermined the fiction of black solidarity—so fundamental to the construction of the narrative of national unity—were of necessity suppressed. However, it was the very fiction of racial solidarity that made askaris so potent as counterinsurgents under apartheid, and it is this same fiction that has shielded them from exposure in postapartheid South Africa. Apartheid-era collaborators have been seamlessly reabsorbed into postapartheid state agencies, thus retaining continuity between apartheid and postapartheid security services.[47] Collaborators and the victims of their actions continue to share this open secret of violence and betrayal. As Dlamini points out, the ongoing silence around this secret, and the protection of the identities of collaborators, has an insidious effect in South Africa's current political climate: allegations of collaboration have been used to silence and delegitimize political rivals, rendering them politically unreliable. The secrets of the past are used to fight contemporary political battles. Subsumed under "a-a-all" the imperfections of the TRC's final report, questions of collaboration were of necessity downplayed during the period of transition. The betrayal narratives that I have discussed bring the figures of the collaborator and the mutineer out of the shadows.

The binarist transition narrative officially adopted by the ANC has provided a linear account in which the events of the past are a series of causalities that lead to freedom and unity. The future is foreclosed—we have attained freedom and are now living in the ever-expanding time of the present. Within this narrative paradigm, the Marikana massacre cannot but be read as repetition, albeit repetition with a destabilizing difference, since the clear ethical and racial paradigms of the past are replaced by murkier commitments, complicities, and betrayals. Formally, the examples of "post-Marikana" narratives that have been the focus of this chapter present an alternative paradigm, where events in the past are nodes in a network of configurations and reconfigurations that continue to have a powerful effect on events in the present. When read within this new understanding, the Marikana massacre is revealed as a persistent symptom of an ongoing and unresolved conflict.

Notes

1　"Necklacing" is a form of kangaroo court execution where a tire that has been doused with petrol is placed around the victim's body and set alight. This practice is often used as punishment for those accused of being political traitors.

2　See the "ANC Submission to the TRC in reply to the TRC's 'Findings on the ANC.'"

3　ANC, "Events leading to the application for an interdict against the TRC."

4　Ibid.

5　See Krog, *Country of My Skull*, 283.

6   I take this image from Mandla Langa's 2014 novel, *The Texture of Shadows*, another recent betrayal narrative particularly preoccupied with the complexity and ambiguity of the figure of the traitor.

7   Nicolson, "Marikana," online.

8   Ibid.

9   Ibid.

10 Mbembe, "SA's Death Penalty Is Not Yet Dead," online.

11 Dlamini, *Askari*, 14–15.

12 Twidle, "The Oscar Pistorius Case: History Written on a Woman's Body," online.

13 Ibid.

14 Allegations that Mokwena was a "deep cover" agent for the South African State Security Agency (SSA) from 2004 until the end of 2012 appeared in the *City Press* newspaper in May 2016. While Mokwena has denied these rumors, it is worth noting that the allegations further serve to construct him as a treacherous figure who has used his training in covert intelligence operations to disempower emerging unions that threaten the hegemonic power of the NUM. See Myburgh, "Lonmin Boss Was a 'Spy,'" online.

15 The appointment of Cyril Ramaphosa, described in the press as "Nelson Mandela's chosen heir," has had the temporal effect of a seeming return to that moment of hope represented by the transition era. However, the budget speech of February 21, 2018, has been slated as anti-poor and evidence of the ANC's entrenched neoliberal economic policies. Nicolson, "Budget 2018," online.

16 Quoted in *Miners Shot Down*.

17 Schutte, "'Miners Shot Down' an Unequal Representation of the Bigger Picture," online.

18 Ibid.

19 Marinovich, *Murder at Small Koppie*, e-book.

20 Ibid.

21 Ibid.

22 Ibid.

23 Badiou, *The Rebirth of History*, 5.

24 Scott, *Omens of Adversity*, 5.

25 Benjamin, *Illuminations*, 223.

26 Thornton, "The Peculiar Temporality of Violence," 55.

27 Quayson, *Calibrations*, 94.

28 Ibid.

29 It is telling that the issue of betrayal is at the heart of Krog's text: she introduces a fabricated affair at the level of the framing narrative, which allows her to stage a personal contestation of truth in tandem with the contestation of truth that emerges through the TRC processes.

30 See Marikana Commission of Inquiry Transcripts, day 273 (August 13, 2014).

31   Davis, "Betrayal Chronicles."
32   Scott, *Omens of Adversity*, 6.
33   Ibid.
34   Quayson, *Calibrations*, 97.
35   Ibid.
36   Ibid.
37   Ibid., 98.
38   Dlamini, *Askari*, blurb.
39   Meg Samuelson notes that apartheid literature "found itself stuck in the urgencies of the present," while the tone of the transitional era was set by the TRC, which "restricted its backward gaze to the recent past." In "post-transitional" texts, by contrast, the "archival turn" is evident, with the Dutch East India Company and British colonial eras "increasingly under scrutiny." This "post-transitional" literature thus draws a wide historical reach into the "now" of an "effervescent and ephemeral present." Samuelson, "Scripting Connections," 114.
40   Dlamini is here citing the phrase from Njabulo Ndebele.
41   Pieterse, "The ANC and the Ancestors."
42   De Villiers, "After the Revolution," 13.
43   Scott, *Omens of Adversity*, 6.
44   Dlamini, *Askari*, 255.
45   Emmet, "A Haunted Struggle."
46   Samuelson, "Scripting Connections," 114.
47   See Dlamini, *Askari*, 53; 252, 259.

Works Cited

ANC. "ANC Submission to the TRC in Reply to the TRC's 'Findings on the ANC.'" October 28, 1998. http://www.anc.org.za/show.php?id=2667&t=Truth%20and%20 Reconciliation%20Commission.

ANC. "Events Leading to the Application for an Interdict against the TRC." n.d. http:// www.anc.org.za/show.php?id=2668.

Badiou, Alain. *The Rebirth of History: Times of Riots and Uprisings*. Trans. G. Elliott. London: Verso, 2012.

Benjamin, Walter. *Illuminations*. Trans. Harry Zohn. London: Fontana, 1973.

Davis, Rebecca. "Betrayal Chronicles: The Agonising Case of Apartheid's Black Collaborators." *Daily Maverick*, December 5, 2014. http://www.dailymaverick.co.za/ article/2014-12-05-betrayal-chronicles-the-agonising-case-of-apartheids-black-collaborators/-.VQF4OUIpzds.

De Villiers, Dawid. "After the Revolution: *Jerusalema* and the Entrepreneurial Present." *South African Theatre Journal* 23 (2009): 8–22.

Dlamini, Jacob. *Askari*. Johannesburg: Jacana, 2014.

Emmet, Christine. "A Haunted Struggle." *SLiPnet*, September 5, 2013. http://slipnet. co.za/view/reviews/a-haunted-struggle/.

Krog, Antjie. *Country of My Skull*. 2nd ed. Johannesburg: Random House, 2002.

Langa, Mandla. *The Texture of Shadows*. Johannesburg: Picador Africa, 2014.

Marikana Commission of Inquiry Transcripts. http://www.marikanacomm.org.za/ transcripts/day273-140813Marikana.pdf.

Marinovich, Greg. *Murder at Small Koppie*. Kindle e-book. Cape Town: Penguin Books, 2016.

Mbembe, Achille. "SA's Death Penalty Is Not Yet Dead." *City Press*, August 16, 2015. http://city-press.news24.com/Voices/SAs-death-penalty-is-not-yet-dead-20150814.

Mhlongo, Niq. *Way Back Home*. Cape Town: Kwela, 2013.

Miners Shot Down. Directed by Rehad Desai. Johannesburg: Uhuru Productions, 2014.

Myburgh, Pieter-Louis. "Lonmin Boss Was a 'Spy.'" *City Press*, May 29, 2016. http://city-press.news24.com/News/lonmin-boss-was-a-spy-20160528-2.

Nicolson, Greg. "Budget 2018: Higher Education Gets R57bn in Budget Slated as Anti-poor." *Daily Maverick*, February 22, 2018. https://www.dailymaverick.co.za/ article/2018-02-22-budget-2018-higher-education-gets-r57bn-in-budget-slated-as-anti-poor/.

Nicolson, Greg. "Marikana: The Day President Zuma Added Insult to Injury." *Daily Maverick*, June 25, 2015. http://www.dailymaverick.co.za/article/2015-06-25-marikana-the-day-president-zuma-added-insult-to-injury/.

Pieterse, Annel. "The ANC and the Ancestors." *SLiPnet*, March 17, 2014. http://slipnet. co.za/view/event/the-anc-and-the-ancestors/.

Quayson, Ato. *Calibrations: Reading for the Social*. Minneapolis: University of Minnesota Press, 2003.

Samuelson, Meg. "Scripting Connections: Reflections on the 'Post-Transitional.'" *English Studies in Africa* 53.1 (2010): 113–17.

Schutte, Gillian. "'Miners Shot Down' an Unequal Representation of the Bigger Picture." *Mail & Guardian*, August 22, 2014. http://mg.co.za/article/2014-08-22-miners-shot-down-where-have-all-the-women-gone.

Scott, David. *Omens of Adversity*. Durham, NC: Duke University Press, 2014.

Thornton, Robert. "The Peculiar Temporality of Violence." *KronoScope* 2.1 (2002): 55.

Twidle, Hedley. "The Oscar Pistorius Case: History Written on a Woman's Body." *The New Statesman*, March 7, 2013. http://www.newstatesman.com/world-affairs/world-affairs/2013/02/history-written-womans-body.

4

Still Waiting? Writing Futurity after Apartheid

Katherine Hallemeier

Nadine Gordimer's "Amnesty" is set in the year of its initial publication, when the person the narrator refers to as "the Big Man" comes "back from prison" (255): a description that strongly evokes Nelson Mandela's release from state incarceration in February 1990. In *A Change of Tongue* (2003), Antjie Krog describes the widespread elation the event elicited from many South Africans: "We could be the most beautiful colour of change the world has ever seen. The man is free and a new time has dawned" (173). For Gordimer's unnamed narrator, however, 1990 is not a year of change, but rather one more year in a history of continual waiting. Nine years earlier, apartheid policies had resulted in the departure of her lover (also unnamed) to the city to search for employment; six years earlier, they had led to his arrest for union work. During his absence, the narrator reports, she did "nothing. Just waiting" (253). This waiting continues after the activist's release: he does not immediately return home from Cape Town, then quickly leaves again to work for the antiapartheid "Movement" (254), leaving him "no time" to get married or to spend with the couple's daughter (256). He barely has enough time to eat. In the final line of the story, the narrator is still "waiting to come back home" (257).

The narrator's ongoing waiting cautions against imagining a national "we" premised upon a shared experience of time, while also troubling a national historiography that anticipates collective transformation. In Gordimer's story, the energetic anticipation of the next nationally significant event, be it Mandela's release or the end of apartheid, is enabled by particular forms of political agency, which "Amnesty" ascribes primarily to urban, educated men, such as the activist, as well as implicitly to the urban, educated author herself, who earlier, in her essay "Living in the Interregnum" (first published in 1983), described a society that was "whirling, stamping swaying with the force of revolutionary change" (21). In an "unreading" of history in Dalit literature from India, Toral Jatin Gajarawala argues that "eventfulness" has been the purview of "a *savarna* historical consciousness" and "a nationalist historiography."[1] "Amnesty" similarly suggests that, in South Africa, a nationalist historiography centered on eventfulness has characterized the consciousness of a particular demographic. The activist in Gordimer's story is represented as fully versed in the goals of the Movement and keenly aware of the fact that in the eyes of the apartheid state the couple "haven't got a home at all": "look at this place where the white man owns the ground and lets you squat in mud and tin huts here only as long as you work for him" (254). The activist looks forward to national transformation because he has come to see his home, or, more precisely, his lack of a home, as a function of apartheid policy.

The narrator's consciousness of home and its lack is, by contrast, not shaped primarily through recourse to national politics. Certainly, the narrator recognizes the importance of the activist's work: "You do it for all our people who suffer because we haven't got money, we haven't got land" (254). Even though the narrator is marginalized from the work of national liberation, it would be inaccurate to claim that she does not look forward to the end of suffering that flows from an unjust regime. She does, however, privately question the degree to which the activist's focus on national transformation is premised upon a blinkered view of the present. Even as the activist decries the existence of a home, the narrator thinks to herself that he is "speaking of my parents', my home, the home that has been waiting for him, with his child" (254). Without denying that national laws have rendered the family legally homeless, the narrator asserts that there are ways of possessing a home that exceed legal ownership, such as daily habitation with others.

Similarly, the narrator offers a vision of dispossession that qualifies the activist's recourse to legal standing in the nation-state as the key to a desirable future. As she looks upon the valley in which she lives, the narrator is struck that the land at her feet is "the Boer's farm," but also that "that's not true, it belongs to nobody" (256). Human dwellings, she apprehends, "are nothing, on the back of this earth. It could twitch them away like a fly" (257). Her sense of ecological vulnerability is reinforced by the presence of an ominous grey cloud that is "eating the sky" (257). The cloud plausibly symbolizes an uncertain political future, but it also concretely marks the industrial pollution that threatens human and nonhuman life in the wake of accelerated modernization. A future with money and land, the narrator foresees, is no guarantee that a home will be even minimally liveable in an era of voracious ecological destruction.

In the narrator's desire for quotidian intimacy and attentiveness to ecological vulnerability, we see the degree to which national eventfulness is an inadequate lens through which to interpret her temporal experience. No national event will ease her waiting, because the vision of the present and the future propounded in national historiography does not address the complexity of the home for which she waits. Waiting is here best understood not as the anticipation of a national event that is yet to come, but an index of how such anticipation entails a narrowed account of the present—and the future. The narrator's waiting calls not for relentless work toward the achievement of the activist's national agenda, but for reflection on how that agenda has been articulated and pursued. The activist extends the promise of homeownership, but in "waiting to come back home," the narrator's home is not exclusively spatial: it is a temporality in which the fullness of the present is not overwhelmed by the necessity of realizing a singular future.

Gordimer's story provides a suggestive interpretive lens for approaching narratives of waiting in contemporary South Africa, where the provision of legal housing has been continually promised since the end of apartheid, but, as Sophie Oldfield and Saskia Greyling observe, in which this "right to access housing translates in practice" for most "to the experience of waiting."[2] At the same time, the antiapartheid movement, whose work included advocating for the right to such housing, has given way to what Asef Bayat has termed a "nonmovement," in which large numbers of citizens negotiate the paradoxical situation of waiting, sometimes for decades, for the state to grant them legal homes, while they are dwelling in informal, illegal settlements in which "waiting for state provided homes is normal, a taken-for-granted, everyday, intergenerational condition."[3] Oldfield and Greyling, synthesizing interviews with residents of Cape Town, describe the ongoing sense of impermanence experienced by those who must negotiate both an ever-changing state bureaucracy and precarious living arrangements: "Living in these uncertain situations is not *living*, interviewees explained, but merely *existing*, getting by on a day-to-day basis, unable to plan for the future, to live fulfilled lives."[4] This experience of stasis may be interpreted readily in terms of national historiography: waiting denotes how the promises of the ANC government to undo the injustices of colonialism and apartheid have yet to be fulfilled. Gordimer's story suggests another possibility: that waiting is symptomatic of how the political vision of present and future national belonging has been reduced to, and so rendered dramatically dependent on, property ownership.

This chapter examines late apartheid and postapartheid nonfiction and fiction that, like "Amnesty," have both invoked and contested the temporality of waiting. I focus especially on works in which waiting is imbricated in the anticipation of apartheid's end, whether that end is defined as the formal dissolution of the apartheid state or as the cessation of its enduring effects. Proceeding from Vincent Crapanzano's late-apartheid ethnography to Njabulo Ndebele's postapartheid writing and a consideration of what comes next, this chapter resonates with a familiar anticipatory narrative form that looks forward to a truly postapartheid national home. At the same time, I struggle against this form. My chosen works foreground how anticipatory narratives generate the time of waiting wherein the present is experienced as stasis, as simply marking time. Counteracting this stasis, the literature suggests, requires narrating time in a way that decenters national events and, indeed, the nation itself, by focusing not on a planned-for national future but on figuring out how to make sense of a complex, chaotic present. More than anticipating a future postapartheid state, these works cultivate an expanded consciousness of the present and thereby multiply possibilities for homemaking in the times and spaces that have been conceived as the nation of South Africa.

Waiting during apartheid

"Amnesty" suggests that the wait for home will continue so long as anticipation of the next national event obscures alternative narratives of the present. By 1990, the representation and critique of a nationalist historiography focused on a singular futurity was well established, perhaps most explicitly in *Waiting: The Whites of South Africa* (1985), Vincent Crapanzano's anthropological study of a South African town in the early 1980s. Crapanzano thoroughly documented and analyzed a defining feature of temporal experience during the apartheid era: "*Waiting,*" he notes, "was a constant preoccupation of the stories I had been hearing, the newspapers I was receiving, and in the literature I was reading" (43). Descriptions of the present were "repetitive, mythic, closed in on [themselves]—a series of variations on a single theme or a small group of related themes" (27). Crapanzano's account focused on detailing the ways in which apartheid policies and their material effects produced the narrative repetition that reduced the present to a time of extended waiting.

Legally precluded from working with nonwhite South Africans, Crapanzano based his analysis exclusively on interviews with white people, whose "rehearsals for the future" compulsively imagined "the day of reckoning" (214, 45). Crapanzano concluded that the "essentialist racism" that structured daily life, which prohibited "any contact with people of different races that might undermine the assumption of essential difference," diminished, for the white South African, the "possibility of a vital relationship with most of the people around" (39), which in turn generated a "primordial fear" (21). "Others" were rendered "unknown and unknowable agents of change" who were "at most the subject of the whites' frozen discourse, of their timeless representations" (41–2). White South Africans, "surrounded by servicing ghosts," waited for the changes these ghosts would enact (22). They perceived that their homes were haunted, besieged even, by "bearers of projected fear" (42), by "mythic object[s] to be feared" (xxii). This fearful waiting in turn enforced the "psycho-ontological dimensions of apartheid" (39). The complex present was "derealized" as it became oriented toward a "constricted" future (44).

Crapanzano's study foregrounded how, as the state permeated psychic life, everyday existence was consequently suffused with a sense of contingency that was both expressed and reinforced through narrative. British imperial fiction, Jed Esty argues, dehistoricized "the European subject as juvenescent" in order to reinforce a project of empire-building that was conceived as never-ending.[5] To reinforce apartheid policy, narratives of the apartheid era similarly dehistoricized the white South African, albeit as a subject who was always and forever running out of time. As J. M. Coetzee made clear in *Waiting for the Barbarians* (1980), such permanent anticipation of attack did not reflect a dramatic reality but did function to promote the state's violent dispossession of others. The "barbarians" never invade, but they are tortured because the Empire anticipates their invasion. The narrow vision of a besieged home, repeated ad nauseam by the beneficiaries of the apartheid state, supported policies that resulted in actual home invasions, forced removals, and precarious, inadequate shelters. As Derek Hook argues in a subtle reading of *Waiting*, Crapanzano's suggestion that a "primordial fear" of "others" is due to a lack of "vital relationship" enforced by segregationist policies, is in some ways a very partial explanation for the "type of deadened and deadening life" that the anthropologist describes.[6] Implicit in Crapanzano's account of narratives that look forward to a "day of reckoning," Hook contends, is a phenomenon never explicitly addressed by Crapanzano himself, namely repressed transgenerational guilt. The fantastical specter of black violence that evidences a sense of "suspended judgement" in white narratives emerges not only through segregationist policies, but also through the repressed knowledge of responsibility for the violent enforcement of those policies.[7] Waiting in fear for the future enables the denial of past and present atrocity; white supremacy awaits its own end in order to sustain its continuance.

The close association between temporal consciousness and oppression suggests the urgency of undertaking the project that Hook describes as "formulating an alternative temporal imaginary."[8] Such a project was undertaken by Crapanzano, who, to counter the temporal consciousness of overwhelming anticipation produced by apartheid, painstakingly detailed the absolute predictability and security of white South African lives. In short, he endeavored to change the temporal imaginary. The white South African experience of waiting, Crapanzano argued, "must be appreciated in all of its banality," despite and against attempts to "mask" the ordinary and "give it importance" through narratives rife with "melodramatic tension" (43–4). White waiting must be understood, not in terms of grand negotiations of "threat," but as the "very ordinary experience" of anticipating the arrival of a narrowly imagined future conceived through a radically restricted knowledge of the present (44). For Crapanzano, the proper representation of this waiting depicts its dull continuance through ignorance, rather than imagining its end. The book may be regarded as successful on this count. As J. M. Coetzee suggested in his review of *Waiting*, the ethnography, though it aspires to the form of the Bakhtinian "plurivocal novel," tends to be quite boring in its faithful transcriptions of repetitive white South African narratives.[9]

By focusing on the banality of the lives of white South Africans, Crapanzano not only offered an alternative temporal account of the present, but also provided the basis for reenvisioning the future of the state. In *Waiting*, the end of apartheid is not defined exclusively by a singular political event but by the innumerable quotidian, subjective events that would inaugurate the end of racist segregation and, implicitly, the repression of ongoing histories of violence and their psychological effects. If the endurance of the time of waiting, Crapanzano contended, depended upon "[t]he failure [of white South Africans] to give conceptual and emotional as well as legal and political recognition to South Africa's majority population" (41), then its end will require the "real recognition of the other" that designates openness "to the complex and never very certain reality" of the present (xxii). Hook allows us to add that it will also require the recognition of the self's repressed guilt that indexes how violent histories persist. As "Amnesty" also suggests, the end of apartheid will be measured not only by legal and political recognition: it will also require that intimate experiences of temporality be transformed.

Waiting after apartheid

The degree to which such transformation has been achieved in postapartheid South Africa is a question that Njabulo Ndebele considers in his 2010 essay "Arriving Home?: South Africa Beyond Transition and Reconciliation," which describes the continuance of a national consciousness that dwells in the suspended time of waiting. Ndebele's analysis suggests a significant split between the degree to which a politics of legal recognition has been realized and the degree to which this recognition has led to a temporal consciousness in which the complexities of the present are fully acknowledged. On the one hand, Ndebele stresses that the political and legal recognition of the majority of the population has indeed resulted in "transformative change." After the formal end of apartheid, "the achievements of the new democratic state were spectacular," and "no area of national life was untouched by new policy: education, tax, housing, health, defense, water, energy, justice, policing, budgeting and others."[10]

On the other hand, Ndebele argues, South Africans had yet to arrive home, in part because the anticipation of future national transformation continues to dominate national narratives of present reality. Openness to alternative narratives of the present have proven elusive, a reading supported by newspaper headlines that regularly declare that South Africans are "waiting" for the government to provide land reform, HIV treatment, and housing.[11] Ndebele characterizes the resultant post-transition politics in terms of deferral and the risk of "inertia": "The masses that marched for freedom in huge numbers over the decades then began to wait for 'redress,' for the benefits of 'affirmative action,' 'black economic empowerment' and, the biggest manna of all, the dream of 'delivery.'"[12] Ndebele goes on to contend that many members of the black elite continue to wait for "whites" to "deliver" to "blacks," in the process downplaying the elite's potential "to induce such delivery."[13] Ndebele does not address white elites directly, but as the predictions of "racial apocalypse" issued in anticipation of Nelson Mandela's death make clear, many white South Africans continue to wait in fear. As Hook contends, "The 'futurity' of Crapanzano's account, and the anxious interchange of an unstable present and an unknown future, could be said to pertain in many ways as much to the contemporary post-apartheid as to the late apartheid context."[14] In an argument that recalls apartheid-era reflections on the temporality of waiting, Ndebele contends that waiting upon external agents for change is among "the postures of a politics habituated by struggle." He concludes that "the strategic mistake is continuing to identify the problems 'out there.'"[15] As Gordimer's novella "Something Out There" (1984) repeatedly intimates, public invocations during apartheid of "somewhere else" (or "something" else) functioned to conceal the "real intimacy" that is "latent" in perceived difference.[16] Ndebele highlights that such concealment persists in contemporary discourses that defer political agency to an apparent other.

To some degree, the claim is startling in an era of accelerated globalization during which "out there" seems to increasingly influence the fate of South

Africans. The emergence of "private indirect government" across the African continent was identified by Achille Mbembe in *On the Postcolony*: "It has not been sufficiently stressed … that one major political event of the last quarter of the twentieth century was the crumbling of African states' independence and sovereignty and the (surreptitious) placing of these states under the tutelage of international creditors."[17] As Jonny Steinberg has argued more recently, the South African government surely waits upon multinational corporations, international markets, and transnational governing bodies.[18] That globalized capital affects not just the capacities of states, but also of individuals, to enact change has been emphasized by Eric Cazdyn, who proposes that global capitalism presents itself as that which must be extended into the future in order to manage the perpetual crises it generates. To this extent, we all live "in the meantime."[19] The pressure of international capital, in other words, certainly affects the state's capacity and willingness to deliver on promised rights, as well as individuals' capacities to claim them.

Kristen Kornienko provides a concrete example of these effects in her account of working with residents of Makause and Harry Gwala, two informal settlements in Ekurhuleni. In South Africa, the right to housing is guaranteed in the Bill of Rights (1996) and the Housing Act of 1997. In interviews from 2008 to 2010, however, residents in Makause and Harry Gwala continued to advocate for, but increasingly despaired of, the administration of "basic dignified service provision and tenure security." These rights were denied, Kornienko suggests, due to "a lack of political will ensuing from capital-driven agendas that render the formal city blind" to the "state of waiting and unfulfilled promises" faced by the urban poor.[20] Internationally backed neoliberal development agendas "continue to undermine the need-based policies of the early post-apartheid years."[21] In a global political economy that does not prioritize the alleviation of ongoing poverty and the reduction of high unemployment rates, options for achieving housing by other means are limited, and, as Oldfield and Greyling aver, "putting yourself on the housing list remains the most likely route to obtain a formal house in the future."[22] Although over three million units of low-income housing have been made available by the postapartheid state to date, demand continues to exceed supply.[23] Of the state-subsidized housing that has been provided, "15.9% households were reported to have weak or very weak walls while 15.3% reported the same for their roofs."[24] Waiting is not a sign of passivity and impotence in contemporary South Africa, but it is a marker of a "constrained form of agency."[25] Given such constraints, it seems reasonable to ask how we *cannot* continue to identify the problems "out there."

Ndebele's project seems to be not to deny that such problems exist, but to insist that the repetitive identification of them does little to produce creative solutions. Other narratives of contemporary South African history are required. In the First Steve Biko Memorial Lecture, "'Iph' Indlela? Finding Our Way into the Future," delivered in 2000, Ndebele acknowledges the sway of global capital on the South African state, linking it to ongoing racialized, neocolonial histories:

> from a black perspective, whatever the economic merits of the case, it is difficult not to see the transfer of capital to big western stock exchanges as "whiteness" delinking itself from the mire of its South African history, to explore opportunities of disengagement, where the home base is transformed into a satellite market revolving around powerful Western economies, to become a market to be exploited rather than a home to be served.[26]

Ndebele also, however, makes a point that he would reiterate in "Arriving Home?": "I am bothered by the phenomenon of a black majority in power, seeming to reduce itself to the status of complainants as if they had a limited capacity to do anything more significant about the situation at hand, than drawing attention to it."[27] The claim reprises Ndebele's call, in his essay "Redefining Relevance," that we must recognize "the oppressed, in the first instance, as makers of the future."[28] Ndebele's recurrent argument is that certain forms of anticipating emancipation, whether from apartheid or a neoliberal global economic order, may in fact work against its achievement.

Rather than reading postures of waiting as signaling the need for ongoing national or global transformation, then, we might reflect on the limitations of how the terms of such transformations are being imagined in order to critique moments in which narratives of anticipation reinforce, rather than challenge, the constraining of state and individual agency intrinsic to global neoliberalism. Narratives of national deliverance and global capitalism are but two alternatives for making sense of the "immense confusion" and "turbulent sea of events" that Ndebele perceives in contemporary South Africa.[29] As such, Ndebele engages with the idea that the stasis of waiting might be more effectively (en)countered in registers other than the national and global, and, indeed, the prospective: he asks what possibilities attend further "breaking down 'the nation'" as it is.[30] In this, Ndebele's project resonates with Crapanzano's *Waiting*, which pointed toward the transformation of quotidian relationships with the self and others as key to breaking down apartheid. At the same time, it is distinctive. While Crapanzano asserted the bathos of white waiting in the late apartheid moment as a necessary basis for challenging a compulsive and narrow vision of the future, his work stopped short of detailing the future temporal alternative for which it called. Ndebele, in contrast, directly engages with how writing may give form to temporal imaginaries, distinctive from (if conterminous with) the experiences of waiting prominent in narratives of South African national history and global capitalism alike.

Penelope's descendants

While this engagement is evident in the nonfiction essays already discussed, it is most fully realized in Ndebele's fictional *The Cry of Winnie Mandela* (2003), in which the narrative arc itself loosens without transcending the temporality of waiting. The work begins with "the blurb of an imaginary book" that "tells the stories of four unknown women, and that of South Africa's most famous woman, who waited" (1). These women are conflated into one woman in the "blurb," as the "woman who has seen all kinds of departures, has endured the uncertainties of waiting, and has hoped for the return of her man. Departure, waiting, and return: they define her experience of the past, present, and future. They frame her life at the center of a great South African story not yet told" (1). This passage imagines the book that could have been written: one in which women's waiting is rendered part of a national narrative, as part of a "great South African story" that highlights women's participation in the anticipation of transformative national events.

Yet, this book remains "imaginary" because the blurb does not describe *The Cry of Winnie Mandela*, at least not when the fiction is read as a whole. Certainly, Part One offers the stories of four women from across South Africa who, recalling Gordimer's narrator, wait as their husbands leave to work in the mines, to study abroad, to work for the movement, or to "sleep around" (36). As Part Two of the fiction will register explicitly, there is "something generic" about the women as they are described in the first half of the text (39). What is generic, specifically, is the way in which the women's stories fit neatly into a nationalist historiography that represents women as those who waited for the end of apartheid. The women are presented as "Penelope's Descendants," that is, as inheritors of the Homeric myth that renders women besieged, suffering, loyal, and chaste. Their personal lives, like Penelope's, are only narrated insofar as they have been affected by or intersect with national politics, which is indexed by men leaving the home to pursue work in the city, education abroad, and national liberation at home.

These narratives of women who wait serve primarily to foreground the intimate, disruptive effects of apartheid. Part Two of *The Cry of Winnie Mandela* suggests that the nationalist historiography of women-in-waiting has been put forward in Part One only so it can be challenged. Ndebele imagines in this section of the work that the four "descendants" have formed an *ibandla labafazi abalindile*, a gathering of waiting women. In this *ibandla*, the four women invite Winnie Mandela "into [their] membership and make her the fifth woman-in-waiting in this room" (46). As each woman addresses Winnie Mandela, she reveals events, desires, and beliefs that have thus far been omitted from "the book that created us" (95). As Winnie addresses the women in turn, the work envisions her not as a public figure, but as a woman who, like the other characters, has lived a life that exceeds the contours assigned to it within national historiographies.[31] Winnie suggests that she is "what politics made me," even as "[w]hat politics made me is not me" (136). As Dirk Klopper argues in his reading of Madikizela-Mandela's testimony before the Truth and Reconciliation Commission, the African National Congress has made Winnie into a deceptive "renegade narcissist" in order to disavow its own fragmentation, as well as its disempowerment of those revolutionary "others" who have been excluded from political and economic power.[32] Ndebele's fiction insists on the partialness of narratives that figure Winnie's life as symbolic of wider national events. Her life requires that the generic stories of apartheid struggle and reconciliation, which together comprise "the great South African story," be broken down.

The result, in Part Two, is a series of narratives that dwell not so much on national events but on peculiar specificities. Each woman is no longer more or less interchangeable with the next, but is introduced by name. The stories of the first, second, and fourth descendants, which are presented in third person in Part One, are related in first person in Part Two. In the exceptional case of the third descendent, Mamello Molete, who is self-professedly "insane" in Part One, the narrative mode remains in first person; Mamello's address to Winnie Mandela in Part Two, however, includes a degree of self-reflection that the more generic story of "insanity" disallows (34). In all cases, as each woman narrates her own story in Part Two, she emphasizes how her life of waiting has exceeded that which is accepted and reiterated within the national imaginary. The women, including Winnie Mandela, reflect on the role of waiting that has been assigned to them in Part One, and how they have lived, embraced, challenged, dismissed, and lived outside that role.

The challenge to a narrative of paralyzed anticipation results in significant differences between the fiction's two main sections. In Part One, for example, the third-person narrator records how the "first descendant," 'Mannete Mofolo, waited for her husband, Lejone, who left their home in Lesotho to work as a miner in

Gauteng. (From the first, Ndebele's "great South African story" is not circumscribed by political borders.) Lejone's visits home become increasingly infrequent, even as he comes to sound and look "definitively urban" (13). Eventually, his visits stop altogether: "what happens to her from now on is one of the great South African stories," in which "she waits" (15). In Part Two, 'Mannete acknowledges that "we've all been profiled in the book that created us," but continues: "I do want to add a few things, though" (95). These few things include how she eventually ceased to wonder about Lejone and, finally, guided by her Christian faith, stopped lying to her children that he was still in touch. She reveals that she no longer feels "obligation" toward her husband, but "serene detachment," an attitude reflected in the fact that Lejone goes unnamed in this section (98). Rather than contemplating the changes that her husband has undergone in their time apart, 'Mannete only imagines how, if he were to return, he would have to reckon with the many changes in her own life. She has "built with my children a new home" (101). Her shop has become so successful that a village bus stop carries her name; several of her children have become professionals in South Africa. 'Mannete's life is inadequately captured through recourse to the temporality of "debilitating" waiting that contributes to "enormous social tensions" (15), as described in the first section, because she has been making her name "become part of the world" (100). Certainly, in Part Two as in Part One, narration proceeds in what David Medalie has described as "anti-realist" and "ostentatiously declamatory and self-conscious rhetoric."[33] The narrative does not move toward a more "realistic" representation of its characters. It does, however, contemplate narrative itself, progressively foregrounding how the narration of individual lives may be contemporaneous with, but not reducible to, a historiography of national eventfulness.

In *The Cry of Winnie Mandela*, reflection on and revision of received narratives of how women have waited promises to nuance generic understandings of South African women's lives in relation to national history and, in so doing, to reenvision the relation of national history to the present. Homi Bhabha's *The Location of Culture* (1994) proposed that feminist literature can reveal the "unhomely" or "unhomed" condition of colonial and postcolonial society by "redrawing the domestic space as the space … of modern power and police: the personal-*is*-the-political; the world-*in*-the-home."[34] Ndebele's fiction, written almost a decade later, does something quite different: it insists that the personal is not only political, and that feminist literature can reveal a home-despite-the-world. This insistence by no means implies that Ndebele's work ascribes women's lives to a private and secluded domestic sphere. Rather, the fiction considers that these lives have always been subject to narration. The featureless "room" in which the *ibandla* gathers is nowhere so much as the narrative space of the fiction itself, which is both private (to the solitary writer and reader) *and* public (as it is discussed by multiple readers). Ndebele's fiction writes against the myth of waiting women not so much by revealing how the domestic registers the violence of a racist state (although it undeniably does) but by challenging the ease with which women are relegated to the space of domesticity and thereby co-opted into national historiographies.

By reflecting on nationalist narratives and imaginatively retelling them, *The Cry of Winnie Mandela* offers not only an alternative account of the past and present, but also of the future. The final section of the book, "A Stranger," imagines the women of the *ibandla* on a road trip to Durban, traveling in a Volkswagen Caravelle with plenty of snacks. This puzzling and delightful vignette—they have "just left the M2 to merge onto the N3 heading east" (139)—is the first to imagine the women together in a particular place. It is also the first section of *Cry* to place the women outside of a specific time. Whereas Part One describes lives during apartheid and Part Two describes reflections on those lives, Part Three takes place in some unspecified time after Part Two. The timelessness of the journey is highlighted by the appearance of Penelope, who appears on the side of the road as a hitchhiker.

It is on a South African road, perhaps in the near future, that Ndebele's book envisions Winnie Mandela and her fellow women-in-waiting as "here now, to stay. At home" (138). This claim to home is as delinked from property ownership as it is from the nation-state and its history of anticipating transformation. The realized "home" does not depend upon the emergence of national (or international) justice, but rather, in Penelope's words, on "affirming new ways of experiencing relationships wherever they emerge" (146).[35] The new ways of experiencing relationships that are forged in the fiction, and perhaps through its reading, are those that exceed the relationships established within nationalist, anticipatory narratives. Penelope's arrival signals liberation from the same old stories: "My journey follows the path of the unfolding spirit of the world as its consciousness increases; as the world learns to become more aware of me not as Odysseus's moral ornament on the mantelpiece, but as an essential ingredient in the definition of human freedom" (145). The fiction itself performs the "increasing consciousness" that prompts the rewriting of a nationalist, masculinist myth that centers on the anticipation of the next big event to one that foregrounds the ongoing contemporaneity of being "fellow travelers in history" (138).

Notably, the resultant sense of contemporaneity is one that contrasts to the anticipatory solidarity of political struggle represented in the antiapartheid era, as well as to the dissociated, individual anxiety of nonmovements represented in the postapartheid present. Not all of the women have ceased to wait, but the retelling of their stories has allowed them to confirm that they are not only waiting. Consequently, the final affective temporal structure of Ndebele's fiction is on par with a temporal experience that multiple characters describe as "mellowness" (49). This mellowness includes "a quality of acceptance. Of moving on without having to respond to blame or any need for self-justification" (59). The "mellow drama" of the fiction brings the women into relationship with each other, without requiring that that relationship take a particular form, be it of judgment, forgiveness, or guilt, for the sake of an anticipated future. "Home" is arrived at through the cultivation of present relationships that are premised, not only on national historical narratives, but also (or instead) on points of connection as random and contingent as those established by the literary encounters the fiction relates. Delisiwe Dulcie S'khosana, for example, has recognized in Madikizela-Mandela's story not only the story of a woman waiting for Mandela's release, but also a story of a woman struggling with "the confusions and banalities of desire" (52). As Mammello takes up Tsitsi Dangarembga's *Nervous Conditions* in the Caravelle, her act promises that the emergence of new forms of relationships will continue, in this case through an encounter with literature set outside of South African borders that is by no means only resonant with the time and place of its setting. In *The Cry of Winnie Mandela*, not much happens, save the reading and retelling of stories, but the work of reading and retelling promises the liberation of the present from the paralysis engendered by constantly anticipating an always deferred future. As Ndebele suggests in the inaugural Steve Biko Memorial Lecture, it would be a mistake to assume that working through existing institutions is necessarily the most effective means to ensure the realization of imagined future. It may be the case, Ndebele contends, that the "search in the realm of consciousness" for "emerging tendencies" may "provide an explanatory context" that will open up room for "new, innovative solutions."[36] It is possible, in short, that changes in consciousness, pursued through the work of reading and writing, will point to paths for real change within organizational structures rather than the other way around.

To this end, it is interesting how the "emerging tendencies" in *The Cry of Winnie Mandela* include not only an experience of "mellow" time but also the material circumstances necessary to support this temporality, including, for example, access to good books and the means to take a vacation. Self-evidently, such circumstances are far from realized in contemporary South Africa. What Ndebele might call the "evoked realities" in the country are of a racist and classist literary culture, high unemployment and poverty, and a tourism industry dominated by wealthy Americans and Europeans.[37] These realities, however, do not discount the contemporaneous existence of what Ndebele refers to in his nonfiction as "emergent phenomena." Such phenomena, Ndebele's fiction suggests, include the means for leisure, the desire to access costly cultural goods such as novels, and the freedom of movement that readily facilitates domestic tourism. In *The Cry of Winnie Mandela*, Winnie Mandela herself embodies these phenomena: even during apartheid, when "tourism is something white people did" (83) and "very few women, especially African women, were to be seen in the driver's seat," Winnie, having ignored Nelson Mandela's instructions during a driving lesson, becomes for one afternoon the "queen of the highways" (115–16). In the postapartheid era, she is chauffeured around in a Mercedes Benz (113). In the imagined future of the Volkswagon Caravelle, she travels with women who are not members of the economic and political elite and passes around her stylish designer sunglasses. In the last instance, she evokes the reality that leisure, wealth, and freedom may be equitably shared.

The Cry of Winnie Mandela highlights that there are present needs, desires, and trends that have not been foregrounded in national narratives, and it raises the possibility that attentiveness to these realities may expand our sense of future possibilities. Notably, the emergent "home" that Ndebele imagines is not one that depends exclusively on state support, although it could certainly be supported (or thwarted) by state policies. Rather, the project of cultivating an emergent, mellow temporality implicates a range of individuals and institutions, from artists and *ibandlas* to publishers and readers to employers, universities, and rental car companies. Rather than waiting together for a global economic system that facilitates the state's delivery of services, we might ask what present realities, including present responsibilities, are occluded in the narrative that postpones home through its narrow definition of what constitutes a "home." In asking such questions, Ndebele's fiction reworks what might be described as a Bakhtinian chronotope of late and postapartheid fiction, or "the intrinsic connectedness of temporal and spatial relationships that are artistically expressed in literature" of those periods.[38] Instead of waiting in or for the legally recognized home, mellow reflection is possible in a home that is represented capaciously as shared space, crisscrossed by a myriad of relationships made depthless by a generic form characterized by imaginative revision.

In "Arriving Home?" Ndebele explicitly examines the relationships that have been recognized and unrecognized in postapartheid South Africa's housing policies. Once again, he suggests that consciousness of the complexity of connections that exist in the present is key to resisting stasis. The provision of housing, Ndebele argues, has not in fact substantially transformed the extractive nature of "dormitory settlements" under apartheid, which were designed so that people would be compelled to invest their labor and creativity in places other than their own neighborhoods: "The statistically successful provision of houses has not extended the horizons of social imagination. When we built houses, we forgot that the building of houses should have been more about building communities" (3). What "has to be broken" is a sense of "permanence": that people must always "export their energies and talents" to elsewhere than where they live (4). What has to be broken, in other words, is the temporality of waiting, during which home remains a promise for the future. Residents of townships do not relate to each other only as fellow citizens of South Africa. There is "strong social bonding among residents living in clusters of about three township streets." There are "numerous forms of social activity," ranging from self-help groups to taxi associations to football clubs, that "have the potential to be organizing principles for the establishment of a complex of institution[s] designed to meet equally complex sets of community needs" (3). A community with its own integrated tax base, in short, would be better equipped to respond to housing needs. Ndebele does not call for an organized movement to demand faster, better housing from the state. He calls for the support and development of community-based institutions that would reconstitute the state.

Ndebele's fiction and nonfiction evidences how creative narratives about the complex present hold the potential to reorient temporal consciousness, such that an experience of waiting gives way to a sense of an actionable present. Importantly, Ndebele highlights that the narratives he offers are by no means authoritative or final. *The Cry of Winnie Mandela* self-reflexively signals that the account of waiting women it offers, wherein women have never only been waiting, must be subject to further retelling. Its evermore nuanced sketch of characters necessarily fails to engender "fully-fledged beings" (39). Winnie concludes her address to the *ibandla*: "If this imaginary book in which we are characters ever gets published, please send me a copy" (138). The book is "imaginary" in this instance because it presents "characters" only, highlighting that increasing consciousness is not a matter of apprehending how things should be but of articulating how they are. In this instance, life, as Judith Butler suggests, "might be understood as precisely that which exceeds any account we may try to give of it."[39] The point is made explicitly in "Iph' Indlela?," in which Ndebele suggests that writing is "a supreme effort at finding your way through immense confusion" but maintains that his effort to identify trends and to make sense of a chaotic present is by no means the "one, single definitive way" (43, 53). Ndebele's work highlights the potential of writing to reaffirm or diverge from dominate temporal narratives. In the specific context of contemporary South Africa, it calls for a form of reading and writing that eschews the anticipatory drive of nationalist historiography and instead contemplates, in some mellowness, the complexities of the present.

Why wait?

By way of conclusion, I consider, through a reading of "Afritude Sauce," a section in Ivan Vladislavić's 2004 linked-narrative collection *The Exploded View*, how this mellow mode of reading and writing might be translated specifically as a method of criticism, of writing about reading. The story is focalized through Egan, a white sanitary engineer who takes a business trip that includes a visit to a Reconstruction and Development (RDP) housing project that he has helped to design. At Hani View, whose very name emphasizes national history and its prospects, Egan notes the surrounding informal settlement that "sprang up overnight," and whose residents travel to the formal municipality for health care and schooling (59). Egan's tour of the new housing project reveals major structural flaws, from too-high manholes to giant cracks in the wall. Egan himself is anxious, defensive, and racist, always vaguely expectant that he will be held personally and violently responsible for the shabby construction. In short, the story may be read as suffused with waiting. Those denied homes under apartheid continue to wait for decent housing, even as Egan believes "that's hardly my fault" (59); Egan continues to wait for a day of reckoning, even as he knows nothing of the people whom he fears beyond stereotypes and conjecture. The story, in this reading, becomes a cautionary tale of how the "new South Africa" remains caught in the temporality of apartheid and the structures that support it.[40]

Ndebele's work, however, suggests an alternative interpretation of the story, which Vladislavić's subtly ironic writing bears. Rather than apprehending a tale of ongoing stasis and entrapment, featuring a protagonist paralyzed by the prospect of future revolution, we might attend to how the story registers a present that cannot adequately be interpreted through the lens of a national historiography centered on apartheid and its end. Such a rereading (or retelling) of "Afritude Sauce" foregrounds the many ways in which no one is waiting for Egan at all, despite his sense that "everyone assumed he was collecting complaints" (61). In fact, at Hani View, Egan stands in for little more than a prop (with sewage expertise) who has been co-opted into a political publicity event he does not fully understand. His actions are coordinated by other stakeholders: Milton Mazibuko, a council official in charge of housing subsidies, two officials from the Residents' Association, a resident named Mrs. Ntlaka, and an unidentified photographer. One might further note that Egan's isolation from these stakeholders need not be traced back exclusively to the enforced segregation of apartheid. Egan also remains clueless at Hani View, as he will remain clueless later at dinner, because of the banal fact that he has not bothered to learn the language he only knows as "Sotho," which is one of the preferred languages of his costumers and business associates.

In this telling, South Africans are by no means waiting upon white recognition and its associated capital and technical expertise. Indeed, as Mrs. Ntlaka poses for the photographer on her toilet seat, which has been installed so high that there is a "marvelous gap" between her shoes and the floor, she is committed to showing the world exactly how "fucked" the situation is (66–7). Her demand for a house that will better accommodate herself and her furniture could not be more different from the introspective contemplation of Gordimer's narrator in "Amnesty," and it is resonate with the "empowering hope derived from action" that Kornienko finds among residents of Harry Gwala and Makause, who are "not waiting."[41] These narratives point toward yet another emergent trend in South Africa, one that Ndebele, citing Muzi Kuzwayo, discusses in "'Iph' Indlela?": "the economic future of this country lies with blacks."[42] It is a future that Egan, in the midst of desiring and resisting "reconciliation" after apartheid, may abet, shape, thwart, exploit, deny, or simply fail to see. It is a future that is not guaranteed to arrive and that may perpetuate, accelerate, or transform global neoliberalism. It is a future, however, that is waiting for no one.

Notes

1 Gajarawala, "Some Time between Revisionist and Revolutionary," 578.
2 Oldfield and Greyling, "Waiting for the State," 1101.
3 Ibid., 1100. Statistics South Africa's 2013 *General Household Survey* states that 13.6 percent of South African households lived in informal dwellings (33).
4 Oldfield and Greyling, "Waiting for the State," 1103. Emphasis added.
5 Esty, *Unseasonable Youth*, 16.
6 Hook, "Petrified Life," 448.
7 Ibid., 453.
8 Ibid., 447.
9 Crapanzano, *Waiting*, xiii; Coetzee, "Listening to the Afrikaners," A3.

10 Ndebele, "Arriving Home?" 1, 10.

11 Ibid., 1. On waiting and land reform, see "Waiting for the Green Revolution"; on waiting and HIV treatment, see Matsolo, "HIV Patients Still Waiting for Easier-to-Take Drugs"; on waiting and housing, see Qabaka, "Housing in Post-Apartheid South Africa: Challenge or Opportunity?"

12 Ndebele, "Arriving Home?," 7, 10.

13 Ibid., 7.

14 Hook, "Petrified Life," 455.

15 Ndebele, "Arriving Home?," 13, 9.

16 Gordimer, "Something Out There," 118–92.

17 Mbembe, *On the Postcolony*, 73–4.

18 Steinberg, "Julius Malema: The Man Who Scarred South Africa," para. 34.

19 Cazdyn, *The Already Dead*, 11.

20 Kornienko, "Waiting, Hope, Democracy, and Space," 40.

21 Ibid., 47.

22 Oldfield and Greyling, "Waiting for the State," 1107.

23 Ibid., 3.

24 Statistics South Africa, *General Household Survey*, 37.

25 Oldfield and Greyling, "Waiting for the State," 1108.

26 Ndebele, "'Iph' Indlela," 52.

27 Ibid., 42.

28 Ndebele, *South African Literature and Culture*, 73.

29 Ndebele, "'Iph' Indlela," 44.

30 Ndebele, "Arriving Home," 10.

31 As a public figure, Madikizela-Mandela has been alternately upheld as the "mother of the nation" and derided as a "corrupt matriarch." For a concise overview of Madikizela-Mandela's public life, with an emphasis on its coverage by members of the US press, see Horwitz and Squires, "We Are What We Pretend to Be," 66–90.

32 Klopper, "Narrative Time and the Space of the Image," 472.

33 Medalie, "*The Cry of Winnie Mandela*", 57.

34 Bhabha, *The Location of Culture*, 15.

35 Ndebele might be included among those thinkers, such as Achille Mbembe, Sarah Nuttall, and Paul Gilroy, whom Ronit Frenkel and Craig MacKenzie (following Isabel Hofmeyer) suggest are "post-resistance," insofar as they "provide the space to reconsider difference as normative to South African cultural life, looking rather to the ambiguities and uncertainties that make a complex post-transitional present" (6). See Frenkel and MacKenzie, "Conceptualizing 'Post-Transitional' South African Literature in English," 1–10.

36 Ndebele, "'Iph' Indlela," 45.

37 Ibid., 49.

38 Bakhtin, *The Dialogic Imagination*, 84.

39   Butler, *Giving an Account of Oneself*, 43.

40   Shameem Black offers a reading of "Afritude Sauce" that suggests the story gives credence to Egan's fear of "the threat of violence": "Egan is helping to construct a system that ultimately will require his own disposal" (15). See "Fictions of Rebuilding," 13–16.

41   Kornienko, "Waiting, Hope, Democracy, and Space," 47.

42   Ndebele, "'Iph' Indlela," 40.

Works Cited

Bakhtin, Mikhail. *The Dialogic Imagination: Four Essays*. Trans. Caryl Emerson and Michael Holquist. Austin: University of Texas Press, 1981.

Bhabha, Homi. *The Location of Culture*. New York: Routledge, 1994.

Black, Shameem. "Fictions of Rebuilding: Reconstruction in Ivan Vladislavić's South Africa." *ARIEL* 39.4 (2008): 5–30.

Butler, Judith. *Giving an Account of Oneself*. New York: Fordham University Press, 2005.

Cazdyn, Eric. *The Already Dead*. Durham, NC: Duke University Press, 2012.

Coetzee, J. M. "Listening to the Afrikaners." Review of *Waiting*, by Vincent Crapanzano. *New York Times*, 14 April 1985.

Coetzee, J. M. *Waiting for the Barbarians*. 1980. New York: Vintage, 2000.

Crapanzano, Vincent. *Waiting: The Whites of South Africa*. New York: Vintage Books, 1986.

Esty, Jed. *Unseasonable Youth: Modernism, Colonialism, and the Fiction of Development*. Oxford: Oxford University Press, 2012.

Frenkel, Ronit and Craig MacKenzie. "Conceptualizing 'Post-Transitional' South African Literature in English." *English Studies in Africa* 53.1 (2010): 1–10.

Gajarawala, Toral Jatin. "Some Time between Revisionist and Revolutionary: Unreading History in Dalit Literature." *PMLA* 126.3 (2011): 575–91.

Gordimer, Nadine. "Amnesty." In *Jump and Other Stories*. London: Penguin, 1991. 247–57.

Gordimer, Nadine, "Living in the Interregnum." *New York Review of Books*, January 20, 1983: 21–29.

Gordimer, Nadine. "Something Out There." *Salmagundi* 62 (1984): 118–92.

Hook, Derek. "Petrified Life." *Social Dynamics* 41.3 (2015): 438–60.

Horwitz, Linda Diane and Catherine R. Squires. "We Are What We Pretend to Be: The Cautionary Tale of Reading Winnie Mandela as a Rhetorical Widow." *Meridians* 11.1 (2011): 66–90.

Klopper, Dirk. "Narrative Time and the Space of the Image: The Truth of the Lie in Winnie Madikizela-Mandela's Testimony before the Truth and Reconciliation Commission." *Poetics Today* 22.2 (2001): 453–74.

Kornienko, Kristen. "Waiting, Hope, Democracy, and Space: How Expectations and Socio-economic Rights Shape Two South African Urban Informal Communities." *Journal of Asian and African Studies* 52.1 (2017): 34–49.

Krog, Antjie. *A Change of Tongue*. Johannesburg: Random House, 2003.

Matsolo, Mary-Jane. "HIV Patients Still Waiting for Easier-to-Take Drugs." *GroundUp*, April 10, 2013. https://www.groundup.org.za/article/hiv-patients-still-waiting-easier-take-drugs_895/.

Mbembe, Achille. *On the Postcolony*. Berkeley: University of California Press, 2001.

Medalie, David. "*The Cry of Winnie Mandela*: Njabulo Ndebele's Post-Apartheid Novel." *English Studies in Africa* 49.2 (2006): 51–65.

Ndebele, Njabulo S. "Arriving Home?: South Africa beyond Transition and Reconciliation." In *In the Balance: South Africans Debate Reconciliation*. Eds. Fanie Du Toit and Erik Doxtader. Johannesburg: Jacana Media, 2010. 1–13.

Ndebele, Njabulo S. "'Iph'Indlela? Finding Our Way into the Future'—The First Steve Biko Memorial Lecture." *Social Dynamics: A Journal of African Studies* 26.1 (2000): 43–55.

Ndebele, Njabulo S. *South African Literature and Culture: Rediscovery of the Ordinary*. Manchester: Manchester University Press, 1994.

Ndebele, Njabulo S. *The Cry of Winnie Mandela*. Banbury: Ayebia Clarke Publishing Limited, 2003.

Oldfield, Sophie and Saskia Greyling. "Waiting for the State: A Politics of Housing in South Africa." *Environment and Planning A* 47.5 (2015): 1100–12.

Qabaka, Vuyisa. "Housing in Post-Apartheid South Africa: Challenge or Opportunity?" *Future Cape Town*, January 3, 2013. http://futurecapetown.com/2013/01/housing-in-post-apartheid-south-africa-challenge-or-opportunity/#.WwWZnSBOlPY.

Statistics South Africa. *General Household Survey, 2013*. Pretoria: Statistics South Africa, 2014. https://www.statssa.gov.za/publications/P0318/P03182013.pdf.

Steinberg, Jonny. "Julius Malema: The Man Who Scarred South Africa." *The Guardian*, February 10, 2012. https://www.theguardian.com/world/2012/feb/10/julius-malema-south-africa-anc.

Vladislavić, Ivan. "Afritude Sauce." In *The Exploded View*. Johannesburg: Random House, 2004. 48–98.

"Waiting for the Green Revolution: Land Reform in South Africa." Africa Research Institute, May 29, 2013. https://www.africaresearchinstitute.org/newsite/publications/waiting-for-the-green-revolution-land-reform-in-south-africa.

5

Precarious Time and the Aesthetics of Community

Sarah Lincoln

In his 2000 inaugural Steve Biko Memorial Lecture at the University of Cape Town, entitled "Iph'Indlela? Finding Our Way into the Future," Njabulo Ndebele considers what he sees as some of the obstacles preventing the full realization of nonracial democracy and economic development in South Africa. Beginning with a description of some "random" events from the preceding transitional decade, including the rise of HIV/AIDS, witch burnings, assassinations, vigilante violence, and the Truth and Reconciliation Commission, Ndebele highlights the various vulnerabilities to which black bodies continue to be subject. He notes also the ambivalence of white South Africans, caught between their longing for "rootedness" and the "white flight" galvanized by their furious defense of their ongoing privilege.[1] In accounting for this contradictory desire, Ndebele takes the "naked, manacled and lonely body of Steve Biko" as an exemplary figure for the precariousness of the black subject under apartheid and for the failure of sympathetic imagination that left white South Africans "cold" to the suffering of their compatriots:[2]

> At this point, the treatment of black people ceases to be a moral concern. Speaking harshly to a black person; stamping with both feet on the head or chest of a black body; roasting a black body over flames to obliterate evidence of murder (not because murder was wrong, but because it was an irritating embarrassment); dismembering the black body by tying wire round its ankles and dragging it behind a bakkie; whipping black school children … these are things one who is white, in South Africa, can do from time to time to black bodies, in the total scheme of things.[3]

The speaker's repetitive grammatical reliance on the present continuous tense ("speaking harshly," "stamping"), and on the contingent temporality of "from time to time," emphasizes the instability and unpredictability of life and death for apartheid's subjects and thus the wildly divergent ways in which time itself was experienced by blacks and whites under the system of racial discrimination and its various regimes of what Achille Mbembe has termed "superfluity."[4] In the aftermath of apartheid, the question of "finding our way into the future" demands a renewed attention to the time frame of lives lived in common, and Ndebele proposes that this collective, democratic future may in fact emerge quite apart from the question of individual life or vitality. Conceiving of a future in community, rather than in (personal or racial) isolation, may entail, he suggests, an acceptance of the potential for harm, injury, or being "undone," in one way or another, by the presence of the other. If times of transition are always implicitly invested in futurity, as Katherine Hallemeier's deft analysis of "waiting" in this volume suggests, the vulnerabilities that attend embodied life and that underpin ethical relation signal a different temporal orientation, one in which the future is neither secure nor predictable, but rather contingent, terminal, and necessarily improvisational. In this respect, amid the exuberant vernal rhetoric that attends it, South Africa's transition also exemplifies the "autumnal" structures of feeling Rita Barnard identifies, in the introduction to this volume, as characteristic of global modernity (8–9).

Ndebele shares Barnard's emphasis on transition as a *practice*, rather than as temporal marker. He concludes his lecture with a striking call for whites to accede to vulnerability as a basis for finding themselves "at home" and claiming a part, however contingent, in the future of the country:

> An historic opportunity has arisen now for white South Africa to participate in a humanistic revival of our country through a readiness to participate in the process of redress and reconciliation.....We are all familiar with the global sanctity of the white body.....The white body is inviolable, and that inviolability is in direct proportion to the global vulnerability of the black body. [...I]f South African whiteness is a beneficiary of the protectiveness assured by international whiteness, it has an opportunity to write a new chapter in world history. It will have to come out from under the umbrella and repudiate it. *Putting itself at risk, it will have to declare that it is home now, sharing in the vulnerability of other compatriot bodies.*[5]

The immediacy of that phrasing—"home *now*"—signals the centrality of the *contemporary* to this ethos that Ndebele sketches: "home" is predicated not upon the claims of heredity or natality—on "identity"—or upon an expectation of the future; it is, rather, "now": provisional, shifting, and profoundly ecstatic, an experience not of security or familiarity, but rather of uncanny unsettlement, the *Heimlich* that is itself rendered *unheimlich* by the intimate, and immediate, presence of the other. To be "home now" precisely admits the possibility of impotence and contingency—of having no, or at least no securely predictable, future in the place and body where one "lives." *Shared* vulnerability, as a conscious practice, opens the door, so to speak, to the emergence of the relational, affective, and communicative networks once impeded by the strictures of apartheid that had protected whites from unexpected harm.

Ndebele's attention to the ethical potential of "putting [ourselves] at risk" begs the question of what this might mean for the work of literary production, or of representation itself, in the postapartheid period. What would an aesthetics of precarity look like, and how might such an investment in subjective insecurity shape an alternative tradition of South African literature? In this chapter, I consider a pair of exemplary South African fictions of the transition that express a similar investment in precariousness not only as a ubiquitous human condition, but also as a practice that sharply exposes the aporias of both ethical and political relations in colonial and anticolonial contexts. These texts locate the tensions between individual subjectivity and communal solidarity in the vulnerable flesh of the body, its porosity and its boundedness, and paradoxically work to imagine a future community in and through a confrontation with the terminal mortality of naked human life. In this respect, these novels articulate what we might see as a powerful ethics—and aesthetics—of the *con-temporary*, in the sense affirmed by Harry Levin, for whom "the word contemporary in its literal meaning signifies being temporary together."[6] My reading here of Nadine Gordimer's *July's People* (1981) and Zakes Mda's *Ways of Dying* (1995) highlights the commitment evinced in literary treatments of the South African transition to the ethical, political, and aesthetic potential of what Jane Chin Davidson terms "affirmative precarity," a willful submission to the vulnerabilities of corporeal life in the face of otherness.[7] Though these are two texts that have received thorough critical attention, including as works concerned with South Africa's transition, the ethical and political stakes of their investment in the con-temporary and in the temporalities of precariousness, have been less well studied. As I will show, the exposure of self to embodied alterity comes to serve as a counterpoint to a kind of political autoimmune crisis that is seen, by some, to have metastasized from the apartheid state into the postcolonial period and thus to threaten the very sustainability of the nation's democratic dispensation.

As works from different points in the country's transition—one from the early 1980s, and the other from the interregnum period of the early 1990s—*July's*

People and *Ways of Dying* also invite consideration of the contemporary resonance of historical examples of future thinking. Though neither text precisely deploys prophecy, their respective visions of South African future, and of the ethical challenges posed by transition, complicate the linear temporality of transitional rhetoric, revealing the complex interdependencies of expectation, disappointment, anxiety, and persistence explored in this collection.[8] Their respective approaches to vulnerability and improvisational survival further highlight the ethical potential of what we might call "precarious time"—an affective-temporal structure that usefully aligns the literature of South Africa's transition with other efforts to come to terms with terminal being, such as life and love in the shadow of HIV/AIDS,[9] ontologies of the Anthropocene,[10] and the fugitive practices of urban survival in Africa.[11]

This con-temporary literature, firstly, evinces profound temporal instability, playing with grammatical tense, narrative mode, and chronology to disorient and defamiliarize the reader and evoke the affective register of terminality, the condition of living under the shadow of an inevitable end.[12] As such, these texts illuminate the narrative temporality of precariousness and its relation to states of transition. Second, images of waste, superfluity, ruin, and decay predominate throughout. Third, this is a literature dominated by figures, experiences, languages and material encounters that are untranslatable and irreducible. It is, in other words, a literature of incommensurability. The singularity of otherness that predicates precarity comes to be expressed, in these texts, through a resistance to interiority, empathetic identification, and novelistic individualism, and an affirmation, instead, of the ethical and aesthetic vitality of encounters with embodied, incommensurable, and abject materiality. Whereas both liberal and radical antiapartheid writing maintained a "steady devotion to the ideal of the empathetic imagination in fiction,"[13] a belief that mutual understanding and compassion could transcend the racial and other barriers imposed by the apartheid system, these precarious fictions reveal a suspicion that such empathetic identification reduces or eliminates altogether what Antjie Krog sees as the singular "strangeness" of the other, the "terror and loneliness of that inability [to really enter the psyche of somebody else, somebody black]."[14] That inability—which might otherwise stand as a case of novelistic or imaginative failure—becomes, for Krog, the very basis of how to "live together"; the novels I consider here share her effort to encounter otherness on its own terms, at risk even of the self, "listening, engaging, observing, translating, until one can hopefully begin to sense a thinning of skin, negotiate possible small openings at places where imaginings can begin to begin."[15]

Epidermal frontiers: Autoimmunity and the threshold of the political

In *A Body Worth Defending*, Ed Cohen traces the intimate connections between the genealogies of the concept of biological immunity and "modern philosophies of personhood," showing how "the modern body aspires to localize human beings within an epidermal frontier that distinguishes the person from the world for the duration of what we call a life."[16] In contradistinction to the premodern corpus, exemplified (as Cohen notes) in the grotesque, porous, incontinent body celebrated by Rabelais and Bakhtin, "the modern body proffers a proper body, a proprietary body, a body whose well-bounded property grounds the legal and political rights of what C. B. Macpherson famously named 'possessive individualism.'"[17] Such proprietary self-containment, the isolation of the self from the alterity of other people, the environment, and its own mortal biology, has become, Cohen shows, fully embedded at the heart of modern notions of biological and existential survival: a survival predicated on a continuous and unflagging state of war between the self and fellow organisms. "[T]he human organism appears," in this immunitarian model of selfhood, "as a defended frontier, bound within an epidermal envelope that establishes the limits of the self, which is both exposed to and opposed to microbial 'others' who threaten to negate its existence."[18] The body, and specifically the "epidermal frontier" that marks the boundary between the self and its environment, thus figures as both the apotheosis and the aporetic limit of modern subjectivity, the site upon which claims of personhood and subjectivity are articulated, and the threatened threshold of their vulnerability.

This "epidermal frontier" has particular resonance, of course, in South Africa, where modern personhood has long been specifically racialized. Political apartheid explicitly represented what Foucault has called "war pursued by other means"[19]: in this case, a "race struggle" in which the rhetorical positioning of the white body and white population as perpetually under siege and under threat played a vital ideological role.[20] The "swart gevaar" discourse of racial peril that brought the National Party to power in 1948 justified the legislation of defensive immunity as the guiding logic of state power. The Population Registration Act (1950), Group Areas Act (1950), Immorality (Amendment) Act (1950), Prohibition on Mixed Marriages Act (1949), and other core legal techniques of the apartheid system introduced during the first term established the protection of (white) racial purity and (white) life itself as its essence and ultimate end. These acts provided the structural foundation and proleptic justification for the

Internal Security Act and other "emergency" legislations that would follow, as antiapartheid resistance threatened the symbolic or material breach of racial barriers.[21] The prioritization of the safety, sanctity, and hygienic maintenance of the individual white body—the need to protect its biological vulnerability against penetration by blackness—metonymically extended to the racial hygiene defended so brutally by the apartheid state, giving rise to what Aletta Norval calls a "'security' psychosis" that saw segregation as an essential immune response.[22]

The result was, as Antjie Krog reflects, a destructive—and self-destructive—militarization of South African society, with whites walling themselves off in an "impenetrable bunker... coming out at times, shooting, destroying, rubbishing, yet sharing nothing."[23] What is known in South Africa as a "laager mentality"—the paranoid sense of being permanently under siege, permanently at war with the other—is readily recognizable in the "immunitarian" orientation described by Roberto Esposito. In his three-volume study, *Bios, Immunitas,* and *Communitas,* Esposito describes the origins of "community" in the *munus* or practice of reciprocal gift-giving, the "obligation that is contracted with respect to the other."[24] Such obligation necessarily entails risk, specifically the "riskiest of threats... the violent loss of borders, which awarding identity to [the subject], ensures his subsistence."[25] "Immunity," then, signals one's exemption from obligatory reciprocity, the radical autonomy of self and property that (Esposito shows) predicates modern subjectivity.[26] For Esposito, the centrality of immunity for modern politics rests upon the presumptive threat that members of a community pose to one another: "the envious desires to acquire the goods of another, and the violence implicated in such a relation."[27]

Judith Butler shows how such immunitarian logics come to define the modern polis, where the geopolitical borders of bodies politic serve as symbolic and material correlates of the skin that is seen to defend human bodies from its threatening environment, its "front line." But as Achille Mbembe points out, even in South Africa, such spaces—material, symbolic, and biological—were always necessarily "tubular," perpetually undermined by the "leakages... lines of flight... fissures and cracks" through which otherness seeped.[28] Butler suggests that the violence that necessarily accompanies the immunitarian defensiveness of, for example, the United States' "war on terror" ultimately symptomatizes a form of political disavowal and projection, given the inevitable porosity and multiplicity of such state bodies. The ferocity with which the apartheid state responded to perceived breaches of racial propriety similarly reflects the insecurity at the heart of white colonial subjectivity, the fear and anxiety provoked when its "imagined wholeness" and purity were revealed as unstable and unsustainable fetishes. The systematic rendering-precarious of black South African life can thus be read as a similar form of disavowal and projection, in which the vulnerability of white bodies was effectively obscured by the violent deracination, isolation, and disposability that characterized black life under apartheid.

This process of isolation, repression, and brutal exception eventually gave rise to a kind of autoimmune storm that would ultimately bring about the terminal crisis of the apartheid system itself. As Stephen Morton shows in *States of Emergency*, the fundamental impossibility of maintaining such hermetic separation of biological bodies from its "others," particularly given the dependency of the colonial system upon the labor of these other bodies, ultimately called into being a "state of exception" that both occludes and highlights the terminal violence needed to maintain this segregationist colonial fiction.[29] Morton shows how the invocation of "security" to justify declarations of colonial emergency represents a form of political autoimmunity, "the mechanism by which an organism works to destroy its own protection, [and] to immunize itself against its 'own' immunity."[30] Like those who depend too obsessively on antiseptics and antibiotics to protect their bodies from illness, but succumb to autoimmune disease as a result, white apartheid society proved unsustainable in the face of its own violent exceptionalism, an irony diagnosed in late-apartheid texts like J. M. Coetzee's *Waiting for the Barbarians* (1980). Increasingly isolated from its racialized compatriots, from the world community, and from its natural environment, white South Africans had become trapped, by the 1980s, in the sterility and vacuity of a "dry white season," fighting an emergency war of immunity that was ultimately destroying the sociopolitical body itself.

Many antiapartheid writers critically documented and indicted the precariousness to which the system subjected those to whom it refused recognition (the novels of Richard Rive, Alex La Guma, Peter Abrahams, and Miriam Tlali, among others, come to mind). But the particular texts I consider here—Gordimer's *July's People* and Mda's *Ways of Dying*—instead contemplate the potential of "affirmative precarity" for both communal ethics and aesthetic production in the wake of apartheid. The communitarian orientation that emerges from fictions of the South African transition refuses the securities of sovereignty and autonomous selfhood in favor of mutual obligation, corporeal porosity, and indignity, affirming interdependency over hygienic isolation despite the risks entailed in such exposure. Confronted by the prospect of an imminent transformation in South Africa's political and social landscape, these "precarious" texts correspondingly choose neither to predict, describe, or secure that future nor to memorialize the traumatic past. Rather, they trace an aesthetic of the temporary and terminal, centered around a subject and, indeed, a language in dissolution, rather than consolidation, affirming the ethical and relational possibilities inherent in a common experience of perpetual loss.

"No Horizons": Immunity and precarity in *July's People*

Written in the violent and anxious aftermath of the 1976 uprisings that spelled the beginning of a new and final phase of resistance to apartheid, Nadine Gordimer's *July's People* contemplated the likely course of events—and the attendant ethical, psychological, and physical challenges—following the collapse of white majority rule. It is a reflection on the precariousness of settler culture and on the ontologies of the temporary that necessarily attend transition. In *July's People*, the liberal Smales family flees their suburban home in war-torn Johannesburg and takes refuge in their servant's rural village. Stranded in a borrowed hut with their three children, without reliable information about the situation "back there," Maureen Smales and her husband, Bam, struggle to adapt to the new situation and the "explosion of roles" brought about by the "blowing up of the Union Buildings and the burning of master bedrooms."[31] Despite their liberal disapproval of overt racism and the ugly brutality of the apartheid state, Maureen and Bam are forced to confront the ways in which their comfortable suburban existence has been predicated upon the security provided by racial segregation and white privilege. Throughout the novel, the existential crisis triggered by the end of apartheid is experienced and figured through the vulnerable flesh of the family's white bodies, most immediately during and after their terrified flight from the burning city and the revolutionary soldiers thought to be hunting white targets. The couple's attachment to the fetishized tokens of their former life—their radio, their gun, their bakkie, their malaria pills—not only bespeaks their inability to let go of the attitudes, identities, and material comforts shaped by apartheid; it also signals the difficulty they face, as whites, in accepting their newfound insecurity as dependents in their servant's village. The thatched roof and porous walls of the borrowed hut that serves as their temporary home indexes their "submission to the elements" (70)—to rain, smoke, heat, insects, animals, and other people. This contrasts vividly with the solid "master bedrooms" that metonymically symbolize the security and impermeability of white life under apartheid, while the family's vulnerability to disease, climate, unwanted intimacy, or discovery by threatening outsiders preoccupy Maureen and Bam's early conversations and ruminations.

This abiding sense of permeability and precariousness radically destabilizes Maureen's sense of self, evoking a perpetual state of indeterminacy in which both past and future are rendered unimaginable and discontinuous with the present. "Since that first morning she had become conscious in the hut, she had regained no established point of continuing present from which to recognize her own sequence" (139), leaving her and her husband feeling like "people in a hospital waiting room" (48), or like jet planes, "between two continents, where crossed date-lines eliminate time and there are no horizons" (99). This sense of temporal disorientation is exacerbated by life in the village, where the passage of time and the inevitability of ruin, departure, and decay are accepted, rather than contested: "Everything in these villages could be removed at the sweep of a bulldozer or turned to ashes by a single match in the thatch; only the earth, worn to the bone, testified to the permanence of the feet that abraded it, hands that tamped it, hearth-fires that tempered it" (114). The people's acceptance of "the same endless dragging of wood" (107), the smells of rot and of bodily decay (156), and their existence "unrecorded in any taxonomy" (148) are anathema to Maureen and Bam, those modern subjects for whom dependency on nature, other people, or their own bodies is a source of shame and disgust. Forced to submit to the charitable hospitality of their servant, Maureen feels like "she was not in possession of any part of her life" (139) and struggles with the intolerable indignity that follows—the indignity of being confronted, inescapably, with the biological immediacy and profound vulnerability of the embodied life. Obsessed with ruin—the rusting remnants of technology in July's village, the mud huts that "sink back into mud," the smoking remainders of South Africa's cities— Maureen struggles against the impermanence, insecurity, and impotence that characterize her new life.

Midway through the novel, as she washes herself "from July's oil drum kept full of river water...with soap supplied by July," Maureen wonders aloud: "Was it like this for him?" (154). Though she now feels the indignity of dependency and precarity with visceral immediacy, she recognizes that she was willfully oblivious to its effects on July's emotional and existential being during his tenure as their house-servant. She prided herself on having "known" him—insisting often that "they understood each other" (13)—and yet her newfound sense of exposure drives home the impossibility of that mutual understanding under the terms of mastery and servitude. Now, however, having put herself in his place (physically and figuratively speaking), Maureen finds it increasingly impossible to "come to terms" with her former servant or with the new state of being "that needed no witnesses" (148) in which she finds herself. Just as she is unable to enjoy the transport of fiction, already being "not what she was" (29), Maureen can no longer trust to the sympathetic imagination as a means for connecting with Mwawate and other black compatriots, for entering into their otherness, and—most significantly—for permitting their otherness to enter into her self. Gordimer's speculation upon the ontological and representational crises likely to follow the terminus of apartheid paradoxically, perhaps, reveals the inadequacies of imagination as a counterpoint to immunity.

Though the novel's famously indeterminate ending—the exemplar of what one critic calls "late apartheid's blank or so-called 'zero endings'"[32]—indicates a kind of pessimism on Gordimer's part as to whites' ability to fully accept the vulnerability demanded of them by the choice to make themselves fully at home in a postapartheid society, the Smales children's willing embrace of the "sweetness and freedom that come from powerlessness" (75) point to the possibility of a future predicated on contingency—on the communitarian potential of the contemporary. Initially disoriented, like their parents, by the sudden relocation to a place without grocery stores, electricity, and white authority, the children rapidly assimilate themselves into the social conventions and hierarchies of the village. They quickly become fluent in the local language (while Maureen and Bam lament their failure to learn an African language [44–5]); share happily in communal meals; and seem "happy among the chickens, hearth ashes and communal mealie-meal pots of July's place" (121). They play with toys crafted from leftover wire and other bits of trash, go without malaria prophylactics, and swim in the river without fear of bilharzia "with children who belonged here, whose bodies were immune to water-borne diseases whose names no one here knew. Maybe the three had become immune, too" (138). Their immunity— or, rather, their *indifference* to the question of immunity and to the claims of self-preservation—and their ability to live improvisationally, from moment to moment without thought or fear of the future, is what facilitates the white children's ability to make themselves at "home" in the black village (121) and what therefore stands, in Gordimer's text, as the basis for a new mode of being and *being-with* other people, the environment, and our own bodies.

Generically speaking, *July's People* represents a kind of anti-*Bildungsroman*, a narrative not of development, growth, and self-consolidation, but rather of shrinkage, dissolution, and crisis.[33] The narrative temporality of precarity—and thus of community—is dominated not by the future aspect, but by a register of terminality. The wasted landscape of their new home—crumbling huts, rusting machinery, contaminated water, and omnipresent filth—indexes the white subjects' new proximity to, and dependence upon, their environment and other people, and the terminality that shadows their consciousness of "living a life that was already over" (147). Here Gordimer elaborates the material and subjective effects of what Athol Fugard refers to as the "violence of immediacy" from which whites like the Smaleses had previously been shielded by their master bedrooms, their consumer objects, and their legal and political protection by the apartheid state.[34] The family's new homelessness—both material and existential—highlights for them the significance of a stable sense of place to the development of subjectivity, even as they are forced to confront the uncanniness of colonial identity itself, a condition wherein black South Africans like July have been made "to feel like a foreigner in the land of one's birth."[35] If the typical *Bildungsroman* tracks the protagonist's maturation and growing independence, this novel depicts Maureen Smales' intense frustration and humiliation at being reduced to a childish, "undignified" state of dependency on her former servant; the erosion of self that follows an immersion in communal life; and the existential crisis triggered by having "lost everything," being a subject who "has nothing, now" (143–4). The novel's much debated ending, in which Maureen runs headlong toward a helicopter without knowing whether it brings "saviours or murderers; and—even if she were to have identified the markings—for whom" (158), and the unusual present-tense narrative mode of the concluding chapter, provide a formal correlative (what Clingman calls a "grammar of identity") for the terminal temporality of the interregnum, unsettling readers with the vertiginous disorientation that attends the precariousness of communal being.[36]

The absence of quotation marks and shifting focalization that characterize the text's postmodernist style further experiment with the possibilities of language and narration beyond the immunitarian subject; the passages that reveal the perspectives of Mwawate or his wife on the new situation offer glimpses into black South Africans' responses to the changing circumstances, but their rarity and these characters' own confusion and disorientation only emphasize the limitations of white readers'— and writers'—imaginative capacities. These failures, along with Maureen's own frustration at her inability to communicate effectively and openly with Mwawate in either colonizer's language or his own, point to what Megan Boler calls the "risks of empathy" in this context.[37] In her essay on the limitations of empathy as a moral response to the suffering of others, Boler points out that empathy is based upon "a fear for oneself": "I know what you are feeling because I fear that could happen to me." The "other" with whom one empathizes is, in other words, affectively secondary to the "reader's [or witness's] fears about her own vulnerabilities."[38] The kind of "passive empathy" that Boler fears as a pedagogical and moral outcome further entails a comforting recognition of an abstract identity between the self and other without imposing any obligation to confront one's implication in the power structures and social forces that have led to the other's pain. There remains, in such encounters, a "safe distance" between the self and the other.[39] Citing Shoshana Felman's work on trauma and testimony, Boler argues instead for a "testimonial" approach to the other, one that entails exposing oneself to the possibility of being "undone" by this encounter: "the imperative of bearing witness," Felman insists, "is itself somehow a philosophical and ethical correlative of a situation with no cure, and of a radical human condition of exposure and vulnerability."[40] Whereas Maureen's compassionate empathy with Mwawate and other black South Africans had once affirmed her liberal credentials and sense of her own moral authority, in other words, she is now confronted with the painful truth that these efforts to put herself in the place of the other—her fantasies of visiting her servant's home village during summer vacations, for example—served to further shore up the "distances that seem to confirm our safety."[41] Now, amid the "aporia" of the "permanent break," these distances are being reduced to zero, uncannily destabilizing the Smales's sense of self: "Us and them. Who is us, now, and who them?" (117).[42] By literalizing the empathetic metaphor of "putting oneself in the place of another," *July's People* reveals the limitations of imagination as a basis for ethical relation, while highlighting the profoundly uncanny effects of a genuinely "testimonial" response.

The novel concludes on an aporetic note—unable to get away, unable to imagine staying, Maureen abandons herself to the contingencies of an unknown and unknowable future, leaving the readers thoroughly unsettled and unsatisfied by the apparent lack of narrative closure. But Gordimer's point is precisely this—that "closure" denotes immunitarian distance, while openness to the other demands that we accede to our own vulnerability, whether to the risk of death itself or, more prosaically, to the risk of being left disoriented and destabilized by the encounter with the otherness of literature itself.[43] As such, it exemplifies what Rita Barnard sees as the "peculiarly African and ... also typically postcolonial" mode of being that Gordimer is outlining: "an open-ended, transient, and migratory existence," an "inversion and critique of novelistic *Bildung*," here couched in the language of precariousness and the uncanny.[44]

Precarious life and the ethics of community: *Ways of Dying*

In *Ways of Dying*, a novel composed some ten years after *July's People*, Mda similarly stages, critiques, and speculates upon alternatives to this immunitarian logic of colonial modernity. But where Gordimer focused on the unsustainability of white settler culture's preoccupation with security, this novel extends the critique to all South Africans, exposing the violent consequences of immunity and its political forms. As its title suggests, *Ways of Dying* bears intensive witness to the precarious lives of South Africans during the transitional period, when "death lives with us everyday" and ubiquitous funerals "give birth to other funerals."[45] People die at the hands of abusive whites and criminal gangs, in accidents, of neglect and starvation, and as a result of endemic political violence; the living, too, inhabit an unpredictable, unstable environment in which homes are bulldozed or burnt to the ground, employment is scarce and contingent, and the means of survival dangerously elusive. The people "liv[e] the life of birds, in fear that they would not see the next day" (65). The protagonist, Toloki, exemplifies this precarious temporality. Having left his rural village and abusive father in search of "a wondrous world of riches and freedom" (59) in the unnamed port city of the novel's setting, Toloki finds his way "dog[ged] … throughout" by violence, death, funerals and disappointment (66). As a migrant, Toloki's predominant experience is of dislocation and instability; his hope for the future is primarily concerned with achieving the stability and autonomy that he sees as synonymous with selfhood, but this aspiration proves intractably elusive.

His dreams of financial security, dignity, and social standing in the city are exemplified initially in the illegal, but cherished, shack that he constructs as part of a land occupation movement by "squatters" denied homes by the apartheid government, and dreams of the day when he would be able to build himself a "real house" (122). Repeatedly bulldozed and proudly reconstructed, his home comes to symbolize the improvisational or "mitotic" process of self-construction, or *Bildung*, that Toloki is undertaking as he grows from penniless youth into solid adulthood.[46]

But once again, the contingency of black existence under apartheid is brought forcibly home to the young entrepreneur when his successful food cart, momentarily left unattended, is declared illegal and summarily destroyed by city council employees. The basis of his livelihood demolished, Toloki loses everything as his savings evaporate, former friends and admirers desert him, and his shack is firebombed by vigilantes when he refuses to pay "protection" fees. For the next twenty years, Toloki sleeps alone in a dockside waiting room, occupying a permanently temporary space and condition; he refrains from sexual contact, political engagement, or any other form of social intimacy, and cultivates an image as an "austere" spiritual ascetic, performatively embodying the corporeal fragility that characterizes black life under apartheid.

Toloki initially chooses his ascetic life of isolation as a gesture of self-preservation against the indignity and suffering he sees resulting from communal being and its vulnerabilities. Throughout the novel, belonging to a group is associated with violence and death. In addition to apartheid's racial classifications, people are relentlessly identified on the basis of membership in one collective or another, from competing school choirs, to places of origin, ethnic identities, or political affiliations. The boundaries of such groupings are policed with brutal intensity, with many of the novel's frequent funerals following from perceived violations of symbolic or material boundaries that trigger immune defensiveness or outright aggression. The fracturing of the social fabric along the lines of such group identifications reflects—and is reflected in—the insular geographies mapped in *Ways of Dying*, where identity is territorialized and mobility a dangerous condition. Toloki's resistance to such collective affiliations is thus expressed not only in his ascetic isolation, but also in his refusal to claim or defend a place of his own. As an emblematic migrant figure, Toloki is perpetually in motion, in transit from one uncertain, tenuous site to another, crossing or even violating borders as he roams the country, wandering from his birthplace in a remote rural settlement, through small platteland towns and on to the city, a journey that itself violates apartheid strictures against black urbanization. Once in the city, he continues to wander, from township to city center, shopping mall to squatter camp, sometimes choosing where he goes but more often forced to keep moving by the social, economic, and indeed military logics that organize the flow of racial bodies across urban space.

After the failure of various attempts to capitalize on the city's consumer economies leaves him homeless, hungry, and desperate, Toloki reinvents himself as a "professional mourner," a spiritual minister to the throngs of mourners who attend the violent city's daily funerals. He insists that this new profession is not simply a way of "making a living": a way of capitalizing, as others have, on the necropolitical economies of the city. It is, rather, a "way of life," an ethos that demands the thoroughgoing remaking of self through the sacrifice and mortification of the body. The hunger, filth, celibacy, and homelessness to which he is subject are refigured as sacrificial practices he performs on behalf of an unappreciative society. He refuses charity and takes pride in his studied independence. His habits "often remove him entirely from the bonds of community or collectivity as he ... shuns more mundane forms of sociality,"[47] even as his work as Professional Mourner "becomes a performance of the substance of community memory—a source of connection between the worlds of the living and the dead."[48]

Toloki's self-reinvention as an austere melancholic can thus be read, in one sense, as a hygienic gesture that attempts to distance him from what he sees as the deadly and degrading effects of bodily flows and communal identity and to recast himself as a singularly modern, "dignified," autonomous subject. But, on the other hand, Toloki's excremental being expresses a refusal to accede to the destructive hygienic logics of immunitarian collectivity: his proximity to dirt, waste, and other remainders testify to the anterior claims of obligation, memory, and materiality that suture subjects to one another and to their environment. As in *July's People*, images of ruin and pollution denote the complex temporalities of transition, and of the embodied vulnerabilities that necessarily attend ethical relation.

After he meets Noria and begins helping her rebuild her shantytown home and her life in the wake of the brutal murder of her son, Toloki reconsiders his aversion to collective being and its violent appetites; instead, he comes to affirm a new philosophy based not on austerity but on generosity. As Mukti Lakhi Mangharam shows of the indigenous ethics of *ubuntu*, the impoverished subjects who share food and other resources in Mda's informal settlements act according to the principle that "a person is a person through other people" (*umuntu ngumuntu ngabantu*). Whereas the consumerist modernity that dominates South African life in *Ways of Dying* privileges the individual and his or her economic and physical security, the spirit of *ubuntu* insists upon the need to risk the self in the face of "(the otherness of) other human beings."[49]

In this novel, overconsumption signifies an indifference to the claims of otherness, exemplified in the corpulent form and overflowing kitchen of Nefolovhodwe, Toloki's father's friend whose success in the city has made him forget his obligations toward his "homeboys." On the other hand, the sharing of food, art, and other pleasures exemplifies the community's generous spirit of *ubuntu*: a concept that, as Esposito reminds us of *community*, originates in the circulation of gifts. In *Ways of Dying*, "love" and "life" are the names given to generosity, and Toloki's skill at "knowing how to live"—that is, love—is what ultimately rekindles material and spiritual life for himself and Noria, and for the "informal" community of which they are part. Whereas both Toloki and Noria, hyperconscious of the risk involved in being in someone's debt, had once refused to "take things from others," their joyous and gentle relationship models the rich potential of interdependency and mutual care.

The contingency of being-in-relation is exemplified in the improvisational arts in which Toloki is expert, and which the novel itself presents as an aesthetic response to precarity. In addition to his self-invented profession, he is a talented *bricoleur*, with a knack for adding value to the discarded remnants of consumer society. Creativity, in this regard, emerges as the essential quality of life lived in common, a gift without which one simply withers away like Toloki's father, who starves willfully to death alone amidst his hoard of iron sculptures.

Improvisation, similarly, defines Toloki's relationship with the city through which he perpetually wanders, as he maps out alternative geographies and challenges spatial or symbolic fixture with his constant motion.[50] The "guileful ruses" that keep Toloki alive in the necropolitical order of the apartheid city are precisely what other characters celebrate when they note that he "knows how to live." This improvisational cunning is a quality associated, as Toloki observes, with the mutual dependency and practicality of women's society, whose perpetual activity in "cooking ... sewing ... drawing water ... closing holes in the shacks ... joking ... fighting ... work[ing]" and parenting hold the "grassroots community" together (175–6). The men of the settlement, on the other hand, "sit all day and dispense wide-ranging philosophies on how things should be," fomenting "empty theories" and taking in food, shelter, and sexual pleasure without reciprocation (175–6). The physical vulnerability to which women are subject belies—or, perhaps, demands—the self-sacrificial, improvisational ethos that represents, in Toloki's view, "the salvation of the settlement" (176).

The generosity that characterizes his relationship with Noria helps Toloki reintegrate himself back into community and his material environment, a process that involves unlearning the disciplinary denigration of the body and its appetites that characterized his austere vocation. The shame and "disgust" he felt toward sexual desire—his own and others'—is a consequence of his insight that "taking pleasure" in this way inflicts a kind of violent harm. Noria gently reveals that desire (whether nutritional or sexual hunger) need not result in consumptive destruction; that it can, in fact, also serve as a kind of *munus* or gift: a basis for the productive coexistence of individual embodiment with a more outwardly directed communal ethos. As Goyal notes, "she shows him how to be part of a community, training him to transform the instinctual and the bodily into something of use for others, thus giving his private rituals and customs public meaning."[51]

This reimmersion in communal life, facilitated though his relationship with Noria, demands not only that Toloki sacrifice some of his prized solitary "dignity," but also that he be willing to expose himself to risk—the risk of emotional or physical injury. After he and Noria cement their mutual dependency by ritualistically washing one another's naked bodies, they sleep together in her shack without dressing, "which was a dangerous thing for both of them to do. Smart settlement people never sleep naked, since they don't know when the next invasion [of murderous vigilantes] will be. When a massacre takes place one should be able to run away fully clothed" (193). The filth, poverty, disease, and insecurity of life for shantytown dwellers pose additional threats to Toloki's life and well-being, yet he chooses to make his life in this place where neighbors "are like two hands that wash each other" (69). In sharp contrast to Nefolovhodwe's suburban compound, with its armed guards and barbed wire, the vulnerability of Noria's shack in the "informal settlement," and the people's precarious lives "like birds," exemplifies the dangers, but also the ethical and relational possibilities, of life lived in common.

The tension within the novel between immunitarian autopoiesis and communitarian exposure is expressed formally through Mda's innovative deployment of narrative voice, focalization, and grammatical tense. Like Gordimer, Mda articulates his investment in affirmative precarity via a kind of textual instability that both bespeaks the insecurity of embodied life and testifies to the "fundamental sociality" that emerges in and from that insecurity. Though focused on, and largely focalized through, Toloki himself, the novel is narrated, unusually, in the collective third person, through the "all-seeing eye of the village gossip":

> Just like back in the village, we live our lives together as one. We know everything about everybody. We even know things that happen when we are not there; things that happen behind people's closed doors deep in the middle of the night.... When in our orature the storyteller begins the story, "They say it happened ..., " we are the "they." No individual owns any story. The community is the owner of the story, and it can tell it the way it deems it fit. (12)

The oral register that dominates the narrative, both in the commentary of the collective narrator and through the extended stories that characters exchange, further reinforces the improvisational and contingent quality of language in this context. In the hybrid discourse that emerges, not only are plural voices in evidence, but oral narratives mingle with more typically prosaic passages, and past and present overlap. This polyvocal narrative voice thereby enunciates the communitarian basis of subjectivity, and the entangled temporalities of transition, that the novel thematizes.

The stories that characters share with each other, and the relations of testimony and witnessing that bring catharsis and healing, provide in one sense a basis for relationality. But they also illuminate the limitations of mutual "understanding" as a ground of identity and identification. Testimonial narrative is key to the novel's articulation of the relationship between past, present, and future in the transitional period, and it also serves as a powerful basis for the development of bonds of care and compassion amongst characters. Mda is careful, however, to avoid presenting such testimony as an "exchange"—characters bear witness to one another's suffering, but the many tragic stories remain profoundly incommensurable and irreducible to easy explanation, as evidenced by the sad silence that characters often share once the stories have been told. While sharing such stories drives home the ubiquity of suffering and loss, the novel emphasizes the obligation (and thus the vulnerability), rather than the identification, that arises from witnessing to the testimony of others.[52]

The return to the experiential qualities of corporeal life—of a kind of "generous" selfhood as it emerges in and through embodied encounters with others and with the environment—is articulated in the novel through a generic disjuncture between prosaic fiction and lyrical sound. The novel's prosaic everyday narrative is interrupted regularly by aural interjections that serve no signifying function but which simultaneously disrupt and intensify the "ordinary" life thematized and generically represented in the text. While the "Nurse" or orator at public funerals presents an account of "how the [deceased] saw his death," Toloki does his mourning work through bodily sound and gesture: sobs, wails, swaying, and groans whose specific qualities are tailored to the circumstances of each particular funeral. And it is precisely through such nonsignifying utterances that the novel emphasizes the untranslatable singularity of individual experience—its inability to serve as grounds for group identity. But it also articulates the irreducibly generous quality of Toloki's vocation, his corporeal identification with—and vulnerability in the face of—the grief of strangers. The lyrical interjections emphasize the improvisational qualities of the kind of communitarian orientation that the novel affirms; whereas the Nurse's testimony works to give order and meaning to otherwise incomprehensible tragedies, and to help in the work of mourning, Toloki's groans express the superfluity of affect and the irreducible persistence of the past in the unredeemed present.

The novel is also punctuated by the "moans and screams" of Toloki's past lovers, by laughter, and by Noria's "meaningless song," which once inspired Toloki's father's artistic energies and set her on the road to a life of destructive consumption where her ability to "give pleasure" served as a token of dehumanizing exchange. Later, though, after she and Toloki have begun their cautiously experimental relationship, this nonsignifying song comes to serve not as a currency of exchange, but as (again) a gift: a spontaneous effusion that "orgasmically" revives Toloki's long-repressed artistic talent. The joyous laughter evoked by Toloki's drawings and by the iron figurines he later inherits from his father testifies to the affective hold they have over others in the settlement. The people's response to Toloki's gifts of art evokes the ethical and social ramifications of generosity—and of aesthetic experience. As such, these gifts represent alternatives to consumerist extravagance on the one hand, and austere, immunitarian self-possession as a kind of hoarding, on the other. In each case, lyrical sound testifies to the experience of "being undone by [the] other," whether through grief or desire—a "mode of being dispossessed, a way of being *for* another."[53]

Like Toloki's talent for finding value and even beauty in the remainders of South African consumer society, his theater of mourning testifies to the aesthetics of precarity that he embodies. This embrace of vulnerability implicitly contests the logics of superfluity and disposability that characterize (post)colonial modernity, and the pressures of group identity that demand the dissolution of difference into sameness. The novel's conclusion on New Year's Eve, amid the "wholesome" smell of burning rubber, marks both the fragile promise of communitarian being and the potentially terminal risk involved in such openness. In this respect, *Ways of Dying* exemplifies the ethics and aesthetics of precarity in evidence in the literature of South Africa's transition. The future being imagined here, as in *July's People*, is uncertain, contingent, and a product not of planning but of improvisation; as such, it testifies to what Graham Pechey sees as "the fragile finitude of all community": the risk and the lyrical potential of a life lived in common.[54]

Notes

1 Ndebele, "Iph'Indlela?" 52.
2 See Butler, *Precarious Life*, especially chapter 2, "Violence, Mourning, Politics." For another recent scholarly attempt to think through the ethical and political potential of vulnerability and unpredictability in the terms I am proposing here, see Tsing, *The Mushroom at the End of the World*.
3 Ndebele, "Iph'Indlela?" 46.
4 See Mbembe, "The Aesthetics of Superfluity."
5 Ndebele, "Iph'Indlela?" 53; emphasis added.
6 Levin, "A Letter to James Laughlin," 7.
7 See Davidson, "Affirmative Precarity."
8 See also Wenzel, *Bulletproof*, and Van der Vlies, *Present Imperfect*.
9 See Motsemme, "'Loving in a Time of Hopelessness'," and Dean, *Unlimited Intimacy*.
10 See Scranton, "Learning How to Die in the Anthropocene," and Ensor, "Terminal Regions."
11 See Mbembe, "The Aesthetics of Superfluity"; Nuttall and Mbembe, *Johannesburg*; Simone, "Globalization and the Identity of African Urban Practices."

12   See Ensor, "Terminal Regions."

13   Romano, "A Novel of Hope and Realism."

14   Krog, *Begging to Be Black*, 267.

15   Ibid., 268.

16   Cohen, *A Body Worth Defending*, 8, 7.

17   Ibid., 7.

18   Ibid., 278.

19   Foucault, *The History of Sexuality*, 93 n87.

20   "The discourse of race struggle functions as a principle of exclusion and segregation, and ultimately as a way of normalising society." Foucault, *Society Must Be Defended*, 61.

21   Norval, *Deconstructing Apartheid Discourse*, 125.

22   Ibid., 203.

23   Krog, *Begging to Be Black*, 266.

24   Esposito, *Communitas*, 5.

25   Ibid., 8.

26   In this respect, the doctrine of immunity can be seen as the opposite of the South African ethics of Ubuntu, in which giving and receiving establishes a basis for communal ethics and for individual being. See Mangharam, *Literatures of Liberation*.

27   Campbell, "Bios, Immunity, Life," 5.

28   See Mbembe, "The Aesthetics of Superfluity," 386.

29   Morton, *States of Emergency*, 9.

30   Ibid., 8. Morton cites Derrida and Habermas, *Philosophy in a Time of Terror*, 150.

31   Gordimer, *July's People*, 117. Further citations are indicated parenthetically.

32   Visser, "Beyond the Interregnum," 61–7; cited in Boehmer, "Endings and New Beginning," 47.

33   See Barnard, *Apartheid and Beyond*, 254.

34   "Poverty = the violence of immediacy/Immediate (dictionary) = (of person or thing in its relation to another) not separated by any intervening medium." Cited in Barnard, *Apartheid and Beyond*, 101. Fugard points out that things like imagination, empathy, and intellectual contemplation are all premised on a certain existential and material security—on not being subject to the "violence of immediacy." Barnard valuably argues for the "importance of material conditions, especially adequate dwelling places, in the shaping of subjectivity and social identity" in Fugard's work (see "A Man's Scenery" in *Apartheid and Beyond*, 95–118).

35   Cronin, "No Unnecessary Noises Allowed, OK?" 9, cited in Barnard, *Apartheid and Beyond*, 105.

36   Clingman, *The Grammar of Identity*, 210.

37   Boler, "The Risks of Empathy," 255.

38   Ibid., 257.

39   Ibid., 263.

40   Felman and Laub, *Testimony*, 5, cited in Boler, "The Risks of Empathy," 262.

41   Boler, "The Risks of Empathy," 269.

42   See Barnard, *Apartheid and Beyond*, 60.

43   See Attridge, *The Singularity of Literature*, especially chapter 9, "Responsibility and Ethics" (123–32). Note also Erica Still's meditations in this volume.

44   Barnard, *Apartheid and Beyond*, 63, 66.

45   Mda, *Ways of Dying*, 98, 160. Subsequent references to the text are cited parenthetically.

46   Barnard, "Of Laughter, the Grotesque, and the South African Transition," 281. Barnard draws on AbdulMaliq Simone and Achille Mbembe in arguing for the emergence of new forms of subjectivity in the "informal settlements" and slums of postcolonial cities. Most significant for this analysis is the insight that such subjects "must live on a kind of temporal verge: 'a cusp where things can happen very quickly'—where fortunes can change in the blink of an eye—even though from the perspective of global capitalism nothing 'seem[s]... to happen at all'" (280–81, citing Simone, "Globalization and the Identity of African Urban Practices," 175).

47   Goyal, "The Pull of the Ancestors," 151.

48   Courau and Murray, "Of Funeral Rites and Community Memory," 93.

49   See Mangharam, *Literatures of Liberation*. Mangharam cites a "lesser-known" translation of the Zulu proverb, proposed in Van der Merwe, "Philosophy and the Multi-Cultural Context of (Post)apartheid South Africa," 76.

50   See De Certeau, "Walking in the City," 93, and, for a valuable account of urban improvisational arts in relation to Toloki's "self-invention," Barnard, *Apartheid and Beyond*, 154–55, and "Of Laughter, the Grotesque, and the South African Transition," 280–81.

51   Goyal, "The Pull of the Ancestors," 153.

52   See, again, Boler, "The Risks of Empathy," 268.

53   Butler, *Precarious Life*, 24.

54   Pechey, "The Post-Apartheid Sublime," 73.

Works Cited

Attridge, Derek. *The Singularity of Literature*. New York: Routledge, 2004.

Attridge, Derek, and Rosemary Jolly. *Writing South Africa: Literature, Apartheid, and Democracy, 1970–1995*. Cambridge: Cambridge University Press, 1998.

Barnard, Rita. *Apartheid and Beyond: South African Writers and the Politics of Place*. Oxford: Oxford University Press, 2006.

Barnard, Rita. "Of Laughter, the Grotesque, and the South African Transition: Zakes Mda's Ways of Dying." *NOVEL: A Forum on Fiction* 37.3 (Summer 2004): 277–302.

Boehmer, Elleke. "Endings and New Beginning: South African Fiction in Transition." Attridge and Jolly. 43–56.

Boler, Megan. "The Risks of Empathy: Interrogating Multiculturalism's Gaze." *Cultural Studies* 11.2 (1997): 253–73.

Butler, Judith. *Precarious Life: The Powers of Mourning and Violence.* New York: Verso, 2006.

Campbell, Timothy. "Bios, Immunity, Life: The Thought of Roberto Esposito." *diacritics* 36.2 (Summer 2006): 2–22.

Clingman, Stephen. *The Grammar of Identity: Transnational Fiction and the Nature of the Boundary.* New York: Oxford University Press, 2009.

Cohen, Ed. *A Body Worth Defending: Immunity, Biopolitics, and the Apotheosis of the Modern Body.* Durham, NC: Duke University Press, 2009.

Courau, Rogier, and Sally-Ann Murray. "Of Funeral Rites and Community Memory: Ways of Living in *Ways of Dying.*" *Ways of Writing: Critical Essays on Zakes Mda.* Eds. David Bell and J. U. Jacobs. Scottsville: University of KwaZulu-Natal Press, 2009.

Cronin, Jeremy, "No Unnecessary Noises Allowed, OK?" *Ingolovane* 2 (1989): 8–12.

Davidson, Jane Chin. "Affirmative Precarity: Ai Weiwei and Margarita Cabrera." *Journal of Visual Culture* 12.1 (April 2013): 130–32.

Dean, Tim. *Unlimited Intimacy: Reflections on the Subculture of Barebacking.* Chicago: University of Chicago Press, 2009.

De Certeau, Michel. "Walking in the City." In *The Practice of Everyday Life*, 3rd ed. Trans. Steven Rendell. Berkeley: University of California Press, 2011. 91–110.

Derrida, Jacques, and Jürgen Habermas. *Philosophy in a Time of Terror: Dialogues with Jürgen Habermas and Jacques Derrida.* Chicago: University of Chicago Press, 2003.

Ensor, Sarah. "Terminal Regions: Queer Ecocriticism at the End." In *Against Life.* Eds. Alastair Hunt and Stephanie Youngblood. Chicago: Northwestern University Press, 2016. 41–61.

Esposito, Roberto. *Communitas: The Origin and Destiny of Community.* Trans. Timothy Campbell. Stanford, CA: Stanford University Press, 2010.

Felman, Shoshana, and Dori Laub. *Testimony: Crises of Witnessing in Literature, Psychoanalysis, and History.* New York: Routledge, 1992.

Foucault, Michel. *Society Must Be Defended: Lectures at the College de France 1975–1976.* Ed. Mauro Bertoni and Alessandro Fontana. Trans. David Macey. London: Penguin, 2003.

Foucault, Michel. *The History of Sexuality*, vol. I. Trans. Robert Hurley. New York: Pantheon, 1978.

Gordimer, Nadine. *July's People.* 1981. New York: Penguin, 1982.

Goyal, Yogita. "The Pull of the Ancestors: Slavery, Apartheid, and Memory in Zakes Mda's *Ways of Dying* and *Cion.*" *Research in African Literatures* 42.2 (2011): 147–69.

Krog, Antjie. *Begging to Be Black.* Cape Town: Random House Struik, 2009.

Levin, Harry. "A Letter to James Laughlin." In *Memories of the Moderns*. New York: W.W. Norton, 1980. 1–12.

Mangharam, Mukti Lakhi. *Literatures of Liberation: Non-European Universalisms and Democratic Progress*. Columbus: Ohio State University Press, 2017.

Mbembe, Achille. "The Aesthetics of Superfluity." *Public Culture* 16.3 (2004): 373–405.

Mda, Zakes. *Ways of Dying*. New York: Picador, 2002.

Morton, Stephen. *States of Emergency: Colonialism, Literature, and Law*. Liverpool: Liverpool University Press, 2013.

Motsemme, Nthabiseng. "'Loving in a Time of Hopelessness': On Township Women's Subjectivities in a Time of HIV/AIDS." *African Identities* 5.1 (2007): 61–87.

Ndebele, Njabulo. "Iph'Indlela? Finding Our Way into the Future." *Social Dynamics* 26.1 (2000): 43–55.

Norval, Aletta. *Deconstructing Apartheid Discourse*. New York: Verso, 1996.

Nuttall, Sarah, and Achille Mbembe. *Johannesburg: The Elusive Metropolis*. Durham, NC: Duke University Press, 2008.

Pechey, Graham. "The Post-Apartheid Sublime: Rediscovering the Ordinary." Attridge and Jolly. 57–74.

Romano, John. "A Novel of Hope and Realism." *New York Times*, April 4, 1982, BR7. http://www.nytimes.com/1982/04/04/books/a-novel-of-hope-and-realism.html.

Scranton, Roy. "Learning How to Die in the Anthropocene." *The Stone, The New York Times*, November 10, 2013. https://opinionator.blogs.nytimes.com/2013/11/10/learning-how-to-die-in-the-anthropocene/.

Simone, AbdouMaliq. "Globalization and the Identity of African Urban Practices." In *Blank_____: Apartheid, Architecture and Beyond*. Eds. Hilton Judin and Ivan Vladislavić. Cape Town: David Philip, 1998.

Tsing, Anna. *The Mushroom at the End of the World: On the Possibility of Life in the Capitalist Ruins*. Princeton, NJ: Princeton University Press, 2017.

Van der Merwe, Willie. "Philosophy and the Multi-Cultural Context of (Post)Apartheid South Africa." *Ethical Perspectives* 3.2 (1996): 76–90.

Van der Vlies, Andrew. *Present Imperfect: Contemporary South African Writing*. Oxford: Oxford University Press, 2017.

Visser, Nicholas. "Beyond the Interregnum: A Note on the Ending of *July's People*." In *Rendering Things Visible: Essays on South African Literary Culture*. Ed. Martin Trump. Johannesburg: Ravan Press, 1990. 61–67.

Wenzel, Jennifer. *Bulletproof: Afterlives of Anticolonial Prophecy in South Africa and Beyond*. Chicago: University of Chicago Press, 2009.

6

Storying Trauma:
Unconfessed as a Site of Political Possibility

Erica Still

In the two decades since its first democratic elections, South Africa has wrestled with the tension between documenting and redressing the recent past and creating the conditions that would make the future significantly different. The numerous temporal descriptors of contemporary South Africa—postapartheid, post-antiapartheid, transition era, and post-transition—suggest the ongoing task of negotiating the relationship among past, present, and future. One aspect of that task has been sustained attention to uncovering the truth about apartheid, leading to the revision and creation of archives and museums, as well as the publication of scholarly historical accounts. Concurrently, recording the past has extended beyond the realm of official, legal, or historical discourse, as numerous creative writers have undertaken literary projects sharing the same impulse, and much of contemporary South African literature has been read in the context of its relation to the national imperative to reckon with the past. Such reckoning has been particularly attuned to the traumatic nature of apartheid—on the horrific acts of violence, the institutionalized constraints regarding employment, residence, education, and relationships, and the everyday reminders of subjugation that shaped the lives of black South Africans under the colonial and apartheid regimes and have lingering effects even now.

Embodied in the constitutionally mandated Truth and Reconciliation Commission, the reclamation of the past became a state-sponsored project aimed at restoring the possibilities assumed to be inherent to the future. Though focused on the past in this instance, the state is, finally, future oriented. By this, I mean that the state relies on the promise of the future to account for its actions in the present; furthermore, the state deploys the specter of the future as the legitimation for its existence—it is through the state that the potential of the future can best be managed (whether that means the state will thwart a dangerous future or that it will fulfill the possibilities of a utopian future). In this light, it becomes easier to see that, for the state, dealing with the past is primarily a pragmatic concern. It must be put in its proper place so that focus can remain fixed on the future. For the state, the concept of trauma becomes a key framework through which "proper" temporal relations can be restored. Generally speaking, trauma is understood as an event (and its aftereffects) that overwhelms the mind's ability to make it comprehensible. "Working through" the trauma is then understood to entail integrating the traumatic event into one's symbolic order so that it is no longer unconsciously repeated or repressed. Understood in this way, attention to trauma and traumatic effects focuses on the past: What happened in the past that continues to interrupt the desired progress attributed to the present? What is hindering forward movement? To the degree that this attitude holds true, we might say that the time of trauma is the past; the problem of trauma is the temporal disruption of the past into the present moment, such that proper attention cannot be directed toward the future, with all its promise. I would argue that this view of trauma animates state-sanctioned truth-telling commissions, and it often results in the fossilization of the past, keeping it subordinated to the demands of the future.

David Scott, in *Omens of Adversity*, cautions against an uncritical acceptance of this kind of reclamation of the past. He attributes the recent scholarly attention toward trauma studies to a larger problem of time. He writes, "There is, I think, a profound sense in which the once enduring temporalities of past-present-future that animated ... our Marxist historical reasons, and therefore organized and underwrote our ideas about historical change, no longer line up quite so neatly ... so *teleologically*—as they once seemed to do."[1] He goes on to suggest that this discontinuity makes the future as an inevitably improved realization of human potential no longer available, such that the "sense of a stalled present, a present that stands out in its arrested movement," prevails. Consequently, "curiously, it is precisely when the future has *ceased* to be a source of longing and anticipation that the past has become such a densely animated object of enchantment."[2] Linking this preoccupation with the past to the discourse of reparatory justice, Scott implies a loss of political purchase or impetus on behalf of those subjected to historical instances of oppression, "because the present can no longer be overcome for a future of emancipation, there has to be an *accommodation* with the past. Truth and reconciliation and its central idiom of 'forgiveness' are the names of a moral politics for an age characterized by being stranded in the present."[3] In this postmodern moment, the present is experienced primarily as absence—the loss of certainty in the moment and of assurance for the future. The turn to the past, then, becomes an attempt to escape the present. That escape comes at the expense of the political, or of the demand for systemic changes that would have an impact on the material, lived experiences of the disenfranchised and marginalized.

Scott's reading of the academic shift toward trauma studies opens important pathways into thinking about the temporality of trauma. I take his point that "an endlessly extending present" unsettles our foundational narratives about temporality and compels us to reimagine the relationship among past, present, and future. I am deeply sympathetic to his concerns that the psychologizing of the past undermines the political possibilities of the present, and I take his excavation of our experience of time and temporality as a persuasive caution against that impulse. At the same time, I want to consider the possibility of engaging with trauma studies in a less dichotomous way. Can we see attention to trauma not as *either* an apolitical escape from the present *or* as a necessary evil that must be attended to in order to move toward a better future? What would be necessary for an attention to traumatic pasts that resists the individualizing of what are social, structural problems even as it acknowledges the singularity of the lived experiences of such problems? Further, what kind of traumatic remembering can resist, even if only in limited ways, the memorializing language of the state *and* the apolitical retreat from the demands of the present?

Through a close reading of Yvette Christiansë's *Unconfessed* (2006), I want to put forward the concept of "storying trauma" as a means of reimagining the temporality of trauma as adamantly attuned to the present. "Storying trauma" is to give narrative shape to an experience that has exceeded the boundaries of language; that narrative shape is always necessarily a fictive, aesthetically crafted account of a past psychological, physical, and/or cultural rupture. More than representing or recording a traumatic event, storying trauma is a process of creating meaning through aesthetically complex arrangements of language, meaning that gives shape to a present irrevocably marked by upheaval or negation of previous cultural or psychic interpretive frameworks. If trauma suggests the eruption of the past into the present, storying trauma acknowledges the consequently blurred temporal lines. It attempts not to recapture the past or to put it to rest, but instead to understand the present in light of the absence of a strict linearity. Storying trauma, rather than memorializing or fetishizing the traumatic past, engages with it in order to acknowledge the suffering of the oppressed, to trace the psychological and material effects of that oppression, and to insist upon action in the present that might ameliorate those effects in experiential, measurable ways. Always present oriented, it is a deeply political effort. At the same time, it is a fundamentally literary effort, highlighting the potential contribution of the speculative to our ongoing efforts toward the political.

Ways of remembering: Slavery and apartheid

Christiansë's attention to the nineteenth-century slave system in the Cape of Good Hope marks an interesting, and increasingly frequent, departure from many of its contemporaries' prominent focus on apartheid. Indeed, as a fictionalized account of an actual slave woman's imprisonment for filicide, the novel participates in the wide-spreading diasporic endeavor to deal with histories of slavery. As Douglas Hamilton, Kate Hodgson, and Joel Quirk explain, "The last two decades have seen a remarkable surge of public, political and intellectual interest in slavery and its legacies."[4] In its narrative focus and innovative approach, Christiansë's text speaks to the global project of reckoning with slavery's troubling histories, and I read it as embodying one means by which such reckoning might be attempted. While its diasporic connections are important, *Unconfessed* is equally at home in the company of a much more local literary community. Scholars have clearly demonstrated that it continues a tradition of South African writing about Cape slavery and in that sense it remains embedded in a particular national undertaking. Margaret Lenta and David Johnson have both contextualized the novel in this way, drawing out important threads and discontinuities within the field. Pumla Gqola also speaks to the relatively recent increased visibility of slave memory specifically in South Africa: "The excavation of slave memory and spaces seen as the repositories for such memories is part of the general project of memory-making in South Africa."[5] Exemplifying such excavation, on a foundational level Christiansë's novel is about the slave experience, as it happened to both a particular woman and the larger enslaved population in a particular place and time. As Lenta notes, the novel is "firmly based on the history of Cape slavery in the period of 'amelioration' and … draws on available documentation."[6] In this instance, slavery supersedes apartheid as the historical event to which memory-making projects must attend; therefore, reading *Unconfessed* within the context of historical fiction and neo-slave narratives, both transnationally and regionally, immediately registers as appropriate and primary.

Simultaneously, however, while expanding the conversation to recognize slavery as integral to the history that must be accounted for, *Unconfessed* participates in South Africa's national project of negotiating the remembrance of a more recent traumatic past. Gqola points out the connection between remembering slavery and postapartheid nation building: "The rendering visible of slavery and colonial history questions some of the tools used to interpret and shape the new nation."[7] In other words, the strategies associated with recovering lost voices and challenging the omissions and assumptions of the historical record regarding slavery have been deployed to interrogate the nation-building process of creating a postapartheid history. Without losing sight of its preoccupation with slavery, then, we can also understand the novel to be about how we remember apartheid. Situated within these contexts of diasporic *and* national memorial efforts, *Unconfessed* stands as a primer for remembering cultural (and personal) trauma resulting from racialized oppression, whether slavery, colonialism, segregation, or apartheid. As it does so, it accomplishes several things: first, it calls attention to an overlooked, silenced experience of a particular enslaved woman; second, it reminds readers that South African history encompasses more than apartheid; third, it functions as an example of how to honor the past without forfeiting the present and/or future; and fourth, it enacts the meaning-making possibilities inherent in literature, suggesting that literary imagination plays a critical role in the cultural work of navigating temporal obligations. All of this is to say that *Unconfessed*, as a particular novel about Cape slavery, participates in the national memorializing project attending South Africa's transition from an apartheid to a democratic state in a way that both embraces and undermines that project. In so doing, it provides a compelling model of the power of the literary to forestall closure, such that the "texture of the now" remains unfinished, ever fraying at the edges.

In contrast (but also as complement) to texts like the TRC Final Report or to institutions like the Slave Lodge in Cape Town or the Apartheid Museum in Johannesburg, *Unconfessed* is a specifically literary undertaking. Though sparked by a historical legal document, the novel itself certainly cannot occupy the same space in the archive—it is, finally, an artfully arranged fiction. As Christianse's attempt to personalize what historical records recount in impersonal, incomplete terms, it is an imagined memory. Rosalind Morris makes a similar point when she notes that "dispersed documents of the legal proceedings brought to bear on Sila provided Christianse with the inciting elements of a narrative without referent, for they were traces of the encounter with power but not, precisely, evidence of a life, certainly not of a subjectivity.... But as to the interiority of the woman who endured these events, one can only speculate."[8] If, as a category, the historical and/or legal document is regarded as definitive and authoritative,

Unconfessed is precisely the opposite. Occupying spaces that are seen as unreliable—imagination and memory—this novel would seem to have little relevance to and authority within the project of constructing a national history.

Nevertheless, Christiansë's imagined memory stands as a necessary corrective to the (equally necessary) form of authoritative history making, such as that represented by the pseudo-legal language of the TRC Report. The literary project seeks to give voice to what remains beyond the realm of these official discourses. Its operating space is the imaginative, the speculative. Within that space, other modes/models of remembering may be encountered. In other words, literature offers the opportunity to imagine ways of remembering what we have in fact never known. In the case of *Unconfessed*, we are invited to imagine the life and memory of a woman whose only remaining proof of existence is a set of names in an historical legal document. Reading it in this light, I contend that *Unconfessed* contains within it a model for remembering traumatic racialized oppression. That model, what I am calling "storying trauma," presents a process that is responsive, reiterative, and recuperative. Through Sila's efforts to give meaning to her experiences, readers encounter a potential template for their own meaning-making strategies. Beyond the personal, however, Sila's process also opens possibilities for national memorializing efforts, especially regarding imaginative contributions to those projects, and therefore I point to Sila as a model for dealing with a traumatic history of racialized oppression. The remembering and narrating she does is a form of storying trauma that makes it possible to reestablish a degree of individual agency (rather than the repetitive acting out of the trauma). *Unconfessed* both embodies and demonstrates this kind of imaginative act. As a fictional account of an enslaved woman's life, it seeks to give voice to trauma and make known what is finally inarticulable. Simultaneously, its portrayal of that fictionalized woman's efforts to give an account of her life reveals the contours of storying trauma in both its successes and failures. In other words, Sila's pattern of remembering the traumatic events of her life provides a model of the work the novel itself undertakes. Understanding Sila's pattern opens up possibilities for comprehending the cultural work a text like *Unconfessed* accomplishes.

The process of shaping a narrative out of a traumatic experience is first of all *responsive*. In the most fundamental sense, it responds to the impulse to communicate one's reality. In this particular context, it also responds to the demand made by racialized oppression to give an account and to be remembered. For Sila, this demand to remember seems to come regardless of her desire for it. Her remembering begins almost against her wishes, when she is waiting for her sentence to be carried out: "She would have told him the truth about how she came to be on Van der Wat's farm."[9] Sila's train of thought is worth noting, for though she begins wanting to explain to the new prison superintendent "the people he would be dealing with" (6), she cannot help but trace her path back to the source of her sorrow, when "she had been a child stolen from her own mother and pushed into a hole with others, only to be pushed out into this world" (13). Sila cannot comment on her present without thinking about the chain of events that led to her imprisonment. She laments her inability to avoid such painful remembering, as memories constantly assert themselves. Even her son's presence, which she welcomes, brings with it memories she has tried to hold off. She tells him, "I have spent today remembering things I have never wanted to remember. Your visits bring me joy, but they also make what should be still shadows crawl. Now that you are back, my son, everything else comes back…I do not want to think of such things. But I must" (108). No matter how distressing it may be, storying trauma answers to the imperative to make meaning of experience—it is responsive to the urge to explain.

Sila's primary preoccupation involves recounting her life story for her dead son, Baro. Though often hurt by what she remembers, she insists on recalling the past because she knows "there are things that hurt when you remember them, but we can still laugh…. I want to remember. And I am afraid of that" (216). Sila knows that calling the past to mind is a dangerous endeavor for someone with such a traumatic background. Nevertheless, she wants to hold on to that past, explaining, "I remember these things because, in this world of lies, the peace of forgetting is a lie too. It is better to remember, even though my longing to forget is as strong as my longing to remember" (218). Sila has learned that forgetting is no easier than remembering, and in fact may be more costly in the end. Given that the effects of life-shattering events will manifest themselves in one way or another, storying trauma provides a self-protective response to the compulsion to make known one's experience.

In addition to being responsive, storying trauma is *reiterative*. It repeats itself, though always with a difference since the nature of trauma, as that which escapes language, resists totalizing or static formulations. Sila provides an example of someone compelled constantly to create and recreate a narrative that will explain and protest her present conditions—six times she offers a history of her movements as a slave, repeating, adding, and developing details until the reader is finally able to piece them together.[10] Such persistence speaks to the repetitive nature of storying trauma. Whether told straightforwardly or meanderingly, it is never finished, never complete in its telling. Over and over again readers witness her attempts to give structure and meaning to her troubling experiences. At times she seems successful. For example, her memories of the community she once experienced with fellow slaves—her "family in this world of demons" (172)—help keep alive her resistance to the overwhelming reality of slavery that would seek to possess her completely, body and soul. In this passage her remembering is clear and well ordered. Other moments are less so, however, and she struggles to make sense of all that is on her mind. In such moments, her remembering is fragmented and disordered. She sometimes gets confused, and she confesses that her hold on meaning is tentative: "I am only slenderly on this side of making sense, even to myself" (207). Furthermore, she recognizes the fragility of her explanations, noting that "there is so much more, but I will try to draw the net in before my greed to catch all explanation makes me lose the bounty of a good few. Some things are delicate in the weaving. Pull too tight and things break, pull and bind too hard and things have no beauty and the eye turns away" (141). Knowing that she must "weave" a thing of "beauty" if she is to keep Baro listening, she persists in trying to engage his interest by returning again and again to her stories of the past. The reiterative characteristic of storying trauma clearly responds to language's failure to convey experience exhaustively, for no matter how much is said, more always remains.

In this light, the third aspect of storying trauma—its *recuperative* nature—perhaps seems unlikely. Despite its incomplete nature, however, giving narrative shape to trauma does in fact achieve a certain kind of restoration of what has been lost. Even as it necessarily and incessantly wanders and repeats, it is also always *closing*. The gerund form matters here, for the ongoing action is crucial—this is a closing or ending always in process, happening rather than finished. Sila's numerous accounts of her life all lead to the slowly unfolding revelation regarding her actions toward her son. At a point later in her narrative section, Sila rehearses again the details of her struggles, focusing more intently on the final days leading up to Baro's murder than she has thus far. Despite her reluctance, she continues to confront memories of the fateful day. By this point, however, readers have pieced together the outline of the story. More important are the conclusions Sila reaches about herself. She explains to her friend that there is a Sila she does not want to be:

> It is her whose name has changed so many times. There are so many of her. She is the woman who looked up at hills and saw them as the horizon rushing away and she is the woman who was made to live like a dog. She is a woman who kills and who has been made to lie in the dirt with men. She is the woman who looked at the hills and forgot everything but being heartsore. That Sila scares me,

Johannes. You did not know her, she is also here. I am not her. I am not a bad person. There is another Sila, the one you knew. (321)

She understands how the world of slavery has created versions of herself that she recognizes but fears. We might call this sense of multiple identities a traumatic splitting, as the "self" is fragmented and distorted by oppressive circumstances and language. Storying trauma helps Sila to reclaim a sense of coherent identity, or of a core being. She retains a vision of who she might have been, who she wants to be. This woman's "other name is Chance. Ja. She is the chance I have not had" (322). Her remembering has brought a moment of self-revelation, and the numerous times she references herself by name in the final pages of her narrative suggest the significance of this revelation. She recognizes the enduring presence of the core identity she has tried to keep from slavery's reach, proclaiming that "there is something in me that has nothing to do with this place or the people who say we are theirs to do with as they will" (205). This "something" has been preserved and in turn has preserved Sila.

That "something" turns out to be the very thing Sila has lamented having: her "heart" itself—that capacity for feeling that makes her vulnerable to slavery's psychic and emotional abuses. As she says late in the narrative, "I have spent a long time trying to run away from my own heart. I have pretended" (333). Nevertheless, despite her best efforts, she cannot deny her heart, and its pain is the explanation she offers for her murderous act. Sila summarizes her deep experience with the "curse" of having a heart in a single word—"heartsore." Questioned in the court, she gives only one answer: "I was heartsore" (247). Her simple sentence leaves much unanswered, for it remains unclear when and for what she is heartsore. Is that the pain that led to her actions? Or is that the pain that her actions have caused? Both? Whatever the temporal connections, her answer clearly locates the *place* of the pain. Sila's heart is broken. And it continues to break, even when she thinks it has taken all it can. When her daughter Debora dies she says, "This is not my heart cracking. There is nothing left to crack" (281), and yet she mourns as she "stood at her grave and saw it was small, too small, and that smallness was a wound in the earth" (285). Though she has lost so many of the people she has loved in her lifetime, and though she has tried to stop her heart from feeling, every new loss comes as a fresh wound. In this way, Sila learns the heart's persistence, for better and for worse. It is not an exclusively painful lesson, as

in this life, I understand that a heart plays a certain game with other hearts. My heart has belonged to my children, and only of late, to Lys, who has taught me that a heart is not something to ignore. A heart, I am learning this late in my life, Johannes, is the very curse that I said it was but more, too. (333)

Having learned to love again, against all her expectations and in the midst of the most unlikely circumstances, Sila accepts all that caring for another entails and gains an even greater recognition of herself.

Mourning Lys's death and thinking of the harm she would like to see come to those who have imprisoned her, she asserts that

> I am Sila, friend and lover to Lys, mother to children who carry the weight of the world on their faces. I am Sila, prisoner—yes, I can say it, I can speak that language of yours that goes across to the town and from the town to that George whose name is repeated so many times they just say, fourth. (339)[11]

She prioritizes her relationships over her imprisonment, even as she realizes they cannot undo the effect of the language that determines her fate even from so far away. "I am Sila"—her declaration reveals the recuperative effect of storying trauma, for only as she has engaged in recounting her story has she been able to open her heart to Lys. It is worth noting that her relationship with Lys also gives her courage to remember; in that regard, storying trauma and love actually seem reciprocal, each one engendering the other. The full meaning of "recuperative" is at work here, for Sila both *recovers from* being overwhelmingly heartsore and *recovers—recoups*—her ability to love herself and others. Her response to Lys's death is significantly different from her response to Baro's suffering, in part, I would argue, because she has learned through storying trauma how to bear heartbreak. Responding to her son's presence and her need to make meaning, reiterating her story in an effort to communicate her experiences, and recuperating her sense of self all enable Sila to love and be loved without desperation and beyond despair.

Very near her narrative's end she says, "Well, Sila van den Kaap, it is time we faced each other. Yes" (345). In that encounter she reflects on the nature of what she has lost. Of the missionaries' teaching about hell she says,

> Perhaps the hell they speak of is the hell in which I, Sila van den Kaap, and my children, my friends, and all of the people who live and have lived like me—if only it could end with me—have lived in this Cape of Good Hope. Perhaps the hell they speak of is the loss of oneself and the knowledge of this. I do not even have the language for that loss or that self any more. (345)

Having named the hell in which everything—community, self, and language—has been lost, Sila refuses to stay there. At the end of that particular section, she concludes, "Then. Let me out of hell. Let me be all that I am as I am now for then I begin where I am, Sila" (345). In this moment of self-confrontation, she is able to imagine self-acceptance and beginning again. Such is the nature of the closing, or ending, that storying trauma makes available. It is not a completion, but a momentary resting. Sila finds rest, not because her circumstances are better, but because she has been able to give voice to her experience, encounter love, and embrace the woman she has become. Closing her narrative, she encourages herself: "Let me be strong now. Sila, whoever Sila is, wherever she has come from, I am telling you, be strong" (349). Within the novel, telling her story leads Sila to a small portion of rest. Her example highlights the efficacy of storying trauma as a means of dealing with overwhelming or devastating experiences.

The limits of story: Language and the law

Telling her story is not, however, without its limitations, and Sila remains highly aware of the steep price of her self-recognition. She has lost everything she holds dear, and even her restored sense of self wavers precariously. As she notes, "I, Sila van den Kaap, I dare to say things that confuse me in a language that has been given me and which strangles all other language, even the language in which my own name lived" (348). That she refers to herself as "Sila van den Kaap" in this moment is crucial, for it reveals her reckoning with the pervasive nature of slavery's logic. Earlier she has spoken resentfully of the renaming that accompanied her life of slavery: "At first they said, Sila van Mozbiek. That was the closest they came to truth. Then it was Sila van den Kaap and that is the one they came to believe since that is the one they believed" (346). Though she knows that her "true" name is not what she has come to be called, she too begins to identify herself through the language of the law, which replaces both her mother's name and the name her mother gave her.

Furthermore, she understands the fragility of her sense of self. "And who I am is loose," she says (348). If on the one hand she has reclaimed herself, on the other she knows how very tenuous that claim remains. She knows too well the dehumanizing effect of slavery and subjugation, and she despairs at the thought that generations following will be reduced to saying, "we are not people, we are things" (343). So while Sila herself attains a kind of resting, she also knows it is a momentary achievement that may not be strong enough to save her generations. Meg Samuelson highlights the temporary nature of what I am calling Sila's rest, along with the long-lasting nature of racialized oppression.

"As emancipation hovers on the horizon of Sila's world," she writes, "Christiansë resists a triumphant ending, forecasting into a fundamentally unliberatory future that may yet be our present.... Christiansë thus renders it impossible to say that the regime of slavery has concluded. Instead, she presents through the voice of Sila an analysis of a future that, while discontinuous with the past, marks slavery's ongoing recurrence."[12] Despite her renewed sense of self, Sila cannot escape the damage done to herself and to her progeny.

She likewise finds little comfort in the prospect of being "written" into memory. Her experience with writing has led to a wariness about how it makes room for her. She recalls Van der Wat's daughter pointing out her name, and her children's names, in the father's ledger, listed with the cows as mere property.[13] She recognizes the uses to which writing can be put, and she knows that it is not always in her favor, more often having served the interests of those who would rule over her. Language itself poses a problem for Sila throughout her narrative, for she knows its power to make her into someone she does not want to be. Reflecting on being forced to learn a new language as a slave, she explains "all the new laws that lived in the new words! *Meid*—a rule lives in that. *Come here*—another law that grows from *meid*. *Clean this*—still another law that grows out of *meid* and *come here*. *Open up*— perhaps the worst law" (148).[14] As David Johnson suggests, "The conflict between instrumentalist legal discourse and Sila's own voice runs through the novel. Sila asserts her subjectivity independent of colonial discourse, distinguishing her authentic self from the identity imposed by her masters and the courts."[15] While I agree that Sila does achieve a kind of self-knowledge, I am less certain that she escapes the colonial and legal discourse that determines her fate. True, the nature of storying trauma as she experiences it leads her in circles as it both asserts and questions itself. But she has also experienced the language of the law, which is linear and definitive. Despite the piecemeal way in which it is dispensed, it is possible to construct a linear account of Sila's life as a slave, beginning with her kidnapping and arrival in the Cape of Good Hope, moving to her time with the Neethlings, Oumiesis, Theron, and so on, concluding with her imprisonment for the murder of her son and the commutation of her sentence to Robben Island. Unlike Sila's meandering, reiterative versions, such an account operates in the language of the law: it provides a record of her movement from one governing body to another (i.e., from slave to prisoner, enslavement to imprisonment) as if she were mere property. In that sense, the language of the law is teleological, marching toward a carefully arranged outcome. Such is the language to which Sila finds herself subjected.

She is also trapped between her dependence on the language and legal code that can guarantee her freedom and her recognition that the same can condemn her to death. She continues to hold out hope that the new superintendent will recognize the legitimacy of her former mistress's will that granted her freedom. And yet, she "know[s] of the thinness of laws and the words that speak them" (77). Hearing her appointed lawyer speaking in the superintendent's office, for her "there was nothing new. She had heard that language of the court before. The 'whereas a female slave named Sila' was not new.... Her life was being summed up in that same language that said how she was:... 'Tried and Convicted of Murder, and had Sentence of Death passed upon her for the same...'" (22–23). Sila is forced to acknowledge the capacity of official language to dismiss and/or distort her own history (and humanity). In this version of events, there are clear causes and effects, as indicated by the use of "whereas." "Whereas" constructs an argument; it sets events in relation to one another in order to lead to a prescribed conclusion. Though she continues to assert her own version of events, she becomes a historical object in that she serves as the topic of the official language without being recognized as its speaking subject.

Rosalind Morris makes the point as well, noting "the degree to which the character whose would-be owners seek to evade the law by misnaming and renaming her nevertheless remains beholden to the fantasy of the proper name and the belief that truth consists in the convergence of name and thing. In this manner, she enacts the desire for law while provoking a recognition of its absence."[16] Sila's only hope rests on the very language that keeps her bound, literally and figuratively. Perhaps this is the point of Christianse's observation that

> tracing Sila's story and seeking the echoes of her own words,...leads one to conclude with a certain melancholy that Sila appears neither within slavery nor the legal system that authorized it. As an archival figure, she responds only to questions and only in the terms and categories posed by those who anticipated their own future recall in the archive.[17]

Christianse goes on to argue that "Sila's action, violent as it is, attempts to summon the law as a full subject might summon it, to question and not merely answer it, to speak and not only confirm what has been heard."[18] The harsh lesson awaiting Sila, reinforced at every turn, is the loss of her right to speak and be heard in any terms that would recognize her subjectivity and personhood.

Not surprisingly, then, Sila likens writing to yet another form of control that erases her own agency:

> My heart is my enemy.... It speaks to me in the language of these demons and it makes me live out their fullest wishes for all of us, as if I am a book that speaks to them of things they like to hear while I—as if I am the language of the book

itself—I must say and do those other things they dare not claim to know or
desire. (348)

Sila's observations suggest that authors write what they themselves want to hear,
overwriting others' voices and realities. As the fictive subject of Christiansë's
actual book, Sila calls into question the very project that seeks to bring her to
life. Her musings highlight the inevitable "mastery" of language—writing makes
objects of its subjects, even when that writing seeks to give the subject a voice.
Maria Olaussen notes this dynamic as well: "There are no South African slave
narratives written by a slave and the use of historical and archival material in
the recreation of the experiences of slavery takes place within a context where
the problems of appropriation and the presence of power structures between
author and subject are highly visible."[19] Through Sila, Christiansë suggests that
her own means of resisting racialized oppression—writing and rewriting—are
the same means by which slavery's pervasive work of erasure and silencing
was accomplished. In the face of such tainted options, any successful rewriting
must necessarily remain partial, fragmentary, and self-questioning. The novel
participates in the now-familiar project of recovering lost voices, and to the
extent that Sila succeeds in reclaiming her voice and self, Christiansë embraces
the kind of memorializing project that seeks to fill in the gaps and silences of
the historical record. Even as she does so, however, the novel raises challenging
questions about the ends and accomplishments of such a project. That is to say,
even as she weaves it, Christiansë registers great reservation about the ability of
story to set Sila free.

Present demands: The political possibilities of the speculative

Given this state of affairs, what remains for those who undertake such rewriting
as an ethical imperative? As Sila herself asks, "Is this all there is"—this
equivocation, this incomplete victory? (349). Yes, I would answer. Christiansë's
project (as well as others like it) is an impossible one, for she seeks to remember
that which is unknown and unknowable to us. In that sense, all she can offer is
an imagined memory of a fictive character. The person named in the archive
remains a mystery. But to acknowledge this unavoidable failure is not to give
up hope. As Christiansë notes in her reflections on writing the novel, "despite
being an inevitably failed gesture, Sila's action nonetheless forced some opening
through which we can glimpse her, perhaps even hear her, some 150 years
later."[20] Christiansë also achieves a remarkable feat, for she models how a cultural

history might be forged. Sila's work of storying trauma becomes a template for how a person and a people might bear the weight of a history of oppression. Such remembering asserts itself against the impulse to forget, reiterates itself against the impulse to simplify and fossilize, and restores those who embrace it by providing a place of resting. In this insistence on remembering even as that task remains impossible, Christiansë's text may be seen as a response to the challenge Sila issues herself: "Let me live up to this, what has been demanded of me. It does not matter who has demanded it. All that matters is that I am the one who knows that something has been demanded of her and I am the one who understands that there is no escape in refusing to answer" (348). Storying trauma, as exemplified in the imagined memory of a fictional character, is, finally, messy, tenuous, and incomplete. But as Sila concludes, "This might be all there is, of necessity, but all there is could be less still" (349).

Unconfessed goes beyond demonstrating through Sila's example this method of narrating trauma, for it embodies the approach to memory that it endorses. Just as Sila's narrative is responsive, reiterative, and recuperative, the novel itself exhibits these characteristics—responding to what might be seen as an ethical imperative to give an account of a period of South Africa's history often ignored or overwritten; reiterating the oppressive nature of slavery; and recuperating the remembrance of a woman long forgotten. Beyond these moves, however, the novel offers one additional characteristic of storying trauma: it is imaginative and speculative. Though based on historical accounts of slavery in the Cape, *Unconfessed*'s representations of how those laws, customs, and interactions might have affected a particular individual are necessarily speculative, which the text calls attention to through its various narrative voices. The first of the novel's three sections presents a third-person narrator, who relays Sila's thoughts and the circumstances she faces from a distant or removed perspective. The second section, which makes up the majority of the book, is Sila's narrative, a first-person address to her ghostly audience. The final section, which consists of a page, directly addresses the reader: "You want to know. What happened to her?" it begins (350). The novel's movement through these different registers suggests both the necessity and limitation of each perspective. We might liken the third-person narration of the opening to the "official" discourse of the law and/or history, which asserts itself as objective and reliably informative. Necessary for establishing a frame of reference, such a perspective also subjects everything to its imposed mastery. In other words, though it (potentially) provides a common ground from which to organize society, it also overwrites the individual experience—especially when that individual belongs to the economically, politically, and/or socially disenfranchised.

In response, the novel's second section rejects the distanced narration, offering Sila's voice in order to personalize what official discourse intentionally generalizes. The intimacy of such a perspective works to overcome the formality of the law, and its audience is invited to presume they are encountering the truth in some meaningful way. The individual voice speaking on its own behalf becomes authoritative in its particularity. Granted access in this manner, the audience finds such revelations satisfying and oddly comforting (even when it involves horrific events or conditions). We might attribute such a response to the power of narrative to supply meaning even when the circumstances defy explanation.

Such satisfaction, however, is challenged by the final section of the novel, which turns the focus directly on the audience itself. Here is the ultimate refusal of the teleology of jurisprudence, as the reader's desire for closure is acknowledged and steadfastly resisted. Sila's story is left unfinished. As Samuelson notes in her reading of the novel alongside Saidiya Hartman's memoir *Lose Your Mother*, "Both authors refuse to draw these 'stories that have nowhere to go' to a redemptive closure.... [t]hey eschew performing the commemorative rites of mourning that would restore linear temporality."[21] Such a claim is in keeping with Christianse's own comments on the potential reading of the novel as a victorious reclamation. She writes:

> There is something that can never be made public in the case of Sila *and* Baro. And this insistent secret cautions contemporary historians against appropriating Sila for the cause of resistance and the history of Western subjects-in-the-making. Deeply private, Baro's death is the factor that will not permit Sila's act to translate itself into resistance, even though this act transgresses the law.... The certainty of Sila's act may transform her by extending her beyond her delegated position, but the fact that Baro bears the full burden of this violence puts the brakes on any runaway "triumphalism" of late twentieth-century readerly practice.[22]

Clearly, Sila's story is not a happy one, and it does not promise or provide the kind of closure—to the story, to the injustice of slavery, or to the legacy of oppression—that some might hope the project of reclaiming "lost" voices would achieve.

Perhaps even more important, her story is revealed as the speculation it must necessarily be. Lulled into familiarity with Sila, the audience is suddenly confronted with the absence of the anticipated resolution. Furthermore, as if to disrupt any pretense of authenticity, the final section deliberately reminds readers of the speculation or imagination prompting the narrative in the first place: "Well, some say she left the island, but there is no agreement on how. Some say...Some say...Some say...Some say..." (350). "Some say" becomes the refrain of the novel's final page, indicating a lack of definitive knowledge. In place of the "Whereas" of the court document, "Some say" announces the uncertainty, the imaginative element, and the multiplicity of the fictive narrative. Here no case is being crafted, but speculation is being indulged, indeed, encouraged. As Lenta puts it, "*Unconfessed* ... continually reminds readers, not only through the representative nature of Sila and what she suffers, the presence of the dead Baro and the multiple endings of the novel, but also in the tone of her thoughts, that the text is an imaginative construct."[23] The account turns on itself, rewriting the ending as a site of possibility rather than completion. Christiansë writes, "And for those long silences or the lines of argument that twist around each other in the air above heads, there is a laughter that might shake an island"—as if to remind the audience that there is "something" to this story, but it is something that remains, finally, beyond their knowing (350).

The speculative nature of storying trauma raises important questions about its efficacy and ethics. To the point of efficacy, we might reasonably ask if such remembering accomplishes enough to overcome its limitation. It is worth noting here the critique David Johnson raises as he considers "whether the novel can be read as an allegory of the end of apartheid." He contends that

> in *Unconfessed*, the resources of lesbian love and fragile moments of solidarity with fellow oppressed help Sila to survive slavery, patriarchal violence and the law's complicity with power.... However, as a political response to post-apartheid inequalities, the literary privileging of a personal/individual "solution" here forestalls critique of the systemic continuities—and the collective struggles against them—in the transition from slavery to capitalism, and from apartheid to post-apartheid society.[24]

Though I take his point, I would also posit that Christiansë achieves a different goal. As a literary text, *Unconfessed* is both less and more than a political response to postapartheid society. It does not reveal structural inequities or collective resistance, as Johnson notes, nor does it map out a path toward strategic political engagement. And yet, it is deeply political in its investment in modeling a particular relationship to the past. Though Sila's "solution" (a tenuous one, at best) is personal, it exemplifies a process by which national memory making might also be accomplished. I have traced the responsive, reiterative, and recuperative nature of Sila's remembering in order to suggest that such characteristics must mark any meaningful remembrance of a traumatic past. Such memorializing is always political, and Christiansë's vision has practical implications for how cultural remembering is undertaken. More than a comment on postapartheid South Africa (though perhaps that too), the novel engages a larger enterprise, namely negotiating the demands made by a history of racialized oppression and the possibilities offered by the future for a just society. It teaches *how* to remember in ethical ways and therefore encompasses a wide range of specific events and agendas that can then be interrogated through particular, contextualized, local means. Put differently, *Unconfessed* offers "storying trauma" as a model of and means by which contemporary audiences (individual and collective) might investigate the political possibilities of the present. The act of creating meaning is always embedded in the present: contemporary conditions shape interpretations and articulations of the past and future. Firmly situated in the moment, "storying trauma" offers an alternative to the state's imposed focus on the future *and* to the apolitical retreat into the past that Scott warns against.

It is my contention that storying trauma is a specifically literary endeavor—to the degree that it keeps alive multiple meanings and possibilities for understanding, it does what "official" discourses cannot do. It is an admittedly risky undertaking, precisely because it does leave open the opportunity for misappropriation and misunderstanding. Likewise, it does not guarantee that engaging in its responsive, reiterative, and recuperative process will lead to closure, to "getting over it," or to clear political agendas and strategies. Nevertheless, storying trauma offers genuine possibilities for reckoning with a troubling past in productive ways. Because it is never final or conclusive, it leaves open, and perhaps even generates, space in which further accounts may be offered. These multiple versions all serve as elaborations and correctives to each other, so that no one telling can lay claim to an exhaustive, infallible authority. The literary makes it conceivable that numerous, sometimes contradictory, statements and understandings can exist simultaneously, and that multiplicity mimics the diversity found within a democratic society. While the "state" *in* transition seeks to make the past a known but distant country, the literary embraces the state *of* transition as a space of uncertainty, pliability, and possibility regarding the past, present, and future. Such a space is necessary to the democratic endeavor, even as it remains locked in tension with the equally necessary pragmatic closure or institutionalization of the "state." If there is such a thing as a literary ethic, I would suggest, it concerns literature's rejection of the claim to authority in favor of an acceptance of responsibility. As a literary discourse, storying trauma does not replace historical, legal, or other disciplinary discourses and authority. Instead, it provides grounds from which to interrogate those official languages. That is the responsibility to which I pointed earlier: the obligation to stand as witness to and against, interpreter of, and alternative to the imposition of the law, which so often works to silence and subjugate. Attuned to its historical obligations and grounded in its contemporary context, *Unconfessed* stages such an interrogation, answers to such responsibility.

Notes

1   Scott, *Omens of Adversity*, 6 (original emphasis).
2   Ibid., 13 (original emphasis).
3   Ibid., 14 (original emphasis).
4   Hamilton et al., "Introduction," *Slavery, Memory, and Identity*, 2.
5   Gqola, *What Is Slavery to Me?* 14.
6   Lenta, "*A Chain of Voices* and *Unconfessed*," 100.
7   Gqola, *What Is Slavery to Me?* 14.
8   Morris, "In the Name of Trauma," 401.
9   Christiansë, *Unconfessed*, 13. (Further references parenthetically in the text.)
10   Ibid., 13, 26–27, 192, 215, 213–18, 301–12.
11   Emphasis is original.
12   Samuelson, "'Lose Your Mother, Kill Your Child'," 15.
13   See Christiansë, *Unconfessed*, 255.
14   Emphasis is original.
15   Johnson, "Representations of Cape Slavery in South African Literature," 557.
16   Morris, "In the Name of Trauma," 406–07.
17   Christiansë, "'Heartsore'," 1.
18   Ibid., 11.
19   Olaussen, "Approaching Asia through the Figure of the Slave in Rayda Jacobs' The Slave Book," 37–38.
20   Christiansë, "Heartsore," 2.
21   Samuelson, "'Lose Your Mother, Kill Your Child'," 39.
22   Christiansë, "Heartsore," 12 (original emphasis).
23   Lenta, "*A Chain of Voices* and *Unconfessed*," 108.
24   Johnson, *Imagining the Cape Colony*, 152.

Works Cited

Bell, David. "The Persistent Presence of the Past in Contemporary Writing in South Africa." *Current Writing: Text and Reception in Southern Africa* 15.1 (2003): 63–73.
Christiansë, Yvette. "'Heartsore': The Melancholy Archive of Cape Colony Slavery." *The Scholar and Feminist Online* 7.2 (2009). http://sfonline.barnard.edu/africana/.

Christiansë, Yvette. *Unconfessed*. Cape Town: Kwela Books, 2006.

Gqola, Pumla. *What Is Slavery to Me? Postcolonial/Slave Memory in Post-Apartheid South Africa*. South Africa: Wits University Press, 2010.

Hamilton, Douglas, Kate Hodgson, and Joel Quirk. "Introduction: Slavery, Memory and Identity: National Representations and Global Legacies." In *Slavery, Memory and Identity: National Representations and Global Legacies*. Eds. Douglas Hamilton, Kate Hodgson, and Joel Quirk. London: Pickering and Chatto, 2012. 1–13.

Johnson, David. "Representations of Cape Slavery in South African Literature." *History Compass* 10.8 (2012): 549–61.

Johnson, David. *Imagining the Cape Colony: History, Literature, and the South African Nation*. Edinburgh: Edinburgh University Press, 2012.

Lenta, Margaret. "*A Chain of Voices* and *Unconfessed*: Novels of Slavery in the 1980s and in the Present Day." *Journal of Literary Studies (JLS/TLW)* 26.1 (2010): 95–110.

Lloyd, David. "Colonial Trauma/Postcolonial Recovery?" *Interventions* 2.2 (2000): 212–28.

Morris, Rosalind. "In the Name of Trauma: Notes on Testimony, Truth Telling and the Secret of Literature in South Africa." *Comparative Literature Studies* 48.3 (2016): 388–416.

Olaussen, Maria. "Approaching Asia through the Figure of the Slave in Rayda Jacobs' *The Slave Book*." *Research in African Literatures* 42.3 (Fall 2011): 31–45.

Samuelson, Meg. "'Lose Your Mother, Kill Your Child': The Passage of Slavery and Its Afterlife in Narratives by Yvette Christiansë and Saidiya Hartman." *English Studies in Africa* 51.2 (2008): 38–48.

Scott, David. *Omens of Adversity: Tragedy, Time, Memory, Justice*. Durham, NC: Duke University Press, 2014.

7

"Reach Forward, into the Past": Nostalgia as Post-Transitional Mode

Erica Lombard

In 2002, Lewis Nkosi declared that "South African literature shows a certain incapacity for generating nostalgia for the past, a *pastness* which can be recreated regrettably as the moment of loss or state of vanished happiness."[1] Rather than "being eternally bathed in a pleasant glow of nostalgia," Nkosi continued, "the past in South Africa is remembered mainly as a bad nightmare fomented by wars of conquests and resistance."[2] Now, in South Africa's so-called post-transitional moment, in the faltering aftermath of political change, where apartheid's demise has been closely followed by the apparent unravelling of the dream of a reconstructed postapartheid future and the discontinuities of a globalizing world, has nostalgia at last begun to emerge from trauma's shadow? What can the literary works that engage with the complexities of nostalgia tell us about the South African present? In this chapter, I explore the textures of nostalgia in recent South African writing, focusing on one of its key literary forms: the novel of an expatriate's postapartheid homecoming. Through readings of Mark Behr's *Kings of the Water* (2009) and Anne Landsman's *The Rowing Lesson* (2007), and touching on the alternative nostalgia of Jacob Dlamini's *Native Nostalgia* (2009), I argue that nostalgia is an ambivalent post-transitional mode in South African literature, concerned both with finding new conceptual resources to ground the present and with preserving the residual "intellectual schemas" through which South Africa has historically been conceived.[3]

The story of the émigré who returns to South Africa some time after the end of apartheid due to the imminent or recent death of a parent has become so widespread in South African fiction since the early 2000s that it is productive to

This chapter was completed during a postdoctoral research fellowship at the University of Johannesburg.

consider it an important period subgenre. Michiel Heyns's *Lost Ground* (2011), a novel that self-consciously inhabits its conventions, contains the following passage:

> [Y]ou have come out here to write a novel about an ex-South African coming back, let me guess, to be by the bedside of a dying parent—yes, the dying parent is obligatory.... We have had about twenty of those, treating us to their momentous return to the mother country and the examination of their own entrails and consciences. The details may differ but the essence is the same: a mixture of self-examination and self-congratulation, with poor tired old South Africa serving as both punch bag and security blanket.[4]

This sardonic comment, made by a black woman, Nonyameko, to the novel's white male émigré protagonist is suggestive of a number of pertinent issues that are at stake in the discussion about the nostalgic mode in contemporary South African literature. The first is the question of repetition and belatedness, expressed in Nonyameko's disparaging comment that "[w]e have had about twenty of those." Secondly, the "momentous return," with its "mixture of self-examination and self-congratulation" suggests a deep suspicion of the motives of such a narrative. Finally, Nonyameko's characterization of "poor tired old South Africa...as both punch bag and security blanket" implies a wariness about sentimental uses of South Africa (the land, perhaps, but also the idea of the nation) to create consoling fictions to shore up identities.

Nonyameko's (and likely Heyns's own) suspicions of nostalgia and its uses in literature are certainly not rare.[5] Commonly understood as a sentimental fondness for, or an idealization of, the past, nostalgia is often seen as an unhelpful if not wholly unethical means of relating to the past, especially in a context such as South Africa, where the object of longing is contained in, or may even comprise, the world of apartheid. Instances of nostalgia are always open to accusations—and indeed are sometimes guilty—of bad faith, historical amnesia, an abdication of responsibility. In aesthetic terms, moreover, nostalgia is frequently assumed to be, if not in the realm of kitsch, then at the very least, conservative, clichéd, or commodified.

Yet nostalgia works in considerably more complex ways than commonsense understandings assume. It is, I would suggest, an inherently transitional phenomenon. As such, it can be read both as symptomatic in South African literature, and also indicative of how South Africa's own transition has been lived. By transitional, I mean, first of all, that as a form of memory and an activity, nostalgia is profoundly concerned with aftermaths, belatedness, and navigating the temporal discontinuities produced by change. Svetlana Boym has described nostalgia as "a defense mechanism in a time of accelerated rhythms of life and historical upheavals," and so suggests that it is "coeval with modernity itself."[6] It is especially prevalent in contexts of temporal rupture, frequently flaring up "in the wake of revolutions, or at times of great, real, or perceived sociopolitical instability and stress."[7] Secondly, the word "transitional" also suggests a *going between*: nostalgia, that is, has an intermediary function.[8] Rather than comprising a temporality in itself, it is a way of mediating between or bringing together different temporalities, including the private times of individuals and the time of history, the past, present, and future.

Here, an introduction to nostalgia's psychical and social operation is in order. At heart, nostalgia may be understood at the most general level as a yearning for unity and continuity of time and identity in times of uncertainty, a longing for an anchor in a world in flux. Operating at both individual and cultural levels, nostalgic activity is an attempt to create this continuity through narratives of memory that reach out from the present, often with affection, and always aching, back to past times and states that are perceived to hold particular value.[9] Significantly, although nostalgia is now associated almost exclusively with lost time, its etymological origins lie in spatial dislocation. Coined in the seventeenth century through a combination of the Greek words *nostos* (the return home) and *algia* (pain or longing), nostalgia literally means homesickness, the longing to return home.[10] Andreas Huyssen contends accordingly that the nub of the issue "is not the loss of some golden age of stability and permanence" but rather "the attempt, as we face the very real processes of time-space compression, to secure some continuity within time, to provide some extension of lived space within which we can breathe and move."[11] Despite its backward glance, therefore, the aim of nostalgia is to find a stable ground, a "home," in the present in which to root identity and the imagination. Such a grounding is crucial for our capacity to imagine the future.

The nature of the continuity sought through nostalgia is significant to the particular forms it takes and their implications. Boym identifies two distinct yet intersecting tendencies to the ways in which we make sense of our nostalgic inclinations, which she names restorative and reflective nostalgia. Restorative nostalgia pursues the actual reconstruction of what has been lost, or thought to have been lost.[12] Emphasizing the *nostos*, it "proposes to rebuild the lost home and patch up the memory gaps."[13] In contrast, reflective nostalgia is more invested in *algia*, the affective experience of longing, and prefers to "delay[] the homecoming—wistfully, ironically, desperately."[14] While restorative nostalgia "spatialize[s] time" through its desire to reinstate the past, its reflective counterpart, enamored of ruins and fragments of memory, "temporalizes space."[15] With this distinction, Boym makes the case that reflective nostalgia can be a catalyst for ethical and creative engagement, a productive means of dealing with the uncertainties of modernity and of relating the past to the present and the future. As I will argue, these different tendencies within nostalgia are instructive of its ambivalent ethical and aesthetic possibilities in contemporary South African literature. It is to this context that I now turn.

Nostalgia after apartheid

Given nostalgia's prevalence during times of social change, the fact that South African culture and literature has contended with it over the past two decades should not be surprising. The years immediately following the transition created an environment especially conducive to the phenomenon, combining the bewildering forces of late modernity, which impressed themselves increasingly upon the country after its reentry into the global economy, with the sociopolitical changes occurring within South Africa itself. Sarah Nuttall has described the postapartheid present as comprising a "complex timescape of entangled and bifurcating layers" of which "modes of nostalgia and melancholia" are a constitutive part.[16] I have earlier used the word "contended" to suggest nostalgia's particularly charged ethical and political status in South Africa over much of this time. The future-oriented nation-building projects of the transition, like the Truth and Reconciliation Commission (TRC), were premised on the assertion of a decisive break with the past, conceiving of it as a domain of trauma from which the country was seeking healing, an oppressed and segregated "other" against which the liberated and unified postapartheid present and future would be defined. Put another way, if "[t]he pressure [was] on ... to 'bind the nation together' and to take its people decisively from a traumatized past to a reconstructed future," in David Attwell and Barbara Harlow's words, there was little room for nostalgia in this public narrative.[17]

Nonetheless, David Medalie has argued that South African literature of the past two decades has shown such a "recurring, even obsessive preoccupation with the past" that it is possible to speak of postapartheid writing as "a literature of nostalgia."[18] The textures and manifestations of nostalgia within this writing have shifted over time. Given the literature of the transition's investment in narratives of the nation and nation building, for much writing of the early postapartheid period, nostalgia was anxiously yoked with trauma. In fiction, the predominant form through which nostalgia was negotiated during the 1990s and early 2000s was the "My Apartheid Childhood Revisited" novel, in which an adult remembers an innocent (white) childhood under apartheid.[19] Frequently coupling idyllic descriptions of childhood with the trauma of apartheid violence, such texts attempt to align the nostalgic impulse with the processes of nation building by dramatizing a political awakening, yet the TRC-style confessional mode they adopt to do so is inconsistent. As Michiel Heyns has suggested, there is a troubling "kind of absolution of form" apparent in these novels through their underlying "presupposition of the myth of prelapsarian innocence."[20] That is, the nostalgic white childhood novel tends to stop short of the kind of thoroughgoing engagement with the complexities of responsibility and complicity that it purports to stage, instead restoring and preserving the idyll of white innocence, which is "the true heart" of the narrative.[21]

Rita Barnard and others have marked "a distinct shift in mood that occurred in the course of Mbeki's presidency," which resulted in a "more disenchanted writing that ... emerged in the new millennium."[22] As triumphalist narratives of the transition have become increasingly threadbare in the years since apartheid's official end, and as uncertainty about the future seems ever more intense, nostalgic sentiment appears to be on the rise among ordinary South Africans.[23] The coming apart of the teleology of linear progress that undergirded the project to produce the new South Africa has begun to open space for literature to explore the elided nuances of the South African past, to conceive of it as something other than the domain of trauma. It has become possible, in other words, to begin disentangling nostalgia not only from trauma, but also from the prescriptions of the national narrative. Boym observes that nostalgia concerns "the relationship between individual biography and the biography of groups or nations, between personal and collective memory."[24] Since the early 2000s, nostalgia has increasingly found expression in texts that privilege the narratives of individuals rather than subordinating them to the biography of the nation.

Jacob Dlamini's *Native Nostalgia* (2009) provides a pertinent example of how nostalgia has been deliberately used to provide a critical counternarrative to South African public discourse as it developed under the African National Congress government after 1994, and especially to the political climate of the late 2000s. Framing his project using Boym's concept of reflective nostalgia, Dlamini suggests that the book, which combines memoir, cultural history, ethnography, and essay, is best seen as "a gathering of fragments of memory, souvenirs of the imagination" that have been assembled into "a fractured whole through which ... to look back at a life, a childhood, spent under apartheid."[25] Dlamini describes his childhood in the township of Katlehong by meditating on various objects and memories through which he fondly evokes "the music, the colours, the sounds, the smells" of the township (108). One of the most memorable of these is his reflection on the radio, through which Dlamini demonstrates that daily life under apartheid was characterized by "shades of grey and zones of ambiguity" (30). It is through the radio that Dlamini, along with the rest of the township, cheered "without reservation" for the white Afrikaner boxer Gerrie Coetzee, whom they considered "a homeboy" (29). In *Native Nostalgia*, the radio emerges as a paradoxical medium, intended for the dissemination of propaganda by the apartheid government, but appropriated in creative and resistant ways by newsreaders and listeners alike. Most significantly, Dlamini emphasizes that radio as a medium provided intellectual and imaginative space and mobility to black South Africans who were otherwise constrained within geographical, cultural, and communal boundaries enforced by the state. Through this relatively cheap technology, black listeners could traverse these limits, enjoying "a freedom of movement and being that the apartheid regime could not take away" (31).

The express aim of Dlamini's project is to use nostalgia to recover the humanity and ordinariness of black South Africans and their communities discursively, to resist their instrumentalization in contemporary political discourse by questioning and complicating the postapartheid public narrative of the struggle. This narrative, Dlamini suggests, is a story of spectacle in which nuance, ambiguity, and the significance of the quotidian have been occluded by an emphasis on the indignity and suffering of black South Africans under apartheid, or their heroic resistance to the system.[26] To remember apartheid-era Katlehong with nostalgia is therefore not to desire to restore the lost world of apartheid, but rather to challenge the "facile accounts of black life under apartheid that paint the forty-six years in which the system existed as one vast moral desert, with no social orders," and which also elide "deep class, ethnic and gendered fissures within black communities" (19, 156). Drawing affective and affectionate connections between the present and the past can serve as a resource in the bewildering present, he suggests, as well as a means of imagining alternative futures beyond the possibilities presented by the postapartheid public narrative.

If *Native Nostalgia* is a groundbreaking example of nostalgia's potential in the post-transitional moment, it is also necessary to recognize that it is in many ways still an exceptional text, not least because nostalgia has continued, for the most part, to be a phenomenon of white writing. Moreover, as with the novel of apartheid childhood, much postapartheid writing in which nostalgia is a prominent element has taken the form of narrative fiction. The novel's narrative drive toward resolution brings to the fore nostalgia's complex temporal mediation. I would therefore like to return now to the novels of postapartheid homecoming, which, as I argued at the start of this chapter, constitute the most prominent "highbrow" nostalgic literary form of the 2000s.

Focused through the figure of the expatriate South African, the narrative of return explores and expresses nostalgia at thematic, formal, and affective levels. Although these texts are less likely to figure the past as a corrupted idyll than the earlier novels of white childhood and coming-of-age, usually taking up a more reflective position, the two forms are not entirely distinct, and many combine tropes of childhood and homecoming. Like the coming-of-age narrative, the novel of return is permeated by a sense of loss—in this case, of a parent, and of the place and time of origin. For the expatriate characters across this literature, the loss of a parent and the loss of home are interlinked: the parent's death threatens to erode the emotional connection to place, to home as a particular geographical locale. The implications for the relationship between place and identity, and especially the idea of national identity in an increasingly transnational era, are also explored in these novels, although their transnationalism usually involves a movement between the fairly typical coordinates of South Africa and the United States or the United Kingdom.

As is the case for many such novels, *Kings of the Water* and *The Rowing Lesson*, which I examine below, are the products of writers who are themselves expatriates, for whom the form arguably has autobiographical resonances as a kind of nostalgic "writing back" to South Africa. But if, as Salman Rushdie has noted, "the past is a country from which we have all emigrated," the returning expatriate text should also be seen as a productive lens through which to focus the question of nostalgia's value—or its risks—in the post-transitional present more generally.[27] Transition is, in fact, a prevailing concern in this writing. Since many of the homecoming novels involve the expatriate's first post-1994 return to the country, they often bring to the fore the various changes that followed the end of apartheid. If we consider modernity to be a state of endless transition, the returning ex-South African further becomes an exemplary figure of modern nostalgia, attempting to create continuity within time and space—to find a home in a discontinuous present and resources for an uncertain future.

Reckoning and recovery: *Kings of the Water*

In Mark Behr's *Kings of the Water*, Michiel Steyn, an Afrikaans man who lives in San Francisco, returns to his childhood farm, Paradys (Paradise), in the Free

State. His homecoming is prompted by the unexpected death of his mother Beth ("Ounooi"), for whose funeral he makes his first journey to South Africa after years of estrangement from his family and country. Focalized through Michiel, the narrative explores the textures of nostalgia in multiple ways: from its thematic preoccupation with memory, loss, recovery, and belonging, to its exploration of the suturing work of nostalgic affect.

We learn through the novel that Michiel fled South Africa in disgrace fifteen years earlier after the discovery of his illicit affair with a male Indian naval officer, which followed his older brother's suicide and Michiel's former girlfriend's disastrous abortion of their child. In fleeing, Michiel cut himself off from his family and South Africa, severing communication for years, and taking up Australian citizenship. For this reason, nostalgia has been an acute problem for Michiel, something that for much of his time away has "demand[ed] constant beating back."[28] He speaks, in fact, of "the tyrannies of nostalgia, loss and guilt" (149). If nostalgia is a means by which continuity of identity is created across time and space in contexts of rupture, Michiel's disavowal of it comes at significant cost. The novel suggests that, despite years of therapy, his physical and emotional estrangement from his home and past has left him unable to integrate either into his sense of identity. He therefore remains out of time and place in the present.

When he is forced to return home for his mother's funeral, he must at last confront the feelings and memories he has repressed. The physical journey to South Africa becomes a passage into the past through memory: "[W]ithin an hour of starting the drive from Jo'burg—no, before, already at tens of thousands of feet—the tumble of memory had begun" (148). On his drive to Paradys, each familiar scene is overlaid for Michiel with vivid nostalgia, which draws the past into the present: "The route on horseback he remembers like lines on his hand, like a story known without quite imagining all that could be found in its reading" (1). "It is," he feels, "as if he has never been away" (1). However, this homecoming is also fraught with ambivalence. On reaching the farmhouse, Michiel finds not the welcome of the prodigal son, but his entry barred by a locked gate, and "a shiny wet stain on the fabric of his suitcase" (17) from one of the farm dogs, which precedes a tense reunion with his ailing father.[29]

On the most superficial level, Michiel's return after many years away highlights the contrast between the old and new South Africa, allowing the novel to register the material and social changes that have taken place since he was last there during apartheid: "Gardens here have been cut off from Church Street's sluiceways and pavements by fences and hedges. A house he remembers with a tin roof now has tiles" (61). The postapartheid country presents itself as a strange and unfamiliar place, rendering him "little more than a voyeur" to "*South Africa's Miracle*" (49), and he feels keenly that "his home—whatever a home is—is no longer here" (50). (That the year of transition falls precisely midway between his leaving and his return suggests that it could be the hidden fulcrum around which Michiel's experience of dissonance pivots.)

The effect of these temporal juxtapositions is that the novel is permeated by a sense of conflicted loss in response to the inexorable passing away of the old, the home that survives now only in memory. This atmosphere, echoed and exacerbated by Michiel's actual bereavement, is explored most vividly through his relation to the family farm, whose name, Paradys, is at once wistful and ironic. Cognizant of the history of land ownership and exploitation in South Africa, Michiel experiences Paradys as both the location of "a youth of near bliss" (82) and a space of conservative politics and racial injustice in which many of the old hierarchies of race and labor have remained active despite the various kinds of transformation happening in the country. The "sluggish no-time" of apartheid has, however, begun leaking out, and, as in many other novels of postapartheid return, the farm's days of prosperity are waning.[30] Its "dilapidated barbed-wire fence" and "leaves drooping over weeds on unplowed fields" prompt Michiel to ask if "[t]hings [are] falling apart" (11). Moreover, after the death of Ounooi, who had administered its workings, the future of Paradys is uncertain. There is disagreement about whether it should be subdivided and turned into a tourist destination, sold off, shared among the workers, or left to deteriorate. With none of the Steyn heirs willing to devote themselves to Paradys, or to subscribe fully to the structures of inheritance and power that such a devotion might require, the loss of the farm and its way of life is inescapable. Given that the farm has often served as a microcosm for the nation in South African literary history, we may read *Kings of the Water* as bearing witness, with an ambivalent sense of mourning, to the inevitable erosion of certain old structures of whiteness in the postapartheid moment—the crumbling of Nadine Gordimer's "house of the white race."[31]

The novel's clear invocation of the *plaasroman* genre is significant in this regard. Numerous critics have argued that the *plaasroman*, a form of white writing associated with a "nostalgia for country ways," seems increasingly ill-fitting in the postapartheid era.[32] Christopher Warnes argues that "socio-political change has overtaken the conditions of possibility for representing the farm as pastoral idyll or locus of identity."[33] It is noteworthy, then, that *Kings of the Water* largely affirms the *plaasroman*'s affective investments. While the farm itself is not idealized, Paradys remains for Michiel (as South Africa did for Behr) a mooring for identity, in some sense, as the place of origin, "where so much of him belongs, is owed" (55).

This is demonstrated in the moment of nostalgic recovery that comes toward the end of the text. Having reestablished his relationships with those he left behind, Michiel experiences a kind of emotional homecoming:

> During the ride with Karien he admitted to himself that rarely, if ever, has he known fulfillment—happiness?—as he has here. Like something suspended that is ignited again. A tiny window or crack opened. Inside all he and she said to each other, her fingers finding his in the jacket pocket, was already a presupposition of knowledge and of lives shared, a language that cannot be had elsewhere. Oh, go on, allow yourself: the sense of belonging, almost; as close as there is to any belonging in life.... Whatever that little crack is ... nowhere but here is it restored, does it remind you of what in your abundance of life, liberty and the pursuit of happiness you live constantly without. And you cannot say that it disappears at the first gate of Paradys or at the airport with its new name, or at the thirty thousand feet above the coast with the seatbelt signs long off. It goes with you. (215)

Here, the *nostos* is rendered in evocative detail. Through his reckoning with both the traumatic and nostalgic memories evoked by his homecoming, as well as his incipient reconciliation with those he abandoned when he fled the country, Michiel regains a "sense of belonging, almost; as close as there is to any belonging in life." In this moment of restoration, Michiel recognizes that this tentative sense of home is anchored in a personal past, the embodied history of "lives shared," whose locus is the farm. The "little crack" that makes this reconnection possible is restored "nowhere but here," through his physical as well as emotional return. More significantly, Michiel feels that this sense of belonging "goes with [him]."

In effect, the estranged self's fragmented sense of home and identity, past and present, is restored through the bridging work of nostalgic affect, which transforms longing into belonging and inducts Michiel, finally, into the present as a belated "new" South African. If "to belong is to be future-directed," as Annie Gagiano has noted, the novel suggests that the positive bonds of nostalgia strengthen one's sense of belonging in the present through the past, which then enables one to move forward.[34] *Kings of the Water* presents the case that nostalgia's productive capacities should not be dismissed, and that it may, in Dennis Walder's words, reflect "not escapism, nor an unwillingness to face the future, but a proper recognition of the importance of the past, and those memories that make up an identity."[35] I will return to the novel's treatment of the question of the future toward the end of this chapter.

In his 1996 article, "A Home for Intimacy," Njabulo Ndebele proposes a redefinition of the concept of home in South Africa, rooting it not in place or time, but in *relation*, which he describes as a kind of intimacy. For Ndebele, regaining a sense of home and belonging is a matter of "enriching ethical consciousness in the public domain," negotiating the "complexity, ambiguity, nuance" of being with others.[36] Ndebele's 2000 Steve Biko Memorial Lecture develops this idea further, shifting the temporality of home from the past to the present, and challenging South African whiteness specifically to "Put[] itself at risk" by "declar[ing] that it is home *now*, sharing in the vulnerability of other compatriot bodies."[37] While *Kings of the Water* engages directly with the question of home in postapartheid South Africa, its concentration on the individual white subject's anxious project of belonging in a changed environment finds a resolution in Michiel's consoling rooting in place and the past, rather than in shared vulnerability or social relation with "other compatriot bodies." That the novel takes a reflexive position in relation to Michiel's nostalgia is noteworthy. His pragmatic brother, Benjamin, dismisses Michiel's scruples about the farm and its black farmworkers as "sentimental crap" (218) that avoids grappling responsibly with the social and economic realities of the present, and we are invited to laugh with him at Michiel's idealistic desire to "hold on to one acre. Maybe the one with the dam and the spring" so that he can "still come, at times, to be in a picture of my own painting, in the tale of my own telling" (219). There is a sense that, as healing and perhaps inevitable as it is, Michiel's nostalgia may not represent a very practical solution. Yet we cannot forget that, as Susannah Radstone notes, "affect and meaning are conjoined" in nostalgia.[38] Despite the text's reflexivity, the affects of restoration and resolution produced in the novel emphasize the significance of Michiel's emotional homecoming, which is ultimately the driving force of the plot. In this sense, even as it records their diminishing relevance, the novel remains within the familiar boundaries of white writing.

Indeed, *Kings of the Water* is notable for its commitment to, and reactivation of, certain other ideas and narratives that have been increasingly regarded as outmoded in post-transitional literature. The first of these is its treatment of the nation and national identity. As Jeanne-Marie Jackson argues, *Kings of the Water* appears at first to use its émigré protagonist to assert a global affiliation, a "worldly identity," but it is ultimately Michiel's emotional bond to the nation that prevails: "South Africa ... begins to look like Michiel's only meaningful source of self-identification, and by extension Behr's only meaningful way of driving the narrative forward."[39] In addition, the story of return, reckoning, and recovery that is staged in the novel bears the traces of the therapeutic movement from revelation to restoration that was so characteristic a narrative of the TRC years, but which has been increasingly questioned since the early 2000s.[40] Lastly, as I have already noted, it is clear that the affective appeal of the pastoral mode remains compelling enough for Behr that the novel may be regarded as a belated *plaasroman*, nostalgically harking back to the form even as it engages critically with its limitations.

I highlight these nostalgic features of *Kings of the Water* to demonstrate how nostalgia by its transitional nature can confound periodizing gestures through its pursuit of continuity between eras. We might bear in mind Meg Samuelson's observation that "the category of the 'post-transitional' cannot be imagined as slicing a clean break into the cultural continuum. Instead, it both bleeds into and draws its sustenance from transitional concerns and apartheid struggles, while re-circuiting these concerns into new engagements."[41] To view the novel in this way is to accept nostalgia's complication of the boundaries between the past and the present.

Memory and private time: *The Rowing Lesson*

Whereas *Kings of the Water* focuses its protagonist's sense of loss directly on the farm and South Africa, Anne Landsman's *The Rowing Lesson* circles further inward, exploring loss at the most personal level, within the dying body of one man. The novel is recounted from the perspective of Betsy Klein, a fine artist who returns from New York to Cape Town to await the death of her father, Harold, a cantankerous family doctor with whom she has had a complicated relationship. The narrative comprises Betsy's imaginative recovery of her father's past and their shared family history, which she addresses directly to the comatose Harold in the second person as she sits beside his hospital bed. In contrast to Michiel, Betsy's nostalgic return is focused not on restoring a literal connection to the past through a particular locale, but rather on entering through the imagination into the private history of her father—an altogether different point of origin—in a complex process of mourning.

The narrative proceeds from the intimate corporeal details of Harold's dying body: "The great saphenous vein, the small saphenous vein, the inferior vena cava ... all your roads are buggered up. I make a left, taking the carotid artery, and now we're driving a car together, the new turquoise and white Vauxhall you bought from Frank de Vos when you turned forty."[42] The operation of nostalgia at this almost microscopic level in the novel is helpfully illuminated by Susan Stewart's account of the souvenir, which is the exemplary nostalgic object. Stewart argues that "[t]emporally, the souvenir moves history into private time."[43] Nostalgia, that is, subordinates the chronology and demands of history to the investments of the private, the personal experiences of lived time and memory. This is "inner, lived time," which, Michela Borzaga suggests, "has to do with the psychic economy of the self, flows of feelings and affects, experiences of pain and pleasure, the precarious negotiation between past, present and future.... It is related to questions of bodiliness, modes of feeling at home or at risk in the world, ... ways of being imbedded in a specific setting or landscape."[44] To delve into the depths of private time is to affirm the embodied experiences of ordinary individuals, along with the affective connections, details, and textures of everyday life that are beyond the scope and teleology of historical narratives. There are clear resonances here with Jacob Dlamini's project in *Native Nostalgia*.

This is not, however, to say that the vicissitudes of history are absent or elided in *The Rowing Lesson*. Rather, they are carefully recorded. As one example, Betsy's memory narrative draws associative connections between the Holocaust and the Sharpeville massacre, embedding her father's life and her family's story within the South African national past and the fraught historical frame of the twentieth century. The effect of this juxtaposition of private biography and history is to create, as Stewart notes of the souvenir, "a time of the individual subject both transcendent to and parallel to historical time."[45] Through its insistent interiority, *The Rowing Lesson* creates an alternative, private temporality that interacts but also contrasts with the narratives of history. Moreover, unlike Michiel, Betsy does not seem beset by "the tyrannies of nostalgia, loss and guilt" of leaving her family and country and is less anxious about her identity as an expatriate, or her relation to South Africa. Landsman, too, is not as overtly preoccupied with the ramifications of South Africa's political transition as Behr. This need not be read as a complete withdrawal from the demands of the South African context; as Meg Samuelson suggests, we might consider post-transitional writing in terms of *rearrangement* rather than *abandonment*.[46] Yet it does signal a moving away from the need to subordinate the personal to a national narrative, the idea that a book about memory in South Africa must necessarily have apartheid at its center, or that, as Barnard puts it, it should further "the project of forging the broad horizontal fraternities of an imagined national community."[47]

Nonetheless, the nostalgic preoccupations of *Kings of the Water*—loss and how to ensure a sense of continuity in time—are also central to the relationship between the past and future that is staged in *The Rowing Lesson*. They are evident in Betsy's preoccupation with documenting and revivifying the disappearing and the extinct, such as through her series of paintings of extinct animals. As with Betsy's art, the nostalgic recovery of the past that is performed in the narrative takes place in the realm of representation, into which fragments of the past are extracted, suffused with significance through an almost painterly building up of metaphorical layers, and used to create meaning in the present. The novel's coelacanth motif provides a particularly resonant example in this regard. The coelacanth, one of Harold's favorite conversation topics, surfaces repeatedly in the narrative, where it is invested with a cluster of associated meanings to do with the relation of the past to the present. Hundreds of millions of years old, this ancient fish was supposed extinct before its rediscovery in South Africa in 1938, during Harold's youth. Like Harold, with whom it is persistently associated in the text, the coelacanth occupies a liminal temporal position. It is a remnant of an earlier age that survives, on the brink of extinction, in the modern world. Betsy's narrative imbues the fish with a kind of atavistic charge, reminding us, in some sense, that the residual continues to live on with the dominant.

The novel's concern with temporal liminality is also evident in its production of "a narrative temporality able draw together past, present and future," as Samuelson argues.[48] The fluidity of this temporal mode is exemplified in the novel's recurrent thematic and formal preoccupation with Ebb 'n Flow, a section of the Touw River that is beloved of Harold, which he visits frequently over the course of his life. As a landmark for Harold, Ebb 'n Flow also becomes a waypoint within the text to which Betsy's account of his life continually returns. The river is a nostalgic narrative space where the linear progression of time breaks down, a zone of memory in which multiple times coexist and interact. It is, in Medalie's words, "a place of endless possibility."[49] Or in Boym's terms, it is an exemplary expression of reflective nostalgia, which conceives of temporality "not as a teleology of progress or transcendence but as a superimposition and coexistence of heterogeneous times."[50] Betsy's description of her parents' honeymoon boat trip is characteristic of this complex temporal situation:

> You reach forward, into the past, then pull your arms and the boat back into the longer future, the older beaches. The canvas tents at the municipal campsite are ghost-grey, and spotted with mould, and nobody's there. A big tree stretches its top branches over the river. A long rope hangs from it into the water. Simon and I are taking turns at the gnarled base of the tree. . . . I swing into the light and I'm so pale and bright that it's impossible to see me. Stella [Betsy's mother] shades her eyes from me, and so do you. (241)

Betsy's parents' past melds here with scenes from her childhood holidays (swinging with her brother on a rope over the river) and the present (or a possible future) in which the campsite has been abandoned. Betsy is at once the narrating adult and the swinging child. Harold's rowing, too, takes on a metaphorical significance, coming to stand for the movement of nostalgia, an active drawing of the past into the present and the future.

Stewart notes that nostalgic narrative "reaches only 'behind', spiraling in a continually inward movement rather than outward toward the future."[51] What we find in *The Rowing Lesson*, however, is a nostalgic narrative that pulls the past into the private present, where it can be imbued with new meanings and become a resource for the future. Here, I echo Medalie's argument that this relationship to the past is an expression of "the modern utopian imagination," which "respects the 'pastness' of the past even as it transforms it into the metaphorical substance of the present."[52] This complex temporality reaches its apogee in the novel's final scene, in which Betsy accompanies her father—through memory, imagination, and narrative—on his last journey up the Touw River toward the moment of his death. Even as the novel acknowledges the irreversibility of time, as Ebb 'n Flow takes on a Stygian function, the narration works furiously to bring together every significant moment in Harold's life in a rich concatenation of embodied memories. On reaching the river's source, Betsy discovers "the crack in the mountain that feeds the river" (277). The image of a crack—which separates the past and present, the here and there—is present in both *Kings of the Water* and *The Rowing Lesson*. Whereas in the former it serves as a bridge through which Michiel's connection to the past and to place is restored, for Betsy the crack is "the source" (277) of the river, and, by extension, the creative power of memory and narrative through which what has been lost to time may be recalled, refigured, and continue, in some sense, to live. Put another way, for *The Rowing Lesson*, "home" is found not in being rooted, but in an imaginative engagement with flux.

Nostalgia and the future

Both *Kings of the Water* and *The Rowing Lesson* end on the cusp of significant change, not only in the lives of their protagonists but also globally. Michiel's trip to South Africa occurs on the eve of the September 11, 2001, attacks in New York: his journey back to America is interrupted by their occurrence, and the novel ends in transit, on the side of the road between Paradys and Johannesburg, as Michiel hears that all flights to America have been canceled. Betsy, we are told in *The Rowing Lesson*, lives in New York within sight of the "giant tuning forks" of the Twin Towers (31). Her return to South Africa in the year 2000—during her first pregnancy and so quite literally on the threshold of the next generation—therefore also takes place at the start of the twenty-first century, with 9/11 imminent. In both novels, then, the return to the past occurs in a transitional space between two significant moments of temporal rupture: one national and one global.

Given that the unrepresented future of the novels is in fact the known recent past for readers (*The Rowing Lesson* and *Kings of the Water* were first published in 2007 and 2009, respectively), a further layer of retrospection is added to the novels' complex temporal situations. Written and read in the aftermath of 9/11 and the disenchantment of the post-2000 years in South Africa, Michiel and Betsy's personal projects of recovery and their transitional preoccupations take place in a historical moment that has been superseded by one that is arguably more fraught, more complex. We know, in other words, that what awaits the protagonists is not a reconstructed future, but greater upheaval. In this, we may detect what Huyssen describes as a "nostalgia for an earlier age that had not yet lost its power to imagine other futures," a nostalgia, perhaps, for the lost alternative futures of the transition.[53]

The temporal vantage point that is produced through these self-reflecting nostalgic structures is reminiscent of Walter Benjamin's angel of history, who gazes out at the catastrophic past piling up before him as he is propelled irresistibly into the unknown future.[54] I would like to suggest that the image of Harold rowing that is so central to *The Rowing Lesson* provides a nostalgic rewriting of Benjamin's figure that gives us a clearer idea of the creative possibilities of nostalgia in this context. If Benjamin's angel can only gaze at the wreckage of history, paralyzed by the storm of progress in which he is caught, Landsman's rower suggests the possibility of a more active and fluid engagement with the past, which here becomes an imaginative resource and not simply a record of devastation. Repeatedly "reach[ing] forward, into the past" (241), the rower draws its fragments into a reflective relationship with the present and "the longer future," creating continuity, and a willing movement toward that future, in which every moment remains an active part.[55]

I have argued that *Kings of the Water* explores nostalgia as a psychical process through which the estranged self may be reconciled to the present and affirm a bond to place. In its nostalgic revisiting of the *plaasroman*, furthermore, we might read an elegy for the old chronotope, and the old "intellectual schemas," bearing in mind J. M. Coetzee's wondering "whether it is in the nature of the ghost of the pastoral ever to be finally laid."[56] *The Rowing Lesson*, turning its nostalgic meditation inward, makes a bold case for the power of the nostalgic imagination to bring the past, present, and future into a creative relationship. In this, it moves beyond the confines of the postapartheid national narrative within which *Kings of the Water* and other postapartheid nostalgic texts have operated. In a literature that has historically found itself constrained within tight political and ideological bounds, where trauma has overshadowed narratives about the past, what is at stake in nostalgia is the issue of freedom, which Svetlana Boym notes is "not a freedom from memory but a freedom to remember, to choose the narratives of the past and remake them."[57]

Coda

In a 2011 essay for the Stellenbosch Literary Project, Wamuwi Mbao contemplated the possibility of a South African version of the American television show *Mad Men*.[58] This "lush reimagining of 1960s Johannesburg" would evince a confident and highly marketable nostalgic aesthetic mode similar to that of *Mad Men*: faithful to the details of retro costumes and set design, but with historical events remaining relatively peripheral to the plot. If such a casual nostalgia for the apartheid past would likely be considered too controversial by the South African national broadcaster, it nevertheless provides Mbao with a useful counterpoint to the literary memory-scape of post-transition South Africa. South African writing has, he argued, been characterized by a "deficit of lightness" and "state of pained watchfulness" in relation to the apartheid past, a compulsion toward cautious self-positioning and self-examination resulting from "so many years of not hearing, of not bearing witness and of not telling." Accordingly, literary engagements with the past have remained within certain "safe" formulaic bounds. In response, Mbao wistfully imagined the creative opportunities that might arise should South African writing one day be able to suspend "the fear of not saying enough," and move beyond the time of somber political and ethical hypervigilance into a state of "ecstatic, flippant *jouissance*." This, he suggested, would be an "illusory space whose power lies in its very indifference to the notion of the real" created through a "shift away from painstakingly showing the inner life, towards an appreciation of less acute sensory impressions."

Mbao's call, in other words, is for an alternative way of apprehending the past, one that can play with artifice, perhaps dwelling on the surfaces and patinas of past eras, rather than succumbing to an exhaustive and exhausting "national-narrative syndrome," as he terms it. Such an engagement would be open to Fredric Jameson's critique of postmodern nostalgia (typified by films such as *American Graffiti*), which in Jameson's mind "displaces 'real' history" by creating only a stylized sense of "pastness" that lacks connection both to the historical realities of the period it purports to represent and to the present.[59] Yet Mbao's comments suggest that the difficulty for postapartheid South African writers in dealing with the past has not been the threat of the loss of historicity so much as its overwhelming influence (indeed, even the term "postapartheid" is inherently historicizing). To evoke the aesthetic style of a past era in the manner proposed by Mbao would involve not a "waning of ... historicity" but a deliberate shrugging off of its weight in the interests of a more frivolous, and perhaps more daring, engagement with the country's history.[60] However, it is not clear that such a flippant nostalgia is possible, or even desirable, so long as the country's historically grounded economic, social, and cultural inequalities continue to ramify in the present. Moreover, we cannot escape the fact that the material substance of the South African past was so thoroughly racialized that nostalgic evocations of it will always risk reproducing or entrenching divisions between racial or group identities in the present. We might read Mbao's proposition as symptomatic of a kind of post-transitional fatigue, an expression of utopian desire for the freedom to imagine ourselves anew as subjects unfettered by the past—or to suspend, albeit temporarily, the ethical demand to remain "inconsolable before history."[61]

Given that the appeal of nostalgia will likely persist as the post-transitional moment continues to unfold with a sense of political and economic instability, the challenge is rather, as Ivan Vladislavić notes, to seek "a self-conscious, critical kind of nostalgia, one that understands the limitations under which it operates, that is, the conditions that make our access to consoling histories so unequal."[62] It is not to flippancy, but to reflective nostalgia's capacity for dissonance and irony that we should look. Nostalgia's "ironic double vision," in Linda Hutcheon's terms, may invoke the affects and affection of nostalgia even as it maintains a clear-eyed and critical focus on history and the present that puts nostalgic longing into perspective.[63] This reflective approach need not be overly earnest or serious; it may be light, playful, or satirical. Here, the logic of the souvenir holds some potential: nostalgia's mediation between history and private time creates the possibility of a narrative of the past that may intersect with, critique, or transcend the set national script. *Native Nostalgia* and *The Rowing Lesson* both take this approach, and, while steeped in history, seem nevertheless to have begun in different ways to move beyond the imaginative limitations of "national-narrative syndrome." If South African literature cannot—or cannot yet—relate to the past with the flippancy contemplated by Mbao, we might read in these examples an indication that writers have begun to forge more complex relationships with what has gone before. In both of these cases, the past is not sealed off from the present, whether as the site of trauma or an object of fetishistic pleasure, but rather exists in a dynamic relationship with it, informing the present even as it is itself subject to reinterpretation.

Notes

1   Nkosi, "The Republic of Letters," 249. It is likely that "regrettably" is meant to read "regretfully."
2   Ibid., 250.
3   Coetzee, *White Writing*, 10.
4   Heyns, *Lost Ground*, 28.
5   Heyns has taken issue with nostalgic writing directly in "The Whole Country's Truth."
6   Boym, *The Future of Nostalgia*, xiv, xvi.
7   Muller, "Notes," 740.
8   See Radstone, "Nostalgia," 187.
9   See Davis, *Yearning for Yesterday*, 34–35, 104.
10 Although varieties of "nostalgic sentiment" had existed well before, the term itself was invented only in 1688, in Swiss doctor Johannes Hofer's dissertation on a pathological condition affecting those who spent extended periods of time away from their home country.
11 Huyssen, *Present Pasts*, 24.
12 Boym, *The Future of Nostalgia*, xviii.
13 Ibid., 41.
14 Ibid., xviii.
15 Ibid., 49.
16 Nuttall, *Entanglement*, 156.
17 Attwell and Harlow, "Introduction," 2.
18 Medalie, "The Uses of Nostalgia," 36.
19 Ibid., 37. Examples include Jo-Anne Richards's *The Innocence of Roast Chicken* (1996) and Troy Blacklaws's *Blood Orange* (2005).
20 Heyns, "The Whole Country's Truth," 50.
21 Medalie, "The Uses of Nostalgia," 37.
22 Barnard, "Rewriting the Nation," 652.
23 See Mattes, "South Africa"; Quinn, "Things Were Better"; Kynoch, "Apartheid Nostalgia."

24 Boym, *The Future of Nostalgia*, xvi.

25 Dlamini, *Native Nostalgia*, 62. Further page references are made parenthetically in the text.

26 Dlamini's project arguably constitutes a postapartheid update to Njabulo Ndebele's influential "The Rediscovery of the Ordinary."

27 Rushdie, "Imaginary Homelands," 12.

28 Behr, *Kings of the Water*, 50. Further page references are made parenthetically in the text.

29 In "Good Reliable Fictions" Zoë Wicomb argues that the *unheimlich*/unhomely is in fact immanent in literary representations of nostalgia.

30 Coetzee, *Doubling the Point*, 209.

31 Barkham, "Author: Nadine Gordimer," 9.

32 Coetzee, *In the Heart of the Country*, 139.

33 Warnes, "Engendering the Post-Apartheid Farm Novel," 51. See also Devarenne, "Nationalism and the Farm Novel"; and Wenzel, "The Pastoral Promise."

34 Gagiano, "Memory, Power and Bessie Head," 54.

35 Walder, "Writing, Representation, and Postcolonial Nostalgia," 939.

36 Ndebele, "A Home for Intimacy," 28.

37 Ndebele, "'Iph' Indlela?" 53; emphasis added.

38 Radstone, "Nostalgia," 189.

39 Jackson, "You Are Where You Aren't," 179, 180.

40 See Graham, *South African Literature after the Truth Commission*, 20.

41 Samuelson, "Scripting Connections," 113.

42 Landsman, *The Rowing Lesson*, 47. Further page references are made parenthetically in the text.

43 Stewart, *On Longing*, 138.

44 Borzaga, "The Present in Pain," 66.

45 Stewart, *On Longing*, 154.

46 Samuelson, "Scripting Connections," 116.

47 Barnard, "Rewriting the Nation," 666.

48 Samuelson, "Scripting Connections," 114.

49 Medalie, "The Uses of Nostalgia," 42.

50 Boym, *The Future of Nostalgia*, 30.

51 Stewart, *On Longing*, 135.

52 Medalie, "The Uses of Nostalgia," 43.

53 Huyssen, "Nostalgia for Ruins," 7.

54 Benjamin, "Theses on the Philosophy of History," 257.

55 Ivan Vladislavić has also invoked and refigured Benjamin's angel in his complex literary engagements with nostalgia. See Van der Vlies, "Towards."

56 Coetzee, *White Writing*, 81.

57 Boym, *The Future of Nostalgia*, 354.

58   Mbao, "What a South African Version of Nostalgia Might Look Like."
59   Jameson, *Postmodernism*, 20.
60   Ibid., 21.
61   Durrant, *Postcolonial Narrative and the Work of Mourning*, 24.
62   De Vries, "Strolling through Troyeville with Ivan Vladislavić." Van der Vlies examines the "critical nostalgia" of Vladislavić's writing on and of memory, which emphasizes the disjunction between the represented and actual past, and is "always grounded in and circumscribed by a particular act of reflection, or recollection, always contextualized, ironized, inevitably flawed" (123–24).
63   Hutcheon and Valdés, "Irony, Nostalgia, and the Postmodern," 23.

Works Cited

Attwell, David, and Barbara Harlow. "Introduction: South African Fiction after Apartheid." *Modern Fiction Studies* 46.1 (2000): 1–9.

Barkham, John. "Author: Nadine Gordimer." In *Conversations with Nadine Gordimer*. Eds. Nancy Topping Bazin and Marilyn Dallman Seymour. Jackson, MS; London: University Press of Mississippi, 1990. 9–11.

Barnard, Rita. "Rewriting the Nation." In *The Cambridge History of South African Literature*. Eds. David Attwell and Derek Attridge. Cambridge: Cambridge University Press, 2012. 652–75.

Behr, Mark. *Kings of the Water*. London: Abacus, 2009.

Benjamin, Walter. "Theses on the Philosophy of History." In *Illuminations*. Ed. Hannah Arendt. Trans. Harry Zohn. New York: Schocken Books, 1968. 253–64.

Borzaga, Michela. "The Present in Pain: 'Temporal Poiesis' in Mongane Wally Serote's *To Every Birth Its Blood* (1981)." *Journal of Literary Studies* 31.1 (2015): 64–81.

Boym, Svetlana. *The Future of Nostalgia*. New York: Basic Books, 2001.

Coetzee, J. M. *Doubling the Point: Essays and Interviews*. Ed. David Attwell. Cambridge, MA; London: Harvard University Press, 1992.

Coetzee, J. M. *In the Heart of the Country*. New York: Penguin, 1982.

Coetzee, J. M. *White Writing: On the Culture of Letters in South Africa*. New Haven, CT: Yale University Press, 1988.

Davis, Fred. *Yearning for Yesterday: A Sociology of Nostalgia*. New York: The Free Press, 1979.

Devarenne, Nicole. "Nationalism and the Farm Novel in South Africa, 1883–2004." *Journal of Southern African Studies* 35.3 (2009): 627–42.

De Vries, Fred. "Strolling through Troyeville with Ivan Vladislavić." *Fred de Vries*, August 19, 2007. http://freddevries.co.za/archive/2007/08/19/stolling-in-troyville-with-ivan-vladislavic.aspx.

Dlamini, Jacob. *Native Nostalgia*. Johannesburg: Jacana, 2009.

Durrant, Sam. *Postcolonial Narrative and the Work of Mourning: J. M. Coetzee, Wilson Harris, and Toni Morrison*. Albany, NY: SUNY Press, 2004.

Gagiano, Annie. "Memory, Power and Bessie Head: *A Question of Power.*" *World Literature Written in English* 38.1 (1999): 42–57.

Graham, Shane. *South African Literature after the Truth Commission: Mapping Loss.* Basingstoke: Palgrave Macmillan, 2009.

Heyns, Michiel. *Lost Ground.* Johannesburg: Jonathan Ball, 2011.

Heyns, Michiel. "The Whole Country's Truth: Confession and Narrative in Recent White South African Writing." *Modern Fiction Studies* 46.1 (2000): 42–66.

Hutcheon, Linda, and Mario J. Valdés. "Irony, Nostalgia, and the Postmodern: A Dialogue." *Poligrafías* 3 (2000): 18–41.

Huyssen, Andreas. "Nostalgia for Ruins." *Grey Room* 23 (2006): 6–21.

Huyssen, Andreas. *Present Pasts: Urban Palimpsests and the Politics of Memory.* Stanford, CA: Stanford University Press, 2003.

Jackson, Jeanne-Marie. "You Are Where You Aren't: Mark Behr and the Not-Quite-Global Novel." *Safundi* 14.2 (2013): 175–90.

Jameson, Fredric. *Postmodernism, Or, The Cultural Logic of Late Capitalism.* London; New York: Verso, 1991.

Kynoch, Gary. "Apartheid Nostalgia: Personal Security Concerns in South African Townships." *SA Crime Quarterly* 5 (2003): 7–10.

Landsman, Anne. *The Rowing Lesson.* London: Granta, 2008.

Mattes, Robert. "South Africa: Democracy without the People?" *Journal of Democracy* 13.1 (2002): 22–36.

Mbao, Wamuwi. "What a South African Version of Nostalgia Might Look Like." *SLiP,* October 16, 2011. http://slipnet.co.za/view/blog/let's-suspend-the-fear-of-not-saying-enough/.

Medalie, David. "The Uses of Nostalgia." *English Studies in Africa* 53.1 (2010): 35–44.

Muller, Adam. "Notes toward a Theory of Nostalgia: Childhood and the Evocation of the Past in Two European 'Heritage' Films." *New Literary History* 37.4 (2007): 739–60.

Ndebele, Njabulo S. "A Home for Intimacy." *Mail & Guardian,* April 26, 1996, 28.

Ndebele, Njabulo S. "'Iph'Indlela? Finding Our Way into the Future'—The First Steve Biko Memorial Lecture." *Social Dynamics* 26.1 (2000): 43–55.

Ndebele, Njabulo S. "The Rediscovery of the Ordinary: Some New Writings in South Africa." *Journal of Southern African Studies* 12.2 (1986): 143–57.

Nkosi, Lewis. "The Republic of Letters after the Mandela Republic." *Journal of Cultural Economics* 18.3–4 (2002): 240–58.

Nuttall, Sarah. *Entanglement: Literary and Cultural Reflections on Post-Apartheid.* Johannesburg: Wits University Press, 2009.

Quinn, Andrew. "'Things Were Better in the Bad Old Days.'" *The Star,* December 11, 2002. http://www.iol.co.za/news/politics/things-were-better-in-the-bad-old-days-1.98663#.VSQR3vnF-uE.

Radstone, Susannah. "Nostalgia: Home-Comings and Departures." *Memory Studies* 3.3 (2010): 187–91.

Rushdie, Salman. "Imaginary Homelands." In *Imaginary Homelands: Essays and Criticism 1981–1991*. London: Granta, 1991. 9–21.

Samuelson, Meg. "Scripting Connections: Reflections on the 'Post-Transitional.'" *English Studies in Africa* 53.1 (2010): 113–17.

Stewart, Susan. *On Longing: Narratives of the Miniature, the Gigantic, the Souvenir, the Collection*. Durham, NC: Duke University Press, 1993.

Van der Vlies, Andrew. "Towards a Critical Nostalgia." In *Present Imperfect: Contemporary South African Writing*. Oxford: Oxford University Press, 2017. 99–124.

Walder, Dennis. "Writing, Representation, and Postcolonial Nostalgia." *Textual Practice* 23.6 (2009): 935–46.

Warnes, Christopher. "Engendering the Post-Apartheid Farm Novel: Anne Landsman's *The Devil's Chimney*." *English Academy Review* 21.1 (2004): 51–62.

Wenzel, Jennifer. "The Pastoral Promise and the Political Imperative: The *Plaasroman* Tradition in an Era of Land Reform." *Modern Fiction Studies* 46.1 (2000): 90–113.

Wicomb, Zoë. "'Good Reliable Fictions': Nostalgia, Narration, and the Literary Narrative (2011)." In *Race, Nation, Translation: South African* Essays, *1990–2013*. Ed. Andrew van der Vlies. New Haven, CT: Yale University Press, 2018. 203–16.

8

Crime Fiction in a Time of AIDS: South African Muti Noir

Brenna M. Munro

The dramatic rise of fiction about crime by South African writers can be read as a reflection of the dystopian nature of the postapartheid present—or, perhaps, its dystopian mood. Crime in postapartheid South Africa is both reality and fantasy; political issue, sensationalist global media trope, and source of everyday anxiety that has changed, according to Jonny Steinberg, the very shape of South Africa's urban world.[1] The lively "muti noir"[2] texts I examine here upend and remix the conventions of crime writing as often as they reiterate them. Their specific textures and temporalities, I suggest, can offer us clues about the shape of the here and now.

If crime fiction is a sign of the times, then the multiple conflicting temporalities produced by these novels—the murderous reach into the present of apartheid in Deon Meyer's *Blood Safari* (2007): the convoluted traffic between a traditionalism presumed dead and the quotidian after-ness of postapartheid life in Diale Tlholwe's *Ancient Rites* (2008); the narcotic present tense of crime in a time of capitalism in Sifiso Mzobe's *Young Blood* (2010); the macabre, futureless repetition of the depiction of AIDS as a serial killer in Kgebetli Moele's *Book of the Dead* (2009); and the magical dystopian near future of Lauren Beukes's *Zoo City* (2010)—point to contemporary uncertainties about the shape of the historical present as it unfolds around us. What has the "transition" brought us toward? How do we, in this moment of disenchantment and disappointment, build a narrative about a better future and the way to get there? David Scott's observations about a widespread "apprehension of temporal insecurity and uncertainty" in the wake of the global failure of socialist and postcolonial hopes for the future is helpful here: "What interests [him] about these catastrophic aftermaths is above all the untimely experience they have provoked of a more acute *awareness* of time, a more arresting *attunement* to the uneven *topos* of temporality."[3] As the grand narratives of history that organize time in legible ways have become less persuasive—whether "revolution," "progress," or "development"—temporality becomes more visible, Scott argues, and this holds true for the novels I am examining, which are all deeply concerned with temporality. If postcoloniality in the neoliberal era means living in the ruins of longed-for futures now become pasts, South Africa's belated postcolonial arrival has also coincided with two phenomena that seemed to have their own separate calendars, incubations, and births and that obstructed the strivings of those attempting to build a new nation and narrate it triumphantly: crime and AIDS.

The AIDS epidemic, no less than crime, has shaken faith in "progress." Kylie Thomas describes the early 2000s quite starkly:

> This was a truly bleak time for the hungry, the cold, and the sick who had been promised houses, security, and comfort, and who were realizing that even if these promises were not false, they would not be actualized any time soon. The fact that the government was refusing to provide treatment and care for people living with HIV/AIDS was the most telling sign of the disjuncture between the promises of the new constitution and the everyday lives of the majority of South Africans.[4]

Like crime writing, literature about the epidemic is often concerned with temporality, with how the illness disrupts individual lifespans, dreams of futurity, and models of "chrononormativity," to borrow and expand Elizabeth Freeman's term, of all kinds. In Ashraf Jamal's short story "Milk Blue," the narrator, a gay artist whose lover has died, makes a piece about their relationship: "two battery-operated circular clocks, side by side like pillows on the bed. He subtitles the piece *Perfect Lovers*."[5] In the gallery, though, he "discovers that the second hands are fractionally out of synch. He says nothing. Desolation grips him ... Synchrony becomes bitter, remorselessly false."[6] Desolate, false synchrony seems a "perfect" image for national liberation in the age of AIDS. Mbonisi Zikhali's poem "N.O.C.U.R.E (No One Can Understand Real Endurance)," meanwhile, imagines the epidemic through images of natural rhythms out of synch, time gone wrong:

> Who waits for the sun to rise
> At the stroke of midnight?
>
> Who waits for the bread to bake
> Before he sets out to harvest the wheat?
>
> Who waits for tomorrow
> when he missed today?[7]

If crime fiction is a genre sensationally asserting its cultural presence, AIDS is a subject in search of form. It makes sense, then, that *Book of the Dead* would attempt to write AIDS through a crime format, while AIDS is a presence in many crime novels. As critics such as Thomas have noted, the epidemic is more often left unspoken than not; indeed, there has been a "monumental failure to mourn the losses of AIDS."[8] Now that that silence is ending, the question of how to give shape to this unfolding history becomes important.

The politics of genre

As a signature genre of the "transition" era, South African crime writing's literary-political significance is currently much debated. Leon de Kock provocatively claims that "as far as 'political fiction' goes, 'crime thrillers' are about the most operative and readable kinds we have going right now," and that part of the genre's political usefulness is in its mapping of the present, its ability to chart "bewilderingly changed political out-theres."[9] Christopher Warnes meanwhile has examined two of the most successful South African crime writers, Deon Meyers and Margie Orford, arguing that their work, while stylistically conventional, is overtly political. Indeed, liberal South African crime fiction is a kind of watchdog genre, taking on important issues "of the day," from sexual violence to political corruption. Michael Titlestad and Ashlee Polatinsky, however, looking at Mike Nicol's work in particular and its shift from "literary" to "genre" in the transition era, critique crime fiction. "Does the proliferation of popular crime fiction in the last decade," they ask, "imply that there is a pervasive abandonment of the complexities of (permanent) transitional politics in favour of the consolations of genre?"[10]

There is, of course, a long-standing critical debate over whether crime fiction as a form is conservative, fictively resolving contradictions in the social order—or, as Warnes argues, managing anxieties about threats, real or imagined—through the reassuring predictability of formula, and plots that solve mysteries, close narratives, and assert the ability to *know*.[11] I want to note the temporality of this form of knowing: the quest of this genre is to know what happened in the past, even as "what happened" is continuing into the present and putting the protagonist who is attempting to know what happened into danger. Literature that addresses the AIDS epidemic, meanwhile, has no comparable genre through which to offer such psychologically satisfying textual transactions, in which a threat is repeatedly evoked and temporary, imaginary resolution offered. Paradoxically, though, crime fiction has also been criticized for its lack of a larger resolution—especially for the more "hard-boiled" version's tendency to present the current state of affairs as insoluble, no matter how many criminals you catch or kill. Where "struggle" writing might have emphasized solidarity or collective action for broad change, conventional crime novels bring a larger world into view, but the protagonist can only make right a very small piece of it, if that. Crime fiction can even exhibit a sort of self-satisfied cynicism. "In a South African crime thriller," De Kock declares, "you no longer beat your breast about the fact that former comrades are boozy sexist fat cats who take out 'hits' on anyone who gets in their way, that professional killers stalk the streets, or that the entire policing and justice system is a stinking, corrupt hellhole. That's just the way things are. Get used to it."[12] Crime fiction of this sort utterly lacks the resistant utopian futurity that José Esteban Muñoz theorized, in which radical alternatives to the present are made imaginable.[13]

This brand of "undiluted political pessimism" fuels both "law and order" politics and racist fears about black political power.[14] To write about crime in South Africa at all may inevitably reinforce a global discourse that associates crime with blackness and violence with Africa. Crime fiction necessarily wrestles with these overdetermined significations. The Oscar Pistorius trial—a murder mystery so dramatic that it seems fictional—to some degree undermines the racialization of crime as black: both the killer and the victim are white; the lead investigator who was, amazingly, pulled off the case when he was separately accused of attempted murder, is also white. Nonetheless, the fact that a national icon committed this act—a man whose international achievements as a disabled sportsman made him a symbol of both South Africa as plucky underdog and South Africa as modern and technologized—reinforces the notion that violent crime is at the center of contemporary South Africanness.[15] Pistorius's trial, however, also made white paranoia about black crime uniquely visible, since his defense rested on his claim that he shot his girlfriend, Reeva Steenkamp, because he mistakenly thought that she was a black armed intruder. As Hedley Twidle points out:

> At first, Reeva Steenkamp's death was presented as a tragic Valentine's Day mistake. The speed with which this narrative emerged in the media was significant. There was a tacit assumption that a domestic crime such as this one was immediately readable. The unspoken perpetrator here was the spectral (black) intruder in the home, a product of a state that could not ensure public safety.

This sort of paranoia is, according to Sianne Ngai, central to the aesthetics of noir and is indeed a key affect of our times: a "sentiment of disenchantment" that is about "obstructed agency" and "one's perceived status as a small subject in a 'total system.'"[16] The sense of being a "small subject" is above all the structure of feeling of the individual in late capitalism, but it also aptly describes how some people experience postapartheid whiteness—a feeling that expresses itself through a sense of intense vulnerability to crime. Steinberg links this to national temporal narratives: "White South Africa's experience of crime cannot be dissociated from the fact that it no longer finds its identity written into the state and that the official narrative of South Africa's futurity is no longer its own."[17]

Historicizing crime

For whites, the experience of violent crime after apartheid *is* new, which is part of why it is a symbol of the postapartheid dispensation—particularly in the crime genre, which in its most conventional form is primarily produced by white writers. While whites "find themselves vastly under-represented among the victims of violent crime,"[18] the body that is imagined to be vulnerable to violent crime is nonetheless often white. Thus, Reeva Steenkamp's killing overshadows the simultaneous, brutal murder of Anene Booysen, and, indeed, the literary representation of rape that instantiates the "new South Africa" is that of Lucy Lurie in J. M. Coetzee's *Disgrace*, rather than the far more statistically likely rape of a black woman.

The historical temporality of the "crime wave" that has been understood as "post-apartheid" is thus complex. As Gary Kynoch points out: "Violent crime and social conflict are not recent developments in the lives of most urban South Africans. Many of Johannesburg's formerly segregated black residential areas, known as townships, have suffered from criminal violence and vigilantism since their inception and attempts to account for the current crisis need to be grounded within this history."[19] Historians have documented the growth of criminal organizations in the chaos of urban industrializing South Africa from the nineteenth century,[20] as well as the lack of state intervention in these developments.[21] Under apartheid, black areas were policed primarily for passbook violations and political dissent, leaving criminality itself unregulated and uncounted, so that black communities had to fashion multiple alternative forms of community policing and justice. After the uprisings in 1976, the local police were ejected from the townships, and the state security forces—who had long backed particular players within township conflicts for their own purposes—became deeply involved with criminality, even as the line between "political" and "criminal" was blurred within the ferment of the 1980s.[22] Beukes's description of an AK-47 in *Zoo City* as "that favorite weapon of revolutionaries, criminals, and revolutionaries-turned-criminals"[23] is indicative of contemporary cynicism about the collapse between those identities and projects. The return of state policing to this environment after apartheid was difficult:

> It was to this terrain—one where security was bought, sold, and bartered, and also exchanged for solidarity and friendship—that the police returned in the early 1990s during the transition … My contention is that they never found sufficient moral authority to rise above the logic of this terrain, nor to refashion it, and that they thus had to negotiate their way into it and join its other players.[24]

For many black people, then, the state of insecurity produced by both crime and an untrustworthy, absent, or hostile police service was ongoing, rather than new. Criminal groups did, however, significantly expand their territory after apartheid, while crime also became more transnational, with the arrival of international crime networks.

While these specific South African genealogies of crime are important for understanding the contemporary moment, one might also see the arrival of these new forms and spaces of crime as part of a larger pattern of capitalist modernity. In John and Jean Comaroff's *Law and Disorder in the Postcolony*, they discuss how "democratization has been accompanied, almost everywhere, by a sharp rise in crime and violence … the latter-day coming of more or less elected, more or less representative political regimes—founded, more or less, on the rule of law—has, ironically, brought with it a rising tide of lawlessness."[25] They argue that crime is not a sign of the inability of the global south to get democracy right, but rather that it is bound up in the contemporary form that democracy takes under capitalism: "criminal violence does not so much repudiate the rule of law or the licit operations of the market as appropriate their forms—and re-commission their substance. Its perpetrators create parallel modes of production and profiteering, sometimes even of governance and taxation, thereby establishing simulacra of social order."[26] South Africa's crime wave, both real and fictional, is thus arguably a sign that the country is becoming more like everywhere else. After all, to a certain extent crime is understood as normal in the global North; you can't turn on the television in the United States or the United Kingdom without encountering policemen, criminals, lawyers, and private eyes. Neoliberal time is global and so is crime fiction.

Postimperial crime writing

The rise of crime fiction, seen from this angle, marks postapartheid South Africa's entrance into the structures of feeling of global capitalism at large. Titlestad and Polatinsky ask, "Is this a dilution of South African literature that will make it at once more global, but also less individuated, less discernible and less significant?"[27] Certainly, much South African crime writing is "generic" in that sense. For Nels Pearson and Marc Singer, however, the current outpouring of the form across the postcolonial world is "formally diverse, flourishing in multiple cultures, and engaged with the production of knowledge and transformation of consciousness within and across societies."[28] Indeed, they argue that postcolonial crime fiction is "a genre in the process of interrogating or defying its own imperial history."[29] If we look back at an earlier moment in South African fiction, to *Drum* magazine's glamorization of the gangster alongside Arthur Maimane's stories about the black detective Chester O. Morena, we can see that both speak back to the imperial archive of writing about the racialized criminal other. As a figure of black masculinity aligned with intelligence and rationality, the enforcer of the law rather than its subject, the black detective challenges racist ideology—even if, like the PIs of hardboiled American fiction, he might be more interested in justice than legality. Meanwhile, the *tsotsi* of the apartheid era is an ambivalent figure of identification and celebration precisely *because* he defies the law in an authoritarian state. South African fiction, like its diverse counterparts across the global South, has long been using the trope of crime to engage with questions of heroism and race, justice, and order.

The law, its making, and its breaking has, after all, been bound up with the history of apartheid and the formation of a new country. Courtrooms have been the stage for great political dramas, antiapartheid prison writing is an important archive that engages with questions of crime in complex ways, and the Truth and Reconciliation Commission (TRC) was all about the uncovering of hidden crimes. The TRC was also a mechanism through which to shift from fighting the police state to becoming a new kind of state. Novels that are not strictly speaking crime novels, from *Disgrace* to K. Sello Duiker's *Thirteen Cents*, examine the creation and transgression of new social contracts. More recently, Imraan Coovadia's *Tales of the Metric System*, which offers a fragmented panorama of South African history from the 1960s through the present through multiple intersecting points of view, presents both spying and thieving as threads that tie South Africa's narratives together: dystopian mood indeed. My definition of "the crime novel" here is a loose one, but I take my cue from the literature itself and its "stretching" of the "boundaries of the genre," to borrow from Christine Matzke and Susanne Mühleisen.[30]

The muti noir novels I examine here definitely challenge the definitions of the genre. *Blood Safari* and *Ancient Rites* are marketed as detective novels, but depart from the city, the conventional scene of crime fiction. *Zoo City* mixes the detective novel with speculative fiction of two kinds; set in a science-fiction-esque dystopian near future, the novel also has elements of "magical realism," and directly borrows from British "fantasy" writer Philip Pullman's *The Golden Compass*. *Young Blood* and *Book of the Dead* are both written from the perspective of the "criminal," and solve no mysteries. All of them offer arresting visions of the shape of the history being lived through.

Blood Safari: Undead histories

Deon Meyer's books are one of postapartheid South Africa's most successful cultural exports.[31] *Blood Safari*, his fifth novel, originally published as *Onsigbaar* in Afrikaans, is a skillfully executed, stylistically conventional work of genre fiction that espouses environmentalist politics. Its protagonist, Lemmer, is a white male "personal security expert," an ex-con who is "new" South African enough to like and respect his lesbian boss. Warnes argues persuasively that Meyer's white middle-aged male detective figures are "transitional," in the sense that they are men who have lived through and beyond the apartheid era, and also that they are old-school tough guys who are working through their emotional wounds. As Warnes puts it:

> The emotionally scarred, alcoholic, violent detective, who in the hard-boiled tradition is unwilling or unable to confront his past, in Meyer's novels yields, cautiously, to the representation of men who find rehabilitation through the processes of detection and protecting vulnerable others…their suffering and their rehabilitation can be read as symptomatic of the challenges and opportunities for white masculinity in the post-apartheid period.[32]

The white bodyguard/detective in this novel has a tense relationship with a black male police detective which ultimately becomes an alliance; in this imagined South Africa, the white man is now a sort of consultant to the newly black state, a relationship that can be beneficial. Lemmer is hired to protect a beautiful white woman who's been attacked just after she thinks she recognizes her long-lost brother, who appeared on television as the prime suspect in the killing of four poachers and a traditional healer. The brother disappeared during the apartheid era when he was working for the military. It turns out that what is ultimately at stake at the end of a very complex plot is the cover-up of the apartheid state's assassination of Samora Machel in 1986; this real-life event, in which the leader of independent, socialist Mozambique died in a plane crash, remains the subject of conspiracy theories of various kinds.

The novel thus uses the thriller's standard temporal form—finding out about the past in order to end its nefarious workings in the present—to produce a specifically South African temporality: apartheid and its crimes continue to shape the transitional present and its history is as yet unfinished. *Blood Safari* is in some ways, then, a TRC novel, given that its message seems to be that painful histories need to be unearthed; but it goes beyond the TRC both in its focus on the crimes committed by the regime outside the country's borders, and on how members of the security forces have since found lucrative new markets for their "skills," rather than being brought to book. This historicizing impulse is substantive and necessary; as we have seen, one cannot understand crime in the present without attending to apartheid histories. However, through this apartheid lens the text quite literally puts whites at the center of the national narrative—they are both those who cause and solve crimes—even as it envisions a certain amount of hope for the crimes of the past being laid to rest, villains contained, and a new multiracial social compact forged in the process. We might draw here on Twidle's critique of the tendency to explain the present through the apartheid past as a "temporality of repetition," in terms of which Marikana is Sharpeville come again, the Secrecy Bill apartheid censorship revivified, and so on. This master narrative "show(s) up the limited repertoire of conceptual shapes available in the public culture as South Africa tries to imagine the relation between past and present."

Ancient Rites: Uncanny returns and renewals

This is not, however, the only "conceptual shape" through which history is being imaginatively organized within crime writing. Diale Tlholwe does not have the global success of Deon Meyer, but *Ancient Rites* won the South African Literary Award debut prize and he has published a follow up in the series, *Counting the Coffins* (2011). *Ancient Rites* offers a vision of postapartheid South Africa in which black people are the cops, the criminals, and the maverick PIs. The past that counts in this novel is not apartheid, but an older, yet still existing "traditional" way of life. Tlholwe tells the story of Thabang Maje, a former teacher turned "security consultant" who takes the case of the disappearance of a female teacher in a remote village, which might be connected to a string of murders of female sex workers who earn their money from truckers. Coincidentally, Thabang and the missing teacher, the beautiful and charismatic Mamorena, were lovers in their youth, but she left him. He poses as a replacement teacher in the eerie village, where everyone seems to be hiding something, including a young girl who looks uncannily like Mamorena. Although he presumes that he is trying to find her killer, eventually he discovers that Mamorena is alive, in a village in a hidden valley; she is a sangoma, and has become a local leader. He learns that she left him, not for other men, but to pursue her calling—an old, personal mystery is solved. Meanwhile, the young girl is her child, and the father is the local bigwig who hired Thabang, but does not want to acknowledge the girl. The killer of sex workers, the black head teacher of the school, is confronted by Mamorena and Thabang, but manages to kill Mamorena, and is then killed by Thabang. The death that the narrator sought to confirm and explain thus belatedly, tragically comes to pass: what had seemed to be an unexpectedly happy ending goes wrong in the final hour.

Ancient Rites has a layered, intricate temporal structure, which could be described as fitful—there are a lot of false endings and alternate beginnings. It opens with a prologue, which throws the reader into the middle of dramatic, disorienting events that are not resolved or explained by the end of the prologue. We are in a dark stone tunnel, we do not know who the narrator is, or what time period we are in. The first chapter then starts the story at a more conventional point, when Thabang is being driven to the village. Here there is a crisp, even bleak particularity; the narrator is in a car on a Monday morning two hours from Mafeking with a Regional Education Director called J. B. M. Tiro. It is clearly postapartheid South Africa. The story takes place over the course of six days, and is told in a linear fashion with the occasional expository narration of past events blended into an otherwise chronological progression. The chapters are organized by and titled with days of the week, from Monday to Saturday—we are in rational, everyday, modern time. The reader is made to wait to catch back up to the opening scene of the prologue, and eventually does find out what was going on. It turns out to have been an important moment of discovery, when Thabang first sees Mamorena again, but is not the end of the novel or the story. The denouement of the plot, when Mamorena dies and Thabang shoots her murderer, is also not the end of the novel. He decides to take her daughter— which Mamorena had asked him to do—and flees the scene in order to evade police scrutiny of his killing. He then meets his city girlfriend on the road, who has come to find out why he isn't calling her, and tells her the whole story. For a moment, they seem to be a proto-happy family, escaping into a potential future, but the girlfriend decides that they should go back to the village to take care of the situation properly—not legally, but culturally. They attend Mamorena's funeral, the local community is pleased that they have done so, and then they leave the girl with them for the meantime, with the promise that they will return for her again.

It's tempting to read these endings that turn out not to be the end as allegorically meaningful: apartheid is over, but the struggle has not finished. More darkly, an unexpected happy ending is swiftly turned into bloodshed. Grand moments of transformation, however, also give way to incremental, slightly awkward continuations, during which important ethical decisions still need to be made. Overall, there is a scrambling of clarity about both historical origins and endings: we are in a zone of temporal uncertainty.

At the same time, however, there are two important temporal modes in conflict in the book, the modern and the traditional, which are mapped to some extent on to the rural and the urban. The prologue, written in such a different style than the chapters, is an interesting foray into the "ancient." These are the first lines:

> From this place …
>
>   I came to a curve in the damp, cold wall of the tunnel, to a moment when the roar of the drums and stamping feet seemed to push me backwards, but the urgent, sweaty heat rolling out of the body of the large, over-muscled man behind me did not let me forget that there was no retreat …. as the tunnel narrowed, an inhumanly large eye seemed to come out of the darkness to examine me … a small boy wearing a loincloth appeared. With slow deliberation he set ablaze the candles that were hanging in recesses cut into the walls, conjuring the full, terrible beauty of a huge female face out of the nothing before my eyes. (9–10)

As if he is going "backwards" in time, the narrator meets a series of surreal primitivist motifs. The passage references imperial writing; the rock tunnels of *King's Solomon's Mines*, the Kipling-esque small boy in a loincloth, the beautiful and imperious black woman, "frightening, erotic, triumphant and disdainful" (10), whose face is on the door and whom moments later he sees on a throne, with one breast bared, which recalls both *She* and Kurtz's "savage and superb" African mistress in *Heart of Darkness*,[33] while the "giant" and "muscled" (10) black man forcing him onward is reminiscent of any number of Ian Fleming villains. When we learn that the narrator—the point of identification for the reader, the observing eye as opposed to the "inhumanly large eye" that emerges from the darkness—is himself African, the racial politics of the literary tradition Tlholwe has summoned up are immediately challenged. We learn, later, that the woman on the throne is Mamoreno, and indeed that the black giant pushing Thabang forward is on the side of good. The status of the "ancient" is positive, not negative, in the novel, and the primitivism of the opening is a kind of red herring, which might prompt the reader to question how traditionalism is usually represented, including its temporal placement as anachronistic and "backwards."

The detective figure is therefore not aligned with modernity against the "ancient," but is temporally hybrid. Although he never loses his wry watchfulness and returns to the space of the city at the end of the book, he goes through something of a renewal through this salving of an old romantic wound, and through contact with a matriarchal traditional culture. Indeed, a certain fantasy of *feminist* traditionalism is in many ways the moral center of the novel, which has a male "hero" but a plethora of powerful intelligent female characters, and a cast of other men who range from the useless to the irresponsible to the murderously misogynist. Thabang comes to be very much on the side of the people who are renewing their traditions, and not the police and the modern state, which seems, in fact, somewhat irrelevant. Interestingly, the police take on three guises in this book: a memory of when Thabang was mistakenly and somewhat vindictively arrested while doing his detective work in the past; an encounter with an intelligent, straightforward black female police officer working on the same case, who subsequently disappears from the plot; and finally, after he has "crossed over" and is to some extent on the run: "A police van leapt out of the darkness behind us, slowed down and crept past. Four hard faces—two black and two white—under blue caps stared at us before the van gathered speed and vanished into the dark again" (161–2). Rather than black against white, the novel casts (progressive) traditionalist ethnic communities against the impersonal, inefficient, multiracial modern state, and crime-ridden contemporary society.

When Mamorena speaks, at the end of the prologue, she uses a kind of archaic poeticism:

> "All those who assume that all things are settled," she said, speaking in a rich contralto that swept towards me and upwards towards the invisible roof:

> 'all questions answered
> all truths revealed,
> all histories recorded …

all wounds healed,
all quests ended,
for all time, are deluded.
Their undoing assured.'
I agreed with everything she said. (11)

Thabang "agreed with everything she said"; indeed, she seems to be articulating the temporal uncertainty of the book in her speech. Paradoxically, this "ancient wisdom" has the distinct flavor of postapartheid political disenchantment and neoliberal disorientation. David Scott suggests that "it is precisely when the future has ceased to be a source of longing and anticipation that the past has become such a densely animated object of enchantment."[34] That could be a description of Mamorena herself, but the village she hides in, too, remains an uncanny space within the novel, inside a cave and yet outdoors, and magically invisible to the modern state. As Scott says, "The past has loosed itself from the future and acquired a certain quasi-autonomy."[35] The turn to tradition in *Ancient Rites* is anti-imperial and feminist, and it offers a site for imagining alternatives to the present, but the novel's sense of futurity is convoluted, continually stalling: the densely animated and enchanting Mamorena, after all, is killed, and her daughter's prospects remain up in the air at the novel's close.

Young Blood: Narcotic capitalism

In Sifiso Mzobe's *Young Blood*, which won the 2011 *Sunday Times* Fiction Prize, the protagonist and narrator, Sipho, commits crimes, rather than solving them. As Grant Farred puts it in his discussion of Victor Headley's *Yardie*, a Jamaican-British pulp fiction novel that has a drug dealer hero, "By bringing the 'cell phone' youth into literary view … Headley opens up the conversation about … postcolonialism on a markedly different terrain, enabling the possibility for new kinds of inquiries, with previously undocumented metaphors, nuances, and literary valences."[36] *Young Blood* indeed articulates an underwritten imagined subaltern perspective—and the township becomes a complex site of generational and class differentiation from his point of view—but the novel is ultimately a story of redemption, so that Sipho is less of a glamorous antihero than D. in *Yardie*. Nonetheless, the novel is an intense foray into the temporality of young men committing crimes—a refusal to consider the likely future consequences of actions so as to acquire pleasure in the here and now.

This temporality is in conflict with a black working-class reproductive futurity underwritten by the ancestors, who, it is implied, save Sipho from ending up "Young Blood."

The story is set in what appears to be the recent past, when Sipho was seventeen, dropped out of school, and began stealing cars with a childhood friend, Musa. Sipho is telling the story, and this enunciative structure creates the expectation of a probable "happy ending" as the story unfolds, although the narrator could be speaking from prison or, borrowing from Phaswane Mpe's *Welcome to Our Hillbrow*, speaking from beyond the grave. Most of the novel relates what happened during this brief, heady, dangerous period of his life in the literary equivalent of a series of long takes punctuated by fades to black. While the narration itself is an act of retrospection, Sipho at seventeen lives his life in the now.

A sense of time coming a-kilter is dramatized from the very beginning: "I remember the year I turned seventeen as the year of stubborn seasons. Summer lasted well into autumn, and autumn annexed half of winter. It was hot in May and cold in November. The older folk in my township swore they had never seen anything like it. Winter nibbled on spring, and spring on summer" (7). These images of the seasons gently but inexorably consuming one another are not quite apocalyptic, but the cycles of nature are nonetheless troubled and even inverted. The horizon of proper temporality has been put into question, while Sipho is refusing chrononormativity. He rejects the regulated time of education by quitting school, and what he later calls the "cycle of nothingness" (101) of his parent's working-class life. His mother, a cleaner at a hospital, tells him that "in this world you don't just give up" (101). She says, "You must keep trying" (101), but he refuses this blue-collar hope in education, hard work, and slow progress. His father is a car mechanic; he steals cars. Sipho describes unfinished renovation work on their house, which "took years to complete, as something of greater importance always seemed to crop up—water and electricity bills, food, school uniforms and shoes. A shopping mall had been built on the outskirts of the township, while the builder's sand grew grass and turned shrubby in our back yard" (10). Commerce—the shopping mall and the houses of the newly rich in the township—has been advancing, but they are left behind. This structure of feeling about time seems deeply linked to the dream deferred of postapartheid democracy, and fifteen years of patience with nation building.

The temporality of crime that Sipho chooses instead is in large part a kind of dreamlike present tense, in which life unspools in unpredictable ways and at varying rates of speed. As he puts it during one of many car journeys, "I fell into a dreamy state, my mind alternating between too fast and too slow. My cellphone was out of airtime. I was already living inside a blur." (86). At one point, he recounts a dream in which he is mired in black tar rain, as if the street itself had become liquid and pulled him into its flow. Plans are always being made by Sipho and his partners in crime, but they are usually last-minute and short-term, often have to be changed as things go wrong, or are abandoned altogether when a more enticing possibility appears, and he skates spontaneously from one situation to the next, without any regularizing schedule. The drugs he takes either speed things up or pleasantly numb reality: "An instant brain scramble hit the center of my forehead, then spread like the tributaries of a river on a map. My lips, nose and tongue felt numb" (138). The narrative relates his activities with vivid yet repetitious specificity: eating, drinking; buying, putting on, and taking off clothes; smoking, taking drugs, blacking out into sleep, waking up again; looking at women, flirting, having sex; making calls and texting; evasively placating his family and girlfriend; and, of course, driving, stealing, working on, spinning, and burning cars.

This is life experienced primarily through consumption; the narrative dwells on hungers that set in and are satiated as quickly as possible, sensations of intoxication and numbness, and specific designer labels and makes of cars. "The 325is was flirtatious under my palms ... Musa, my waiter, supplied cooler-box-cold beer. Under a yellow streetlight, two shapes waved in silhouette. All I could make out were curves" (17). Cars and girls are interchangeable and sexualized; female bodies are consumable, and car theft is sexual mastery—"I held it firm, traced the slash, turned the tool" (115)—and all of this "risky behavior" inevitably summons up the specter of AIDS. After an ominous sexual encounter with a woman whose name he cannot remember, Sipho says, "I met my ghost again, a few months later, in a dream so violent that the rain in it was blood. Her ass was still as firm, the rest of her a decade older" (104). The sped-up aging of his "ghost" is perhaps a trace of the ruined bodies of those with the illness, entangled here with the violence of the criminal world: both are possible futures that Sipho disavows—repressed knowledge that returns in dreams—in order to continue getting what he wants in the present.

Crime is thus a form of youth-driven capitalist consumerism, which Graeme Reid puts in historical perspective: "The political transition has been coupled with ... a renewed emphasis on fashion and style after the austere struggle years and the consumer boycotts that characterized the last phase of militant struggle against apartheid. ... The status symbols of the new order are aptly summed up by the 'three Cs' (cash, car, cell phone)."[37] While *Young Blood* is definitely engaging with contemporary youth culture and the materialist aspirations of young men with no capital, crime is not just consumerism in this novel—and criminals are not just youths. Crime is also presented as a form of *work*, a trade and a craft that involves skill, focus, knowledge, and dedication; it is, as the Comaroffs point out, an appropriation of the forms of the market rather than a rejection of them. Sipho's friend Vusi looks like a rap video gangster, but is a model worker when it comes to retooling stolen cars, and Musa, who grew up even poorer than the others as an informal settlement kid, expresses utter scorn for a gang called the Cold Hearts because they simply "take" with excessive violence and, crucially, do not pay other criminals for work done. Sipho's crew sees car theft as both pleasure and business, albeit illegal, and they work for and take advice from older gangsters.

While crime in this novel is initially presented as a new, youth phenomenon, it turns out to be a tradition, with long-established local specialties, rituals, and lingo, as seen in this exchange about gang symbols and tattoos: "We are brothers, you and I, money lover. The very thumb you raise up, I was raised on it. My body is a gallery of medals" (31). We learn that Sipho's father was a gangster in his youth:

> I knew what the stars tattooed on my father's shoulders stood for. I knew that the stars were emblems from his past life as a lieutenant in the 26 prison gang. I knew that the 26 gang was for the money. Dad looked at me with regretful eyes, shook his head, and said, "It is just a fairy tale, son. My boy, never believe in fairy tales." (33)

The older generation that stayed in the crime business and survived—for whom the "fairy tale" of financial success is happening, albeit at brutal cost—is more than capable of running the new shadow economy "In dress, Mdala was old school, with formal shirts, creased trousers and shiny shoes. In the game of money, though, he was post-future school. He owned two mansions in the townships. His taxis always looked new. Mdala was what we in the township call a 'razo'—a classic old-time rider" (73). Crime isn't new, but it has been renewed in "post-future school" South Africa.

Within the criminal worlds of the novel, conflicting temporalities are to some degree mapped onto younger and older generations, and the central image of the car speaks to both. An older gangster-cum-businessman admires Sipho's "drive," and both cars and thieves are valued for their speed: "If you have ever seen a car thief at work—and you probably never have—the only word to describe it is 'swift'" (85) There is repeated emphasis on the smooth, easy movement of expensive cars, which might be interpreted as fulfilling a desire for social mobility—Sipho can literally travel effortlessly between radically different locations in and beyond the city. However, this speed is also associated with stasis. As Sipho says, "I don't remember the speedometer and rev counter. The gauges on the dashboard ceased to exist for the moment. All I recall is the car and the road" (77). The young men like to "drift"—driving fast, and then freezing the car's movement with the brake, and spinning in the air in suspended, ecstatic motion. The accumulation of cars and money is a kind of false progress. Money piles up, is spent, or is exchanged in fluid and confusing deals, piles up again, and then is taken in one fell swoop by the police. This form of capitalism then, which mirrors an official version, is not progress, but a form of stasis, an eternal present tense with no political alternative.

Sipho is eventually pulled back into a more traditional circuit of temporality, however. As Vusi's mother says to him, "We know it is hard for you but this is no way to live. Parents should not bury their children—it is the other way round. Money may rule everything, but it is not the beginning and end" (146). He is given multiple signs about the fates that might befall him. Musa's stories of prison are horrifying, and Vusi sees his Uncle Sazi, a former gangster dying of AIDS, as an embodied warning:

> "He stays with us now, a shadow of himself. I'll tell you something about this HIV, my friend: it hinders progress. I think sometimes, of where uncle Sazi could be if he were not sick. What we are doing now he did ten years ago." ... "At least he lived a little, he tasted things, drove the flyest," I said ... "It is the violence with which he is dying that I worry about." (91)

Vusi himself is killed, and then Sipho is pulled over by cops when he is driving a stolen car with drugs in it. Miraculously, he makes a deal with the cops, and a series of strokes of luck save him from the men who asked him to sell the drugs. Sipho discovers that his long-suffering girlfriend is pregnant; he is thus fully pulled back into reproductive futurity—as opposed to the queer brotherhood of car thieves—and legal working-class time. Strangely, though, the pregnancy turns out to be a false alarm. The final lines of the novel are Sipho reflecting on his ability to conform to educational time: "From my first class at the technical college, I realized that my mind no longer drifted into a maze of tangents. I concentrated for the forty minutes the class lasted ... I knew that I concentrated in class because of everything I saw in the year that I turned seventeen" (227–8). He has been "scared straight."

All this luck, it would seem, comes from the intervention of the ancestors, to whom Sipho's father had made him appeal through the family's traditional healer: "What do you think goes on in the night? You think you roam the streets alone? As you walk, bad spirits are on your left and right, back and front" (57). His father argues that he should get protection from the ancestors because "life is progress, my boy" (57). Muti is not linked to "primitivism" but to continuation, to pragmatic survival within dangerous modernity. The novel thus stages a conflict between the seductive but deathly time of crime/capitalism—the time of the present—as opposed to the continuous and collective time of the ancestors, which underwrites national "progress."

The Book of the Dead: The accumulative present tense

In Kgebetli Moele's *The Book of the Dead*, the first half, "Book of the Living," focalizes the point of view of Khutso, a man who has been infected with HIV by his now-dead wife, through an omniscient narrator. In a passage just before the end of the first part of the book, however, an "I" begins speaking, and speaks for the entirety of the second half, "Book of the Dead," in an act of narrative infection, possession, and hijacking:

> I live amongst you, waiting like a predator … You lovingly summon me. I don't break in. My schemes are not like that. I am willingly invited in, and only then do I take up my position and do my work. Don't get me wrong, I love my work—it is my work and I do it with pride … Many think that I am only for the poor, and that I will never come for them, but I am walking with two legs amongst you. Smiling back at your smile. Laughing at your jokes. You can think that I am not coming for you, but I will eat you out and leave what's left of you for death. (77)

An implacable force made animate through those it infects, the illness describes itself in this assaultive direct address to the reader as a kind of criminal "predator," "breaking in" like a thief, but also a con artist or lover. This structure echoes Angela Makholwa's *Red Ink* (2007), a more conventional crime novel that opens with the repellant first-person voice of a male serial killer and then alternates between third-person narration of his point of view and the point of view of the female journalist investigating him. The illness takes control of the angry and grief-stricken Khutso after he decides not to kill himself, and the two of them begin a mission to infect as many people as possible by having unprotected sex with them. Khutso's first act is to buy a notebook that he designs: "a leather-covered journal with five hundred unnumbered pages—each page divided into two columns—with two golden pages at the beginning and two at the end" (82). He tells the sales clerk that he's going to use it to investigate his male lineage, and the clerk says, "And here I was thinking that you are a serial killer, and you wanted to record the names of your victims" (153). Of course, that is what he's going to do. Khutso is in a sense the "serial killer," but he is also just the instrument, someone whose own voice has been snuffed out by a more powerful force. AIDS is cast here as a sardonically evil criminal, a tokoloshe that possesses people, and a macabre accountant.

The "book of the dead" is an accounts ledger, in which important information about the disease's victims are recorded. Although the entries become brutally short and personal—"*15 August 2008: Daisy Fay. Done. Liberal white woman!*" (155)—they begin and end with Khutso's numbers:

> *03 October 2002: Khutso*
> *Age: 41 years*
> Height: 1.74 metres
> Weight: 107.6 kilograms
> Status: HIV positive
> *CD4 count: 650.* (89)

The book's gold color is repeatedly emphasized, and evokes the bloody history of the acquisition of gold in Southern Africa; disease is thus a form of accumulation and acquisition, and infection is a form of workmanship, akin to the craftsmanship of thievery in *Young Blood*. Finance capitalism is serial murder, it would seem, and its allure is infectious. The social world that Khutso seduces his way through is primarily that of affluent black South Africa. As the disease puts it:

> The average entry was seven women a week, one for each day of the week, but the record was sixteen in a week: 23–29 June 2003. That was when Khutso was at his peak. We were dangerous then. How? Money and women. They mix in ways that even I don't understand. And Khutso, well, he had enough money, and he could kick it the way he liked. (153)

Although Khutso's life has a very definite arc, and he dies at the end of the novel, like Sipho in *Young Blood* he exists during the era of his possession in an accumulative present tense.

This is also a deeply masculine mode of acquisition—the notebook does establish his "male lineage" in a sense—and while the novel presents a male subjectivity built on the conquest and domination of others as villainy, it also steers dangerously close to persuading the reader that the judgments Khutso and the disease make about women—that they are all, without exception, faithless and seducible—are correct. There is no room in this novel for sex positivity, or indeed for forgiveness, since the epidemic is represented as a form of interpersonal *crime*, rather than the product of human fallibility; eight years on from *Welcome to Our Hillbrow*, it offers a very different politics to Mpe's ethics of forgiveness. Whether the narrative voice infects us or is so repellant as to incite critique remains questionable.

Within the space of the novel itself, there is no vision of redemptive futurity akin to *Young Blood*'s black working-class heteroreproductive futurity rooted in the continuity of the ancestors. There is, however, a continuation of the present condition. Both *Young Blood* and *Book of the Dead* have a repetitive aesthetic, one conquest happening after another quickly and serially, and in *The Book of the Dead*, the disease's only goal is to keep existing: "I am alive, but I have no dreams or visions; I have only a purpose" (77). There is an interesting echo here of Coetzee's *Waiting for the Barbarians*:

> One thought alone preoccupies the submerged mind of Empire: how not to end, how not to die, how to prolong its era. By day it pursues its enemies. It is cunning and ruthless, it sends its bloodhounds everywhere. By night it feeds on images of disaster: the sack of cities, the rape of populations, pyramids of bones, acres of desolation.[38]

Empire is a social system built and potentially unbuilt by humans; part of the horror of AIDS is that it seems outside the human amphitheater of politics and struggle, even though the responses to the disease, which have crucially shaped the epidemic as it has unfolded, are in fact deeply political. This novel of AIDS as crime and as capitalist accumulation thus emphasizes how the neoliberal order of the present aspires to be beyond and outside history, with no disruption from politics. *Book of the Dead* does not imagine an alternative to this accumulative present tense, but it forces the reader into an intense and disturbing intimacy with it.

Zoo City: Modernity as magical dystopia

Zoo City is speculative fiction—by definition, then, dealing with futurity or possibilities beyond the "now." The novel, which contains an array of precise dates, is set in the very near future to its time of publication. Its dystopianism lies in its intensification of the negative aspects of the present: the struggle for money rules, and political activism is absent. The plot begins with the disappearance of one of a pair of twin teen pop stars, Song and S'bu, who are photogenic, talented AIDS orphans; Song reappears, but is killed toward the end of the novel, reproducing a temporal plot arc from *Ancient Rites*. The detective and narrator is a black woman, Zinzi December, and the villain turns out to be a white male record company mogul. Beukes's semi-parodic deployment of multiple other forms of contemporary writing within her novel—the tabloid newspaper article, the online movie review, the music magazine interview, and the academic paper—lends the novel a familiar modern discursive texture. The material and social inequality of this world is also not that far from reality—along with the ineffective, uninterested police force, which Beukes introduces early on with noir nonchalance: "A dead zoo in Zoo City is low priority even on a good day" (11). This speculative future that shadows the present, then, marks the difficulty of imagining radically different futures right now. Where the novel fully departs from realism is in its central trope of the "animalled."

Some time in the 1980s, people who had committed crimes mysteriously began to develop "Acquired Aposymbiotic Familiarism" (AAF), or, more colloquially, become "zoos"—and the phenomenon came into global public consciousness in 2002. Zoos are deeply connected to an animal, from which they cannot be separated without pain, and they acquire unique powers; they will also eventually succumb to "the Undertow," and will die. Being "animalled" is a visible stigma, depending on the obtrusiveness of your animal. As Zinzi says, "In China, they execute zoos on principle. Because nothing says guilty like a spirit critter at your side" (16). In South Africa, however, they are constitutionally protected from medical experimentation (156). This imaginary form of otherness is a way of bringing to vivid life the social divide between those marked as "criminals" and those considered to be (good) citizens. Zinzi herself is a zoo; a former addict, she was responsible for her brother's death because of her involvement in drugs. Her animal is a sloth, while her supernatural power is the ability to find people's lost things. That is what makes her a detective, but she is still a criminal—her poverty and debts force her to participate in 419 scams, about which she feels mounting shame over the course of the novel, as well as her ongoing sorrow about her brother. From the start, then, the reader is positioned to feel sympathy for zoos.

Being animalled also works as a metaphor for multiple forms of difference— addiction, disability, sexuality. Characters talk of coming out of the animalled closet, and a rapper pretending to be a zoo says, "It's not like being gay. We don't have some magic zoodar to detect other zoos" (308). In the South African context, of course, it also evokes racism; being "animalled" is a way to describe being racialized as black, and the racist association between blackness and criminality underscores this mapping. It also, however, operates just as powerfully as a metaphor for being HIV positive. Zindzi acknowledges this parallel and yet dismisses it, saying that the animalled "patient zero" is like Gaëtan Dugas, but is not him, because this is "an epidemic that had nothing to do with disease" (80). This welter of parallel, intermixing stigmas that do and do not stand for one another, with AIDS at the center, might be connected to the complex historicity of the novel.

The novel opens with a dystopian image tempered with bathos: "Morning light the sulphur color of the mine dumps seeps across Johannesburg's skyline and sears through my window. My own personal bat signal. Or a reminder that I really need to get curtains" (7). Morning is dawning, but imperial histories are contaminating and dirtying the present, like the ecological fallout from mining. The importance of animality in the novel is brought into the frame through the reference to bats, raising the question of whether the narrator is a rich, white male superhero, which of course she is not. The narrator then draws our attention to the black male body in her bed, his feet "like knots of driftwood" that "say he walked all the way from Kinshasa with his Mongoose strapped to his chest." Black African masculinity is "strapped" here to exotic wild animals, gnarly nature, feats of strength, walking barefoot, the specter of war and poverty. In other words, in a similar move to the opening of *Ancient Rites*, the imperial temporalities of race in which blackness is both primitivity and animality, thus existing outside culture and history, are summoned up. But the mongoose is curled up on a laptop "like a furry comma." The animal is at home in technologized modernity, and is likened to a fragment of language; it is part of a discursive system of meaning that Beukes is archly calling into question. Benoit, the man in her bed, is the most morally centered person in the novel. Reader, you might think you know what time it is in (South) Africa, but you don't.

Zoo City is told in a fairly straightforward chronological order, and its mystery is solved and resolved at the end; Huron, himself animalled with a huge crocodile, has been having homeless zoos killed for the *muti* power they endow, and in the novel's denouement, he arranges a murderous ritual to rid himself of his animalled status, in which Song is killed by a hyptonized S'bu. The person engaging in "ancient," "dark" practices is, it turns out, the white man, whose white female minion forces a black boy to stab his sister: black "crime" is orchestrated by white people. Unlike *Blood Safari*, Huron is not a remnant of the apartheid security state; on the contrary, he smuggled guns for struggle activists, and "in the 80s, he was one of a handful of white producers ... who were willing to take a risk on black artists at a time when the apartheid government frowned sternly on such 'crossover' projects" (170). His club, employing animalled dancers, is called Counter Revolutionary, described as "Great Gatsby by way of Lady Gaga" (232). Huron is thus a symbol of the betrayal of revolutionary values in a new gilded age. With the help of magical email messages from a murdered transgender animalled sex worker—a frail figure with a sparrow who we glimpse wandering the street at the beginning of the novel—Zinzi figures out and survives Huron's plot to make her the fall guy for his crimes, and persuades his rejected crocodile to eat him.

Zinzi's gift of being able to find lost things—or rather, to feel them, as they pull at her like "the tendrils of an anemone" (13)—orients her to what has gone, and indeed each person's animal is a reminder of deeds committed in the past. The novel is about the near future, but it is also about how the past shapes us and stays with us, and is preoccupied with moments of epochal change. Zinzi refers to the time before she herself became animalled as her Former Life (FL), and the time before and after the appearance of the animalled across the globe is the important historical shift in the novel's universe—not the coming of democracy in South Africa. The parallel to AIDS again suggests itself, but the animalled epidemic is also connected to ecological degradation and nuclear fallout, and can be read as a sign that we are living in the time of environmental apocalypse— that this is how future historians will translate our era. The question of which historical period we are living in, which overlapping crisis will define our times, where it began, and what it will become is central to the book.

At the end of the novel, the plot is completed, but there are threads that have not been gathered. Benoit has been injured helping Zinzi, and is thus prevented from traveling to find his long-lost wife and children among the refugee camps of Kigali. Zinzi decides to go and find them in his place. In the last lines of the book:

> I have an amaShangaan bag full of fake cash, I have a bundle of photographs. I have print-outs of emails from a UN aid worker. I have Benoit's family's names and ID numbers and application papers for asylum in South Africa.
>
> What I do not have is permission to leave the country in the wake of a multiple homicide/serial killer investigation.
>
> Celvie, Armand. Ginelle. Celestin. It's going to be awkward. It's going to be the best thing I've done with my miserable life.
>
> And after that? Maybe I'll get lost for a while. (366)

Unconventionally for a crime novel, then, *Zoo City* is open-ended, leading into the unknown. While to a certain degree a "wild continent" beyond South Africa is being exoticized here, this is also an interesting moment of Muñoz-like utopianism: a world outside the dystopian modern state is being imaginatively entered into, in a move that also goes beyond the confines of the genre, and alternative fates thus come onto the horizon.

Conclusion: In search of historicity

These South African "muti noir" texts remake crime fiction—and many of them also transform magical realism, disorienting the ways in which the "magical" is usually situated outside "modernity" and within its own genre. This formation also begins to write the AIDS epidemic. Titlestad and Polatinsky, as we have seen, suggest that crime fiction turns away from a serious engagement with history; I would argue that in these texts, it goes in search of historicity. The temporal variations, including the failures of futurity, that they enact tell us a great deal about the difficulties of imagining political alternatives in South Africa right now. However, the liveliness of these textual imaginings and their original stretching of genres indicate a creative mobility that bodes well for South African politics, history, and literature—all of which are far from being over.

Notes

1   See Steinberg, *Thin Blue.*
2   The term comes from Lauren Beukes's description of her novel *Zoo City* in an interview; see Ansell, "Behind All the Monkey Business."
3   Scott, *Omens of Adversity*, 2, 12.
4   Thomas, *Impossible Mourning*, 2.
5   Jamal, "Milk Blue," 41.
6   Ibid., 42.
7   Zikhali, "N.O.C.U.R.E. (No One Can Understand Real Endurance)," 110.
8   Thomas, *Impossible Mourning*, 9.
9   De Kock, "Roger Smith and the 'Genre Snob' Debate."
10   Titlestad and Polatinsky, "Turning to Crime," 270.
11   Warnes, "Writing Crime in the New South Africa," 983.
12   De Kock, "Hits Keep Coming But It Ain't Enough."
13   See Muñoz, *Cruising Utopia.*
14   Titlestad and Polatinsky, "Turning to Crime," 267; de Kock, "Roger Smith and the 'Genre Snob' Debate."
15   As Rautenbach puts it in "To Write Poetry after Pistorius Is Insufficient," "consider the elements of this story: 'Bullet in the chamber,' Nike's unfortunate campaign

slogan, was on the day of the shooting still plastered on billboards above Johannesburg's major highways, alongside a larger-than-life Pistorius running on his aluminium blades. Meanwhile, in Cape Town, the stage was set for President Jacob Zuma's State of the Nation Address, two weeks after the grotesque rape and disembowelment of 17-year-old Anene Booysen, an event which called for greater state action against gender violence."

16 Ngai, *Ugly Feelings*, 2, 5, 13.
17 Steinberg, "Crime," 27.
18 According to Steinberg, "while 1 in 9 South Africans is white, 32 out of 33 murder victims are not" ("Crime," 27).
19 Kynoch, "Crime, Conflict, and Politics in Transition-Era South Africa," 493–514, 494.
20 See Glaser, *Bo-Tsotsi*; Kynoch, *We Are Fighting the World*; and Steinberg, *The Number*.
21 Kynoch, "Crime, Conflict, and Politics in Transition-Era South Africa," 497.
22 Ibid., 502.
23 Beukes, *Zoo City*, 249. This and other muti noir novels under discussion referenced parenthetically hereafter.
24 Steinberg, *Thin Blue*, 110.
25 Comaroff and Comaroff, *Law and Disorder in the Postcolony*, 1.
26 Ibid., 5.
27 Titlestad and Polatinsky, "Turning to Crime," 270.
28 Pearson and Singer, "Introduction: Open Cases: Detection, (Post) Modernity, and the State," 2.
29 Ibid., 7.
30 Matzke and Mühleisen, "Postcolonial Postmortems," 2, 3.
31 Warnes, "Writing Crime in the New South Africa," 986.
32 Ibid., 987.
33 Conrad, *Heart of Darkness*, 60.
34 Scott, *Omens of Adversity*, 13.
35 Ibid., 13.
36 Farred, "The Postcolonial Chickens Come Home to Roost," 295.
37 Reid, *How to Be a Real Gay*, 262.
38 Coetzee, *Waiting for the Barbarians*, 133–34.

Works Cited

Ansell, Gwen. "Behind All the Monkey Business." *Mail & Guardian*, May 6, 2011. http://mg.co.za/article/2011-05-06-behind-all-the-monkey-business.

Beukes, Lauren. *Zoo City*. South Africa: Jacana, 2010

Coetzee, J. M. *Disgrace*. 1999. London: Vintage, 2000.

Coetzee, J. M. *Waiting for the Barbarians*. New York: Penguin, 1980.

Comaroff, Jean, and John Comaroff. *Law and Disorder in the Postcolony*. Chicago: University of Chicago Press, 2006.

Conrad, Joseph. *Heart of Darkness*. London: William Blackwood and Sons, 1902.

Coovadia, Imraan. *Tales of the Metric System: A Novel*. Athens, OH: Ohio University Press, 2014.

De Kock, Leon. "Hits Keep Coming But It Ain't Enough." *The Sunday Independent*, February 14, 2010. http://www.leondekock.co.za/wp-content/uploads/mike_nicol.pdf.

De Kock, Leon. "Roger Smith and the 'Genre Snob' Debate." *Stellenbosch Literary Project*, January 9, 2012. http://slipnet.co.za/view/reviews/crime-fiction-the-'new-political-novel'/.

Duiker, K. Sello. *Thirteen Cents*. Cape Town: David Philip, 2000.

Farred, Grant. "The Postcolonial Chickens Come Home to Roost: How *Yardie* Has Created a New Postcolonial Subaltern." *South Atlantic Quarterly* 100.1 (2001): 287–305.

Glaser, Clive. *Bo-Tsotsi: The Youth Gangs of Soweto, 1935–1976*. Cape Town: David Philip, 2000.

Jamal, Ashraf. "Milk Blue." In *Nobody Ever Said AIDS: Poems and Stories from Southern Africa*. Eds. Nobantu Rasebotsa, Meg Samuelson, and Kylie Thomas. Cape Town: Kwela Books, 2004. 40–44.

Kynoch, Gary. "Crime, Conflict, and Politics in Transition-Era South Africa." *African Affairs* 104.416 (July 2005): 493–514.

Kynoch, Gary. *We Are Fighting the World: A History of the Marashea Gangs in South Africa, 1947–1999*. Athens, OH: Ohio University Press, 2005.

Makholwa, Angela. *Red Ink: A Novel*. Northlands, South Africa: Pan Macmillan, 2007.

Matzke, Christine, and Susanne Mühleisen, eds. *Postcolonial Postmortems: Crime Fiction from a Transnational Perspective*. New York: Rodopi, 2006.

Meyer, Deon. *Blood Safari*. New York: Atlantic Monthly Press, 2009.

Moele, Kgebetle. *Book of the Dead*. Cape Town: Kwela Books, 2009.

Mpe, Phaswane. *Welcome to Our Hillbrow: A Novel of Post-Apartheid South Africa*. Athens, OH: Ohio University Press, 2001.

Muñoz, José Esteban. *Cruising Utopia: The Then and There of Queer Futurity*. New York: New York University Press, 2009.

Mzobe, Sifiso. *Young Blood*. Cape Town: Kwela Books, 2010.

Ngai, Sianne. *Ugly Feelings*. Cambridge, MA: Harvard University Press, 2005.

Pearson, Nels, and Marc Singer. "Introduction: Open Cases: Detection, (Post) Modernity, and the State." *Detective Fiction in a Postcolonial and Transnational World*. Eds. Nels Pearson and Marc Singer. Farnham: Ashgate, 2009. 1–13.

Pullman, Philip. *The Golden Compass*. New York: Alfred A. Knopf, 1995.

Rautenbach, Anneke. "To Write Poetry after Pistorius Is Insufficient: Rapture, Rupture and Narrative Non-fiction in South Africa." *Africa in Words*, September 30, 2013. https://africainwords.com/2013/09/30/to-write-poetry-after-pistorius-is-insufficient-rapture-rupture-and-narrative-non-fiction-in-south-africa/.

Reid, Graeme. *How to Be a Real Gay: Gay Identities in Small Town South Africa.* Scottsville: University of Kwa-Zulu Natal Press, 2013.

Scott, David. *Omens of Adversity: Tragedy, Time, Memory, Justice.* Durham, NC: Duke University Press, 2014.

Steinberg, Jonny. "Crime." New South African Keywords. Eds. Steven Robin and Nick Shepherd. Johannesburg: Jacana, 2008. 25–34.

Steinberg, Jonny. *The Number: One Man's Search for Identity in the Cape Underworld and Prison Gangs.* Johannesburg: Jonathan Ball, 2004.

Steinberg, Jonny. *Thin Blue: The Unwritten Rules of South African Policing.* Johannesburg: Jonathan Ball, 2008.

Thomas, Kylie. *Impossible Mourning: HIV/AIDS and Visuality after Apartheid.* Lewisburg, PA: Bucknell University Press, 2014.

Titlestad, Michael, and Ashlee Polatinsky. "Turning to Crime: Mike Nicol's *The Ibis Tapestry* and *Payback*." *Journal of Commonwealth Literature* 45.2 (June 2010): 259–73.

Tlholwe, Diale. *Ancient Rites.* Cape Town: Kwela Books, 2008.

Tlholwe, Diale. *Counting the Coffins.* Cape Town: Kwela Books, 2011.

Twidle, Hedley. "The Oscar Pistorius Case: History Written on a Woman's Body." *New Statesman*, March 7, 2013. http://www.newstatesman.com/world-affairs/world-affairs/2013/02/history-written-womans-body.

Warnes, Christopher. "Writing Crime in the New South Africa: Negotiating Threat in the Novels of Deon Meyer and Margie Orford." *Journal of Southern African Studies* 28.4 (December 2012): 981–91.

Zikhali, Mbonisi. "N.O.C.U.R.E. (No One Can Understand Real Endurance)." *Nobody Ever Said AIDS: Poems and Stories from Southern Africa.* Eds. Nobantu Rasebotsa, Meg Samuelson, and Kylie Thomas. Cape Town: Kwela Books, 2004. 110.

9

Queer Returns in Postapartheid Short Fiction: S. J. Naudé's *The Alphabet of Birds*

Andrew van der Vlies

"Isn't it strange where ex-South Africans pop up these days and which subjects and worlds they join together?"[1] This arresting question is posed by a character in S. J. Naudé's debut short story collection, *The Alphabet of Birds* (2014), in a story where not a great deal happens, at least in the narrative present. Two expatriate white South African men meet at a party in a crumbling villa in Milan; they spend the night together; one leaves the following morning with an object belonging to his hosts. Yet the longing and loss the question expresses, the incommensurability of diasporic subjects and worlds it indexes, and the stasis in which its speaker seems trapped, make the story—and the collection as a whole—emblematic of a rich recent trend in contemporary South African fiction.

This trend features the representation of bad feelings—most notably disappointment—that attest to an anxiety about the condition of contemporary South Africa: its incomplete transition to fully postapartheid state.[2] For some white writers in particular, these feelings are bound up with a sense of complicity in the wrongs of a past from which it seems impossible to escape, a condition often staged in the recurrent narrative of the émigré child who returns to the scene of a parent's deathbed in South Africa.[3] In many such cases, these children are also queer, pointing to another characteristic or manifestation of the affective structure I am tracing. Queer longing lies athwart the reproductive logic implicit in standard metaphorical renderings of the nation as family. It is a longing that desires fulfillment—and has every right to expect it (since queer citizens, in theory, enjoy full constitutional protection)—but one that is also structured by a strange pleasure located in disavowal or postponement. I will explain more fully what I mean in due course; suffice it to say that a constellation of desire, dysphoria, and dislocation features in all of the stories in Naudé's collection, many of which also have queer protagonists.

Formally, the short story is well suited to times that seem out of joint. The linked short story collection or cycle in particular has, for a half-century or more, been noteworthy for articulating structural critique of apartheid's grand narratives. Key examples include Bessie Head's *The Collector of Treasures* (1977), Njabulo Ndebele's *Fools and Other Stories* (1983), and Miriam Tlali's *Footprints in the Quag* (1989). The cycle, "a form positioned somewhere between the coherence of the novel proper and the disconnectedness of the 'mere' collection of autonomous short stories," Sue Marais noted in 1995, evidenced "a dualism" that rendered it "particularly well suited to the representation of that tension between centripetal and centrifugal or entropic impulses." While present in any modern society, she noted, these were especially heightened in late-apartheid South Africa, with its "conflict between community, solidarity and national unity, on the one hand, and dissociation, segregation and Apartheid, on the other."[4] The "ambivalent" nature of stories conceived as a unit and featuring a shared, overlapping cast of characters, enabled the genre to indict the psychic and social divisions that existed because of apartheid, while also defying apartheid by emphasizing the bonds that persisted, regardless.[5] Zoë Wicomb's *You Can't Get Lost in Cape Town* (1987), in which the stability and coherence of the world occupied by diverse stories' characters cannot be assumed (a mother figure assumed dead midway through reappears in the final story), and Ivan Vladislavić's *Missing Persons* (1989), whose stories are linked only by their location in a country whose absurd politics marks everything as surreal, signal a departure from Ndebele's and Tlali's cycles in their self-aware strategies.

Naudé's stories are less tightly interlinked than Wicomb's, though characters do reappear. The stories are not as concerned to foreground their own status as texts, although they do engage throughout with the performative. They are, however, no less invested in the elaboration of what Marais identified in the earlier period's key cycles as "existential" breakdown. One of their innovations is to take *South Africa* as marker neither of hoped-for community, as Ndebele or Tlali (perhaps also Wicomb) did, nor absurd performance, as in Vladislavić's work, but rather as the name for an elsewhere, indeed another temporality, for characters unmoored by migration and globalization, racially or ethnically inflected senses of guilt, and processes of coming to terms with their sexuality. For Naudé's protagonists are, in the main, expatriate white Afrikaners, and *The Alphabet of Birds* was first published in Afrikaans in 2011 as *Alfabet van die voëls* (and subsequently translated into English by Naudé). Indeed, in the Afrikaans original of "The Noise Machine," Chris does not imagine "ex-*South Africans*" (34) but instead ex-*Afrikaners* turning up all over the world, tying together subjects, spaces, and lost time.[6] Here two observations—the first about language (and translation) and the second about locatedness (and cosmopolitanism)—are germane. Each one points to the potential of the short story, and particularly examples that engage as Naudé's do with the trends and tropes I am describing, as a potentially *queer* genre, if by that description we name that which disrupts, challenges, and prompts reconceptualization of the status quo.

Some of the dialogue in Naudé's Afrikaans text was originally composed in English and later translated for the first publication.[7] *Alphabet/Alfabet* thus embodies an intriguing negotiation of the process of textual and linguistic translation at the same time that it thematizes much about the postapartheid period in relation to translation as metaphor. The stories feature the physical translation of characters between different geographical spaces,[8] as well as temporal translations among various pasts, presents, and imagined futures. They treat the issue of the transmission of shared experience, including of culture, between generations, and even figure death as the translation of the soul from life to whatever might follow. Also at issue is a *failure* to translate, of the imaginative leap required to conceptualize a means of communication beyond or around that which might be linguistically intelligible. Here the stories' references to nonverbal communication are significant. Birds are a recurring leitmotif (the meaning of their songs periodically prompting reflection), while other modes of encounter including music, dance, cooking, travel, nursing, and sex, all similarly in excess of language, enable and impede translation in various ways. Performance operates in indecipherable alphabets that offer glimpses of modes of care somehow more appropriate than words for engaging with the dissolution of family and the aftermath of apartheid. It is the great success of Naudé's stories to effect a representation of the failure of language *in* language.

The language of first publication naturally puts Naudé's collection in conversation with Afrikaans-language progenitors, perhaps preeminently those in the antiestablishment border-literature (*grensliteratuur*) tradition, including work by Etienne van Heerden, Alexander Strachan, and especially Koos Prinsloo, in whose groundbreaking stories antiapartheid, antimilitary critique meets the erotics of queer desire.[9] Here my observation about language and translation segues to that about locatedness and cosmopolitanism, for Naudé's focus, in contrast to the precursors mentioned earlier, is no longer a particular location— South Africa, or the South West African (Namibian)/Angolan border—but a world in which South Africans, even if of a particular ethnicity, find themselves no longer exceptional yet forever marked by their origins. The seven partially linked stories in *Alfabet/Alphabet* offer vignettes from the lives of characters whose ties to a homeland are unraveling: the reader follows them from Johannesburg to Dubai, London to Phoenix, Arizona, Vietnam and Japan to Pretoria, from South Africa's rural Free State province to Paris and Milan. While Naudé claims that he did not "set out to create a suite of cosmopolitan stories" but "simply wrote about characters and places" like those from his own experience (a "childhood in South Africa," an "adult life elsewhere," several years working as a corporate lawyer in London and New York),[10] he has done precisely this.

In an insightful survey essay on fictions of the early postapartheid nation, Rita Barnard observes about the emerging strain of transnationalism in the period that while South African writers "often spanned the dual imaginary locations of home and exile" during the apartheid years, "they are now fully and voluntarily diasporic; the geographical and thematic range of their work has been broadened accordingly." Referencing the polemical question posed by Leon de Kock (in an essay entitled "Does South African Literature Still Exist?"), Barnard observes that some of the most engaging early postapartheid fiction has moved "so far beyond the national concerns of the struggle years that a new conceptual framework [...] will be needed to replace our ultimately politically motivated critical project of viewing works by South African-born writers as contributing to an (only theoretically and tenuously unified) national canon."[11] The stories in Naudé's debut collection engage this provocation uncommonly well. The unfinished and forestalled in the experience of characters no longer at home in South Africa but unable to claim to be from anywhere else, challenge both heteronormative constructions of the postapartheid national family and narratives of South African exceptionalism. My analysis in what follows has an eye on the ramifications of the stories for understanding what the term "South African" names in the present—in relation to subject, affect, and cultural product.

"Loose shards, infinite performance"

The first story in the South African editions of *The Alphabet of Birds*, "Van" ("Die mobile" in *Alfabet van die voëls*), follows Sandrien, a white farmer's wife recently trained as a nurse, as she struggles to care for poor (black) patients dying from AIDS-related causes, battling against corruption, nepotism, and intransigence in the Eastern Cape provincial health department. Sandrien herself is dying of cancer. In other stories, "VNLS" and "Mother's Quartet" ("Moederskwartet"), we meet the second key female protagonist in the collection, Ondien, an ethnomusicologist-turned-performer and composer who travels to the same lodge in the Free State at which Sandrien stays (as described in "Van").[12] The Ondien narratives are moving and insightful in their engagement with the discontents of the diasporic condition of some young white Afrikaners. They also stage in engaging manner what the label "South African" is made to serve abroad: Ondine's troupe, the Victorian Native Ladies' Society (VNLS), in the story of that title, finds itself in Lesotho, from whence Ondine reflects on how their music has changed according to context, morphing from "a reasonably coherent fusion of Western club music [...] with kwaito and township elements" (170) to something more easily able to be apprehended by foreign audiences as "African." Back in South Africa, Ondine seeks to challenge local audiences, improvising, quoting "[p]recise little fragments of Schoenberg or Webern" (172) when Cape Town crowds or "art-festival types" (173) settle too comfortably into a dance rhythm. She gives the *foreigners* something to challenge assumptions about the stasis of black "tradition," and *locals* some alienating high modernism. The story's central engagement with art's power to unsettle expectations is suggestive *about* and is also an allegory *for* what happens to South African writing in the process of translation, both metaphorically (to a world audience) and, in some cases, textually (into a world language), into a version that circulates, and inevitably one that returns. Much as these linked Sandrien-Ondine stories reveal about such processes, I want to focus on four of the five remaining stories that feature explicitly or implicitly gay protagonists.[13] I will discuss these in detail in what follows, in two pairs.

In the first story in the British and American editions of the English-language translation, "The Noise Machine," we meet two "lapsed South African[s]" (18).[14] Chris, the story's focalizer, is a London-based art historian, while Tom is a freelance photographer based in New York, who gradually comes into focus for Chris as a figure from his youth, "Tommie from his school days," to whose "reckless aura" he had been intensely attracted (24). Tom tells Chris about having been a war reporter, as well as about reporting from small-town Pennsylvania on a missing child subsequently found drowned, a child with whom Chris later significantly identifies, dreaming that he is "looking through the eyes of the dead child in Tom's story," trapped in a frozen canal "below the ice" (33). It is tempting to have recourse here to the formulations of the antisocial thesis in North American queer theory, to invoke its refusal of a heteronormative investment in the child as somehow a theoretical analogue for the gay Chris's fascination with the stalled childhood of the (literally) frozen child.[15] The dead child here also suggests the queer child whose future is—or has been—forestalled in apartheid-era South Africa, a time and place in which Christiaan (as he was) and Tommie's halting attraction could go nowhere, could only be disavowed. A refusal of the logic of production is tied to capital in the story's present, too: the decaying villa's owners, Tita and Fredericke, call it a "lesbian nest among the machines," a "crumbling barricade against the merciless march of production" (18).

The morning after their night together, Chris discovers that Tom has left without farewell, just as he suddenly moved away when they were children. Where he had once stolen the young Christiaan's bicycle, in the present Tom has stolen a rare futurist noise machine belonging to musicologist Tita. She tells her guests that what the futurists "could not predict was what would follow noise, the silence that comes after collapse" (31). The silence that comes after the noise that the futurists imagined, the challenge to convention, the unsettling of the bourgeois and normative, silence as the antithesis of communication, is replicated here by the silence that follows Tom's departure. It reflects the stasis in which all other characters seem trapped. Conditioned by his childhood, perhaps, to want what is refused him, Chris is left with an "ache in his bones," "a longing for Tom to return, and to bring with him a vanished world" (36). Is this the South Africa of their childhood, a lost place *and* time? "Our youth is a no-man's-land" (27), Chris thinks at one point, and the resonances of war-zone rhetoric and of the refusal of the imperatives of gendered role-playing might be heard in this description. Fredericke indeed remarks that her South African guests appeared to be "battered," like "walking wounded left in the aftermath" (28). "How impossible […] to return to it," Chris thinks, meaning both the time and place that was the South Africa of their childhood; what "remains is a void to be filled with the wonders of the world" (27). Yet, it is in this world—*overseas*, where one goes to escape South Africa temporally and spatially—that Chris finds himself apparently trapped in terrible stasis, like the child under the ice; "when you are frozen," he thinks to himself, "you're unable to move; you can only wait to be found" (36).

What attracts Chris to Tom is precisely that which appears *un*-South African, that there was "no room for the wearisome kind of questions and tales with which exiled South Africans sometimes approach each other when they meet in foreign parts" (21). Tom has managed to slough off something that marks him as South African, and this seems at once desirable but also impossible for Chris to achieve. If what Chris has lost is a world in which desire had to be postponed, such waiting might in fact preserve the potential for change—just as the promise of liberation from apartheid promised so much more than has been, or perhaps could ever could be, delivered. Such present stasis is the best for which Naudé's characters can hope; whether anyone might in fact deliver respite—communication, affiliation, communion—is the question posed in each of the stories that follow. Incidentally, "The Noise Machine" occupies the final position in the Afrikaans collection and in the English version published in South Africa. If in first position it inaugurates the collection's interest in an Afrikaner diaspora, drawing in the non-South African reader,[16] in the final slot its refusal of resolution seems resolutely *less* hopeful, even as the open ending retains the hypothetical possibility of Chris and Tom's paths crossing again.

Silence and the longing for something to loosen what Chris experiences as an ache in the bones recur in the story that occupies the final position in the British and American edition, "Loose," which concerns the relationship between an unnamed focalizing protagonist and a younger mixed-race dancer, Sam, and begins with what must be one of the most arresting opening sentences in contemporary Afrikaans literature: "He dreams he is doing ballet with a Japanese man at the Voortrekker monument" (260).[17] The monumental stone structure commemorating the movement of proto-Afrikaner colonists into the interior of South Africa in the 1830s, erected in the late 1930s at a moment of heightened Afrikaner nationalist mythopoeia, is ironically apt for a dream that subverts heteropatriarchal stereotypes.[18] It is also suggestive for its juxtaposition of immobility and movement, specifically a performance that promises to unlock something that has been trapped, to thaw what has been frozen (a metaphor that recurs in the stories).[19] The man in the dream "puts his arm around" the protagonist's dream self: "Besides firmness, there is empathy in the man's grip, in the manner in which he is steering them. It is simultaneously without doubt and without insistence" (260).

The protagonist has returned to Pretoria on sabbatical from a high-powered finance job in London to find his family riven by "death and divorce and other forms of heartache" (272). He watches a production of student theater work at the university and is drawn to Sam, noticing his refusal to be constrained by gender norms or ethnicity. Sam is the antithesis of our returnee's sense of restriction and stasis; he practices a Japanese dance form, Butoh, which is "about the more difficult stuff behind emotions" (281). His movements offer his older lover a vocabulary in excess of verbal expression and of social institutions (monogamy, heteronormativity), promising a reconnection with the body and with desire. And Sam is willing to share his gifts widely, helping the protagonist's sister, who is in the midst of a "traumatic divorce" (276), to express her emotions on stage in a way that mirrors her brother's sense of reawakening.

However, the refusal of commitment that is part of Sam's "New Age clarity" (282) becomes difficult for our protagonist to bear. He wants more than clichés about movement and shape. At the story's end, also the end of the collection in the British and American English edition, we find both men attending a bohemian artists' gathering in a disused office block in downtown Pretoria, on a street plastered with rotting jacaranda blossoms and within earshot of the hyenas in the zoo. This is a space that is the very antithesis of the Voortrekker Monument, that symbol of settlement and a normative Christian nationalist "civilization" invoked in the opening lines. The protagonist here finds himself deeply skeptical of the lack of structure and certainty that Sam represents, even as that forestalled intimate relationality is precisely emblematic of a certain postapartheid affective temporal structure:

> Sam is not *with* him, he thinks, and he is, similarly, not with any of the people in this fatherless little crowd, none of whom he will ever see again after this evening. [....] Loose. They are all loose—loosened from each other. He turns around, observing the scene. He withdraws from the light, inching his way backwards. His hands search the wall behind him for the exit. (292)

Our protagonist has hitherto not known whether the romantic entanglement with Sam was "moving forward" or "edging loosely sideways, crab-like." How might he "push it into a direction," he wonders, sensing too however that it is "the absence of direction," the "[l]oose shards, [and] infinite performance" (281) that has in part been the attraction. While these meditations might be taken as a salutary lesson for South Africans, loosened by the traumatic past from investment in belonging and in any number of group identities that always inevitably become imbricated with exclusionary categorization, they also bespeak a longing for something else—without definitively inviting the reader to regard this desire either as a failure or as itself desirable. The original title, "Los," it should be said, conveys a wider range of meanings that includes *loose*, in the purely descriptive, material, as well as metaphorical sense (which is to say "promiscuous"), as well as the imperative "*let go!*". What does it mean to let go? What are the costs?

The protagonist's disappointment with Sam suggests a tentative insistence on utopian possibilities even if these inhere, paradoxically, in what Ernst Bloch called the inevitable disappointability of hope. Hope must make allowances for the possibility of failure, Bloch insists; it must hold "the condition of defeat precariously within itself."[20] Hope's "not-yet," Bloch observed, is a time imagined as "a place where entrance and, above all, final content are marked by an enduring indeterminacy."[21] This suggestive time-place is one in which many of Naudé's characters find themselves, and it is in the very uncertainty of the open ending, one radically indeterminate rather than merely gesturally so, of the longing *for* longing *itself*, that hope appears to inhere. Failure, stasis and longing are paradoxically reconstituted as hopeful rather than hopeless.

The anthropologist Hirokazu Miyazaki, offering a gloss on Bloch, notes that he understood that the only way to recapture the temporal structure of hopeful moments was to reproduce "another hopeful moment" and to offer this "moment of hope" in writing itself.[22] Though Naudé is not working in the same mode as Bloch (or Miyazaki), there are many moments in the stories of the representation of writing, as well as of listening and of performance that is either unfinished or evanescent (thus, expressly not objectifiable), to which the reader might return in order to experience, repeatedly, the holding open, the promise of the loose end(ing). Naudé's stories frequently insist on reminding readers about their status *as* writing. The epigraph at the head of "Loose," from Richard Schechner's *Performance Theory*, for example, reflects that "empathy with the performer rather than with the plot" is what allows particular kinds of Asian ("rasic") theater

> to explore detours and hidden pathways, unexpected turns in the performance. [...] The partakers' interest is not tied to the story but to the enactment of the story; the partakers do not want to "see what happens next" but to "experience how the performer performs whatever is happening." (260)[23]

This emphasizes this story's own performance *as text* (something which might have a paratext), while also suggesting a way of reading the whole collection by inviting reflection on both the nature of the performativity described and the nature of the collection's texts as collective performance.

The unmoored protagonist in "Loose" finds that he can only bear to be in Pretoria—once the center of white executive and military power—so long as "the strangeness that Sam is enabling him to feel" lasts, which is to say that "Sam makes it a different place, a nowhere place" (279). Sam's otherness is pure antithesis, his affect "inscrutable"; he looks to the man at one point "like an angel of dark glass" (281). It is not fanciful to imagine Sam's dark angelic otherness and the nowhere-place longed for by the protagonist to be in conversation with Walter Benjamin's imagination of a static *Jetztzeit* (or "now-time"), in which past moments of utopian potential might—indeed *must*—actively be revivified in a flash in the face of a disappointing present. Benjamin's injunction that we pause to seek an alternative to narratives that cast history as unremitting progress (which in our day often serve neoliberalism), seems both salutary and appropriate, and not only in postapartheid South Africa.[24]

It is surely not unwarranted either to invoke a Benjaminian understanding of *Jetztzeit* to describe Chris's stasis at the end of "The Noise Machine" or to make a connection between that which this metaphorics helps us apprehend and Antonio Gramsci's characterization of the morbid body politic that lingers in the interregnum. Gramsci's famous diagnosis of capitalism's discontents, the "great diversity of morbid symptoms" famously invoked by Nadine Gordimer in relation to late-apartheid society, was used as epigraph to *July's People* (1981), and for the title of (and Gordimer's analysis in) "Living in the Interregnum," an essay in which she looked beyond what seemed then a terrible stasis toward a future that perhaps could not arrive during her lifetime.[25]

Invocations of Gramsci's tropic figuring of the unforeseeable consequences of the apparently interminable convulsions of an old order continue to resonate in the affective landscape of contemporary South African. Gramsci's metaphorics—and the legacy of Gordimer's citation of them—can be observed in the specific trope of the dying parent that has recurred with great frequency in postapartheid literature, at least since Coetzee's *Age of Iron*, whose protagonist, a retired classics teacher dying of cancer in Cape Town in the winter of 1986, writes a letter to a daughter who has lived outside South Africa since 1976. Mrs. Curren hopes her child will return but knows that she will not.[26] The dying parent, serving metonymically perhaps for the generation that benefitted most from apartheid rule, also features in Naudé's collection, most powerfully in the stories "A Master from Germany" and "War, Blossoms."

Sic transit: Writing returns

"A Master from Germany" begins and ends in the present, with a formerly expatriate protagonist (referred to as "he" throughout) back in South Africa for his mother's final illness. At the beginning of the story, he remembers coming upon her naked, just before she died, and how both mother and son pretended this "never happened" (94). A scene of profound vulnerability is focused through the pain of imminent loss but connected with that which cannot be spoken. Later, as the story circles back to this period, the days of her treatment and slow, painful decline, the incident comes to stand for much else, not least the protagonist's sense of alienation from a former identity, his sense that a boundary has been crossed. His mother's pain evokes his own, the landscape of her body his own vulnerability but also the landscape of another country, one as burdened with racialized mythography as the South Africa to which he returns. He recalls:

> It is during this time that he gets such an unprotected view of his mother in the bathroom. The retina will not let go of the image, he realises after a while. It stays with him. He wonders what it means, the lingering. Yes, it does carry something in it of *then* and *now*, the man before and after the event. How he is to construe the respective selves, however, he will never know. But he knows it is a dividing line, a flash of light in the blindness of which all protection is torn away. And it superimposes her body indelibly over his German trip, a defenseless landscape on the edge of collapse. (124)

Memories of this German journey occupy the largest part of the story, guiding the reader backward as if a box were opening to reveal others concealed within: "Let's first go back in time, a few months" (94); "let's go back a week further" (95). In these episodes, we see the protagonist and his enigmatic—and, it transpires, ill—German partner, Joschka, visiting Joschka's sister's family in a partially restored castle ruin near Nuremberg, then in Berlin, a week before that. We return thereafter to Bavaria, where the protagonist learns of his mother's illness and from whence he travels to South Africa (105). While a series of backward glances is staged, in each of the German scenes the protagonist also feels he is constantly being left behind, being or looking *backward*—and here I mean to echo Heather Love's invocation of both senses of the word in her writing about queer history and literary historiography.[27] The focalizer-protagonist feels that he is somehow belated (a feeling associated with the *backward*), engaged in a counter-motion to a forward-dawning futurity in which he senses he has no place. (Here we might again invoke the antisocial thesis in queer theory and its casting of the child as representative of a heteronormative investment in the [re]productive.) In Bavaria, in his recollection of events, we first see him "halfway down the cellar stairs, looking up at Joschka," who is "hesitant, calling him back" (94). In Berlin, as he trails Joschka through a nocturnal pleasure-scape of dance clubs, bars, and apartment parties, he has "the feeling, and not for the first time, that Joschka is leaving him behind" (97), "is not within hearing distance" (99), "that he cannot catch up with him" but "can only follow" (97). Who is Orpheus, who Eurydice in these encounters is open to debate; Orpheus is a key figure of some queer tropologies,[28] and a link to *Alphabet*'s meditation on music as alternative mode of communication.

The reader encounters multiple imagined queer spaces in Berlin in which Joschka functions as another dark angelic (and Mephistophelean) figure, in which time is routinely out of joint: "There are times when they linger—sometimes it feels like an eternity, sometimes like seconds—in apartments all over town" (96). What happens in Bavaria, however, is most germane to the story's imbrication of German and South African landscapes as affective settings. During their stay in the ruined castle, one haunted by the specter of nineteenth-century nationalist invocations of Teutonic knights and other heroes (Bayreuth is not far away), the protagonist receives two phone calls from his distant homeland. During the first, his mother, whom he suspects called to break other news, tells him only that a crabapple tree growing on the inherited family farm ("They rarely go to the place nowadays; it is no longer safe" [109]) is dying, that it is having to be grafted onto "the trunk of a hardened European apple tree" to be saved (110). Soon thereafter, Joschka tells the protagonist that he should be tested for HIV: they inadvertently wounded each other during sex a week previously (111). Unsettled by both revelations, the protagonist walks alone into the forest, which, he thinks, despite its idyllic calm, is a space in which "one could perhaps even, with sufficient concentration, stir up all the twentieth-century European horrors" (118). While in the forest he receives the second call, in which his father relays his mother's cancer diagnosis. Time seems to stand still:

> He stops, looks up, listens for birds. All he can hear are the lines, something from his school days, which he now starts reciting:
>
> *Über allen Gipfeln*
> *Ist Ruh,*
> *In allen Wipfeln*
> *Spürest du*
> *Kaum einen Hauch;*
> *Die Vögellein schweigen im Walde—*
>
> The voice of a bird, somewhere above the pines (they will not venture into the dead dusk down here), sweeps away the calm peaks and windless treetops of the poem: "*Sie bricht herein! Sie bricht herein! Die dunkle Nacht der Seele…*"
> "Don't bother," he says, "with the warnings and the mockery. It's already enveloping me from all sides."
> He gets bored of being lost. (119)

The poem is Goethe's "Wanderer's Nightsong," regarded by some as among the most perfect Romantic lyrics in German. It extols the sensation of calm above the mountain summits, the absence of wind in the trees, and the silence of the birds, and was supposedly written on September 6, 1780, on the wall of a gamekeeper's lodge on the Kickelhahn mountain near Ilmenau, about 170 km from Nuremberg, thus sufficiently near to Joschka's family's ruin to come to mind. The protagonist "walks past a small wooden hut, a forest ranger's house" (117) immediately before the episode in which he understands the birds to be repeating Goethe's words.

While the Romantic poet's description of being alone in the forest emphasizes calm, there is darkness here, too. What breaks in (*Sie bricht herein*) is the "dark night of the soul," the mystical, transformative experience of negation shared by many religious and analytical traditions, from Catholic mystic St. John of the Cross (whose term it is) to Buddhism, in or after which the sufferer experiences a transcendent sense of unity. The lyric invocation of quiet is rendered hollow, the peace promised is unequal to an enveloping darkness: "soon the sun will set" (119); Naudé's original runs "binnekort is dit skemer,"[29] *soon it will be twilight*, with its possible echo of Wagner's *Götterdämmerung*, the twilight of the gods. Indeed, the protagonist loses his way as he tries to navigate back to the castle through what had earlier seemed "the cliché of the German forest," in which he might find himself in a "quadruple exposure" bringing together the ideological and performative: "myths and music, history and landscape. A richly decorated *Szene*" (118). Yet if the forest is imbued with codes, they are such as he cannot understand, "illegible beneath the floor of pine needles" (118) and immaterial to those who live there. He encounters a sign blocking passage, "*Zutritt verboten*," and stumbles on a modern housing estate where skinheads spit-roast bratwurst (120).

The aesthetic proved unequal, too, to the horrors that would follow from the version of romantic nationalism enacted by the Nazis, but imagined first, some would argue, by Wagner. Here Goethe and birdsong are juxtaposed with the overarching invocation of a deathliness that stalks the protagonist in Germany. Indeed, the story's title is a nod to Paul Celan's famous 1944 poem "Todesfuge," a love song and an elegy, a threnody in the shadows of the Holocaust's gas chambers, in which the words "Tod ist ein Meister aus Deutschland" ("death is a master from Germany") are repeated four times (and echoes clearly in the Afrikaans title, "'n Meester uit Duitsland").[30] The drawing together of meditations on the limits of language (and verbal aesthetic objects), of metaphors of stasis and illness, of the resonances of ideological constructions put upon landscape, and of the aftermath of racist nationalisms, are compounded for the reader who might know that the oak tree under which Goethe reputedly wrote "Wanderer's Nightsong" was later enclosed in the grounds of Buchenwald concentration camp, that it caught fire in an Allied raid, and survives now only as a stump near the former crematorium.[31] The juxtaposition of Goethe's lyric with news of the sick tree on the protagonist's mother's family's abandoned farm works powerfully to emphasize the conflation. All come together again in the story's final pages, when, during his mother's last illness, her pain seems to the protagonist to be both "a strange country" and "an impenetrable language," one that surely evokes once more Celan's politics of memorialization, imbued as it is with the poetics of ever-forestalled—and thus nonmessianic (or, in Benjamin's formulation, *weak* messianic[32])—return: "Not a Germanic language barked in a menacing voice, but a set of soundless signs. Like aleph, the unvoiced Hebrew consonant. Or what he hears when the birds fall silent" (123–24).

In transit: Writing's returns

"War, Blossoms," the middle story in both orderings (the British-American English version; the Afrikaans original—where it appears as "Oorlog, bloeisels"— and the South African English-language edition, which maintains the order of the Afrikaans version), features a range of similar engagements with the figure of the returnee, here only implicitly queer, with the mother dying of cancer, and the nature of the loose ending. Also, rather more overtly than "A Master from Germany," it meditates on the nature of writing itself, foregrounding writing (and reading) as performance. This story's protagonist, another young man who has worked in London, also returns to tend his mother, but their negotiation of her care is complicated by her refusal to eat, which he construes as "a kind of war" (129). Cancer, as Susan Sontag reminds us, has long been conceptualized in relation to "the language of warfare"; even treatment is described in military terms ("patients are 'bombarded' with toxic rays" in radiotherapy, treated with "poisons" in a kind of "chemical warfare" in chemotherapy).[33] Into this tense standoff, this "series of escalating skirmishes" (129), comes Hisashi, a Japanese friend the protagonist had come to know in London and who has taken seriously a vague invitation to visit. Hisashi rebuffs the protagonist's refusals of help with his mother, coming to the house and coaxing the dying woman to eat. The visits prompt reflections on the part of the returnee-protagonist, who thinks of himself as one of a "diaspora of fearful, grim, white children from South Africa" (132), of his travels with Hisashi to Japan and Vietnam years before. He begins to write a belated report of the journeys, sitting in the garden while "trying to remember, to figure out what happened [...] and what it has to do with what is happening here now" (149). "What he has forgotten, he makes up"; "[h]is pen takes them to places they have never been" (153).

Like each of Naudé's other stories, this one speaks to the ongoing sense of being in transit. It deals with the pain of loss, the difficulty of consolation, and the anxieties occasioned by displacement. "A Master from Germany" concludes with the protagonist similarly unmoored, hearing several months after his mother's death that Joschka has returned to Berlin, that he is no longer taking his medication and "is withering" (127), though "[l]ife goes on"; "[t]hings could be worse" (128). In that story, the protagonist buys a ticket to Berlin and we are left to wonder what sort of reconciliation might take place, what the ending might be given that he has neglected to find out the results of his HIV test, that we see nothing beyond yet another departure.

In "War, Blossoms," the ending is the writing itself—a writing that can only imagine the imagined writer's own end. What the returnee protagonist recalls and what he invents in his travel reminiscences we do not know for certain, although each episode is suggestive, perhaps none more so than a visit to Aokigahara, the Japanese forest on the slopes of Mount Fuji associated with suicides and with the practice of abandoning aged parents. Later he imagines himself dying with his mother, timing his own withering away to coincide with the precise moment of her death, whereupon birds will come in from the garden to "whirl around their heads," to "write an ending on them" (165). Earlier, he had noted that a bird trapped indoors left excrement on the walls "[l]ike Eastern calligraphy," and speculated that this might offer an "ending" to his travel journal, or indeed his life: "Let the birds write it" (154).

In the cancer in both stories we note an instance of the morbid symptoms of the interregnum referenced earlier. Siddhartha Mukherjee observes in his celebrated account of the disease that cancer is "expansionist," invoking both the language of warfare, colonization, and diaspora in his description of how "it invades through tissues, sets up colonies in hostile landscapes, seeking 'sanctuary' in one organ and then immigrating to another."[34] No wonder cancer has been so suggestive an illness to South African writers. What is more, it has been associated, at least since Wilhelm Reich, with a failure adequately to *feel*, with "a steady repression" of emotion.[35] One is reminded of Coetzee's diagnosis of white South Africans' failure to love *all* the peoples of the country, or at least to love *enough* (to love *in general*), in his "Jerusalem Prize Acceptance Speech" (1987).[36]

The queer remainder: A coda

Is it significant that so many of Naudé's characters are queer? Queer characters are unsettling to genealogical and national narratives of belonging, traditionally strangers to the family, "outsider rather than citizen," as Brenna Munro reminds us.[37] Yet queer figures have served in South African writing for three decades as figures of disruption in the revised national script.[38] In Naudé's stories, we encounter queer characters whose awkwardness, recalcitrance, and messy desires insist on remaining inassimilable either to domesticating narratives, or indeed narratives of the freedom and progress for which they stand in one accounting of the liberal postapartheid nation's constitution. If their range of bad feelings marks them as exemplary in nonspecific ways, as figures of a desire for nonnormative utopian spaces that might serve for queers as for *all* subjects of the precarious neoliberal present, *The Alphabet of Birds* surely also frames a critique of complicities between queer universalism and neoliberalism without eliding the utopian, or indeed that which simply refuses, that which counters and negates.

It is worth noting that Naudé's subsequent work has continued this project. A novel, *Die derde spoel* (2017), published simultaneously in the author's English translation as *The Third Reel*, reads in part as an elaboration of the scenarios explored in the *Alfabet/Alphabet* stories: a white, gay Afrikaner escapes conscription in late-apartheid South Africa for a new life in London and Berlin, though inevitably is unable to leave his past behind. There is illness and death, stasis and longing, departure, return, disappointable hope, and moments of *Jetztzeit* in which futures past are constellated, in a flash, in the present. The novel ends, indeed, with just such a Benjaminian moment, as the protagonist, Etienne, his eyes closed, imagines again his dead lover, and both are transformed into queer angels of history:

> On the inside of his lids, the black wall next to his and Axel's vegetable garden in Berlin appears. In a flash he is *there*, his nose pressed against the wall. His feet lift off the ground. Slowly he rises, until his eye is aligned with the bright spot.
>
> It is a peephole, he realizes. And there, on the other side—so close and yet not—Axel is standing. Alone and fierce. In a land of pure light, where, if Etienne were to join him, time's strongest winds could never blow them from each other's arms again.[39]

*

Sara Ahmed suggests that pessimism on the part of queer characters, and in particular about political action, is best understood—indeed "matters"—as skepticism of "a certain kind of optimism," as "a refusal to be optimistic about 'the right things' in the right kind of way."[40] We might reframe this, given my discussion earlier, as a genre of perverse—or perversely—educated hopefulness.

To understand it in this way is to take seriously a potentially politically progressive determination to be ambivalent about those things that we are told we *should* desire. We should be asking (Ahmed contends), "how queer fiction attributes and locates unhappiness" and "how queer fiction might offer different explanations of queer unhappiness rather than simply investing its hope in alternative images of happy queers."[41] To find ourselves unhappy is not necessarily to despair, nor to imagine that things cannot be different. In fact, we are often too eager to read negative affect as apolitical, whereas the everyday registers the political in profound ways we have perhaps to train ourselves to read better.

Turning to texts like Naudé's with these injunctions in mind allows us to ask how we might bring representations of and about supposedly South African experience into conversation with the body of affect-studies and queer-theoretical work that attends to the political valences of backwardness, melancholia, and other bad feelings. I have in mind Lauren Berlant's work on what she calls "cruel optimism," Heather Love and Elizabeth Freeman's on queer temporalities, as well as queer theory's antisocial thesis *pace* Lee Edelman and others.[42] Naudé's stories offer occasions for working through the lessons of some of this work for postapartheid South African subjectivities more broadly. But they are not simply legible in these terms in an uncomplicated way. That Naudé's characters' experiences are inflected by race and sexuality, marked by multiple forms of displacement and alienation (whether on account of local historical circumstances or globalized conditions of late-capitalist modernity), makes of them exceptional *and* representative, singular *and* allegorical. Naudé's queer figures live lives that speak of the drawing together of the so-called First- and Third-World experience that Gordimer understood as necessary and inevitable in "Living in the Interregnum." His stories enact something like a reprise of her call in that essay to "cosmic obstinacy to believe in and work towards the possibility of an alternative."[43] What that alternative might be is something the reader of a collection like *The Alphabet of Birds* is invited to contemplate.

Notes

1   S. J. Naudé, "The Noise Machine," in *The Alphabet of Birds*, 34. Parenthetical references throughout are to this edition.

2   For an extended engagement, see Van der Vlies, *Present Imperfect*, which expands on many of the ideas explored in this chapter in relation to the work of writers including Ingrid Winterbach, Zoë Wicomb, Ivan Vladislavić, Marlene van Niekerk, Masande Ntshanga, Songeziwe Mahlangu, and J. M. Coetzee.

3   Examples include: Marlene van Niekerk, *Agaat* (2004); Anne Landsman, *The Rowing Lesson* (2007); Mark Behr, *Kings of the Water* (2009); Eben Venter, *Wolf, Wolf* (2013). See also Erica Lombard's chapter in this volume.

4   Marais, "Getting Lost in Cape Town," 29.

5   Ibid., 31. Dorothy Driver observes that the short story's resources of fragmentation and ambiguity "helped give birth to an African modernism on South African soil as distinctive, if also as variable, as that of the Harlem Renaissance, but open to a non-ethnic definition of 'African,'" although such "experimentalism was short-circuited by increasing demands for social realism in Black Consciousness writing of the 1960s to the 1980s." See Driver, "The Fabulous Fifties," 388–89.

6   Emphasis added. In the original Afrikaans story, "Die lawaaimasjien," the observation reads: "Ja, is dit nie koddig waar eks-Afrikaners deesdae opduik en watter onderwerpe en wêrelde hulle byeenbring nie?" Naudé, *Alfabet van die voëls*, 234.

7   "I had been away from South Africa for so long that I simply no longer knew how people spoke." Naudé, "Into the Open Sea."

8   Naudé has also addressed the metaphorical suggestiveness of thinking of emigration and return as a kind of translation. See "In Conversation."

9   Examples include Van Heerden's *My Kubaan* (My Cuban) (1983), Strachan's *'n Wêreld sonder grense* (A World without Borders) (1984), Prinsloo's *Jonkmanskas* (Youngman's Wardrobe) (1982), *Die hemel help ons* (Heaven Help Us) (1987), *Slagplaas* (Farm of Slaughter/Abattoir) (1992). See Viljoen, "Afrikaans Literature after 1976," 458–59.

10 Naudé, "In Conversation."

11 Barnard, "Rewriting the Nation," 670–71.

12 The Ondien stories are also the most intertextual, with direct references to Van Niekerk's *Agaat* and allusions to Coetzee's *Age of Iron* (1990) and *Disgrace* (1999).

13 I omit "Mother's Quartet," in which Ondien's gay brother, Cornelius, features.

14 In the original, each is a *former* South African, "'n voormálige Suid-Afrikaner." Naudé, *Alfabet van die voëls*, 221.

15 Much queer theory has been concerned with negative affect, often in relation to temporality and political action, preeminently Edelman's *No Future* and Halberstam's *The Queer Art of Failure*.

16 This was the publisher's rationale for the rearrangement, according to Naudé (personal communication, September 2014).

17 In the original, "Hy droom dat hy saam met 'n Japannese man by die Voortrekkermonument ballet doen." Naudé, *Alfabet van die voëls*, 84.

18 See Delmont, "The Voortrekker Monument: Monolith to Myth," 76–101; Coombes, *History after Apartheid*, 25–53.

19 See, for instance, the freezer full of prepared food in "War, Blossoms," discussed below.

20 Bloch, "Can Hope Be Disappointed?" 341.

21 Ibid.

22 Miyazaki, *The Method of Hope*, 23. See further Van der Vlies, *Present Imperfect*, 13–14.

23 Punctuation, ellipses original.

24 See Benjamin, "On the Concept of History," 389–400. The protagonist is also like Benjamin's angel of history at the end of the story, "inching his way backwards" (292).

25 Gordimer, "Living in the Interregnum," 263.

26 On *Age of Iron* as intertext for representations of stasis, diaspora, and cancer, see Van der Vlies, *Present Imperfect*, 45, 52.

27 Love notes that "queers have embraced backwardness in many forms: in celebrations of perversion, in defiant refusals to grow up, in explorations of haunting and memory, and in stubborn attachments to lost objects." *Feeling Backward*, 7.

28 Ibid., 5. Love reads "figures of backwardness as allegories of queer historical experience" and cites, among key literary-philosophical representations, Orpheus turning back to look at Eurydice in the underworld, and Benjamin's angel of history looking back at the wreckage of the human past (ibid.).

29 Naudé, *Alfabet van die voëls*, 76.

30 Celan, *Selected Poems*, 64. This poem was much referenced by the artist Anselm Kiefer, whose work the protagonist of "A Master from Germany" recalls seeing in a Mayfair gallery (117).

31 Garton Ash, *The File*, 51. Naudé's protagonist thinks: "In this air, one could perhaps even, with sufficient concentration, stir up all the twentieth-century horrors" (118). The Afrikaans original uses the word "konsentrasie," which functions similarly for the act of concentrating the mind, adding as resonance the Anglo-Boer War-era concentration camps in which many white Afrikaner women and children died of disease. Naudé, *Alfabet van die voëls*, 74.

32 See Benjamin, "On the Concept of History," 390.

33 Sontag, "Illness as Metaphor," 66.

34 Mukherjee, *The Emperor of All Maladies*, 38.

35 Sontag, "Illness as Metaphor," 23.

36 See Coetzee, *Doubling the Point*, 97.

37 Munro, "Queer Family Romance," 398.

38 See also Munro, *South Africa and the Dream of Love to Come*.

39 Naudé, *The Third Reel*, 346. Both editions have as epigraph Benjamin's statement that no document of civilization is not always also one of barbarism. There are echoes of and allusions to Benjamin throughout.

40 Ahmed, *The Promise of Happiness*, 162.

41 Ibid., 89.

42 Berlant, *Cruel Optimism*; Freeman, *Time Binds*.

43 Gordimer, "Living in the Interregnum," 283–84.

Works Cited

Ahmed, Sara. *The Promise of Happiness*. Durham, NC: Duke University Press, 2010.

Attridge, Derek and David Attwell, eds. *The Cambridge History of South African Literature*. Cambridge: Cambridge University Press, 2012.

Barnard, Rita. "Rewriting the Nation." Attridge and Attwell. 652–75.

Benjamin, Walter. "On the Concept of History." Trans. Harry Zohn. In *Selected Writings: Volume 4, 1938–1940*. Eds. Howard Eiland and Michael W. Jennings. Cambridge, MA: Belknap Press, 2003. 389–400.

Berlant, Lauren. *Cruel Optimism*. Durham, NC: Duke University Press, 2011.

Bloch, Ernst. "Can Hope Be Disappointed?" Trans. Andrew Jorn. *Literary Essays*. Stanford, CA: Stanford University Press, 1998. 339–45.

Celan, Paul. *Selected Poems*. Translated with an Introduction by Michael Hamburger. [1988]. London: Penguin, 1995.

Coetzee, J. M. *Age of Iron*. London: Secker and Warburg, 1990.

Coetzee, J. M. *Doubling the Point: Essays and Interviews*. Ed. David Attwell. Cambridge, MA: Harvard University Press, 1992.

Coombes, Annie E. *History after Apartheid: Visual Culture and Public Memory in a Democratic South Africa*. Durham, NC: Duke University Press, 2003.

Delmont, Elizabeth. "The Voortrekker Monument: Monolith to Myth." *South African Historical Journal* 29 (1993): 76–101.

Driver, Dorothy. "The Fabulous Fifties: Short Fiction in English." Attridge and Attwell. 387–409.

Edelman, Lee. *No Future: Queer Theory and the Death Drive*. Durham, NC: Duke University Press, 2004.

Freeman, Elizabeth. *Time Binds: Queer Temporalities, Queer Histories*. Durham, NC: Duke University Press, 2010.

Garton Ash, Timothy. *The File: A Personal History*. New York: Random House, 1997.

Gordimer, Nadine. "Living in the Interregnum." *The Essential Gesture*. Ed. Stephen Clingman. 1988. London: Penguin, 1989. 261–84.

Halberstam, Jack. *The Queer Art of Failure*. Durham, NC: Duke University Press, 2011.

Love, Heather. *Feeling Backward: Loss and the Politics of Queer History*. Cambridge, MA: Harvard University Press, 2007.

Marais, Sue. "Getting Lost in Cape Town: Spatial and Temporal Dislocation in the South African Short Fiction Cycle." *English in Africa* 22.2 (1995): 29–43.

Miyazaki, Hirokazu. *The Method of Hope: Anthropology, Philosophy, and Fijian Knowledge*. Stanford, CA: Stanford University Press, 2004.

Mukherjee, Siddhartha. *The Emperor of All Maladies: A Biography of Cancer*. London: Fourth Estate, 2011.

Munro, Brenna. "Queer Family Romance: Writing the 'New' South Africa in the 1990s." *GLQ: A Journal of Lesbian and Gay Studies* 15.3 (2009): 397–439.

Munro, Brenna. *South Africa and the Dream of Love to Come: Queer Sexuality and the Struggle for Freedom*. Minneapolis: University of Minnesota Press, 2012.

Naudé, S. J. *Alfabet van die voëls*. Cape Town: Umuzi, 2011.

Naudé, S. J. *The Alphabet of Birds*. Translated by the author. London and New York: And Other Stories, 2015.

Naudé, S. J. *Die derde spoel*. Cape Town: Umuzi, 2017.

Naudé, S. J. "In Conversation: S. J. Naudé and Ivan Vladislavić." *Granta*, December 11, 2014. http://granta.com/in-conversation-s-j-naude-and-ivan-vladislavic/.

Naudé, S. J. "Into the Open Sea: Translating *The Alphabet of Birds*." *Asymptote*, January 2015. www.asymptotejournal.com/article.php?cat=Criticism&id=85.

Naudé, S. J. *The Third Reel*. Cape Town: Umuzi, 2017.

Sontag, Susan. "Illness as Metaphor." [1977]. Reprinted in *Illness as Metaphor and AIDS and Its Metaphors*. London: Penguin, 1991. 1–87.

Van der Vlies, Andrew. *Present Imperfect: Contemporary South African Writing*. Oxford: Oxford University Press, 2017.

Viljoen, Louise. "Afrikaans Literature after 1976: Resistances and Repositionings." Attridge and Attwell. 452–73.

10

History and the Genres of Modernity:
Marlene van Niekerk's *Agaat*

Lily Saint

History helps narrate the inexplicable passage of time. Organizing time into discrete periods, we speak of times of war, times of peace, times of transition, middle ages, golden ages, dark ages, and times of revolution. Each of these historiographic categories—or genres—is identifiable by a specific set of narrative elements. Revolutionary periods, for instance, are described in terms of hope, despair, revelation, damnation, upheaval, violence, and change; histories of oppressive eras feature characters we call variously tsar, dictator, zealot, warlord, worker, peon, peasant, and boss, while its time is lived fearfully, anxiously, or with action held in abeyance. During peaceful times, diurnal or seasonal narratorial temporalities dominate alongside historians' metaphors of prosperity, fecundity, and haleness.

Given this propensity of historians to construct recognizable narrative genres of history, genre theory allows us to grapple with the implications of these constructed historical typologies. This chapter shows how Jacques Derrida's cautionary tale about the *law of genre's* impulse to categorize, separate, to name and cordon off, or to place apart (as in apartheid), may also be the danger of *the law of historical genre*. This law also seeks to apportion and separate off period from period, thereby banishing evidence of continuity, contiguity, exception, indeterminacy, and contingency from the historical register. My argument delves into this analysis of the conjunction between literary genres and historical genres through a look at Marlene van Niekerk's *Agaat* (2004, trans. 2005), a novel preoccupied with the overlap between narrating the history and the present of twentieth-century South Africa and the construction and deconstruction of narrative genres.

Of course, if anything could be said to be *the* problem of contemporary South African literary studies, it is precisely this problem of how to grapple with the historical. Whether we understand history to be a concatenation of isolated stretches of time organized into clearly distinctive periods such as the Mfecane, the colonial period, the apartheid era, the Interregnum, the postapartheid moment, and so forth; whether we instead emphasize the palimpsestic character of history; or whether we understand history as both rupture and continuum, event and duration, *kairos* and *chronos*; howsoever and with whichever conceptual figure we represent the passage of time, what persistently vexes the South African present is how the time of apartheid and its legal abolition is to be understood in its cultural and aesthetic responses as well as its material effects.[1]

The temporal concept-metaphors commonly deployed to describe this present can be loosely divided into three types: the first indicates lateness, or aftermath, as in the term "post-apartheid"; the second indicates rebirth or renovation, as in the term "New South Africa" or Thabo Mbeki's "African Renaissance"; while "transition," the third framework for understanding the present, represents the contemporary as a perpetually ambiguous moment of in-between—Walter Benjamin's Janus-faced angel of history, gazing back at the traumas and nostalgias of colonialism and apartheid, while simultaneously careening forward into the anxieties and desires of future *teloi*. As Milla, *Agaat*'s central narrator, puts it, when she describes winding up a grandfather clock, this multidirectional view of history is: "time that streams away backwards, time that ticks on ahead, time being wound up for the running down."[2]

How relevant are these extant temporal apparatuses to South African literary studies today?[3] If the postapartheid era is a failure in many *material* ways, its disappointing anticlimax paradoxically succeeds at highlighting how the neat division of time into *befores* and *afters* reduces experience to linear time that, as any individual or national history makes plain, is rarely the lived experience of time. Thus, the postapartheid "failure" provides evidence of the rich complexity of lived time, presenting us with an opportunity to reassess terms of analysis (as Jacob Dlamini's work on nostalgia and many chapters in this volume have done) and, possibly, to disassemble them.[4] This chapter questions the impulse to periodize, since cordoning off literary works from one another in the sanitized terminologies of imperial, modern, postmodern, neoimperial, and so forth, might be a critical impulse that unwittingly echoes segregation's own system of social-engineering-by-division.

In *The Sense of an Ending*, Frank Kermode's exploration of humans' compulsion for form, he suggests that "we re-create the horizons we have abolished, the structures that have collapsed; and we do so in terms of the old patterns, adapting them to our new worlds."[5] This impulse of historians and critics alike, to create "necessary fictions," is one way we respond to, or stave off the palpable threat posed by time's amorphous and unrelenting contingencies, allowing us to argue instead that they have definable form and character. One such fiction is precisely this idea of aftermath or belatedness, the "post" of postapartheid, expressed most convincingly in the term itself, if not by those who inhabit the time it means to explain. Is it possible, then, for critics and writers to rise to the challenge presented by the failure of the postapartheid, and to recognize the inherent danger of the categories of genre and historical genre? In other words, in the reconfiguration of racial dynamics after the formal end of apartheid, was there also a reconfiguration of historiographic genres, both literary and academic, and if so, how does *Agaat*, as one particular instance, grapple with the challenges of narrating the contemporary?

Agaat deploys myriad formal strategies to make manifest the difficulty of narrating the contemporary in South Africa. In its false starts, its preambles ("the preamble is just as important as the action itself" [14]), its pending but often delayed revelations and morbidities, its asynchronous plot development, and its multiple narrative modes, the novel exposes the irreducibility of South Africa's contemporary reality to any set of generic conventions. Yet, paradoxically it also shows this irreducible reality to be only expressible via a complex but carefully ordered architectural fiction. At the heart of this novel is the tension between *Agaat*'s—and Milla's—insistence on the solidity of fixed markers of generic and racial identity, and its persistent rejection of form and race as inadequate to the task of narrating individual and historical existence.

The novel's structure can be compared to something that has been clearly mapped out in advance—as in an embroidery pattern, or a paint-by-numbers kit. Indeed, Milla's overriding preoccupation for the first half of the novel is to review a map of her property, and in such a way Van Niekerk renders both the longing for form along with form's persistent absence a central *theme* of *Agaat*'s plot. The novel itself has a clearly mapped structure consisting of four recurring narrative modes framed by the prologue and epilogue, which are narrated by Milla's son, Jakkie. These are not always included in the same order, but all four modes appear in each chapter except the last; they can be described as follows:

1. Milla's first-person present-tense narrative, told from her invalid's bed as her body becomes increasingly incapable of communicating or moving. These sections are set after the formal end of apartheid;

2. An unidentified second-person narration—possibly Agaat's, but more likely Milla's self-justificatory and self-involved internal dialogue—concerned

with relating to Milla the early years of her marriage to Jak and her
relationship with Agaat;

3. A series of much shorter italicized first-person interludes, lacking regular
   punctuation and narrating Milla's fraught stream-of-consciousness, as she
   tries to understand when and why her sickness began. These are set in the
   1990s;

4. Milla's diaries, read to her by Agaat, which cycle from 1960 through 1979,
   and then shift back from 1953 to 1960.[6]

When one starts the book, it takes some time to become acquainted with the
rhythm of these four narrative modes; they serve, thus, to divert the first-time
reader from her narrative expectations, while also subtly nudging her along
a very carefully manicured path. Though Milla intones: "Timing. Chance.
Coincidence. From the beginning it had flowed strongly through the whole
history," we might wonder how much Van Niekerk's writing project is itself
marked by these contingencies (545). Are there loose threads in the novel that
are not also intentional loose threads?

Milla's desire to revisit the map of her farm expresses her longing for
containment, an urge to locate order within "slippery, supple, subtle, silvery
time" (69). Much like genre, maps restrain with their clear spatial demarcations,
reassuring Milla that there is an underlying structure to reality. "Maps attend
lifetimes," she suggests, and then goes on to ask a question I want to focus
on: "What is an age without maps?" (69). Can history be written without
some necessary enclosing formalism? Or better: How can historiography be
spatially or temporally organized and yet remain conscious of the fictional
nature of its own construction?

Kermode quotes Iris Murdoch: "Since reality is incomplete, art must not be
too afraid of incompleteness." He continues: "We must not falsify [reality] with
patterns too neat, too inclusive; there must be dissonance."[7] Modern literature,
for Kermode, is that which moves from attempts at mimesis or the imitation
of reality, to precisely the recognition, by writers, of the impossibility of art
reflecting or imitating the world. Such writers are consciously aware that they
construct fictions or fabrications, and though they require forms and paradigms
within which to do so, these come into being along with the recognition that
reality cannot be contained by them.[8] Form is certainly necessary for the
representation of reality's heterogeneous forms, leading us to deduce that it is
indeed fiction that accepts its own failures to adequately represent reality that is
necessary for the representation of that which we live everyday. In other words,

fictions are the only forms in which to represent the nonfictional. *Agaat*'s attempt at comprehensiveness (Rita Barnard calls the novel "encyclopedic") reminds us that all narratives of the South African present are fictions—including political, academic, and journalistic ones—since all narratives necessarily demand that certain incidences of "Timing. Chance. Coincidence" be disregarded in order to impose a structure on that reality (545).

In one of Milla's disquisitions on farming we hear her nostalgic *ars poetica*, a longing for a different narrative mode which "retain[s] control" of the narrative, as of the land and the country:

> You don't just blunder into a thing, you examine it from all sides and then you make an informed decision and plan it properly in distinct phases, always in tune with the seasons. And then you round out the phases one by one, all the while keeping an eye on the whole, the rhythms, the movements, just like rehearsing a piece of music.
>
> That's how you retain control, that's how you prevent irksome delays at a later stage. (14)

The writer, as much *homo faber* as a farmer, begins with the raw material and, through effort and planning, turns it into something else, something "made up" or artificial, but no less real for being fabricated. This is the "control" she can exercise within "slippery, supple, subtle, silvery time"—the construction of ordered fictions out of disordered reality. Recognizing, then, the artifice of fiction's ordered forms, however self-consciously disordered they are, should not deter us from simultaneously acknowledging such fictions as mete, if compromised, forms of historical and literary representation.[9]

Genre and nation

The temporal and narratorial fragmentation of *Agaat*'s four-part structure suggests its allegiances to the modernist novel, yet obviously I am striving here to avoid too rigidly categorizing *Agaat*. I do, however, appreciate the aims of writing that Neil Lazarus refers to when he defines "*modernist writing after the canonization of modernism*" as that which "does what at least *some* modernist work has done from the outset: namely, says 'no'; refuses integration, resolution, consolation, comfort; protests and criticizes."[10] In this vein, *Agaat* cleverly limns the divide between our desire to imagine history, life, and narrative as following some neat emplotment and structure, and our parallel recognition of the sheer impossibility of such completion and order.

Continued debates over South Africa's own contested history, in literary and other public and private spheres, attest to this impossibility. *Agaat* therefore approaches its story from different angles, so that the resulting effect on the reader is one of familiarity (the plot unfolds, the secret is revealed), tempered by the reminder that there are endless ways to tell and know the tale. None is sufficient alone, Milla's several stories tell us, and only in tandem might they begin to more accurately represent the various temporal modalities of South Africa's historical and discursive realities.[11]

Set on a farm in the Western Cape, *Agaat* tells the story of Milla de Wet's adoption of a colored child, whom she names Agaat. When the novel opens, Agaat is caring for an elderly Milla, who is dying from amyotrophic lateral sclerosis (ALS), also known as Lou Gehrig's disease. While Milla has lost all motor function, she remains mentally alert, and thus her interior monologues convincingly comprise a large part of the narration. Milla's various narratives describe the rupture at the heart of the plotline: when, finally, after thirteen years of being childless, she gives birth to her only son, Jakkie, Milla expels Agaat from the main house to a room outside, effectively tearing asunder the relationship of mother and child previously established between them. Agaat's exile, and Milla's subsequent attempts to repair the damage it causes while contradictorily forcing Agaat to assume the normative role of colored maid, farmhand, nurse, and all-around dogsbody, suggests, as Mark Sanders has pointed out, that "the making of this ambivalent mother—repaired and retributive, good and bad—is what the novel is about."[12]

Agaat is also self-consciously about South Africa. From its very first page it compels the reader to think of the novel as a representation of the nation, or as the nation itself. Central dates in South Africa's notorious history haunt the novel, though it is rarely explicit about its apartheid context. When historical markers (capital H) are occasionally mentioned (and not as part of the diary entries), they are years such as 1948 (election of the National Party, birth of official "apartheid"), 1960 (formation of the Republic of South Africa; Sharpeville massacre), and 1993 (death of Chris Hani; selection of Mandela and de Klerk as Nobel Peace Prize recipients).[13] This national concern is declared from the start in the choice of sources for the three epigraphs introducing the novel: the *National Anthology of Song of the Federation of Afrikaans Culture Organizations*, *Embroider Like This*[14] (with its introduction by Mrs. E. Betsie Verwoerd, wife of apartheid-era prime minister H. F. Verwoerd), and the *Handbook for Farmers [Boere] in South Africa* (with its foreword by J. G. C. Kemp, minister of agriculture). These quotations synthesize the novel's preoccupation with the production and reproduction of the Afrikaner nation, foregrounding, in particular, how the nation is brought into being and reinforced via generative cultural acts like singing, sewing, farming, and reading.

These introductory books are the same ones Milla leaves for Agaat in the "outside room" she assiduously prepares for Agaat shortly before Jakkie's birth. Each is driven by a discourse of teleological, even eschatological intent, in its dream for the production of the ideal nation. From the song book:

> This new volume [of songs] seeks to interpret the growth, passion and expansion of the soul of the nation. May the indefinable element—the force and flavor of this Southland—be found, felt and experienced, then the nation will press it to their hearts and adopt it as their own.

From the sewing book:

> That is the beauty, the value of this [embroidery] book: that it was born out of love and inspires to love, that nobody can doubt. And with that a great service is done to the nation, for who feels for beauty, on whatever terrain, has a contribution to make to the cultural development of the nation.

And from the farming manual:

> Just as the Bible points the way to spiritual perfection so will this Handbook also point to ways and means to more profitable farming and to great prosperity for every farmer in every part of the country. (ix–x)

The song anthology hopes to be a vehicle for the "growth" and "expansion" of the nation, the embroidery manual "has a contribution to make to the cultural development of the nation," while the farming guide invokes another eschatological *ur*-text, the Bible, an inspiration which "points the way to spiritual perfection" for the more prosaic activities of sowing and reaping on South African soil.

As if to reemphasize the importance of these texts for Van Niekerk's novel, Milla tests out the room she prepares for Agaat by drinking "Agaat's" rooibos tea and reading "Agaat's" books there:

> took all A.'s other reading matter out of the crate where I had put it away & so read the introduction by Her Honour Mrs Dr. Verwoerd in the embroidery book & must say was really quite inspiring: The book conceived in love for the development of the nation & the homely atmosphere that embroidery creates because it's the mark of a culturally conscious nation underlined the words & wrote in the front: May this book provide you with much pleasure yet in the empty hours on G[rootmoeders]drift. (62–63)

After singing some of the songs from the song book anthology and reading from the farming manual, again Milla records: "Underlined in pencil for A. the sentence in the Foreword that says that the Handbook will help the farmer in his material growth just as the Bible helps him in his spiritual growth" (64). Milla's "underlining" acts as compensatory overstatement: she seeks to ward off the sneaking possibility that the ideals are themselves empty by constantly reaffirming their truth. Yet it is not only Milla who returns repeatedly to these texts, but Van Niekerk herself, who chooses to begin her own book, *Agaat*, with these selfsame quotations, reappropriating and transforming their fantastical temporalities of perfectibility.

Apartheid was, of course, the engine driving these Afrikaner utopian ideals. While the international community retrospectively memorializes apartheid as the ultimate racist dystopia, in its political, discursive, and ideological instantiation of Afrikaner power, apartheid as doctrine served to solidify and entrench Afrikaner identity. To say that *Agaat* is a novel grappling—in Afrikaans—with the problem of narrating the South African present is also, inevitably, to say that it is a novel about the unraveling of the apartheid fantasy and, by extension, the destabilization of Afrikaner identity.[15] I return to this below.

Apartheid and genre

Paul Gilroy's *The Black Atlantic: Modernity and Double Consciousness* (1993) famously recasts standard historical periodization by positioning black experience at the center of modernity. For Gilroy, what unites writers in the Black Atlantic is their shared sense that modernity itself "was founded on the catastrophic rupture of the middle passage."[16] Similarly, in *Rewriting Modernity* (2006), David Attwell refuses the racist monochromaticism of narratives of Western modernity, recognizing instead how modernity in colonial and postcolonial spaces emerged as a series of concurrent, "fugitive," modernities.

Both scholars examine how black *genres of modernity* explore and communicate shared, group experiences. Furthermore, as these are genres forged in the contact zones of slavery, colonialism, and apartheid, they are thus characterized by syncretism and hybridity. Gilroy posits W. E. B. DuBois's *The Souls of Black Folk* as the prototype of the Black Atlantic modern tradition; Attwell begins with Tiyo Soga. Describing such works, Gilroy writes:

> The genre of modernist writing [Du Bois] initiated in *The Souls of Black Folk* and
> refined further in his later work, especially *Darkwater*, supplements recognizably

sociological writing with personal and public history, fiction, autobiography, ethnography, and poetry. These books produce a self-consciously polyphonic form that was born from the intellectual dilemmas that had grown alongside Du Bois' dissatisfaction with all available scholarly languages.[17]

A more recent South African example of this type of writing can be found in Jacob Dlamini's "recollection," *Native Nostalgia*, which the author describes as follows:

> not an ethnography of Katlehong, a systematic study of its culture, even though there is some of that. Nor is it a conventional retelling of Katlehong's history, with events flowing neatly into a chronological whole. There is no recounting of dates like the beads of a rosary. The book is neither a memoir nor indeed even a cultural biography of Katlehong. But it contains elements of both. This book is best understood as a gathering of fragments of memory, souvenirs of the imagination. I have collected these fragments into a fractured whole through which I hope to look back at a life, a childhood, spent under apartheid.[18]

The cross-pollination of genres characteristic of both Du Bois' modernism and Dlamini's depiction of life under apartheid, insists upon a writerly dynamism characterized by collage and serendipity instead of adherence to convention or rule. Such an approach to writing about black experiences undoes strict generic categories, producing a more honest form of mimesis, mirroring back reality's refractions, contaminations, and imperfections albeit through the grammatical structures of written language.

For Mikhail Bakhtin, of course, the novel is always already dialogic in its inclusion of multiple voices that cross registers, including high and low discourses, poetic and prosaic. *Agaat*, too, exhibits the heteroglossia that Bakhtin says is inherent in the novel. Yet for Bakhtin, the heteroglossia of novels is an unintentional consequence, or component, of novel-making, but Van Niekerk's work purposefully makes explicit this multitude, or mass, of voices, rendering polyvocality South African literature's theme as well as its form, going so far as to imply that the problematizing of genre is the formal task at hand for the contemporary South African writer. To undo apartheid is to undo what Derrida calls "the law of genre" that restricts and draws boundaries, ushering in "norms and interdictions." The writer can level a challenge by exposing the heterogeneity undergirding the apparent limits genre reifies. This heterogeneity, or "principle of contamination," discretely resides within all genres, and is in fact, for Derrida, "the law of the law of genre."[19]

What Gilroy and Attwell identify as the mark of black modernity—in *their* terms, "polyphony" and "transculturation," respectively—could thus describe many other literary traditions. Yet it is not merely this mélange of textual and extra-textual materials that permits Gilroy and Attwell to identify a class of texts that represent their own generic intervention in and as *black* modernities, but also their shared centripetal working through, in, and around slavery and apartheid.

Van Niekerk's work also foregrounds generic heterogeneity while placing the idea of historical rupture and racial displacement in the heart of the country at the heart of the novel. Embracing myriad genres including shopping lists, songs in Afrikaans and English, German *lieder*, passages of first-person lyrical stream-of-consciousness, diary entries and poems, alongside other miscellany, *Agaat* is quintessentially polyphonic.[20] Yet can Gilroy's terms describing black contributions to modernity apply to a white Afrikaans writer's novel? Does such a claim co-opt a theoretical specificity for broader application, thereby divesting it of its original usefulness? Or do Gilroy and Attwell's theories deserve to be updated now that an Afrikaans writer appears who is as concerned with the centrality of apartheid and polyvocality as the black and colored writers preceding her?

As Andrew van der Vlies explains in his essay on the English translation of *Agaat* (the edition I use here), the attempt to turn *Agaat* into "world literature" by translating it into English undermines the book's focus on the specificity of Afrikaner identity and language. While *Agaat* narrates the gradual dissolution of Afrikaner identity through language (what Van der Vlies calls "the novel's insistent identification as an *Afrikaans* text"), Michiel Heyns's choice to translate it for global audiences by changing local high and low cultural Afrikaans references into English canonical ones (T. S. Eliot is the emblematic figure for this in Van der Vlies's estimation) renders the text more accessible and transparent for the Anglophone reader, but divests the novel of its particular difference that is central to its thematic and formal concerns.[21]

In what way, then, can *Agaat* function as an "'archive' of particular sets of out-of-use Afrikaans vocabulary," and can that archive be transmitted beyond Afrikaans, Van der Vlies implicitly asks?[22] Can the novel transcend its local particularities to convey something of those particularities to global readers? Relatedly, how might the specifically local contexts of Gilroy and Attwell's discussions about black literary modernities apply in our understanding of Van Niekerk's own destabilization of modern genres? Joining Van der Vlies's assertion that *Agaat* is a novel that aims "to be encyclopedic in relation to words that have fallen out of use in current Afrikaans usage" with Attwell and Gilroy's repositioning of blackness at the center of literary modernisms, I suggest that

Afrikaner identity, at least as represented in Van Niekerks' wider oeuvre, is as strongly bound up in its relation to racial ideologies—and to apartheid—as it is to Afrikaans.[23] While Gilroy absents Africa in his discussion of the Black Atlantic except to analyze it as a "mythic counterpart to modernity in the Americas,"[24] his arguments apply in the South African context as well. Certainly, and in direct response to his oversight, one can usefully deploy Gilroy to discuss South African modernities and thereby insist that the concept of black Atlantic modernity should include writing produced in and about Africa by Africans. Yet, it is his placement of slavery at the center of the project of Western modernity that directs us to similarly situate colonialism, segregation, and apartheid at the center of various South African modernities, much as Attwell himself does. This reconfigured understanding of modernity undermines the long-dominant vision of it—and its associated genre, modernism—as a merely derivative, Western mode, replacing it with multiple, or "fugitive," versions of modernity, determined by racist ideology and practices.[25]

Van Niekerk's oeuvre consistently places colonialism and its offspring, apartheid, at the center of Afrikaner identity, rather than seeing these historical phenomena as adjuncts to a preexisting Afrikaner culture. *Triomf*, her earlier novel (published in Afrikaans in 1994), demonstrates her concern with Afrikaner identity, but it is with *Agaat* that the *interdependence* of racial identities takes center stage. In *Agaat*, racial divisions are both clearly defined and all mixed up. Indeed, the book's plot as much as its form emphasizes what Breyten Breytenbach has famously called the *bastardization* characterizing Afrikaner identity. "We are a bastard people (bastervolk) with a bastard language [bastertaal]. Our nature is one of bastardy [basterskap]," he writes, in *Season in Paradise*.[26] The unorthodox familial arrangement between Agaat and Milla thus pales in comparison with Breytenbach's definition of Afrikaner identity, which locates heterogeneity, or impurity, at its very origin. In this sense Milla's adoption of Agaat is an "Afrikaner" thing to do, if we accept the definition of "Afrikanerskap" as a hybrid *volk*.[27] Milla's symbolic defense of a pure Afrikaner blood in her rejection of Agaat in favor of her genetic heir, Jakkie, is, therefore, no more than another act of psychological overcompensation: "like all bastards" writes Breytenbach, "uncertain of their identity—we began to adhere to the law of *purity*. That is apartheid. *Apartheid is the law of the bastard.*"[28]

Despite Milla's reluctance to relinquish this "law of purity," hybridity remains essential to her—if such a contradictory phrase be allowed—as, for instance, in her approach to her African farm, and noticeable when she tells Jak, her new fiancé, "we must make of Grootmoedersdrift what it can be, a textbook example of mixed farming" (23), combining crops and livestock. This mixture, inherent in Afrikaner culture, language, and practice, is as central for Du Bois, Dlamini, and Soga's stylistics and formalisms, as it is for Van Niekerk's, who grapples with otherness at the level of language as well as structure and form. Echoing Lazarus, Derek Attridge names this turn-of-the-century responsiveness to the demands of otherness "modernism after modernism."[29] While Van Niekerk's style in *Agaat* may not be as dissonant or minimalist, as, say, late Beckett, the novel hovers, generically, precisely at that edge between the law of the novel and the breaking of the law of the novel to foreground the laws themselves: the laws of the literary, as well as the laws of the land.

That *Agaat* undermines generic categories may be implied by Rita Barnard's designation of the novel as "encyclopedic," since the encyclopedia is a form that must always fall short of its own ambition.[30] Indeed, despite its enormity, *Agaat* is also the story of failing to tell a story: "All your life you've wanted to record it," the second-person narrator tells Milla: "Just for yourself, to try to gain some clarity. But you never got round to it. It was a skipped chapter. You couldn't bring yourself to do it" (79). And this theme of the unnarratable returns in the final chapter: "The beginning you never recorded. You couldn't bring yourself to it... There was in any case something cryptic about the beginning" (544). An explanation (of sorts) is offered for this narrative lacuna:

> Now you understand the actual reason. Or one of them.
>   It wasn't meant for the diary.
>   Nothing about it was meant for a diary.
>   It would have to be taken up into the family saga direct: Grootmodersdrift, farm, house, man, wife, child.
>   First child.
>   From the beginning. It was never a story on its own.
>   Especially not the early beginnings.
>   You thought you could make of the whole Agaat a separate chapter. You thought you could quarantine it in this way. As if it were a thing you could tend in an isolation-pen so that nobody need experience your failures and your mistakes at first hand. (544)

Despite the four narrative modes, none is sufficient since the story was always more than a story—always exceeding the "quarantine" of formal limits. Similarly, *Agaat* fails to adequately convey Afrikaner identity (and as Van der Vlies shows, this is even more true of its English translation). While the book goes to great lengths (in terms of exertion as well as sheer size) to include all the details of life on an Afrikaans farm, it is self-conscious about its failure to accomplish any total explanation of Afrikaner culture, language, and identity. Much as Milla strains to assert a commitment to the ideology underlying the opening epigraphs while contradicting it through her behavior, so too, the more *Agaat* includes, the more the absence of things, narratives, and words is implied. No matter the extensiveness of the archival documentation, Milla notes, it may in fact often leave out the most important parts of the story.

Certainly the four strategies of narration work in tandem to represent the experience as adequately as possible—from different voices and points of view—as if the multiplicity of consecutive stylistic and generic approaches could better honor the heterogeneity of contemporary South African experience. But if South African modernity has a genre of its own narration, if it is to be represented by any genre, it is best represented by the genre that calls into question the idea of genre itself.[31] Van Niekerk's novel troubles the restrictions and edicts of "the law of genre," and by doing so, in the South African *national* context, the novel promotes the undoing or destabilizing of distinctions and boundaries. Another way of putting this is to say that *if genre was the fantasy of apartheid, writing, in the post-apartheid moment, is dreaming of something else.*

Milla too, has a dream that calls for our attention. Here is her transcription:

(Jan 10 1954) Dream I pull out her tongue like an aerial, one section, two, three, longer and longer I pull it out, my hands slip as I try to get a grip on it, there's no end to it, she laughs from the back of her throat, thousands upon thousands of red tonsils wave like seaweed, her tongue shudders in my hands, like a fishing rod, there's something heavy biting and tugging at the line, pulling me off my feet, drawing me in, into her mouth, then I wake up screaming. (402)

In Milla's dream, Agaat's tongue resembles an antenna—a receiver and transmitter of other people's words. But this is no passive conduit of information. Instead, Agaat's dream-tongue possesses a nightmarish magnetism that is so forceful it threatens to draw in and engulf Milla entirely. Milla's quasi-maternal, quasi-pedagogical project of the daytime (Agaat, she relates during her waking hours, is "brave, as open as possible to receiving everything transmitted to her") is challenged by the repressed material exposed in the dream (109). She knows Agaat will never merely receive her knowledge, nor obediently transmit it. Instead, Agaat's agency is unpredictable, like a radio frequency gone haywire that transmits information that may or may not mean something intelligible. Again, Van Niekerk cautions us against too readily taking her own transmission—*Agaat*—as a transparent archive of postapartheid Afrikaner identity.

This imagery of a failed, or skewed transmitting device occurs elsewhere in the novel, when, for instance, Milla describes the sounds she listens to from her bed, that suggest someone pacing in the house "[a]s if somewhere a recording has been made of all the times that I've walked in the passages and rooms of my house, as if it were now being played back to me on a worn audiotape, a record without clear information" (85). Much of what constitutes the novel's present-tense narration is about Milla's failure to properly communicate to Agaat her desire to revisit the map of Grootmoedersdrift. Milla wonders to herself: "Perhaps telepathy works better through piss in the pan than transmitted in waves through the air into the rock-hard skull of Agaat" (69). In other words, even after their many years together, Milla fails to grasp how meaning crosses between herself and Agaat.

As Mark Sanders notes of Van Niekerk and Adriaan van Zyl's *Memorandum* (2006), the "conduit…model," which this work's narrator initially believes to be a possible way of telling a story—that a human being can simply transmit the words of others—proves vastly oversimplistic when considered through the frameworks of mimesis and literary representation.[32] That Agaat (as well as *Agaat*) does not and indeed cannot merely transmit Afrikaner history, knowledge, and culture is as self-evident as Milla's recognition of her own texts' inadequacy when it comes to accurately representing reality. Here we might recall Kermode's conviction that the best writers of modern fiction are those most conscious of its mimetic limits. And indeed, Van Niekerk alerts us also to the way that Milla's "stories" are not only flawed representations of her experience and the world around her but also haunted by those stories not told by Agaat herself, coeval but unarticulated in the space of the novel.

Perhaps, however, Agaat's dances tell us something about the unsayable. Certainly, contemporary South African and "postcolonial" literature remains inflected by the unsaid, the genres of mime or silence. In addition to being a story about Milla's failure to tell a story, *Agaat* is, of course, also the story of the absence, or exclusion, of Agaat's story. Van Niekerk's book testifies to the tyranny of Milla's textual predominance, as well as to the author's reluctance to speak as, or for, Agaat. Sanders concurs that "to the extent that [Agaat's] narration depends on citing what Milla has written, Agaat cannot *narrate* a crucial part of her story, although, throughout her life, she has *symbolised* it in a number of ways"[33]:

> A. is on the mountain in her new uniform! … Could make hr out clearly with J.'s binoculars. *Can't see what she's getting up to there* odd steps & gestures against the slope … That to-do on the hill *I can't figure out.* Sideways & backwards knees bent foot-stamping jumping on one leg jump-jump-jump & point-point-point with one arm at the ground. Then the arms rigid next to the sides. Then she

folded them & then she stretched them. Looked as if she was keeping the one arm in the air with the other arm & waving. (126, emphasis added)

How strange … Hr head in the air, looking up at hr little arm as if it's a stick. *Walking stick? Fencing-foil?* Then again held still in front of hr, palm turned down palm turned up. *Judgment? Blessing? Over the hills over the valley along the river? A farewell ritual? Where would she get it from?* So weird it all is I can't put the images out of my head I think of it all the time. *Why up there? What could she have wanted to see? … Could the binoculars have been playing tricks upon me? Hr arm a pointer? Pointing-out pointing-to what is what & who is who? An oar? A blade? Hr fist pressing apart the membrane & the meat as if she's dressing a slaughter animal?* But not a sheep, as if she's separating the divisions of the night. Or dividing something within herself. Root cluster.

Far-fetched Milla! Your imagination is too fertile for your own good. But surely one couldn't think it up. A. in hr working clothes in the moonlight in the middle of the night doing a St Vitus's dance. I could surely not have dreamt that. There must be a simple explanation. Perhaps she's working herself up to running away. I suppose I'll get to the truth of the matter one day. (127, emphasis added)

Although Agaat's dance remains indecipherable to Milla and the reader—we never "get to the truth of the matter"—it too requires formal expression to make itself known at all, even as an enigma. Milla's questions and guesses permit for multiple interpretations without any conclusive one triumphing over others:

W•H•A•T W•E•R•E Y•O•U D•O•I•N•G F•I•R•S•T N•I•G•H•T O•N M•O•U•N•T•A•I•N I•N Y•O•U•R U•N•I•F•O•R•M, question mark. S•A•W Y•O•U W•I•T•H B•I•N•O•C•S, full stop. F•U•N•N•Y S•T•E•P•S + L•A•T•E•R W•I•T•S•A•N•D E•A•R•L•Y M•O•R•N•I•N•G I•N Y•O•U•R C•L•O•T•H•E•S I•N W•A•V•E•S, full stop. S•A•T•A•N•I•C R•I•T•E•S, exclamation mark. M•A•I•D•S S•A•Y Y•O•U A•R•E P•O•S•S•E•S•S•E•D W•A•N•D•E•R A•R•O•U•N•D A•T N•I•G•H•T + L•E•A•V•E M•E H•E•R•E A•L•O•N•E, full stop. N•O•T T•A•K•E•N I•N B•Y Y•O•U•R I•N•N•O•C•E•N•C•E, comma, W•I•T•C•H, exclamation mark. = M•Y D•E•A•T•H N•O•T E•N•O•U•G•H F•O•R Y•O•U, question mark. O•N W•H•A•T C•L•I•M•A•X A•R•E Y•O•U S•E•T, question mark, swearword. (371)

We can return to Gilroy here, and to his observation that modes of resistance, or what he calls "politics," under slavery had to be hidden from the overseers, and thus

invoked by other, more deliberately opaque means [than language]. This politics exists on a lower frequency where it is played, danced, and acted as well as sung and sung about, because words … will never be enough to communicate its *unsayable claims to truth. The willfully damaged signs which betray the resolutely utopian politics of transfiguration therefore partially transcend modernity, constructing both an imaginary anti-modern past and a postmodern yet to come.*[34]

Agaat's power to "transfigure" also haunts Milla's dream. In addition to synecdochically representing Agaat as a faulty conduit of information, Agaat's dream-tongue exerts an unexpected counterattraction on Milla threatening to bring about her complete annihilation. Milla pulls on Agaat's tongue much as she pulled Agaat from her childhood immiseration only to find that her exertions have consequences far exceeding her expectations. It is Agaat who, in Milla's dream, is on the brink of a sort of transubstantiation through her near-incorporation of Milla, proving that her unspoken acts—and the threat of speech which her tongue also represents—exerts an equal, perhaps even stronger, power of transformation than Milla's logorrhea.[35]

Milla's dream also recalls two key events in (post)colonial literature: first, the ending of Coetzee's *Foe* (1986), in which the speechless Friday opens his mouth to let out a stream which "runs northward and southward to the ends of the earth" and, second, "Ariel's song" from William Shakespeare's *The Tempest*: "Nothing of him that doth fade,/But doth suffer a sea-change/Into something rich and strange."[36] If the "trans" of Agaat and Milla's transubstantiations is also the "trans" of transition, we might, rather than trying to determine which *form* contemporary South African cultural production should or will take, use this opportunity to relinquish residual attachments to the fantasies of genre that are the remainder of colonial and apartheid law, accepting instead the undoing, or at least trans-*form*-ation of literary categories after apartheid. Perhaps the "richness" and the "strangeness" of *Agaat* prove this point.

Agaat closes predictably with Milla's anticipated death. Nonetheless, to follow Kermode, Van Niekerk successfully uses peripeteia to fulfill our readerly "wish to reach the discovery or recognition by an unexpected and instructive route."[37] Narrating the transition yet ending the story, the form is itself at odds with a key thematic concern. It is this abrasive disjuncture—between the inevitability of ending and the continuity of Agaat's story and the nation's history—that creates one further challenge to genre. By holding the predictability of the ending in tension with the ongoing time of a wandering, unpredictable transition, the neat thread of narrative and historical linearity is undone, forcing us to trace historical experience through its frangible amorphous forms. The same is true of the ending of Milla as emissary of Afrikaner ideology, which stands in tension with the continuation of Afrikaner culture and language in the transubstantiated form of *Agaat*.

Of course, there is a paradox at the heart of my argument (and Kermode's), since this narrative ethics of Van Niekerk's, one that seeks to render transparent the mimetic and ethical failures of narration itself, depends on those selfsame forms and genres of historical narrative in order to expose its flawed—and even dangerous—effects. Where Van Niekerk chooses the rather conventional formal structure of the frame narrative to house her far less conventional inner novel, I too have adhered here to generic conventions, albeit academic ones. In solidarity, then, with attempts to keep the tension between form and deformation explicitly palpable, I return once more to Kermode's quotation of Iris Murdoch: one "must not be too afraid of incompleteness."[38]

Notes

1   On history as rupture, see Michel Foucault, *The Archeology of Knowledge*. Frank Kermode uses *kairos and chronos* to explain how humans turn to form in order to make sense of that which is actually senseless—namely, the endless "tick" "tick" "tick" of time, which we supplement with a "tock" to provide us with a "sense of an ending." Part of the problem with the term "apartheid" is that it may be better understood as a conceptual rather than as a historical term, evidenced by its use, for example, to describe twenty-first-century Israeli policy.

2   Van Niekerk, *Agaat*, 55. This edition is referenced parenthetically in the text hereafter.

3   There are important critical precedents reevaluating extant terminologies. Recent work by Leon de Kock, for instance, has called into question the category of a unitary and unifying national "South African" literature, while the question of the modern is carefully treated in books by Derek Attridge and David Attwell, who both force us to reevaluate the usefulness of the historicizing categories of modernity and postmodernity in the South African context.

4   Dlamini, *Native Nostalgia*.

5   Kermode, *The Sense of an Ending*, 58.

6   The years represented in Milla's diaries are: 1960, 1961, 1964, 1965, 1966, 1967, 1968, 1971, 1972, 1973, 1974, 1978, 1979, and then from 1953, 1954, 1955, 1956, 1957, 1958, 1959, 1960. In the final chapter, Milla tells us that it was Agaat who determined the structure of their representation in the novel: "a sequence determined by her. With so many omissions and additions that nobody, not even you, would ever be able to ascertain the true facts" (545). The last chapter (Chapter 20) excludes the diary entry.

7   Kermode, *The Sense of an Ending*, 130.

8   Ibid., 168.

9   The novels (and fake novels) listed on page twelve remind us again that the slippage between the forms of fiction and the forms of life is almost imperceptible. Van der

Vlies alerts us to various inconsistent renderings in the English translation of the novels listed in the Afrikaans original.

10 Lazarus, *The Postcolonial Unconscious*, 31. For more on current debates about the definitional borders of the modern, particularly outside the Euro-American tradition, see Attwell, *Rewriting Modernity*; Gilroy, *The Black Atlantic*; as well as Wollager and Eatough, *The Oxford Handbook of Global Modernisms*, and GoGwilt, *The Passage of Literature*.

11 Jamal refers to South Africa as a site of "radical heterogeneity" beset by the problem of how to best address the "multiple"-ness of South African identity and history (xii).

12 Sanders, "Miscegenations," 20.

13 Milla "showed [Agaat]... the representations of our History the ships of Van Riebeeck & the distribution of the first farms on the Liesbeeck & the fat-tailed sheep that the Free Burghers exchanged with the Hottentots for beads & cloths & the Voortrekkers & the Oxwagons & the Boer War & the History of Gold & Diamonds." When she teaches Agaat how to sew, she explained, "It's like that with every art form ... You start with the simple & then you practise faithfully every day until you're ready one day to tackle the scenes from Hist. & then Heaven" (143).

14 This book was actually translated into English as *Embroider Now* by Esther Geldenhuys; the title included here is likely Heyns's translation.

15 In a letter Breytenbach wrote to *Die Burger*: "I hate and abhor apartheid with all of its implications, and if it is representative of Afrikanerdom, if the two cannot be separated, then I see no future for the Afrikaner in our beautiful country." Quoted in Lazarus, "Longing, Radicalism, Sentimentality," 159.

16 Gilroy, *The Black Atlantic*, 197.

17 Ibid., 115.

18 Dlamini, *Native Nostalgia*, 62.

19 Derrida, "The Law of Genre," 59.

20 Michiel Heyns's English translation takes this even further, by finding "equivalents from English poetry" to replace *Agaat*'s references to "mainstream Afrikaans poetry," and by "extending the range of poetic allusion ... generally without acknowledgment," rendering the novel, in English, even more polyphonic and polygeneric than the author herself made explicit. Quoted in Van der Vlies, "MêME DYING STOP CONFIRM ARRIVAL STOP," 195.

21 Ibid., 192.

22 Ibid. (quoting Marlene van Niekerk in interview in Van der Vlies's translation).

23 Ibid., 204. See also Van der Vlies, *Present Imperfect*, chapter 3.

24 Gilroy, *The Black Atlantic*, 113. This oversight is addressed in part in Bystrom and Slaughter's *The Global South Atlantic*.

25 For Attwell, black South African modernities are "fugitive" in the sense that their "investment in modernity ... was never complete or unguarded ... it always sought ... to define itself outside of received, colonial versions of authority."

Fugitiveness, in this sense, has less to do with flight ... than with the fugitiveness of being in-and-out simultaneously." Attwell, *Rewriting Modernity*, 23–24.

26 Breytenbach, *A Season in Paradise*, 156. For Breytenbach it is the heterogeneity and hybridity that renders Afrikaner identity "good and beautiful."

27 In a 2008 talk, Breytenbach spoke of Afrikaans as a soon-to-be extinct language that he uses, at times, as a deliberate way of thinking against orthodoxy (in this case, the orthodoxy of English), in order to maintain diversity ("Reading Series").

28 Breytenbach, *A Season in Paradise*, 156.

29 Attridge, *J. M. Coetzee and the Ethics of Reading*, 5.

30 Barnard, "World Literature, World Music, and the Encyclopedic Novel."

31 This is not unlike Kermode's definition of modernists as those authors most self-aware of the failure of their writing to adequately reflect reality. This turn to generic instability (in the work, for example, of Ivan Vladislavić, on which see Chris Holmes's chapter in this volume; see also Marlene van Niekerk's collaboration with an artists on *Memorandum*) is at the same time accompanied by a resurgence in popular genre fiction (crime novels in particular). Does this indicate a nostalgia for apartheid or for the rules of genre, a disquiet around the instability of the present? Authors in *Safundi*'s special issue "Beyond Rivalry: Literature/History, Fiction/ Non-Fiction," 13.1–2 (2012), took up some of these questions.

32 Sanders, "Mimesis," 108.

33 Sanders, "Miscegenations," 23 (emphasis original).

34 Gilroy, *The Black Atlantic*, 37.

35 Earlier in the novel, Milla describes Agaat's process of cleaning her tongue via a similar, if reversed, image of Milla pulling out Agaat's tongue in the dream: "The little mole-hand nuzzles out my tongue ... I feel a tugging at my tongue. The grip tremors with a faint temptation: Where is it fixed? how firmly? with what strings? how long is it?" (53).

36 Friday's mouth opens to let out a stream which "passes through the cabin, through the wreck; washing the cliffs and shores of the island, it runs northward and southward to the ends of the earth. Soft and cold, dark and unending, it beats against my eyelids, against the skin of my face" Coetzee, *Foe*, 157; Shakespeare, *The Tempest*, 1173.

37 Kermode, *The Sense of an Ending*, 18.

38 Ibid., 130.

Works Cited

Attridge, Derek. *J.M. Coetzee and the Ethics of Reading: Literature in the Event.* Chicago: University of Chicago Press, 2004.

Attwell, David. *Rewriting Modernity: Studies in Black South African Literary History.* Athens, OH: Ohio University Press, 2006.

Bakhtin, Mikhail. *The Dialogic Imagination.* Ed. Michael Holquist. Austin: University of Texas Press, 2002.

Barnard, Rita. "World Literature, World Music, and the Encyclopedic Novel: Reflections on Marlene van Niekerk's *Agaat*," November 3, 2010. Unpublished talk, New York: New York University Postcolonial Colloqiuim.

Breytenbach, Breyten. *A Season in Paradise.* 1976. Trans. Rike Vaughan. 1980. New York: Harcourt Brace, 1994.

Breytenbach, Breyten. "Reading Series: Breyten Breytenbach and Dubravka Ugrešić." Public reading, unpublished. 92nd St Y, New York. September 23, 2008.

Bystrom, Kerry, and Joseph Slaughter, eds. *The Global South Atlantic.* New York: Fordham University Press, 2018.

Coetzee, J. M. *Foe.* New York: Viking, 1987.

Derrida, Jacques. "The Law of Genre." Trans. Avital Ronell. *Critical Inquiry* 7.1 (1980): 55–81.

Dlamini, Jacob. *Native Nostalgia.* Auckland Park, South Africa: Jacana, 2010.

Foucault, Michel. *The Archeology of Knowledge.* New York: Routledge, 2002.

Gilroy, Paul. *The Black Atlantic: Modernity and Double Consciousness.* Cambridge, MA: Harvard University Press, 1993.

GoGwilt, Christopher. *The Passage of Literature: Genealogies of Modernism in Conrad, Rhys, and Pramoedya.* New York: Oxford University Press, 2010.

Jamal, Ashraf. *Predicaments of Culture in South Africa.* Pretoria: University of South Africa Press, 2005.

Kermode, Frank. *The Sense of an Ending: Studies in the Theory of Fiction.* New York: Oxford University Press, 2000.

Kruger, Loren. *The Drama of South Africa: Plays, Pageants and Publics since 1910.* London: Routledge, 1999.

Lazarus, Neil. "Longing, Radicalism, Sentimentality: Reflections on Breyten Breytenbach's *Season in Paradise*." *Journal of Southern African Studies* 12.2 (1986): 158–82.

Lazarus, Neil. *The Postcolonial Unconscious.* New York: Cambridge University Press, 2011.

Sanders, Mark. *Complicities: The Intellectual and Apartheid.* Durham, NC: Duke University Press, 2002.

Sanders, Mark. "Mimesis, Memory, *Memorandum*." *Journal of Literary Studies* 25.3 (2009): 106–23.

Sanders, Mark. "Miscegenations: Race, Culture, Phantasy." *Journal for the Association for the Study of Australian Literature* (2008): 10–35.

Shakespeare, William. "The Tempest." In *William Shakespeare: The Complete Works.* Oxford: Clarendon Press, 1988. 1167–89.

Van der Vlies, Andrew. "'MêME DYING STOP CONFIRM ARRIVAL STOP': Provincial Literatures in Global Time, the case of Marlene van Niekerk's *Agaat*." In *Institutions of World Literature: Writing, Translation, Markets.* Eds. Pieter Vermeulen and Stefan Helgesson. London: Routledge, 2015. 191–208.

Van der Vlies, Andrew. *Present Imperfect: Contemporary South African Writing*. Oxford: Oxford University Press, 2017.

Van Niekerk, Marlene. *Agaat*. 2004. Trans. Michiel Heyns. 2005. Portland, OR: Tin House Books, 2010.

Van Niekerk, Marlene. *Triomf*. 1994. Trans. Leon de Kock. Woodstock: Overlook, 2004.

Van Niekerk, Marlene, and Adriaan van Zyl. *Memorandum: A Story with Paintings*. Trans. Michiel Heyns. Cape Town: Human & Rousseau, 2006.

Wollager, Mark, with Matt Eatough, eds. *The Oxford Handbook of Global Modernisms*. New York: Oxford University Press, 2012.

11

Transition as Democratic Form:
The Unfinishable Work of Ivan Vladislavić

Christopher Holmes

Few terms have been as central to the description of the political state of postapartheid South Africa as *transition*, and few have been so ambiguously defined. The shift to majority rule occupies a space of uncertain temporality despite the precise dating of the capital-T Transition. Born with the release of Nelson Mandela and the beginning of peace talks in 1990, marked by violence and great uncertainty in the run-up to elections, and nominally concluded with the elections of 1994, the transition names a historical era of becoming—namely, becoming democracy. Understanding the transition as a manifestation of becoming poses definitional problems for a term that continues to be reborn in various contested "post-transitional" forms, with the parameters for what this radical change might look like in the everyday political and sociocultural life of the country remaining uncertain.[1] Transition, as a broader historical marker in any number of national and global contexts, is often a stand-in for a set of ambiguous rhetorical concepts that bear little relationship to the actual work of political change. Monica Popescu rejects it as "a magic word—a word that is hardly expected to explain the status quo, but which provides a convenient label to positively connote an evolution and mask and justify a social, economic, or political 'lack.'"[2] And it is to this lack that critics of the political state of postapartheid South Africa consistently return when diagnosing the protracted postponement of democracy's arrival. "Novels"—Peter Hitchcock argues—"should not be expected to solve the riddles of nations (and neither should nations for that matter)."[3] I propose that nations might look to novels—and the work of the aesthetic more broadly—to help negotiate among the many discursive forms those social and political riddles take, and the contexts they hold in dynamic tension.

As a response to the unfinished business of democracy, and the problems of defining a historical period that is by definition in flux, a genre of transition writing has emerged.[4] While this literary intervention has been largely understood as a counter to the historical representation of transition as a political limbo that disregards the ordinary, evolving relationships that individuals have to life in post-apartheid South Africa, very little has been said about the value of literature's embracing the uncertainty and incompletion of transition. This chapter will investigate literature's role in shifting the significance of transition from an ambiguous contextualization of the democracy yet-to-come, to a form of dynamic change and adaptation that, in fact, better describes the work of ongoing democracy. Looking to the work of Ivan Vladislavić, in particular the relationship between *The Restless Supermarket*, the novel he completed during the transition, and a collection of unfinished writings published in the post-transition years, the chapter suggests that the fictions of transition instantiate a form with which to understand democracy as transition and literature as democratic.

The Loss Library and Other Unfinished Stories (2012), Vladislavić's most peculiar work in a canon marked by radical experimentation, is a collection of fragments, fits and starts, notebook excerpts, and "stillborn schemes" imagined during the transition period but left unfinished, unpublished, or unrealized. In the pages of *Loss Library*, Vladislavić sets about like the archeologist of these unpublished pieces, excavating and deciphering the "unsettled accounts" and "case studies of failure" that are the remainders of literary miscarriages attempted during the transition, and pointedly, trying to understand why the historical moment itself made the ideas and concepts of these pieces so difficult to bring into being.[5] While it is easy to cordon off *Loss Library* as *sui generis* among Vladislavić's considerable catalogue of novels, short stories, and creative nonfiction given its temporal strangeness, I argue that it is merely the most explicit of his transition works. As I will demonstrate in a reading of *Restless Supermarket*, the crisis of linguistic representation in/of a period of radical political and social change, to which no definitive outcome can be ascribed, acts as a catalyst for the formal experiments in Vladislavić's fiction; what begins in the completed narrative of the *Restless Supermarket* is expanded and theorized (not to say "completed") in *Loss Library*'s incomplete narratives. Indeed, *Loss Library* functions as Vladislavić's inchoate, transitional novel, an embryo in the state of emergence, not yet formed, but capable of meaning nevertheless. This chapter will make clear that *Loss Library*'s relationship to *Restless Supermarket* reveals Vladislavić's understanding of transition's relationship to democracy.

By composing and publishing a book of unpublished and unpublishable stories, journal entries, and wandering ideas, Vladislavić makes his most radical political statement on not only South Africa's state of democracy in its nascent form, but also the relationship of fiction to the process of exploring and rediscovering the value of transition. And in discovering transition anew, as a form and function of democracy, *Loss Library* becomes a conceptual model for rereading *Restless Supermarket* not simply as a representation of the anxieties of transition, but as an attempt to create space for new forms of transitional democracy. In this way, *Loss Library* is not a wayward diversion to recollect failed narratives of a historical moment that had yet to find its context; rather, it is the instantiation in form of democracy's always-transitional nature. As we will see, the unlikely emergence of a book of self-proclaimed failures by one of South Africa's most important novelists signals the necessity of literature's transitional forms as a bulwark against the drive to contextualize transition as a failure of democracy.

Turning away from context

In her dramatically titled article "Context Stinks!" Rita Felski argues that a "repudiation of context can result in a rarefied focus on poetic language, form, and textuality," and in the process raises questions about the supposed "clarifying power of" the historical.[6] While being careful to avoid essentializing aesthetics at the expense of being willfully naïve about the ideological implications of reading only in the present, Felski rejects what she says is the implicit metaphor at the root of much historicism: the box of history. "One of the main obstacles," she writes of contextualizing the literary, "lies in the prevailing picture of context as a kind of box or container in which individual texts are encased and held fast."[7] Levying the work of Bruno Latour, an arch provocateur of doctrinaire historicism, Felski reads the social scientist as rejecting "society," at least as it is used to describe "a distinctive, bounded totality governed by a predetermined set of structures and functions."[8] This rejection of society as a set of prefab structures makes Felski's argument about context particularly useful for thinking through literary form as the incomplete or unable to be completed analogue to what, in *The Loss Library*, Vladislavić calls the history that was "hard to ignore" (2) in the transition to democracy in late twentieth-century South Africa. The social, and therefore de facto the context, is for Latour and Felski the

> act and fact of association, the coming together of phenomena to create multiple
> assemblages, affinities, and networks. It exists only in its instantiations, in the
> sometimes foreseeable, sometimes unpredictable ways in which ideas, texts,
> images, people, and objects couple and uncouple… The social, in other words,

is not a preformed being but a *doing*, not a hidden entity underlying the realm of appearance, but the ongoing connections, disconnections, and reconnections between countless actors.[9]

Notice how context shifts from the box that contains to the instantiation of "doing," understood as a *dynamic* of associations, coupling and uncoupling, connection and disconnection. Such a social context cannot be contained or completed, but operates in the realm of the "ongoing," a realm to which Vladislavić aspires. Grappling with literature's relationship to the "doing" of social context, Felski asks whether, "in doing better justice to...transtemporal impact, we might usefully think of texts as 'nonhuman actors.'" In calling for an "experiment with other forms of reading" that eschew context in favor of the ongoing connections of many social actors, Felski arrives at her most valuable formalist insight on context. In the "name of history," she writes, we may have well inculcated a "remarkably static model of meaning, where texts are corralled amidst long-gone contexts and obsolete intertexts, incarcerated in the past," subjected to "an all-determining contextual frame."[10] The loss that she posits for such overdetermined framing—couched in the dramatic language of imprisonment, suffocation, police, and the coffin—is movement and dialogue between the manifold social actors, and between failure and instantiation, in the transitional space that is better understood as the figuration of thought itself. And while literary texts, for Felski, "gain vitality from their co-actors," she argues we might be best served to begin to think of novels "not as things to be known, but as things to know *with*."[11] This axiom provides an unwitting anticlimax to her argument, as context already contains "*with*-text" etymologically, but perhaps this is precisely the point. Felski does not wish to dissolve context, as much as she texts to form and reform contextual boxes into the more socially minded dynamics of everyday interaction.

Understanding Felski's own internal contradictions opens the box of context and allows transition to speak differently. My argument about literature's relationship to transition follows on from South Africanists working at the nexus of form and politics, text and context. These include Stephen Clingman, whose "grammar of identity" seeks to "keep a whole series of contexts in view: all the way from the processes and possibilities within the individual"; Sarah Nuttall, who investigates the past's multilayered entanglements with an as-yet-unsettled present; and Derek Attridge, who argues that the singularity of a novel resides in "its open[ness] to change in new contexts" as it is read by new readers, with new and dynamic contexts of their own.[12] In none of these studies is the value of context for the literary work isolated from the contingency and ephemerality of its vantage; indeed, each seeks to forestall the closure of a text's meaning by a monolithic contextualization, or what Felski calls the "coffin" of context. They locate in the interchange between context and text models of what Susan Stanford Friedman calls "exercises in comparative thinking" that lead to new modes of comparison, which expand and evolve previous understandings of historical, political, and generic context.[13] Using these thinkers and the transition writings of Ivan Vladislavić to complicate Felski's wariness of overwhelming context, I propose turning from what Felski calls the "all-determining contextual frame" in our attempts to understand South African literature's representation of transition, and toward the unsettling of our terms of engagement, a process whereby one might claim many contexts in an unfinished dialogue between modes of thinking. In order to make space for a theorization of transition, it is necessary to examine the tacit matter of transition's supposed endpoint for South Africa, the perceived motivation for completing and concluding transition: democracy. But what is the relationship between transition and democracy, and can literature negotiate between the two in a legible form?

Democracy as transition

In the wake of the so-called Arab Spring, the media consumer in the West is warned daily that the formlessness of transitions in the Middle East is dangerous and antidemocratic. Such transitions, often revolutionary departures from dictatorship, tyranny, and theocracy, are interpreted according to the West's latent desire to frame and constraint those transitions within definitive temporal and cultural boundaries, even as the nations and peoples involved are themselves unsure of what democracy—the "rule/power of the people" (gk: *dēmos kratos*)— will look or act like. The rush to contextual judgments brand chaos and upheaval, dynamism and precariousness, polyphony and revolt as signs of the failure to sustain democratic institutions, the damning critique lobbed at nearly every governmental shift in Latin America, the Middle East, and Africa in the twentieth and twenty-first centuries. The Middle East is but the most immediate twenty-first-century example of the postcolonial pessimism that dominates Western commentary on political transition in the global South. Even the briefest periods of transitional amorphousness are adjudged according to a framework of interpretation that prescribes a categorical and speedy resolution of uncertainty— with democracy inevitably coded as Western, secular, capitalist, and complete-able. Forgetful of the fact that democracies have all historically emerged in fits and starts, have broken and refashioned themselves, and are constantly in a state of tension and dialogue in Europe and the United States, Western appraisals of democracy in the global South dismiss anything other than recognizable structures and tropes of capitalist democracy.[14] The recounting of "failures" to bring about democracy in countries that, we are told, have no history of democratic institutions, are too many to elaborate; media outlets of every stripe are guilty of this bland and largely ignorant reduction of democracy to a static, infinitely reproducible form of Western capitalism.[15] Achille Mbembe most prominently reminds us that any approach to the quandary of defining the postcolonial nation must "enclose multiple durées made up of discontinuities, reversals, inertias, and swings that overlay one another."[16] The movement implicit in Mbembe's description—"reversals" and "swings," and even the paradoxical overlayering of "inertias"—furthers this definition of democracy as an event, rather than a state of affairs: as something on the move, but without a definitive direction.[17]

In a 2011 *New Yorker* article on the future of democratic governance in the Middle East, David Remnick writes: "Democracy is never fully achieved. At best, it's an ambition, a state of becoming."[18] Remnick's theory of democracy as a state of perpetual becoming offers us another way into the negotiation of transitional forms, the doing and now the "becoming" of what I argue are the thinking processes of literature and democracies. *The Restless Supermarket* and *The Loss Library*—Vladislavić's finished and unfinishable fictions, respectively—are in this way both explicitly about the ordinary sociopolitical lives of South Africans in the transition period, and examples of fictions that enacts transitionality as a form, speaking back to the rhetoric of lack and failure to complete. As we will see, the event of democracy allows for a return to the failed context in *The Loss Library*, and the overwhelming context in *The Restless Supermarket*, this time understood according to its birth pains, its embryonic dynamism, rather than its unfinished commentary on transition. If the unfinishable qualities of democracy—the perpetual movements that keep questioning, that stay unsettled—are its greatest assets, might not the same be true for the literatures of democracies? This state of becoming is the mode with which Vladislavić's fictions engage the movements of people and language, and, in doing so, dramatize and complicate what Jacques Rancière has called democracy's primary necessity: to *dis-order language* as a process of allowing new forms of thinking that will make space for the voiceless. It is blatantly idealistic, but it also points to one reason why democracy, even in putatively democratic nations, is often elusive:

> Democracy is first and foremost the invention of words by means of which those who don't count make themselves count and so *blur the ordered distribution of*

speech and mutism that made the political community a "beautiful animal," an organic totality.[19]

Rancière's project in *The Politics of Literature* fixes upon the "mistakes" of literature, the blurred lines that allow for disagreement with the tacit ordering of bodies and words. Disagreement thus engenders the ability to "invent names, utterances, arguments and demonstrations that set up new collectives where anyone can get themselves counted."[20]

In order to further develop the conceptual model of democracy as an unfinishable form not unlike *The Loss Library*, I'll turn briefly to Thomas Docherty's audacious—and to my mind transformative—attempt to define democracy as an "episodic" feature of cultural-aesthetic transformation, rather than as a recognizable state of political affairs. Docherty conceives of democracy as inseparable from culture, both of which he understands as states of becoming that allow for the extraordinary to exist within ordinary circumstances. This allows him to sketch a democratic temporality that cannot be limited by historical context, and which depends on the transitional movements of culture between individuals to create new forms of community. The event of democracy is thus "conditioned by alterity" and made legible by the aesthetic:

> "culture" names an event in which the ordinary—a manner of living—discovers or reveals a foundation that is extraordinary, and whose extraordinariness makes possible a different manner of living. Culture can be defined as that event of perception—the root sense of "aesthetic" (*aisthanomai*)—that calls a human subject to differ from itself… It therefore names the possibility of a transformation, a change in our ordinariness that occasioned by aesthetics or art.
>
> Democracy is extraordinary
>
> By this second statement, I mean to suggest that democracy, like culture, is not a constant, not a state of affairs, not a political mode of being; rather, democracy—episodic and rare—names those moments in which the possibility of an ethical respect for selfhood, a selfhood that is marked by cultural change, discovers or reveals itself to be conditioned by alterity, or by our condition of being-with-otherness. The name that we give to this, usually, is "becoming."[21]

Breyten Breytenbach's *"groot andersmaak"* ("great Othermaking") offers a South African precedent for precisely this theorization of democracy. Breytenbach writes of the struggle to build a new community apart from the brutal monolith of apartheid rule as a "process of becoming," where "South Africanhood passes through a breaking down of apartheid and a helping to build the great Other making." And while he does not name this process "democracy," as such, he sharpens Docherty's point about culture in his declaration that "we *make* each other."[22]

Understanding form as democratic facilitates a way of reading political fictions without making the narrative subservient to an already-fixed and singular understanding of what those politics should look or act like within the contextual box. Democracy as an event of dynamic linguistic change allows us to read the history that was "hard to ignore" in Vladislavić's *The Loss Library* as a failure to complete, but a failure that paradoxically enables the text's greatest possibility for interaction with the polyphony of narratives of South African transitional democracy. Since, in the case of Vladislavić's oeuvre, failure to complete represents a primary mode of engagement, we must not expect it to solve problems or riddles. Such an impulse to capture the literary text in a state of stasis and stillness instrumentalizes form, propelling transition toward an endgame. We must deny ourselves the consolation of easy answers—answers too easily ordered in a manner that destroys pluralism in the name of *realpolitik*, reconstituting older modes of colonial power—in favor of difficult, unfinishable questions about how to model forms of thinking through transition, context, and failure.

Becoming restless

I now turn to Vladislavić's most immediate engagement with transition, *The Restless Supermarket*, his "completed" novel set in the waning days of apartheid. My aim is not to differentiate *The Restless Supermarket* from *The Loss Library*, but rather to understand the two as concerned with the same formal project. Both texts reimagine the context of transition as a dynamic movement that, as Caitlin Charos writes, is notable for its "'open-endedness' and resistance to 'closure.'"[23] Being thus purposefully incomplete and incompletable, the two texts can be understood as aware of the inadequacy of their form as a context, and equally of the potential of form as negotiation. The seeming counterintuitiveness of a negotiation without end precisely describes what the failure to settle or complete looks like and acts like in both these texts. I am compelled by negotiation's temporal exceptionalism, its constant restructuring of meaning in an oscillation between failed resolutions—in short, its transitionality. Derrida points to the less-sanguine etymology of negotiation: "neg-otium, not-ease, not-quiet...no leisure."[24] Difficult and constant negotiation gives us a conceptual model to read a novel's performance before that performance has come to an end, at the perpetual Act II of the event of the novel itself. This is explicitly a question of how we interpret the relationships between aesthetics and politics in the novel, and any answers we might derive from negotiated reading must not dissolve one into the other. As such, we might look to Rancière to imagine how the discourses of politics and forms are always negotiating the terms of their engagement as a polyphony: "It is this negotiation between the forms of art and those of non-art which makes it possible to form combinations of elements capable of speaking twice over: on the basis of their legibility and on the basis of their illegibility."[25] Rancière's "beautiful animal" of language politics does double duty in the case of Vladislavić's transitional fictions: it describes his multiple voicing of the stories in the narrative and retrospective commentary, and it validates illegibility as but one stage of the interchange between discourses of historical, political, and literary context, context that does not rest or settle.

Vladislavić envisions the project of *Restless Supermarket* first and foremost as a rejection of a single static vantage from which the reader can claim understanding of South Africa's transition. As with much of Vladislavić's writing on South Africa, vantage is constituted in language, not visual perspective. In a 2002 interview with Mike Marais and Carita Backström, Vladislavić describes his narrative style as a process of "keeping an ironical movement going," as a bulwark against what he imagines as the reader's desire for a "quiet place in the novel where we can stand and put it all together." Self-negotiation is the underlying mode in what is described by the interviewers as Vladislavić's striking "emphasis on the nature of the creative process," in which he "responds to questions not only as writer, but as a reader of the novel," moving back and forth between inspiration and interpretation.[26] The reader's encounter with the unrest (or "not-ease," returning to Derrida's negotiation) of the novel preserves the nature of transition from the imposition of that quiet vantage point. Vladislavić equates a too-easy reliance on stable context with the epistemological ordering of people and things under apartheid. To thus finalize a context for an emerging South Africa is merely "establishing a new vantage point from which you can then judge everything in this orderly way, put everything into its category."[27] The idea that a system of "substitution or replacement" of one political system of categorization by another does not, for Vladislavić, take into consideration the "community at work," that he sees at ground level in Johannesburg. "I'm referring to a community which recognises the contingency of its own values and codes, and therefore its ultimate *incompletion*."[28] Negotiation's unsettling of expectations about how South African literature should appear newly democratic, especially when the material lives of everyday people have not been bettered, prompts a dialogue about the possibilities for as of yet unknown forms of dissent and community, some of which may still be called democracy. This is what David Atwell calls the necessity of "transla[ting] the terms of this current version of modernity in ways that are appropriate to the country's political, social, and cultural priorities."[29] In this we find Vladislavić in accord with Bruno Latour's preference for movement over the "homogenizing gestures" of contextualization, which equates with stasis: "Context is simply a way of stopping the descriptions when you are tired or too lazy to go on."[30] Not at ease, not settled, *restless*.

The Restless Supermarket imagines Felski's nonhuman actors not, as she does, at the level of whole texts, but at the atomic level of language, grammar, and phoneme. Aubrey Tearle, Vladislavić's politically retrograde narrator, is a retired proofreader, most recently of the telephone directory, living in years just preceding the formal end of apartheid. He whiles away his days writing letters to the editor of the local newspaper decrying the lack of standards in the prose and font choices, disputing the misalignment of across and down clues in the crossword, and ignoring the crashing tide of political change breaking just at his horizon. An enemy of error in all forms, Tearle reduces Johannesburg's violent response to the waning days of apartheid to a series of lexicographical errors, obsessively searching for what he calls the "corrigenda," those things that "await his correction."[31] He describes his occupation as the holding up of "examples of order and disorder, and thus contributing to the great task of maintaining order where it already existed" (98). For Tearle, the misuse of language equates to "so much barbarism," a word that carries a double meaning of "uncivilized" and "stuttering" (153). Tearle's search is not, however, limited to texts; he "mines" the clientele of his daily haunt, the absurdly named Café Europa, for "misuse" of dictionary English (182). "I never lost sight of my main purpose," Tearle writes of his occupation, "which was to hold up examples of order and disorder, and thus contribute to the great task of maintaining order where it already existed" (98).

This incessant ordering of language according to the *Concise OED*—a volume substantial enough to ultimately deflect a bullet away from Tearle's heart—allows him to imagine a world where difference can be edited out, deleted from the final categorization of words and things. All the "spoilt material, repetitious and dull verbiage, misplaced stops, misspellings, solecisms, anacolutha" might be drawn through the "insatiable and unshuttable maw" of the proofreader's delete mark (188). Tearle's fundamentalism is veiled by "a sincere wish to document, so allowing for comparison and improvement" (97). But it is no benign matter, the corollary Tearle establishes between comparison and the possibility of editing out error, for at the very least it plays at linguistic eugenics. Note the slippage from editorial deletion to pogrom: "Imagine, if you can, the mountain of delenda purged from the galleys of the world. Who would build on such a landfill?" (188). Tearle's vision of linguistic purity squeezes the world through that delete mark's "insatiable maw" in order to ensure that the proximate can always be the known, and the disorder ordered. We recognize this as the contextual imperative parodied at the extremes of the colonial epistemology of order, limit, edit, and deletion.

It is of course the dictionary that rests at the heart of the matter. As an ordering structure that must rationalize exclusion on the basis of correction, Tearle's *OED* discounts language that cannot be read, and subsequently categorized. He sorts out otherness as a kind of error in the programmatic use of language; he corrects for democracy. Thus, cultural heterogeneity, operating so often outside the prescriptive rules of dictionary language, is adjudged by its uncivilized error, rather than by its performance. Language as a source of cultural knowledge is, indeed, beside the point for Tearle, who brags: "I myself once proofread the Pentateuch in isiZulu, against the original (I don't have a word of the language) *and* against the grain—and made only one error" (327). The question remains, how would he know? How would error present itself when every *matter* of the text is closed to him? His revelation, that sometimes "it is better not to know the language at all," exists for Tearle as one of the "saddest things," and indeed it is the pathos of the novel that the form of misunderstanding, the grain of knowledge that is foreign to us, must preserve itself against the systems of comparison that will amend or delete those corrigenda that resist correction (329).

How then does *The Restless Supermarket*, a novel that cannot narrate the end of apartheid except as a "massive disturbance that resisted correction," preserve some matter of cultural democracy, the "great Othermaking," from the proofreader's mark (219)? My argument lies with the restless interior of the novel, the purported life's work of Aubrey Tearle: his "Proofreader's Derby." Tearle has composed the Derby as a testing ground, a game of hunting out errors with which the would-be proofreader might hone his craft. Written as a piece of short fiction meant to contain untold *purposeful* errors, Tearle has imagined the Derby as a place of possible perfection where corrigenda have slipped in like the traces of an illicit visitor. Corrigenda are again the stand-in for the demographic shifts in Johannesburg that Tearle despises, and here in the text they are grossly anthropomorphized as the racial and economic other: the "lexical world was overpopulated with scrawny, open-mouthed schwas, like hordes of hungry little pitas waiting for their stomachs to be filled" (95). The reader has already been playing proofreader for Tearle by the time he or she reaches the Derby section— Tearle's letters and turns of phrase are plagued with the play of false etymologies and solecisms ("*wanton* dumplings" and "*muslin* fundamentalists"), which color and ironize his descriptions of his Hillbrow neighborhood—but now the reader negotiates between Tearle's lexicographical tyranny and Vladislavić's transitional form (227).[32]

The Derby section holds the middle of the novel, but it is better understood as confined, constrained, and ghettoized between the two sections of narrative devoted to Tearle's life at the Café Europa. According to Tearle, the Derby functions as a narrative prison for every manner of linguistic criminal that might creep into prose; it is a holding pen for Johannesburg's new democratic languages of transition. Crucially, the Derby takes the guise of a fiction, for the novel form, according to Tearle, represents the only perfectly hermetic container for error: "An error in the pages of a novel ... may be compounded by reproduction, sometimes tens of thousands of times. Yet despite this wasteful abundance, the error itself seldom transcends the covers between which it is caught like a slow-moving insect" (107). Yet despite the centrality of this section of the novel, "The Proofreader's Derby" itself is the book of errors that we never meet; it is the material text at the heart of the novel that, as we will see, moves the narrative with the most pronounced vitality and dynamism, with a transitional form that beguiles the would-be proofreader, for its errors are entirely imaginary and immune to correction. As we will see with *The Loss Library*, narrative failure in *Restless Supermarket* is penned in by paratext, but in this case Vladislavić makes it clear that the failure to complete the derby is its potential as a form—its resistance to the single vantage point from which Tearle would correct it.

When, as readers, we approach the middle section of the novel, "The Proofreader's Derby" is presented to us in its "corrected" version, cleansed of its errors, and already "put to the proof" (339). The proofreader's copy we encounter as the fifty-page delay in the narrative arc of Tearle's life is meant to be the ordered, edited-clean copy guarding against the prolific error that might spill over into the other two sections of the novel.[33] It has been purified and sanitized according to Tearle's own system. One might say it has been denovelized, made un-new and nonfiction. The novel has been tamed and contained. The narrative arc that has promised us Tearle's raison d'être offers instead the specter of untold errors that we will never read, the remainder of a text that cannot be known except by its narrative effect. Tearle himself describes the Derby as "a scrap of canvas hacked from the frame" (124).

The great bugaboo of Tearle's quotidian life, the comically named grocery, the "Restless Supermarket," plays its eponymous error across the three sections of the novel, most potently in the "corrected" Derby section. Named by its

Greek owners for its late-night convenience, its rest-less-ness (and here we recall negotiation's restlessness and lack of leisure), Tearle cannot abide by the supermarket's unwitting pun. In the age of transition, he cannot stand for restlessness. Confronted by Tearle in the first section of the narrative, the owner defends the name: "My friend, we ollaways open. You come any day, twenty-four hour ... [and Tearle's retort] 'Restless Supermarket', it creates the wrong impression. One thinks of mess ... of groceries jumbling *themselves* together, of willful chaos" (93). What Tearle describes is a space of uncertainty where difference can coexist, coinhabit in a willful chaos, and do so without the eventual assimilation to common ground. This is a democratic community of others contained in language, but not defined by its container. When we return to the supermarket in the "Proofreader's Derby" section of the novel, canvas without its frame, we encounter translation as the dynamic feature of the restless form:

> The interior of the Restless Supermarket was barely recognizable. The entire space was seething, alive with an indiscriminate, indefatigable jumble ... all mingled into one substance, whose textures eluded them, being simultaneously soft and hard, fuzzy and sharp, perishable and indestructible. Each element remained vividly itself for as long as they focused on it, and then dissolved back into the irreducible compound as soon as they relaxed their attention. It was like trying to watch one wing in a wheeling flock. (246)

This scene reads easily as an allegory for the political and demographical changes in Tearle's South Africa, but as allegory it refuses a static form; it is willful chaos. This is the prison house of language, but in full riot. The allegory is split and on the move; its language has both a social and a linguistic significance that refuses to collapse into one or the other.

The Restless Supermarket and Vladislavić speak with one voice on this matter of new language. In the failure to find context with which to resolve questions of what has not yet settled recognizably into one mode of politics or society, they warn against etymology and category, two impulses that trade dynamism for a sclerotic eye. The Derby section retains what Carita Backström calls "a volition of its own," or, in the terms of this argument, an enactment of its unfinishability, its negotiation without rest. And so we read not the wing but the wheeling, the becoming and doing of democracy, rather than its container, whether that is the store, the chapter, or the context. The contained Derby section ironically offers us the formal event of democracy in a novel whose protagonist wants nothing more than to lock away that linguistic becoming. The final section of the novel will indeed prove to Tearle that, while he is no longer the proofreader of Hillbrow's transformation, he can still live restlessly.

The temporality of loss: Measuring democracy

I will turn now to Vladislavić's unfinishable or transitional writings that could not exist during the official transition period, *The Loss Library*. These vestiges of Vladislavić's previously unpublished writings come together in a form that is beguiling in genre and narrativity, even for a master of the bent and broken literary form.[34] The flyleaf introduces *The Loss Library* as "an unusual text, a blend of essay, fiction, and literary genealogy," but the text and illustrations within prove even less easily categorizable. Vladislavić's incomplete—and in some senses incompletable–literary stem cells are set chronologically and topically during South Africa's transition period, stretching from the nominal end of apartheid to popular elections in 1994. They are framed so as to highlight their response to the uncertainty and anxiety of that violent and politically fraught period before the ultimately peaceful movement to popular government. The gathered pieces are in fact recognizable as partial fictions—characters are introduced, a plot unfolds, denouements are described, albeit with a particular and peculiar form—but their failure *to complete*, as it were, a failure to arrive in a timely fashion, offers Vladislavić a way out of what he describes as the impossible bind of writing the historical present in a moment of profound uncertainty. Incompletion, as such, is the impetus to thinking through the dilemmas and possibilities inherent to the concept of cultural and political transition.

The question of why this book exists at all, why it was published in the amoebic post-transition, is the catalyst for my evaluation of South African literature's relationship to uncomfortable temporalities. Vladislavić's answer to his own inability to complete writings about a transitional moment in South African political life is to offer those writings both as an explicit failure of contextualization and as the possibility for uncertain sociopolitical temporalities to be meaningful as a competing form of progress. Read in concert with the completed novel of transition, *Restless Supermarket*, *Loss Library* becomes a conceptual model with which to rethink Vladislavić's experimental representations of South Africa's changeover to democracy and a way to conceptualize transition as a literary form. *Loss Library*, understood doubly, reads as both the exemplar of the failure of transition to describe the complications of a particular historical moment in South Africa accurately, and as a formal mode for negotiating uncertainty in the competing discourses of a work of fiction.

Let's look at precisely what allows Vladislavić dramatic temporal passage from that which he describes as "the frozen life of the book" with "frostbitten pages" (the writings during the historical transition), to the facility of "words on the page" to make "anything possible," the publication of his post-transition collection (1). The thawing agent involves a "warm-blooded reader breathing air" into the potential of his unfinished pages, and a brief scan of *The Loss Library* shows Vladislavić performing an obsessive reanimation of the collected fragments of story. Alongside the visual collages of the artist Sunandini Banerjee, Vladislavić reinserts himself into these unsettled accounts as the historian of his stories' failed instantiation (113).[35] In this way, the unfinishables are reauthored, voiced by a third-person narrator (Vladislavić) who is determined to find perspective on his own convoluted representations of South Africa's transitional moment. When the narration proves equally flawed in its effort to contextualize the failure of the stories to come to fruition, additional frames are added, annotating the narrative but moving, ironically, further from completion.

It is precisely *The Loss Library*'s interest in the value of failures that drives this examination of Vladislavić's work as a chronicler of the transition period. Each unsettled account commences with a brief introductory remark on the germ of the story, though the tone and style of these introductions remind one of a sudden fiction or a Buddhist koan as much as anything else. They are notable for their brevity, hermetically complete as if to further highlight the fragmentary nature of what is to come. Most of the introductions are followed by a parenthetical date—1992, in the case of "The Last Walk"—placing each story precisely on the historical continuum from emergency to interregnum to transition. In an evocative example, this lyric line plays at interpreting the story, "The Last Walk": "As if they know it, his last words are already on the wing, flocking around his steaming head like birds of passage" (7). But rather than being introductory, the pun on death and birds of *passage* demands a rereading of this framing device, circling us back to the start again, further away from anything like an explanation of the story.[36] Occasionally, these introductions allude to Vladislavić's writer's block, as is the case with "Gravity Addict," in which a "woman means to write a book…a serious book," but is distracted by the contingencies of modern life, in particular a cartoon on the television. As with "The Last Walk," the description of the story fragment resolves with a lyric turn—cartoon animals, one "after another step off a window ledge or hurr[y] over a cliff…and the creature plummets, ears raised in surrender, through the bottom of the frame into our hard-edged reality"—and we are asked once again to consider whether we have just read a self-contained fragment, rather than an introduction to a failed story, or whether we have simply fallen through the frame (69).

Thus, visualized with collage, rationalized by the terms of their failure to be published, finished, or recovered, and periodized with a particular date in the years of transition, Vladislavić adds to the fragments the generic perversion of academic endnotes and headnotes, demarcating a vague historicity with quotes from literary and historical texts. These citations are largely drawn from colonial travel narratives, themselves a perversion of historical context. The treatment of 1927s *Dragon Lizards of Komodo: An Expedition to the Lost World of the Dutch East Indies* as a citable source purposefully undercuts the very idea of historical source material, and Vladislavić pushes the parody by quoting slight, whimsical fragments and grammatical anomalies that make meaning only in their self-negation: "there are women, women," "doubtless their naughtiness," and "there is nothing very strange" (118). These citations prove to be yet another unfinishable form, their promises of revelation ultimately empty, fragmentary, illuminating neither source nor story, as in this list-quote from *The Story of San Michele*: "wood pigeons, thrushes, turtle doves." If the historical intertext is wholly unengaged, why have it there at all? For an answer one looks to the interaction between unfinished narrative and failed context, and finds the carryover of dialogue between the two—a transitional temporality that makes meaning from the unfinishable forms. Contextual overload brings an exquisite awareness of a meaning-making process that oscillates simultaneously between unresolvable perspectives.

What drives the *The Loss Library*'s contextualizing-impulse? Why burden already-failed stories with aimless literary-historical context? In part, it is the failure of these stories to gain a vantage on a moment when "history was hard to ignore" that draws them to the promise (in this case false promise) of context. In his preface, Vladislavić remarks upon the "heady year or so" during the violent transition when he fancied himself "some sort of historian" (2). Indeed, he reminds us that "the years of negotiations were among the bloodiest in South Africa's history." History's onerousness at the moment of transition is implicitly a rationale for the stories' failure to exist as completed pieces; it speaks, as well, to a particular burden on the South African writer to deal with the paradox of the apartheid optic: the exaggerated declarations of its pastness, matched against its continued ability to eclipse alternative historical discourses. The result of this paradox, however contrary, is *The Loss Library*'s palpable, even sensuous, desire for abject context: images, introductions, dates, and footnotes, framing devices that signify historicity while ironically doing little to place these failed stories in a particular historical moment. Rather than recovering history or enacting a Greenblattian communion with the dead, the useless context and failed narrative shed light on a particular mode of thinking that values context differently: thinking in motion.[37] Thinking in motion is the great promise of form contained within these unfinished pieces; it is the capability of texts to engage context differently by refusing to settle at a point of common understanding.

Such a principle makes it clear that when Vladislavić gathers his failed narrative pieces—stories and ideas that were meant to cast history in amber—he does so as a conscious instantiation of their dynamic relationship to history, and to negotiating democracy. As such, the fragments' failure to rest and thereby complete a representation of a particular historical moment, problem, or idea, allows for a facility of the thinking process that context can too easily harden.

Vladislavić elucidates this meaning-making process in his notes for the story "Frieze." The story, sparsely detailed, but sketched broadly in narrative notes for *The Loss Library*, concerns an artist who created a "series of friezes depicting scenes from South African history (what else?)," and who in his old age must "explain his choice of subject matter to this hostile—or merely curious—interpreter" (50). The story's title cannot help but resonate trebly for the reader of this collection: as architectural decoration, as history captured in the aesthetic, and as the frozen process of creation, what Vladislavić calls a work *"frozen* in words" (29). In the same vein, the "(what else?)" embedded in his descriptions of the art freezes, lexicographically and in its parenthetical state, a reminder of the impossibility of avoiding history in any fictional representation of the transition, and more pointedly of the burden of the ungraspable history that remains weighty in the writer's imagination. It is also a literal question operating apart from its syntactical context. It expresses a desire for something "else," something more than, or at least other than, history. Indeed, *The Loss Library* treats the historical subject matter of the imagined friezes as the primary impediment to a full instantiation of the story. Here his notes recount the struggle to free history from its bind: "Should the friezes show representative scenes from colonial history or explore a single theme?" and "What about episodes from the history of apartheid focused on something specific like the Soweto uprising?" (50). A newspaper clipping acting as a supplement to his notes highlights the particular historical worry that in "the early 1990s, when I was trying to write 'Frieze,' change was in the air. The expression 'the new South Africa' was on everyone's lips" (51). To embed his ekphrasis of the friezes in a particular context explicitly contradicts the dominant historical discourse of change and newness during the transition years. For to *frieze* it, as such, is to contract the very idea of change, to capture the moment through a forced stasis. One might read the story as a vestigial record of postapartheid status or even failure, but I want to argue that Vladislavić's reanimation of his problematic transition stories prepares us for a different mode of thinking through history in literary representation, one that highlights the liminal event of transitional periods.

The notes imagine the works themselves as "stolen or destroyed…buried somewhere," or perhaps "never produced at all" (52). Anxiety about the historical focus of the sculptures—in one permutation of the story, the sculptures are informed by Afrikaner nationalism—is paired with Vladislavić's stated desire to have a conflict arise in the retrospective response to the art after the end of apartheid, a "layering of speculations, revisions, judgments and defenses" of friezes that no longer existed, but which had been deemed historically important. The resultant modernist polyphony might begin to reveal, he hoped, the essence of history as the inevitable, if ineffable, condition of experience:

> Five versions of the absent artworks collide: the Journalist's *skeptical* interpretation, the Artist's *self-serving* defense, the Assistant's *business-like* descriptions, mediated across three generations by the Poet's *lyrical* recollections and the Historian's *clinical* analysis. All the adjectives being tentative, of course [...]. (52–53)

The necessity of history as the frame in which the story would be meaningful to South Africans' contemporary circumstances comes into direct conflict with the contingency of historical interpretation of works of art: "all the adjectives being tentative, of course."

This series of failed attempts to contextualize ekphrastic, discursive, polyvocal forms of literary representation, sets the stage for *The Loss Library*'s performance of an internal literary criticism. Turning inward, the text animates the process of questioning form's ability to complete the meaning-making process. Rather than resting at a definitive contextual position, the text as framed by Vladislavić's narrative preoccupations with history makes drawing meaning unthinkable or at least incompletable. Instead, the failure of context to settle mirrors the story's incompletion, leaving the residual forms of possibility incomplete but circulating in the text. Vladislavić's retrospectives on South Africa's transition to democracy beg a lasting question: Is it the transition period that needs a historical revision, even a renaming, or is it democracy itself that has been hemmed in by definition? It is Thomas Docherty who again reminds us that we are best served by literature that engages us in the democratic process of being "conditioned by alterity," even when that process involves loss, and even when it remains unfinished.

Notes

1   For Ronit Frenkel, "[t]he term 'post-transitional' can be read in much the same way as the term 'post-feminist', with its attendant conceptual shifts that do not necessarily imply that the ideals of feminism have been attained and are now to be taken for granted." "South African Literary Cartographies," 26.

2   Charos, "'The End of an Error,'" 24, quoting Monica Popescu's doctoral dissertation, "South African Literature in Transition," University of Pennsylvania, 2005.

3   Hitchcock, *The Long Space*, 144.

4   For a more comprehensive accounting of transition-era literature, see Barnard, "Rewriting the Nation."

5   Vladislavić, *The Loss Library and Other Unfinished Stories*, 1. This edition referenced hereafter parenthetically in the text.

6   Felski, "Context Stinks!" 574.

7   Ibid., 577.

8   Ibid., 578.

9   Felski, "Context Stinks!" 578, emphasis added.

10 Ibid., 590.

11 Felski, "Context Stinks [lecture]."

12 Clingman, *The Grammar of Identity*, 11; Nuttall, *Entanglement*; Attridge, "Context, Idioculture, Invention," 681–99.

13 Friedman, in Felski and Friedman, "Introduction," vi.

14 While I do not support his ultimate conclusions about a prescribed order for the emergence of democracy, Francis Fukuyama places an importance on the great uncertainty and *longue durée* of the transition from nation-states to democracies in Europe, a point of history lost on most chroniclers of the so-called failure of democratic institutions to find footing in the Middle East, and in critiques of South Africa during the transition. Fukuyama, "Is There a Proper Sequence," 308.

15 Witness, for example, the tautologies present in this comment about Egypt from the *National Review*: "Democratic processes—elections, referenda, constitution-drafting—must be conditioned on a preexisting democratic culture. Otherwise, in a majority-Muslim country like Egypt, you end up giving totalitarianism the patina of democratic legitimacy." McCarthy, "Elections Are Not Democracy."

16 Mbembe, *On the Postcolony*, 14.

17 My argument about democracy's event dynamic owes something to Žižek's philosophical fashioning of an "event" as "something out of joint" that "interrupts the usual flow of things," and as "an *effect that seems to exceed its causes*" (*Event*, 4).

18 Remnick, "Threatened."

19 Rancière, *The Politics of Literature*, 40, emphasis added.

20 Ibid., 41. Zoë Wicomb also frames South Africa's negotiation for the present democracy as a grammatical-progressivism that must respect the unsettled accounts of linguistic, as well as social transition: "How will we […] invent a new language for reconstructing ourselves to replace the fixed syntagmas of the discourse of oppression," she asks. "Culture Beyond Color?" 28.

21 Docherty, *Aesthetic Democracy*, xii.

22 Quoted in Sanders, *Complicities*, 131.

23 Charos, "'The End of an Error,'" 26.

24 Derrida and Rottenberg, *Negotiations*, 1.

25 Rancière, *Aesthetics and Its Discontents*, 46.

26 Backström and Marais, "An Interview," 121.

27 Ibid.

28 Ibid., 127.

29 Attwell, *Rewriting Modernity*, 6.

30 Backström and Marais, "An Interview," 127.

31 Vladislavić, *The Restless Supermarket*, 98. This edition referenced hereafter parenthetically in the text.

32 Here is Vladislavić describing Tearle's fundamental misunderstanding of language: "and etymology is precisely the last place you should look to establish a fixed meaning for a word," it is "where you look to establish the fluidity of meaning." Backström and Marais, "An Interview," 125.

33 Vladislavić confesses that the copy of the Derby we encounter as readers was initially chock-full of linguistic errors that he had plumbed from his daily observation of written language in Johannesburg, or had made up himself, but that "to expect the reader to cope with typographical errors, along with formatting errors … and spelling mistakes in every line, was going to be impossible" ("Interview," 125). In consultation with his editor, the architecture of the grammatical errors was razed, flatting the visual landscape of the "Proofreader's Derby" to allow a simpler traverse for the reader.

34 In a public conversation with the writer Teju Cole, Vladislavić told an audience at 192 Books in Chelsea that he began writing in the 1970s in part as a response to what he felt were the underdeveloped forms at play in the political realism of novels of the apartheid era. He spoke of an ideology of necessary-realism epitomized by the political novel that "deeply limited the imaginative possibilities for literary forms," and of his desire to "test the limits of the novel form, and then break them" (Vladislavić, public discussion).

35 Vladislavić's commentary on the function of visual art, particularly on the photography in literary work by André Breton and W. G. Sebald, helps to conceptualize Banerjee's collages within the book's larger project. He writes of the value of these visual insertions as counter-instrumental when used most effectively: "They are always less than or more than illustrative; they do not live up to the text or they carry an excess that demands explanation. Their purpose is less to define than to disrupt, to create ripples and falls in the beguiling flow of the prose" (*Loss Library*, 54). In brief, I follow Vladislavić's claim in my own reading of these tangential visuals (they are literally tangents, attached only at the top corner of the print, and otherwise clinging loosely, perhaps desperately to the page. A "hanging-chad" of mixed-media). At first glance, the Banerjee piece composed to accompany the story "The Last Walk" appears to be an impressionistic rendering of the major plot element described in Vladislavić's fragment, the death of the Swiss writer

Robert Walser. There's a tight pen and ink sketch of a man lying on a photographic image of a snow bank, and birds (a feature of many of the fragments, and notably a motif in *The Restless Supermarket*) drawn in silhouette, float above the body. But the image is in excess of its illustration of the scene, with typed text under erasure at the top of the print, illegible, but commanding of our attention.

36 The collection as a whole ends in a Joycean wrap-around, refusing anything like a conclusion, and presenting instead the possibility of a nonteleological narrative that begins and ends with the potential of new readings: "Yet words on a page make all things possible. Any line, even this one, may be a place to begin" (*Loss Library* 114).

37 See Greenblatt, *Shakespearean Negotiations*. The chapter on exorcism offers a good introduction to new historicism's trope of speaking with the dead. I have further developed this theory of the novel's dynamic thinking in an article on the reception of Zadie Smith's experimentations with forms of realism in Holmes, "The Novel's Third Way."

Works Cited

Attridge, Derek. "Context, Idioculture, Invention." *New Literary History* 42.4 (Autumn 2011): 681–99.

Attwell, David. *Rewriting Modernity: Studies in Black South African Literary History*. Athens, OH: Ohio University Press, 2005.

Backström, Carita, and Mike Marais. "An Interview with Ivan Vladislavić." *English in Africa* 29.2 (October 2002): 119–28.

Barnard, Rita. "Rewriting the Nation." In *The Cambridge History of South African History*. Eds. Derek Attridge and David Attwell. Cambridge: Cambridge University Press, 2012. 652–75.

Charos, Caitlin. "'The End of an Error': Transition and 'Post-apartheid Play' in Ivan Vladislavić's The Restless Supermarket." *Safundi: The Journal of South African and American Studies* 9.1 (January 2008): 23–38.

Clingman, Stephen. *The Grammar of Identity*. Oxford: Oxford University Press, 2009.

Derrida, Jacques, and Elizabeth Rottenberg. *Negotiations: Interventions and Interviews, 1971–2001*. Stanford, CA: Stanford University Press, 2002.

Docherty, Thomas. *Aesthetic Democracy*. Stanford, CA: Stanford University Press, 2006.

Felski, Rita. "Context Stinks." Lecture, Brown University, Providence, 2010.

Felski, Rita. "Context Stinks!" *New Literary History* 42.4 (Autumn 2011): 573–91.

Felski, Rita, and Susan Stanford Friedman. "Introduction." *New Literary History* 40.3 (Summer 2009): v–ix.

Frankel, Ronit. "South African Literary Cartographies: A Post-Transitional Palimpsest." *Ariel: A Review of International English Literature* 44.1 (2013): 25–44.

Fukuyama, Francis. "Is There a Proper Sequence in Democratic Transitions?" *Current History* (2011): 308–10.

Greenblatt, Stephen. *Shakespearean Negotiations*. Berkeley: U of California Press, 1988.

Hitchcock, Peter. *The Long Space: Transnationalism and Postcolonial Form*. Stanford, CA: Stanford University Press, 2009.

Holmes, Chris. "The Novel's Third Way: Zadie Smith's Hysterical Realism." In *Reading Zadie Smith: The First Decade & Beyond*. Ed. Phillip Tew. London: Bloomsbury, 2014. 141–54.

Mbembe, Achille. *On the Postcolony*. Berkeley: University of California Press, 2001.

McCarthy, Andrew. "Elections Are Not Democracy: A Lesson from Egypt." *National Review*, July 6, 2013. https://www.nationalreview.com/2013/07/elections-are-not-democracy-andrew-c-mccarthy/.

Nuttall, Sarah. *Entanglement: Literary and Cultural Reflections of Post-Apartheid*. Johannesburg: Wits University Press, 2009.

Rancière, Jacques. *Aesthetics and Its Discontents*. Cambridge: Polity Press, 2009.

Rancière, Jacques. *The Politics of Literature*. Cambridge: Polity Press, 2011.

Remnick, David. "Threatened." *The New Yorker*, March 12, 2012. https://www.newyorker.com/magazine/2012/03/12/threatened.

Sanders, Mark. *Complicities: The Intellectual and Apartheid*. Durham, NC: Duke University Press, 2002.

Vladislavić, Ivan. Public discussion with Teju Cole. 192 Books, New York. November 4, 2013.

Vladislavić, Ivan. *The Loss Library and Other Unfinished Stories*. London: Seagull Books, 2012.

Vladislavić, Ivan. *The Restless Supermarket*. Cape Town: David Philip, 2001.

Wicomb, Zoë. "Culture Beyond Color?" *Transition* 60 (1993): 27–32.

Žižek, Slavoj. *Event: A Philosophical Journey Through a Concept*. New York: Penguin, 2014.

12

Conclusion: Reading in Transition

Tsitsi Jaji

This closing gesture is a meditation on how the practice of reading and writing South Africa over the past two decades has enabled the "rediscovery of the ordinar[iness]" of belonging to Africa.[1] Taking Solomon Plaatje's historical novel *Mhudi* (1930) as my starting point, I consider a series of shifting frontiers and their effects on periodization, canonization, and the project of a national literature. While scholars have attended to the numerous narratives about the spatial frontiers of 1830s in South African fiction and film (including Harold Shaw's 1916 *De Voortrekkers,* the considerably more problematic 1938 *Die Bou van 'n Nasie,* and André Brink's 1996 novel, *Imaginings of Sand*), I am more interested in the way that frontiers work on a metanarrative and therefore also a temporal level.[2] For much of the twentieth century, apartheid's dissolution marked the horizon of "freedom" and served as an essential temporal frontier that determined how successive generations imagined futurity. While the struggle toward that frontier was unforeseeable in duration, the temporal-political orientation it defined held out the hope of an end to the present of colonial segregation and apartheid. However, since the coming of democracy, a new and rigid attitude toward the border between South Africa and the erstwhile Frontline States has come to structure contemporary imaginings of the nation and has provided a new view of frontiers.[3] Prompted by the rise of violence directed at immigrants from other African countries, border checkpoints and urban neighborhoods with concentrated foreign-born populations have in recent years come to serve as a conceptual frontier against which national belonging is framed.

To be sure, this attitude has been subject to critique. Post 1994 literature by writers as diverse as Nadine Gordimer, Phaswane Mpe, and Keorapetse Kgositsile has worked to restore South Africa to a full awareness of its belonging in Africa as a continent and to undo apartheid-era notions of exceptionality as well as their neoliberal extensions. However, rather than formulating entirely new grounds for belonging, works like Gordimer's *The Pickup* and Mpe's *Welcolme to Our Hillbrow* have (in continuity with earlier writers like Plaatje) engaged with the other side of both the temporal and spatial frontiers of 1994 and the Limpopo (in conversation with Frontline writers).[4] In this chapter, I hope to illuminate the interconnections between these novels and *Mhudi* to suggest thereby that these foundational texts be mobilized to do new kinds of work in the wake of South Africa's democratic elections and the reconstruction of nationhood. I propose that writing—and reading—in transition (to play here with the collection's title) should assume a plurality of frontiers, a plurality of states that need to be traversed and transitioned. This kind of writing and reading constitutes a critically potent and, I would say, politically exigent approach to South African writing—as part of broader conversations in African writing and in literature of the global South.

By anchoring my readings of post-transition novels to the narratives about the 1830s, I build on Jennifer Wenzel's elegant interpretation of South African and, more broadly, colonial temporalities. Wenzel highlights a symbiotic relationship between "*remembered prophecy*" and "*prophetic memory*," the latter being of particular relevance here. *Mhudi*, she notes,

> narrates the remembrance in the 1910s of prophecies articulated in the 1830s. I am equally concerned with what I call *prophetic memory*, remembrance of a moment that, viewed retrospectively, offers a glimpse of a future that bears upon the present. This need not be a memory of literal, explicit prophecy, but rather a recognition of a relationship between moments in time: the past, viewed from the present, seems suddenly to limn a future.[5]

However, I want to consider the historical setting of *Mhudi* not only to figure "prophetic memory" but in order to engage a term introduced some forty years before Wenzel in the dark days of apartheid: "future memory." The term belongs to the late Keorapetse Kgositsile, the first poet laureate of the democratic South Africa, who explained it as follows in an early interview, "[i]n my usage, *memory* is more an assimilated aspect of your every day living and thinking. In that sense, *memory* can be, or it is, all time – i.e., it is past, it is present, it is future, too."[6] But how does future memory serve as a means of crossing the temporal frontier of "freedom" and what happens to such a flexible orientation toward temporality in the wake of 1994?

Plaatje: Father of SADC literature?

Solomon Plaatje's esteemed place in the history of South African writing as the first black novelist to publish in English is uncontested. However, it is seldom recalled that his historical novel, *Mhudi: An Epic of South African Native Life a Hundred Years Ago*, is not only an account of the formation of an ill-fated alliance between the Barolong nation and the Boers on the Great Trek in their struggle against Matabele leader Mzilikazi, but also a story of how Mzilikazi came to migrate from South Africa, eventually settling in modern-day Zimbabwe. Indeed, the *izibongo* honoring Mzilikazi encodes precisely this migration as the core of his legacy:

> UMkhatshwa wawoZimangele!
> Okhatshwe ngezind'izinyawo,
> Nangezimfushazanyana ....
> Uband'abalubande balutshiy'uZulu.
> Inkom'ethe isagodla yeluleka
>
> [You are the son of Simangele who was kicked!
> Who was kicked by long feet and by the short ones ....
> You are the log from which the Zulus cut firewood until they left it.
> You are the cow that, while it was just emerging made progress.][7]

Taking Plaatje as a father of a regional, rather than only a South African, literature, enables us to read against the enduring exceptionalism of South Africa, to rediscover the ordinariness of its borders and suture South Africa back into a body of continental African literature. It allows us also to think carefully about the relation between canon formations and literary criticism. Here we should recall the many pointed calls early in the transition period for a renewal of critical conversations along international axes. These sought to expand upon the deep and diligent work of scholars like Michael Green, Stephen Gray, Tim Couzens, Brian Willan, and others on Plaatje's place within the context of South Africa, and anticipated the work of scholars like Laura Chrisman and Bhekizizwe Peterson in reading Plaatje as a more global figure.[8] Plaatjie's work, I would argue, suggests that the temporal frontier at the end of apartheid was prefigured and troubled from both sides of the borders dividing Frontline States and South Africa. It invites, moreover, the following question: How might normalized diplomatic and economic relations between nation-states provide grounds for a comparative regional approach to Southern African literature? And how might this conceptual frontier crossing permit us to rethink the notion of "transition."

Though my chapter's transit between temporal and spatial frontiers is an experiment in reading, the premise of my approach is by no means new. Among a set of future-oriented articles reflecting on the coming transition in *Current Writing* in 1992, A. E. Voss observed:

> if … we can look forward to South Africa being viewed as a country like any other, we will also be in a better position to recognize similarities between our "historical concreteness" (Clayton, 1991) and that of other nations from whom we may learn. Perhaps most important of these will be other African countries and their literatures.[9]

I will suggest additionally that the return to broader contextual conversations to which Voss and others looked forward also constitutes a return to the roots of an anti-racist project in constructing a national literature: a project clearly called for in *Mhudi*. Given Plaatje's leading role in political and cultural life and, particularly, his innovative use of protest and petition in *Native Life in South Africa*, it is not at all surprising that he is celebrated as having inaugurated a new phase in South African national literature. What has more seldom been noted is that he might also be read as a foundational figure for a more regional transnational literary imagination, precisely because the history fictionalized and chronicled in *Mhudi* is one that predates the national borders separating South Africa from Lesotho, Swaziland, Namibia, Botswana, Zimbabwe, and Mozambique.

Among Plaatje's stated aims was correcting the erasure of black subjectivities and interethnic, intra-racial political histories in his counternarrative. In recounting the decade of the 1830s, Plaatje portrays the region at a moment of tremendous flux, indeed, in transition from the hegemony of the Matabele to the new ascendancy of the Boers. Plaatje figures the violent arrival of technologized modernity in the transformation in instruments of war from the hand-held weapons and athletic physique of the Matabele to the guns wielded by the Boers and their allies. Thus, the Trek and the end of Mzilikazi's dominance entail not only a temporal shift (a terrifying collapse of the duration of hand-to-hand battle into the instantaneity of gunfire) but also, with it, the inauguration of a new temporal regime in which racial inequality was mediated via time. As Michael Hanchard has put it:

> Unequal relationships between dominant and subordinate groups produce unequal temporal access to institutions, goods, services, resources, power, and knowledge, which members of both groups recognize. When coupled with the distinct temporal modalities that relations of dominance and subordination

produce, racial time has operated as a structural effect upon the politics of racial difference.[10]

One of the most striking portrayals of the advent of racial time occurs as Ra-Thaga decides on a homeward journey to stop at the Boer camp and visit his friend Phil Jay. Plaatje writes: "Tired and thirsty as he was, he saw a vessel full of cold water and at once proceeded to help himself."[11] Ra-Thaga is immediately assailed by the loud protests and epithets from the camp, and only the stern admonishment of a community elder saves him from the angry crowd. Ra-Thaga delays revisiting the Boers' camp, but when Phil Jay visits him, he offers as an explanation that "Boers at their own homes never allow black people to drink out of their vessels. The Boers cannot understand why black people when visited by white men show no scruples" (127). In other words, Ra-Thaga has neglected to defer to the ideological principle of inequality, nor does he institute a temporal gap between his own body's needs and those of visiting Boers (the "scruples" to which Plaatje refers). It is this presumption that black and white operate in the same racial time, rather than in a time out of joint in which one is forced to wait for goods, services, and resources according to power differentials that fills the Boers in this scene with such anxiety.

As the novel closes, a parallel scene plays out as Mhudi and Annetje (alongside their husbands) take leave of each other. Annetje's reflection at first appears to show that her sadness at parting from Mhudi reflects a true intimacy: "Annetje too had fallen in love with Mhudi" (197). However, it quickly becomes clear that she imagines herself and Phil Jay in a dynamic temporal flow where they continue to move to the next stage of married life, but sees Mhudi frozen in a static timeless state that is further unmoored from the novel's present by its sudden multilingualism:

> She said if she lived to have little ones of her own, surely they would be proud to have for an ayah, such a nobel *mosadi* [woman] as Mhudi. But, unlike the two men, they knew not each other's language, consequently she made a less favourable impression on Mhudi than Phil did on her husband. (197)

In highlighting the linguistic gap between the two women, Plaatje reminds us of the many hours that Phil Jay and Ra-Thaga have spent together in order to master each others' languages, and the fact that Annetje and Mhudi have not occupied a synchronized or simultaneous time of relation calcifies their relation as being out of joint. Mhudi's relation to Phil Jay, however, is one that confirms her unique ability to explode the gendered cyclical time with which the novel opened. If, in the first pages of *Mhudi*, we learn that "a woman's work was never out of season ... [and fulfilling] these multifarious duties of the household was not regarded as a drudgery by any means, on the contrary, ... as an art" (23), Plaatje reminds us in the end that Mhudi's heroism has always been rooted in her refusal to stay behind in the safety of the circular time of the domestic sphere. Instead, she has always preempted the injunction to wait, venturing into the lion-infested wilderness, the Matabele-dominated unknown, and the space of encounter with the Boers. Phil Jay honors Mhudi as "the only Rolong woman who had been to the front" by offering her a "*permanent* and useful souvenir of her *own* adventure" (197, my italics), a wagon, its gear, and two bullocks to be used as payment to repair the wagon. The wagon, an icon of the frontier, is a highly symbolic gift, but this gift is a Trojan horse of sorts, both a sign of the arrival of technologized modernity and a commodity already inescapably embedded in relations of exchange, production, and obsolescence. Thus, it serves both to recognize her own modernity and to recruit her into a set of temporal relations of wage work and rationalized labor.

Ethnic nationality is central to Plaatje's historical imaginary and lexicon; in his preface he declares that the novel grew out of collecting oral history, and examines the events precipitating the Matabele, a "fierce nation," "unleash[ing] the war dogs [on] the Barolong nation" (11). However, he is also working between a fictionalized past in which nations did not map onto fixed territorial spaces or complex state systems, and a present moment of writing in which he sees the national literary patrimony of the Setswana nation in peril. As he notes in the preface, his express intention is to raise money to publish a collection of Setswana folktales "to arrest this process [of forgetting] by cultivating a love for art and literature in the Vernacular." His introduction makes clear that he sees himself intervening in the ideological state apparatus of "Bantu Schools," a model of education that Plaatje presciently critiqued long before the more formalized depredations that would follow with the Bantu Education Act in 1953. By recounting the history of the 1830s in English; choosing to provide a fragmented narrative where the narrative perspective shifts constantly, focalizing Barolong, Matabele, Boer, and other perspectives at various moments; and privileging exceptional individual characters over group stereotypes, Plaatje's intervention as "a Native venture" in "South African literature [that] has hitherto been almost exclusively European" (11) reconstructs a past that in hindsight presages the revalorization of South Africa's linguistic and cultural multiplicity in Rainbow Nation rhetoric.

Writing in the 1910s, and in the wake of his 1916 critique of the Native Lands Act, Plaatje was well aware of the significance of territorial frontiers, and indeed

Mhudi closes with the migration of Mzilikazi to the antipodal north to found a new Gu-Bulawayo across the Limpopo; however, his version of South Africa (which, as Stephen Gray cannily notes, includes not a single British voice despite being written in English) is a resolutely multiethnic one. No invented past of pan-African peace features here, but I do want to argue that, in foregrounding three successful marriage plots in the domestic relationships of Umnandi and Mzilikazi, Annetje and Paul, as well as Ra-Thaga and our heroine, Mhudi, Plaatje offers a striking parity in the possibilities for empathic readings of the Matabele, Boer, and Barolong pasts that might serve as a "future memory" to be activated on hindsight. Reading Plaatje over a century after he wrote, in this extended moment of a state of transition, we may now, I suggest, read his opening salvo into South African literature as a proposal to read nation-ness as a process rather than a state, and identity as deeply contingent, mobile, and always already under revision. Thus, the Matabele military dominance of the 1830s is uncoupled from stereotypes of baseless brutality (even while a sustained critique of sadism runs through the entire narrative) and couched within a larger world-historical process of struggle over land and resources. *Mhudi* is consequently not merely an epic of South African life, but of Zimbabwean, MoSotho, Botswanan life, an epic of the *fiction* of territorial national identity, and a declaration of a deep skepticism at the legitimacy of those fixed national frontiers at which, more recently, the divide between the Rainbow Nation and *makwerekwere* have become so fraught.

Today's frontier narratives are of an entirely different order. While the mines and other new industries drew workers from across the nation, and the infamous series of Native Lands Acts, Group Areas Act, and other forced relocations made territorial belonging a deeply vexed grounds for claiming rights, cross-border migration was also a constitutive dimension of the rise of South African capital. One has only to remember that no less an icon than Clements Kadalie, founder of the Industrial and Commercial Workers Union of Africa, was born in what was then Nyasaland and only migrated to South Africa in his twenties. Nevertheless, as Jean and John Comaroff have noted:

> Part of [a process] of bolstering the nation against assertive claims in the name of [religious, linguistic, sexual, and other competing affiliations to national] identity, is to appeal to the primacy of autochthony: to the unambiguous loyalties, the interests and affect, that flow from *place of birth* .... as a *national* claim against aliens, its mobilization appears to be growing in direct proportion to the sundered hyphenation of the sovereign polity, to its popularly perceived porousness and impotence in the face of exogenous forces.[12]

Paradoxically, such a turn coincides with the liberalization of trade and rise of the very transnational capitalism that limits local opportunities for meaningful work in the face of globalization's cruel calculus. Hence, since 1994, the Department of Home Affairs has spawned extensive bureaucratic machinery to police the arrival (and deportation) of growing numbers of (im)migrants from other Africa nations near and far, and alongside this state apparatus, a more virulent and disturbing popular trend toward exclusion, discrimination, and nationalist protection has repeatedly erupted in episodes of violence targeting African immigrants.

Plaatje's novel informs Peter Abrahams' *Wild Conquest* (1950), both inscribing African perspectives on the 1830s, bearing witness to the multiple experiences of displacement and migration in the wake of both the Mfecane and the Great Trek. It destabilizes a myth of timeless autochthonous attachment to the land that would, paradoxically, exclude the Barolong, Matabele, Sotho, Tonga, Swazi, and other groups from a world-historical perspective and would privilege Boer and other European immigrants as the "actors" of history. By portraying a longue durée process of fluid relationships to the land (without obscuring the vast differences in power and moral right driving such movements), it offers a counternarrative to the nativist logics driving xenophobic tendencies in contemporary South Africa. Its lesson in history is one newly relevant in the preset prolonged state of transition, and I want to end by tracing a line to some post-1994 works that do similar kinds of work.

Lost in transition: *Makwerewere* and other migrants

For authors like Phaswane Mpe, in *Welcome to Our Hillbrow* (2001) and Nadine Gordimer in *The Pickup* (2001) the temporal horizon of freedom has collapsed but the everyday banality of border enforcement imposes an urgency on plots in which time is otherwise suspended, whether in the endlessness of death or the illusory euphoria of love. Mpe's quasi-epistolary diegesis is defined by its belatedness, as the novel opens: "If you were still alive, Refentše, child of Tiragalong, you would be glad that Bafana Bafana lost to France in the 1998 Soccer World Cup fiasco."[13] The too-soon-deceased Refentše seems to have learned how to navigate "Hillbrow: The Map" (as the first section is entitled) as a network of rumors and street knowledge; however, we also know, from the very start, that he has been dead wrong. Thus, the pavement newspaper's spurious connections between AIDS and the "foreign germs that travelled down from the central and western parts of Africa," and that, according to "Tiragalong's authoritative grapevine on all important issues [concluded from media reports] that AIDS's travel route into Johannesburg was through *Makwerewere*; and Hillbrow was the sanctuary in which *Makwerewere* basked" (3–4) are subject to a preemptive critique that extends to similar homophobic ideas about same-sex intercourse and AIDS.

Mpe's strongest critique of xenophobic discourses turns on a collective amnesia. As the narrator puts it:

> There are very few Hillbrowans, if you think about it, who were not originally wanderers form Tiragalong and other rural villages, who have come here, as we have, in search of education and work. Many of the *Makwerekwere* [accused] of this and that are no different to us—sojourners, here in search of green pastures.... You would want to add that some *Makwerekwere* were fleeing their war-torn countries to seek sanctuary here in our country, in the same way that many South Africans were forced into exile in Zambia, Zaïre, Nigeria and other African and non-African countries during the Apartheid era. (18–19)

Mpe turns here to a time when territorial frontiers signified differently for collective identity and status to work out an ethics for how to navigate the unknown new ground of the New Dispensation. This move, a projection of pre-transition historical narratives onto post-transition maps and boundaries of national becoming, is one of the recurring tropes in how to *use* history in a state of transition. Indeed, this trope of turning to history as a resource for navigating the present suggests that we might read not only Plaatje's historical novel but also works by Olive Schreiner, Thomas Mofolo, Magema Fuze, the Dhlomo brothers, Peter Abrahams, and others as *transition* literature.

The irony here is that ideas about the contamination risked in trafficking across borders are almost exactly mirrored in Zimbabwean discourses about South African sojourns. As the young poet Mgcini Nyoni writes in "Ten Years Across the Limpopo":

> After ten years
> across the Limpopo
> what he brought back home
> is this:
> a fruit knife
> known as okapi
> the clothes on his back
> a small radio
> and the deadly

disease that's eating him.
Delirious rumblings
of a good time
in Jozi.[14]

Clearly, crossing the border is a spatial transit that looms large in imaginations on both sides of the Limpopo, and suggests that the national frontier itself remains a live and therefore fertile zone for excavating future memories of reconciliation. And one such future memory might return us to a more fluid imaginary of the border's material substance, an invitation to float through the murky waters of citizenship, regional and global dialogue, countering the uneven ways in which capital flows unimpeded while bodies are checked at borders, assigned treatments through territorial administrations, and ultimately abandoned to a fate whose timing may delay but whose terminal certainty is an inescapable sentence. How would narratives of the Limpopo, and by extension, other national frontiers, resonate differently if sounded in the same breath as Kgositsile's 1969 paën to Nina Simone, "Ivory Masks in Orbit" (from which the phrase "future memory" is drawn):

88 times over lovely
ebony lady swims in this
cloud like the crocodile
in the Limpopo midnight
hour even here speaking
of love armed with future
memory: desire become memory … [15]

Kgositsile's choice to include the poem in his 2004 collection surely speaks not only to his long-overdue return to a South African reading public after decades as a banned writer, but also to his sense that its message was newly urgent in the extended moment of transition, that "even here … speaking/of love armed with future memory" could, and must, renavigate the Limpopo, diverting it into a broader network of affiliations and alliances; from the Mississippi he hails to the Zambezi, Congo, and other rivers his exile traversed.

Nadine Gordimer's *The Pickup* ranges over equally expansive space. The protagonist Julie, a young woman who has grown up in Johannesburg's affluent suburbs, spends much of her time lingering in the open-ended temporality of the EL-AY Café with a trendy interracial set of friends. As Gordimer describes it, the café is the place where [Julie] would habitually meet, without arrangement, friends and friends of friends, whoever turned up ... a place for the young; but also one where old survivors of the quarter's past, ageing Hippies and Leftist Jews, grandfathers and grandmothers of the 1920s immigration who had not become prosperous bourgeois could sit over a single coffee.[16]

Julie grapples with the unevenness of immigration's meanings, noting that for the many European friends in her father's social set "re-locating" is both a euphemism for fleeing the economic or political consequences of transition and a sign of the global reach of race and class, accessible to them in a way that is impossible for her accidental lover, who introduces himself as Abdu. In fact, her first outing with Abdu brings to the fore the challenge of a friendship across unequal regimes of time and space:

If I were driving a new car, someone else on the road could fail in some way, and that could kill me—so?

That would be your fate, but you would not have—what do I say—looked for it.

Fate.

She was amused: Is there such a thing? Do I believe in it? You do, then.

To be open to encounters—that was what she and her friends believed, anyway, as part of making the worth of their lives. Why don't we have coffee—if you're free?

I'm on lunch. (10)

Where for Julie fate seems a matter of such abstraction as to be amusing, for Abdu it is a familiar metaphor for the numerous ways in which the conditions of his life seem beyond his control. Knowing it is only a matter of time before he is discovered and deported, every moment is invested with a weighty consequence. Their worlds (and schedules) intersect at The Table, a moveable and unending feast for Julie, and a break off the clock for Abdu. In other words, open-ness as ethos, timetable, and freedom of movement are givens for Julie, where Abdu is hemmed in by the walls of his back room and auto-mechanic overalls, and always waiting for the news of his immigration status being terminated. As their relationship develops, Abdu's life migrates to Julie's flat, and it is only when he receives notice from Home Affairs, that the difference in their senses of urgency expose the seams that tenderness and novelty have obscured.

After moving to Abdu's unnamed home country, Julie finally discovers his full name, Ibrahim ibn Musa, a name that inscribes his familial identity as a son, both literally and functionally. Ibrahim finds in the return to his family household a set of strictures on his spatial movements that make the open horizon of time lacking meaningful work unbearable. Yet Julie discovers in the desert's endless reach a new absence of frontiers that beckons her for long walks and transformative meditation. Conversely, the rhythms of family life and the cyclical nature of domestic labor appeal deeply to her, and participation in these cycles is one of the only ways that she can develop a relationship with Ibrahim's family given her language limitations. The novel closes with Ibrahim departing for a new round of the immigrant's life and Julie remaining behind, unwilling to abandon the routines of his home for an unknown landscape and the uncertain fate of newcomers. Ibrahim is caught off guard to discover how close Julie is to his mother (who sees in Julie an ally luring her son back home) and another woman in their household, Khadija:

> Khadija put an arm round [Julie] conspiratorially, smiled intimately and held out the bunch of sweetness, smooth dark shiny dates. She spoke Arabic, the foreigner understands enough, now.
> –He'll come back—
> But perhaps a reassurance offered for herself, Khadija thinking of her man at the oil fields. (268)

I would argue that for Julie, this is the moment when she is most fully an African woman (or as Michael Hanchard might put it, an Afro-modern one); this is the moment she becomes implicated in the same temporal structure of waiting, waiting on the other side of a border, that defined so many (black) women's lives in South(ern) Africa throughout the twentieth century. The fact that she chooses this life, defying Ibrahim's expectations (and indeed those of his community), demands that we read this as an existential choice rather than a patriarchal imposition. Julie can afford to "re-locate" but she chooses radical empathy with those women who have no choice but to wait.

Imagining frontiers after 2004

While both Gordimer and Mpe offered fresh and challenging new ways to think about migration, xenophobia has continued to be a concern. Writing in 2004 as part of the commemorative *Democracy X* volume, Guy Berger noted the progress in representation of black South Africans in the media since a 1998 Human Rights Commission had sensitized journalists to extant stereotypes and assumptions. However, Berger saw a continuity between apartheid media's "devaluing of all things black" and the contemporary situation in which:

> Too much media in South Africa is focused on this country as if Africa were another continent. Xenophobia towards black people from elsewhere on the continent is frequently present in gratuitous references as in "Nigerian drug-dealers" or "Zimbabwean criminal syndicates," tarnishing entire nations in the process.[17]

In contrast to this brief and rather muffled critique, the one other contributor who seriously addressed the rise of such attitudes, Keorapetse Kgositsile, wrote far more forthrightly and, I would argue, in the tradition of Solomon Plaatje. Like Plaatje, who hoped to fund a Setswana proverb collection with the proceeds from *Mhudi*, Kgositsile wrote in English, but was informed by an understanding of Setswana as a living language, intimately bound up in the contemporary epistemological and ethical crises of his day. Kgositsile saw a link between neo-traditionalist pieties about origins and authenticity, on the one hand, and the forgetting of more recent world-historical practices, networks, and interdependencies that testified to the fact that South Africa had never been anything other than a part of Africa. In turning to Setswana as his "mother"-tongue, he also shared the womanist perspective seen in the prominence and agency of Plaatje's Mhudi, noting that

> some of my fathers, those patriarchs who are the uncompromising upholders of tradition and custom which, as I hope by now we understand, privileges the patriarch, will not like this *mother*-tongue madness. They believe themselves to be the authentic custodians of our language—there is even a Grade V reader by A.T. Malepe entitled *Setswana Sa Borre* ("Our Fathers' Setswana")—though everyone knows who has customarily remained with the children and brought them up and who has taught the language, the foremost repository of cultural values.[18]

As I have discussed more fully elsewhere,[19] Kgositsile formulated an argument against xenophobia that was grounded in a Setswana concept of civic belonging rooted in residency rather than lineage, noting that the verb "*go agisana/agisanya*" (from which the word "*moagi*" or resident was derived) implied shared needs ("in the same breath") and shared goals ("building together"), whereas the badge of national belonging, the passport, emerged from colonial borders instituted as "expressions of the greed and plunder of diverse European nationalisms."[20] Furthermore, Kgositsile calls into question his readers' memories, noting that those who would like to gloss over his objections to a rainbow formulation of reconciliation as "black and white together" and those resentful of African immigrants alike seemed to forget the role of the Frontline States and other allies. He asks whether, "[d]uring our struggle for national liberation[,] had other African countries been wrong or misguided to give us the welcome, the solidarity and support which enabled us to execute our struggle?"[21] He goes on to critique the parallel between such nativist discourses of protection and "the way the US refers to Mexican people who cross into Southern California, without pieces of paper, as illegal aliens," making a point that the Comaroffs have echoed more recently.[22]

What is most striking, however, is Kgositsile's repeated invocation of a question of temporality that resonates not just with continental Africa, but with a broader pan-African world to which South Africa's poet laureate has long and consistently been a bridge. The essay is entitled "Race: What time is it?" and alongside his recourse to history as a reproach for abandoning ties of solidarity, the phrase repeated like a refrain, "What time is it?" transposes a question common in the late 1960s and early 1970s among Black Arts writers and activists in the United States, whose customary response—It's nation time!—Kgositsile leaves to his readers. The tone of his essay, issuing a call to continue striving for a society that values human rights despite the risk of distortion, "a decade into democracy,"[23] implies that Nation Time is yet to come, or rather that it is necessarily an unfinished project, most vital in its waiting potential. Kgositsile's essay effectively makes a case for why Nation Time in South Africa necessarily entails taking full cognizance of the enduring inequalities racial histories continue to sustain, while also using the work of the Black Consciousness movement and others who "politicized [the concept of blackness] and turned it into a philosophical alternative that was powerfully anti-racist."[24]

A new dispensation does not entail disregarding the realities of unequal power and resources in the interests of a public discourse of rainbows and reconciliation, so much as a renewed understanding that "racial time," as Michael Hanchard terms it, structures the everyday experiences of national subjects in distinctive ways. Hanchard, while cognizant of the important differences between racial regimes in the United States and the global south, notes that the lived experience of inequality is apparent not only in spectacular acts of violence but also at the level of the ordinary, the routine, the banal, the given:

> Violence, meted out by the state and by those whom the state vests with qualitatively superior citizenship, structures the process of temporal inequality. In both the colonial and postcolonial contexts, racial difference was the premise for maintaining inequality between U.S. whites and blacks, as well as between

Africans and Europeans.... The experiential knowledge of human time that is peculiar to certain groups in given situations is the actual basis of collective consciousness—whether of race, nationality, gender, or other forms of conscious collective activity.[25]

Hanchard analyzes three conceptual ways in which racial time, as a response to the impact of inequalities on experiences of duration, has been seized by Afro-modern subjects: waiting, temporal appropriation, and a millenarian understanding of the ethico-political relations between time and progress. In Kgositsile's question ("Race: What time is it?"), we are reminded that waiting for justice is no meek accommodationist stance. Rather, waiting becomes a *critical position*, a vantage point from which "subordinate groups objectively perceive the material consequences of social inequality, as they are literally made to wait for goods and services that are delivered first to members of the dominant group"[26] and gather energy to appropriate time in public acts of collective protest. This stance is driven by a conviction that the "New Day" must never foreclose hope nor allow shadows to overwhelm that first light which Aimé Césaire heralded, "au bout du petit matin," that miraculous weapon in the wee hours of the morning, that righteous reversal. If states of transition are to have any meaning, they must be permanent, ongoing, and excessive, spilling over temporal boundaries and territorial frontiers, as the ever-approached and never-reached limit in the calculus of liberation.

To be sure, I am not arguing for a permanence of transition that would disguise and even sustain an inertia dragging against fundamental changes in the structures and assumptions that perpetuate Euro-centric, propaganda-bound, or other systems of value and institutional reproduction. Rather, I want to summon the late Édouard Glissant's elegant phrase: "J'écris en presence de toutes les langues du monde," and to suggest that local, national, regional, continental writers most essentially join him *writing in the presence of all the languages of the world*, in ethical relation to those whose differences are neither forced into a washed out transparency nor allowed to obscure their shared humanity in confronting the toll of hydra-headed racial and capitalist violence.[27] We should recall Njabulo Ndebele's proposition that any effective transition will necessarily entail upending spatial distributions of resources that assign some locations a perpetual "dormitory" status where little creativity is expected or fostered. Ndebele names "resilient factors" as those elements that pose a challenge to social transitions because they resist change

by simulating it in such a way that in the end there is only the impression of change. It is a form of resistance that goes hand in hand with good intentions.

The risk that resilient factors pose is that within a short space of time, a country in transition, such as South Africa, may enter into an unintended state of inertia in which change is genuinely sought, but the complexities of transition delay movement beyond it, such that the sense of transition actually becomes permanent. The state of inertia may generate its own politics, which may be as vibrant as any but actually dances on the same ground.[28]

As Ndebele shows throughout his essay, the distorted spatial distribution of resources is one of the most obvious afterlives of apartheid; he urges that new ground must be broken. I have sought to demonstrate in this chapter that the work of overcoming resistance to transition also entails connecting such processes of exclusion internal to the nation to transborder exclusions that operate out of a similar neocolonial logic of race, contamination, and risk. If enforcing borders, frontiers, and trade tariffs is the real-politik behind such euphemistically named agendas as the African Renaissance, the reading and writing of South African literature in the presence of all the languages of the continent demonstrates literature's potential to offer an alternative vision of cross-border, pan-Africanist solidarity, a site from which to project the future memory of a truly continental commitment to human rights, dignity, and openness. This, to my mind, is the final frontier across which South African literature is in transit. We are all *makwerewere*.

Notes

1   The phrase borrows from Njabulo Ndebele's well-known essay "The Rediscovery of the Ordinary: Some New Writings in South Africa," first published in 1986.

2   See Petzold, "'Translating' the Great Trek to the Twentieth Century."

3   The Frontline States were a regional group of Southern African states—Angola, Botswana, Lesotho, Mozambique, Tanzania, Zambia, and, following its independence in 1980, Zimbabwe—that actively supported the antiapartheid struggle.

4   Rob Nixon's essay, "Border Country: Bessie Head's Frontline States," offers a beautiful reading of Head's work and biography as an example of this cross-border dynamic (between Botswana and South Africa).

5   Wenzel, *Bulletproof*, 125.

6   Quoted in Rowell, "'With Bloodstains to Testify,'" 31.

7   Anon., "Izibongo ZikaMzilikazi KaMatshobana/The Praises of Mzilikazi, Son of Matshobana."

8   See, among others: Couzens and Gray, "Printers' and Other Devils"; Green, *Novel Histories*; Willan, *Solomon Plaatje: South African Nationalist*; Chrisman,

9   Voss, "Reading and Writing in the New South Africa," 7.

10 Hanchard, "Afro-Modernity," 253.

11 Plaatje, *Mhudi*, 126. Further references parenthetically in the text.

12 Comaroff and Comaroff, "Nations With/Out Borders," 97.

13 Mpe, *Welcome to Our Hillbrow*, 1. Further references parenthetically in the text.

14 Nyoni, "Ten Years Across the Limpopo."

15 Kgositsile, "Ivory Masks in Orbit," in *This Way I Salute You*, 13.

16 Gordimer, *The Pickup*, 5. Further references parenthetically in the text.

17 Berger, "Media in the Mix," 207.

18 Kgositsile, "Race: What Time Is It?" 145.

19 See Jaji, *Africa in Stereo*, 241–46.

20 Kgositsile, "Race: What Time Is It?" 147.

21 Ibid., 149.

22 Comaroff and Comaroff, "Nations With/Out Borders," 104–05.

23 Kgositsile, "Race: What Time Is It?" 149.

24 Ibid., 146.

25 Hanchard, "Afro-Modernity," 266.

26 Ibid., 256.

27 Glissant, "J'écris en présence de toutes les langues du monde."

28 Ndebele, "Arriving Home? South Africa beyond Transition and Reconciliation," 57.

Works Cited

Anonymous. "Izibongo ZikaMzilikazi KaMatshobana/The Praises of Mzilikazi, Son of Matshobana." Zimbabwe page for Poetry International. http://www. poetryinternationalweb.net/pi/site/poem/item/5799.

Berger, Guy. "Media in the Mix." Oliphant, Delius, and Meltzer. 203–20.

Chrisman, Laura. *Rereading the Imperial Romanceereading the Imperial Romanceweb. net/pi/site/poem/*. Eds. Schreiner Haggard and Plaatje. New York: Oxford University Press, 2000.

Comaroff, Jean, and John L. Comaroff. "Nations With/Out Borders: The Politics of Being and the Problem of Belonging." In *Theory From The South: Or, How Euro-America Is Evolving Toward Africa*. Boulder: Paradigm, 2012. 91–107.

Couzens, Time, and Stephen Gray. "Printers' and Other Devils: The Texts of Sol T. Plaatje's *Mhudi*." *Research in African Literatures* 9.2 (1978): 198–215.

Glissant, Edouard. "J'écris en présence de toutes les langues du monde." *Congrès Eurozine 2008: Crosswords X/Mots croisé* http://sens-public.org/IMG/pdf/ SensPublic_EGlissant_Toutes_les_langues_du_monde.pdf.

Green, Michael. *Novel Histories: Past, Present, and Future in South Africa*. Johannesburg: Witwatersrand University Press, 1997.

Hanchard, Michael. "Afro-Modernity: Temporality, Politics, and the African Diaspora." *Public Culture* 11.1 (1999): 245–68.

Jaji, Tsitsi. *Africa in Stereo: Modernism, Music, and Pan-African Solidarity*. New York: Oxford University Press, 2014.

Kgositsile, Keorapetse. "Race: What Time Is It?" Oliphant, Delius, and Meltzer. 145–50.

Kgositsile, Keorapetse. *This Way I Salute You*. Cape Town: Kwela/Snail Press, 2004.

Mpe, Phaswane. *Welcome to Our Hillbrow*. Pietermaritzburg: University of Natal Press, 2001.

Ndebele, Njabulo. "Arriving Home? South Africa beyond Transition and Reconciliation." In *In the Balance: South Africans Debate Reconciliation*. Eds. Fanie Du Toit and Erik Doxtader. Johannesburg: Jacana Media, 2010. 55–73.

Ndebele, Njabulo. "The Rediscovery of the Ordinary: Some New Writings in South Africa." *Journal of Southern African Studies* 12.2 (1986): 143–57.

Nixon, Rob. "Border Country: Bessie Head's Frontline States." *Social Text* 36 (1993): 106–37.

Nyoni, Mgcini. "Ten Years Across the Limpopo" on Poetry International Zimbabwe webpage. https://www.poetryinternationalweb.net/pi/site/poem/item/18097/auto/0/TEN-YEARS-ACROSS-THE-LIMPOPO-Mgcini-Nyoni.

Oliphant, Andries, W. Peter Delius, and Lalou Meltzer, eds. *Democracy X: Marking the Present, Re-presenting the Past*. Pretoria: University of South Africa Press, 2004.

Peterson, Bhekizizwe. "Petitioning Selves and the Ethics of Suffering in Sol Plaatje's *Native Life in South Africa*: Melancholy Narratives." *Journal of Commonwealth Literature* 43.1 (2008): 79–95.

Petzold, Jochen. "'Translating' the Great Trek to the Twentieth Century: Re-Interpretations of the Afrikaner Myth in Three South African Novels." *English in Africa* 34.1 (2007): 115–31.

Plaatje, Solomon. *Mhudi: An Epic of South African Native Life a Hundred Years Ago*. Jeppestown: AD Donker/Jonathan Ball, 1989.

Rowell, Charles. "'With Bloodstains to Testify': An Interview with Keorapetse Kgositsile." *Callaloo* 2 (1978): 23–42.

Voss, A. E. "Reading and Writing in the New South Africa." *Current Writing: Text and Reception in Southern Africa* 4.1 (1992): 1–9.

Wenzel, Jennifer. *Bulletproof: Afterlives of Anti-colonial Prophecy in South Africa and Beyond*. Chicago: University of Chicago Press, 2009.

Willan, Brian. *Solomon Plaatje: South African Nationalist*. London: Boydell and Brewer, 1988.

Index

Lightning Source UK Ltd.
Milton Keynes UK
UKHW021528111219
355136UK00003B/169/P

Limit Order Books

A limit order book is essentially a file in a computer that contains all orders sent to the market, with their characteristics such as the sign of the order, price, quantity and a timestamp. The majority of organized electronic markets rely on limit order books to store lists of the interests of market participants in their central computer. A limit order book contains all information available on a specific market and it reflects the way the market moves under the influence of its participants.

This book discusses several models of limit order books. It begins by assessing the empirical properties of data, and then moves on to mathematical models in order to reproduce the observed properties. It finally presents a framework for numerical simulations. It also covers important modelling techniques including agent-based modelling, and advanced modelling of limit order books based on Hawkes processes. The book also provides in-depth coverage of simulation techniques and introduces general, flexible, open source library concepts useful to readers in studying trading strategies in order-driven markets.

The book will be useful to graduate students in the field of econophysics, financial mathematics and quantitative finance. The contents of this book are taught by the authors at CentraleSupélec (France) for a course on "Physics of Markets". A short course based on the content of this book has been taught at the Graduate School of Mathematical Sciences, University of Tokyo (Japan), and it will be used at the Université Paris Saclay (France) for a course in quantitative finance.

Frédéric Abergel is a Professor and Director of the Chair of Quantitative Finance, CentraleSupélec, France. Beginning as a CNRS scientist at Université Paris Sud Orsay, he acquired several years of industrial experience in investment banking at BNP Paribas, CAI Cheuvreux, Barclays Capital and Natixis CIB. His research interests include financial markets, pricing and hedging of derivatives, quantitative finance and empirical properties of financial data.

Marouane Anane is a Quantitative Analyst at the BNP Paribas, Paris. His research interests include market making strategies, price dynamics and automated technical analysis.

Anirban Chakraborti is a Professor and Dean of the School of Computational and Integrative Sciences, Jawaharlal Nehru University, India. He has held academic/research positions at the Saha Institute of Nuclear Physics, Helsinki University of Technology, Brookhaven National Laboratory, Banaras Hindu University and the Ecole Centrale Paris. He is a recipient of the Young Scientist Medal of the Indian National Science Academy in 2009. His research areas include econophysics, statistical physics and quantum physics.

Aymen Jedidi is a Quantitative Analyst at HSBC Bank, Paris area, France. His research interests are quantitative risk management and stochastic order book modelling.

Ioane Muni Toke is an Associate Professor and Dean of studies at the Université de la Nouvelle-Calédonie, New Caledonia. He has held academic/research positions at the Ecole Centrale Paris and University of Texas at Dallas. He has research interests in financial markets modelling and microstructure, quantitative finance, statistical finance, applied mathematics and applied probability.

Physics of Society: Econophysics and Sociophysics

This book series is aimed at introducing readers to the recent developments in physics inspired modelling of economic and social systems. Socio-economic systems are increasingly being identified as 'interacting many-body dynamical systems' very much similar to the physical systems, studied over several centuries now. Econophysics and sociophysics as interdisciplinary subjects view the dynamics of markets and society in general as those of physical systems. This will be a series of books written by eminent academicians, researchers and subject experts in the field of physics, mathematics, finance, sociology, management and economics.

This new series brings out research monographs and course books useful for the students and researchers across disciplines, both from physical and social science disciplines, including economics.

Kausik Gangopadhyay
Professor of Economics
Indian Institute of Management, Kozhikode,
India

Taisei Kaizoji
Professor of Economics
Department of Economics and Business,
International Christian University, Tokyo, Japan

János Kertész
Professor of Physics
Center for Network Science, Central European
University, Budapest, Hungary

Parongama Sen
Professor of Physics
University of Calcutta, Kolkata, India

Victor Yakovenko
Professor of Physics
University of Maryland, College Park, USA

Giulia Iori
Professor of Economics
School of Social Science, City University,
London, United Kingdom

Kimmo Kaski
Professor of Physics
Dean, School of Science, Aalto University,
Espoo, Finland

Akira Namatame
Professor of Computer Science and
Economics Department of Computer
Science, National Defense Academy,
Yokosuka, Japan

Sitabhra Sinha
Professor of Physics
Institute of Mathematical Science, Chennai,
India

Physics of Society: Forthcoming Titles

- *Macro-Econophysics: New Studies on Economic Networks and Synchronization* by Yoshi Fujiwara, Hideaki Aoyama, Yuichi Ikeda, Hiroshi Iyetomi, Wataru Souma, Hiroshi Yoshikawa

- *Interactive Macroeconomics: Stochastic Aggregate Dynamics with Heterogeneous and Interacting Agents* by Mauro Gallegati, Corrado Di Guilmi and Simone Landini

- *A Statistical Physics Perspective on Socio Economic Inequalities* by Victor Yakovenko and Arnab Chatterjee